Traditional approaches to creating employment and economic growth
have failed in the 1990s. A new understanding of what creates jobs and
drives growth has emerged in a cross-disciplinary approach which
combines industrial organization, the economics of technological
change, and international economics. The new approach focuses on the
dynamics of firms and industries as sources of innovation (and conse-
quently increased competitiveness, job creation, and economic growth),
and emphasizes the shift in economic activity based on traditional
factors of production to being based on new economic knowledge.

   Innovation, Industry Evolution, and Employment edited by David
Audretsch and Roy Thurik brings together leading scholars to present
important and original research in this exciting new area. With case
study material taken from countries including France, Germany,
Holland, Canada, and the US. *Innovation, Industry Evolution, and
Employment* will be vital reading for policy makers, researchers, and
students.

DAVID AUDRETSCH is the Ameritech Chair of Economic Develop-
ment and Director, Institute for Development Strategies at Indiana
University. His publications include *Innovation and Industry Evolution*
(MIT Press, 1995); *Innovation and Small Firms* (MIT Press, 1990), *Small
Firms and Entrepreneurship: An East–West Perspective* (CUP, 1993).

ROY THURIK is Professor of Industrial Economics and Entrepreneurship at Erasmus University Rotterdam. He also works at EIM Small
Business Research and Consultancy in the Netherlands. He has previously edited *Small Businesses in the Modern Economy* (with Zoltan
Acs and Bo Carlsson) (Basil Blackwell, 1996).

Innovation, Industry Evolution, and Employment

Edited by
DAVID B. AUDRETSCH
AND A. ROY THURIK

CAMBRIDGE
UNIVERSITY PRESS

CAMBRIDGE UNIVERSITY PRESS
Cambridge, New York, Melbourne, Madrid, Cape Town, Singapore,
São Paulo, Delhi, Dubai, Tokyo, Mexico City

Cambridge University Press
The Edinburgh Building, Cambridge CB2 8RU, UK

Published in the United States of America by Cambridge University Press, New York

www.cambridge.org
Information on this title: www.cambridge.org/9780521142717

First published 1999
First paperback printing 2010

A catalogue record for this publication is available from the British Library

Library of Congress Cataloguing in Publication data
Innovation, industry evolution, and employment / edited by David B. Audretsch
and A. Roy Thurik.
    p. cm.
ISBN 0 521 64166 7
1. Technological innovations – Economic aspects.
2. Economic development.   3. Job creation.   4. Industrial organization.
I. Audretsch, David B.   II. Thurik A. R. (A. Roy)
HC79.T4I5466   1999
331.12'4–dc21   98–35101   CIP

ISBN 978-0-521-64166-1 Hardback
ISBN 978-0-521-14271-7 Paperback

Contents

vi   Contents

Contributors

David Audretsch *Indiana University*
Roy Thurik *Erasmus University Rotterdam and EIM Small Business Research and Consultancy, the Netherlands*
Bee Yan Aw *Pennsylvania State University*
Geeta Batra *The World Bank*
John Baldwin *Statistics Canada*
Mohammed Rafiquzzaman *Statistics Canada*
Martin Carree *Erasmus University Rotterdam*
Marcel Lever *Ministry of Finance, the Netherlands*
Henry Nieuwenhuijsen *EIM Small Business Research and Consultancy, the Netherlands*
Jacques Mairesse *l'Institut National de la Statistique et des Etudes Economiques, France*
Bronwyn Hall *University of California at Berkeley and Nuffield College, Oxford*
Lee Branstetter *University of California at Davis*
Bruno Crepon *l'Institut National de la Statistique et des Etudes Economiques*
Michael Fritsch *Bergakademie Freiberg, Germany*
Rolf Lukas *Bergakademie Freiberg, Germany*
Bo Carlsson *Case Western Reserve University*
Pontus Braunerhjelm *Research Institute of Industrial Economics, Sweden*
Paula Stephan *Georgia State University*
Luuk Klomp *Statistics Netherlands*
Joachim Wagner *Universität Lüneburg, Germany*
José Mata *Banco de Portugal*
Pedro Portugal *Banco de Portugal*
Enrico Santarelli *Universiti di Bologna, Italy*
Marco Vivarelli *Universiti Cattolica di Piacenza*
Leo Sleuwaegen *Catholic University of Leuven, Belgium*
Micheline Goedhuys *Catholic University of Leuven, Belgium*

1 Introduction

David Audretsch and Roy Thurik

1 The employment and growth challenges

Economic growth and employment creation are the twin horns of not just the European dilemma but of what looms as the major challenge confronting the West.[1] Unemployment in the European Union is twice as high as that in Japan and the US together. Over 11 percent of the workforce in the European Union was unemployed in 1996, ranging from 3.3 percent in Luxembourg and 4.4 percent in Austria, to 15.3 percent in Finland and over 20 percent in Spain.[2] Germany, Europe's biggest labor market, experienced 12 percent unemployment, a number that has proven difficult to reduce. Individual countries have responded to the twin horns of the growth–employment dilemma with a broad spectrum of policy approaches. Led by France and Germany, continental European countries have generally pursued policies of maintaining the status quo, while the United Kingdom and The Netherlands have been bolder at reducing the role of the state.

The continued rising unemployment coupled with moderate growth in Europe has triggered a plea by policy-makers for rethinking the policy approach that ushered in European prosperity during the post-war era. The resulting policy debate has been cast in terms of an inevitable tradeoff between greater employment but at the sacrifice of lower wages, on the one hand, versus the maintenance of wages and living standards but at the cost of less employment, on the other.

---

[1] For example, *The Economist* (11 May, 1996, p. 86) points out, "Ask any European what is today's biggest policy problem, and without hesitation he will say: unemployment. Ask an American economist the same question, and you will hear something about flagging productivity growth."

[2] OECD (1997), standardized rates.

1

According to this debate, the Anglo-American solution has been the former, while the continental Europeans have chosen the latter.

The purpose of this book is to suggest that this policy debate has been miscast. There is an alternative. This alternative involves structural change, and in particular shifting economic activity out of traditional moderate-technology industries and into new emerging knowledge-based industries. In other words, it involves innovation, industry evolution and their consequences for employment creation.

2   Globalization and the telecommunications revolution

The cold war combined with internal political instability rendered potential investments in Eastern Europe and much of the developing world as risky and impractical. During the post-war era most trade and foreign direct investment was generally confined to Western Europe and North America, and later a few of the Asian countries, principally Japan and the Asian Tigers. The comparative advantage was generally attained through large-scale production, which facilitated low-cost production through exploiting scale economies. Large-scale mass production was essential to gaining the comparative advantage. The relatively small domestic markets in most European countries seemed to pose a serious threat to European competitiveness during the post-war era. However, three strategies were quickly developed to compensate for a small domestic market. The *first* strategy has been that of the creation of a larger and more coherent domestic European market. The *second* strategy was to internationalize by developing markets outside of the domestic market. The *third* was to rely on skilled labor and high levels of human capital to produce goods that, although they might cost more, were of superior quality. Large transnational corporations such as Philips Electronics thrived on this dual strategy basing the comparative advantage on large-scale production made possible by superior management and organization combined with high-skilled labor. The comparative advantage of Europe lay in large-scale production of moderate-technology products in traditional industries, such as machine tools, automobile parts, and metal working.

This comparative advantage has been lost in the high-cost countries of Western Europe and North America in the last decade for two reasons. The *first* has to do with globalization or the advent of competition from not just the emerging economies in Southeast Asia but also from the transforming economies of Central and Eastern Europe. The production costs, and in particular labor costs, are considerably lower in these countries.[3] At the same time, the potential labor force of about 500 million persons in China and 350 million persons in India will put a continuous pressure on any upward lift of the wage rate. While the uncertainties of the cold war and the internal political instabilities in Eastern Europe rendered transnational activities prohibitively risky during the first four post-war decades, this is no longer the case.

The *second* factor triggering the loss of the traditional comparative advantage in the advanced developed countries of Western Europe and North America has been the communications revolution. The new communications technologies have triggered a virtual spatial revolution in terms of the geography of production.[4] The marginal cost of transferring information across geographic space has been reduced to virtually nothing. Information can be transferred around the globe via e-mail, fax machines, and cyberspace, making it not only feasible but even desirable to shift economic activity out of the high-cost locations in Europe to lower-cost locations in Central Europe and Asia.

Confronted with lower-cost competition in foreign locations, producers in the high-cost countries have responded by pursuing four distinct options: (1) maintain wages and suffer a loss in global market shares, (2) reduce wages and other production costs sufficiently in the home country to compete with low-cost foreign producers, (3) substitute capital and technology for labor in the home country to increase productivity, and (4) shift production out of the high-cost location and into the low-cost location.

Pursuing the first option will generally lead to the demise of the firm. The second option is generally not viable in Western Europe where wage rigidities prevent such drastic reductions. The most common response has been the third and fourth options, both of which reduce employment in the home country.[5] Substituting capital and technology for labor,

---

[3] For example, the daily earnings of labor have been estimated to be $78.34 in the European Union, but only $6.14 in Poland, $6.45 in the Czech Republic, $1.53 in China, $2.46 in India, and $1.25 in Sri Lanka (Jensen, 1993).

[4] According to *The Economist* ("The Death of Distance," 30 September, 1995), "The death of distance as a determinant of the cost of communications will probably be the single most important economic force shaping society in the first half of the next century."

[5] For example, about 70 percent of Sweden's manufacturing employees work for large multinational corporations, such as Volvo, which through outward foreign direct investment have been constantly shifting production out of the high-cost domestic location and into lower-cost countries. Between 1970 and 1993 Sweden lost 500,000 private sector jobs, and unemployment reached 13 percent of the workforce in 1995. Sweden is not an exceptional case; every third car that is manufactured by a German company is actually produced outside of Germany. Similarly, Lufthansa recently shifted

along with shifting production to lower-cost locations, has resulted in waves of corporate downsizing throughout Western Europe and North America. At the same time, it has generally preserved the viability of many of the large corporations. As record levels of both European and American stock indexes indicate, the profitability of the large companies has generally not suffered.[6]

Corporate downsizing triggered by the shifting comparative advantage as a result of globalization has not been restricted to just a few countries. Rather, the response to globalization has led large corporations to downsize throughout the OECD countries. For example, between 1979 and 1995 more than 43 million jobs were lost in the United States as a result of corporate downsizing.[7] Similarly, the 500 largest US manufacturing corporations cut 4.7 million jobs between 1980 and 1993, or one quarter of their work force (Audretsch, 1995). Perhaps most disconcertingly, the rate of corporate downsizing has apparently increased over time in the United States, even as the unemployment rate has fallen. During most of the 1980s, about one in 25 workers lost a job. In the 1990s this has risen to one in 20 workers.

This wave of corporate downsizing has triggered cries of betrayal and lack of social conscience on the part of the large corporations.[8] Such accusations are misconceived. It is a mistake to blame the large corporations for this wave of downsizing that has triggered massive job losses and rising unemployment in so many countries. These corporations are simply trying to survive in an economy of global competitors who have access to lower-cost inputs.

3   The shifting comparative advantage

There is a fifth response to the twin forces of globalization and the telecommunications revolution in order to revitalize the capitalist engine (Nelson, 1990). This alternative does not require sacrificing wages to create new jobs, nor does it require fewer jobs to maintain wage levels and the social safety net. This alternative involves shifting economic activity out of the traditional industries where the high-cost countries of

the location of a number of office functions, such as telephone operators, out of high-cost Germany and into India.

[6]   "Big is Back," *The Economist*, 22 June, 1995 and "The Year Downsizing Grew Up," *The Economist*, 21 December, 1996.

[7]   "The Downsizing of American," *New York Times*, 3 March, 1996, p. 1. These 43 million jobs include 24.8 million blue-collar jobs and 18.7 million white-collar jobs.

[8]   As the German newspaper, *Die Zeit* (2 February, 1996, p. 1) pointed out in a front page article, "When Profits Lead to Ruin – More Profits and More Unemployment: Where is the Social Responsibility of the Firms?"

Europe and North America have lost the comparative advantage and into those industries where the comparative advantage is compatible with both high wages and high levels of employment – knowledge-based economic activity. In the Silicon Valley region of the United States, 15 percent more jobs were created between 1992 and 1996, and at the same time the level of wages rose to a level that is 50 percent greater than the national average. By shifting to knowledge-based economic activity the seemingly inevitable tradeoff between wages and employment can be avoided.

The emergence of geographic regions where both wages and employment are expanding, such as Silicon Valley in California, Research Triangle in North Carolina, and Cambridge in the United Kingdom, may seem surprising and even paradoxical in a world increasingly dominated by global telecommunications. The conventional wisdom would have suggested that the telecommunications revolution combined with globalization would make location irrelevant. The resolution to this paradox lies in a crucial distinction between knowledge and information. Information consists of facts, such as the price of gold in Tokyo, or the weather in New York, which can be costlessly transmitted around the globe. By contrast, knowledge, and especially tacit knowledge, consists of ideas that are subjective, uncertain, and difficult to explicitly write down (Nooteboom, 1994). Many of these ideas arise as a result of face-to-face contact and interchange.[9] Many of the most creative ideas have been the result of chance meetings at a social event in a supportive environment (Nelson, 1995).

Economic activity based on new ideas and tacit knowledge cannot be easily copied by competitors located far from the original source nor easily transferred to lower-cost countries by multinational corporations. While the processes and organizational methods required to produce automobiles can be transferred from Stuttgart to Hungary, it is not so easy to transfer innovative work in biotechnology around the globe.

The global demand for products in emerging knowledge-based industries is high and rapidly growing; yet the number of workers who can contribute to producing and commercializing new knowledge is limited to just a few areas in the world, largely in North America and Western Europe. Economic activity based on skills that can be found throughout large parts of the world is doomed to generate lower wage rates as a result of global competition. By contrast, economic activity based on new knowledge will generate higher wages and greater employment

---

[9] For further explanations of the distinction between information and knowledge, see Audretsch and Feldman (1996) and Audretsch and Stephan (1996).

opportunities reflecting the exploding demand for new and improved products and services.

There are many indicators reflecting the shift in the comparative advantage of the high-wage countries toward an increased importance of knowledge-based economic activity. For example, Kortum and Lerner (1997, p. 1) point to "the unprecedented recent jump in patenting in the United States," as evidenced by the rise in applications for US patents by American inventors since 1985, which exceeds the increase in other decades in this century. Throughout this century, patent applications fluctuated within a band of between 40,000 and 80,000 per year. By contrast, in 1995 there were over 120,000 patent applications. Similarly, Berman, Bound, and Machin (1997) have shown that the demand for less-skilled workers has decreased dramatically throughout the OECD, while at the same time the demand for skilled workers has exploded.

Why has it proven so difficult to shift economic activity out of the traditional industries where the products are now fairly standardized and where production can be easily transferred to lower-cost locations?[10] The present collection of studies attempts to present an answer starting from a macroeconomic-labor-industrial organization synthesis.

4   The macroeconomic-labor-industrial organization synthesis

In order to shed light on the links between innovation, industry evolution, and employment generation, the Tinbergen Institute of Erasmus University Rotterdam, the School of Policy Studies at Georgia State University, and EIM Small- and Medium-Sized Business Research and Consultancy in Zoetermeer, the Netherlands hosted a two day conference on the subject in Rotterdam and Zoetermeer, 29–30 August, 1997. The chapters included in this volume reflect a carefully edited and revised selection of the papers of this conference. What the papers have in common is that they link some measure of economic performance to technology and innovation, and they do it using a dynamic framework based on a longitudinal database that tracks micro-observations over time. By and large, the emphasis is on how various measures of performance, such as wages, growth, productivity, and survival, for different units of observations such as industries, firms, regions, and

---

[10] What *Der Spiegel* ("Wer ist der Nächste?: Angst um den Arbeitsplatz," number 5, 1994, pp. 82–83) concludes for Germany is equally valid for much of Europe: "Global structural change has had an impact that only a short time ago would have been unimaginable. Many of the products, such as automobiles, machinery, chemicals, and steel are no longer competitive in global markets. And in the industries of the future, like biotechnology and electronics, the German companies are barely participating."

individuals, are shaped in an evolutionary context by technology and innovation. Within this general framework, the focus of chapters 2 through 5 is on productivity and wages while that of chapters 6 through 9 is on innovation. The last five chapters generally deal with industry evolution.

This book begins with "Wages, firm size, and wage inequality: How much do exports matter?" by Bee Yan Aw and Geeta Batra. This *second chapter* examines the links between wages and different types of labor, with a particular focus on the role of exports, all within the context of an Asian Tiger, Taiwan. The authors use the longitudinal Census Data Base to track the performance of over 80,000 Taiwanese firms spanning ten manufacturing industries. The empirical evidence suggests that the gap between production and non-production workers varies substantially between exporting firms and non-exporting firms. In particular, exporting firms pay their production and non-production workers higher wages than do non-exporting firms, even after controlling for firm-specific characteristics identified in the literature as being highly correlated with wages. The cross-industry mean wage premium associated with exporting over non-exporting firms is about 30 percent for non-production workers and 14 percent for production workers. In general, exporters in all ten industries are also associated with higher wage inequality between the non-production and the production workers relative to their counterparts in the domestic market. Thus, the evidence from Taiwan clearly suggests that the propensity for some firms to export while others do not accounts for a considerable amount of the wage gap between production and non-production workers.

The source of wage differentials is also the subject of *chapter 3* on "Trade, technology, and wage differentials in the Canadian manufacturing sector," by John R. Baldwin and Mohammed Rafiquzzaman. As in most other countries, the authors point out that the wage gap between skilled and unskilled workers has increased in Canada during the last decade. In particular, Baldwin and Rafiquzzaman use a comprehensive longitudinal database from the Canadian Census of Manufactures to examine the impact of technology use on the structure of worker wages. Like in the previous chapter by Aw and Batra, Baldwin and Rafiquzzaman focus on the gap in wages between production and non-production workers. The authors find that the effects of technology have not been felt equally in all segments of the labor market – the wages of non-production workers have risen relative to the wages of production workers. While the evidence suggests that some of the increased wage gap is attributable to changing trade patterns, a key finding in this chapter is that the use of new technology has also contributed to the growing wage gap. Most strikingly, the premium paid to non-production labor was the greatest during the 1980s, when capital intensity and labor-enhancing technology use was the highest.

In *chapter 4* Martin Carree and Roy Thurik examine "Industrial structure and economic growth." While a number of studies have identified a systematic shift in economic activity in the OECD countries away from large firms toward small enterprises, virtually no study has been able to identify any light on the welfare implications of this shift. That is, is this shift welfare enhancing and therefore to be fostered by government policy, or does it lead to reduced economic welfare and should therefore be impeded by government policy? Carree and Thurik use a longitudinal database consisting of 13 manufacturing industries in 12 European countries to identify the impact of this shift on economic growth. The evidence clearly suggests that countries which have experienced greater rates of growth also experienced the greatest shift in economic activity toward small enterprises. The authors point out in their conclusions that the evidence in the chapter provides support for specific policies introduced during the 1980s and 1990s in European countries stimulating small enterprises.

Chapter 5, by Marcel Lever and Henry Nieuwenhuijsen, focuses on a slightly different measure of economic performance – productivity. In particular, in their "The impact of competition on productivity in Dutch manufacturing" the authors examine the relationship between the degree of competition and productivity growth in Dutch manufacturing. They estimate a Cobb–Douglas production function, incorporating several distinct measures of competition using a longitudinal database consisting of nearly 2,000 Dutch manufacturing firms between 1978 and 1993. The authors find considerable evidence suggesting that economic performance, in this case productivity growth, responds positively to the degree of competitive pressure.

A considerably different measure of firm performance, investment, is the focus of *chapter 6*. Bronwyn Hall, Jacques Mairesse, Lee Branstetter, and Bruno Crepon examine "Does cash flow cause investment and R&D? An exploration using panel data for French, Japanese, and United States scientific firms." In this chapter the authors examine the impact of financial institutions and corporate governance on the performance of industrial firms. Using a panel data version of the vector autoregressive (VAR) methodology, they test for the causal relationship between sales and cash flow, on the one hand, and investment and R&D on the other. This test is undertaken using three large longitudinal databases of firms in the scientific (high technology) sectors in the United States, France, and Japan. The evidence suggests that both investment and R&D are more sensitive to cash flow in the United States than in France and Japan. Their findings imply that the different institutional structure in France and Japan enables firms to avoid liquidity constraints experienced by their counterparts in the United States. Thus, there is substantial reason to believe that the institutional structure, in terms of financial institutions and corporate governance, shapes the dynamic performance of firms.

Chapter 7, by Michael Fritsch and Rolf Lukas, is concerned with economic performance at a different unit of observation than the firm – the region. Focusing on the performance of regions is important because ultimately economic policy makers are responsible for the economic welfare of what is called in Germany, the *Standort*, or location, rather than for particular firms. In "Innovation, cooperation, and the region," Fritsch and Lukas ask the question why the extent of cooperation and linkages among firms varies from region to region. They develop a new source of data to identify the extent and nature of regional cooperative linkages in Germany. This new database enables them to identify the characteristics of businesses engaging in cooperative relationships. They find that the regional distribution of cooperative partners suggests that, in particular, public research institutions and non-vertically related firms within a given region tend to constitute key elements of the regional innovation system. The authors also find that there are pronounced differences with regard to the propensity to cooperate as well as with regard to the locational structure of cooperation partners which may have an impact on two key measures of regional performance – innovation and growth.

Economic performance for the unit of observation of regions is also the focus of *chapter 8*, "Industry clusters: biotechnology/biomedicine and polymers in Ohio and Sweden," by Bo Carlsson and Pontus Braunerjhelm. Using data from the United States and Sweden, Carlsson and Braunerjhelm address a series of questions about the nature of the innovative performance in regions: (1) What are the origins, extent and composition of the technological system surrounding innovative activities in each region? (2) Who are the main actors both in the industrial/commercial area and in the science, research, and institutional infrastructure? (3) What is the nature of industrial clustering within each region? (4) What are the characteristics of regional networks? (5) What has been the role of public policy in shaping these clusters? And (6) what are the policy implications for both private firms and public policy? An important finding in this chapter is that the universities apparently play an important role in generating new knowledge for commercial development within the region.

While David Audretsch and Paula Stephan are similarly concerned with the linkages between knowledge sources and commercialization, in *chapter 9* they shift the unit of observation away from firms and regions to the individual. In addressing the questions, "How and why does knowledge spill over in biotechnology?" they focus on the incentives confronting scientists to appropriate the expected value of their knowledge considered within the context of their path-dependent career trajectories. In particular, they focus on the ability of scientists to appropriate the value of their knowledge embedded in their human capital along with the incentive structure influencing if and how scientists choose to commercialize their knowledge. They use a longitudinal database tracking the career paths of scientists over time and use a hazard model to estimate the duration over a scientist's career to starting a new biotechnology firm. They conclude that the spillover of knowledge from the source creating it, such as a university, a research institute, or an industrial corporation, to a new-firm startup facilitates the appropriation of knowledge for the individual scientist(s) but not necessarily for the organization creating that knowledge.

Firm survival, as well as growth, are also the performance measures in *chapter 10*, "Do services differ from manufacturing? The post-entry performance of firms in Dutch services" by David Audretsch, Luuk Klomp, and Roy Thurik. While a large literature has emerged focusing on the post-entry performance of firms, in terms of the links between growth, survival, size, and age, virtually all of these studies are based on manufacturing. In this chapter, the authors fill this gap in knowledge of the role of non-manufacturing in the dynamics of industrial organization. They suggest there are theoretical reasons why the relationships between firm age and size, on the one hand, and survival and growth, on the other, may in fact not be the same for services as they are for manufacturing. They use a longitudinal data base for Dutch firms in the retail and hotel and catering sectors to identify around 13,000 new-firm startups and 47,000 incumbents in the services and track them over subsequent years. The results suggest that the most fundamental relationships between firm size, firm age, survival, and growth are strikingly different for services than for manufacturing. In terms of the dynamics of industrial organization, services may, in fact, not simply mirror the manufacturing sector.

Audretsch (1995) suggested and found empirical evidence from a large longitudinal database of US firms that "Who exits and why?" is determined by the existence of two distinct models of industry evolution. The first is the *model of creative destruction,* where new entrants displace the large incumbents and the second model is that of *the revolving door*, where most new entrants exit from the industry within a short period. In *chapter 11*, "Who exits from German manufacturing industries and why? Evidence from the Hannover Firm Panel Study," Joachim Wagner pursues the same question using a large-scale longitudinal database of German firms. In fact, on the basis of the evidence presented in this chapter, Wagner rejects both of Audretsch's models and instead proposes a third variant – the *Darwinian model*, or the survival of the fittest. Wagner argues that this new variant is more consistent with the evidence from Germany, because firms, independent of age, that do not grow in terms of size or productivity or earn higher profits are confronted with a greater risk of failure than their fitter counterparts.

In *chapter 11*, "Technological intensity, demand conditions and the longevity of firms," by José Mata and Pedro Portugal, performance is again at the unit of observation of the firm and is measured in terms of the ability of firms to survive. In particular, the authors focus on the impact of demand and technological conditions on the likelihood of survival of Portuguese firms. They use a large longitudinal database of Portuguese firms and find that both demand and technological conditions influence firm performance.

In "Does start-up size influence the likelihood of survival?" in *chapter 13*, David Audretsch, Enrico Santarelli, and Marco Vivarelli also measure performance in terms of survival. In particular, they use a large longitudinal database in Italy to track new-firm startups and their subsequent post-entry performance over time. After comparing the results with those from the United States, they conclude that there is evidence supporting two very distinct views about the economic role of small firms. While the evidence between firm size and performance, measured as the likelihood of survival, supports the evolutionary view of small firms in the United States, the evidence from Italy is more consistent with the static network view of small firms.

The final chapter, *chapter 14* of the volume, "Barriers to growth of firms in developing countries: evidence from Burundi," by Micheline Goedhuys and Leo Sleuwaegen, also measures firm performance in terms of growth and survival. However, as the title suggests, the context is very different and is in terms of a developing country, Burundi. It shows that a learning process shapes the growth of firms in the developing world as it does in the developed world. However, this process is hampered by institutional and environmental conditions specific to the developing world.

12   David Audretsch and Roy Thurik

References

Audretsch, David B. (1995), *Innovation and Industry Evolution*, Cambridge, Mass.: MIT Press.
Audretsch, David B. and Maryann P. Feldman (1996), "Knowledge Spillovers and the Geography of Innovation," *American Economic Review*, 86(3, June): 630–640.
Audretsch, David B. and Paula E. Stephan (1996), "Company-Scientist Links: The Case of Biotechnology," *American Economic Review*, 86 (3, June): 641–650.
Berman, Eli, John Bound, and Stephen Machin (1997), "Implications of Skill-Biased Technological Change: International Evidence," Working Paper 6166, National Bureau of Economic Research (NBER), Cambridge.
Davis, S.J., J. Haltiwanger, and S. Schuh (1996), *Job Creation and Destruction in U.S. Manufacturing*, Cambridge, Mass.: MIT Press.
Jensen, Michael C. (1993), "The Modern Industrial Revolution, Exit, and the Failure of Internal Control Systems," *Journal of Finance*, 68: 831–880.
Kortum, Samuel and Josh Lerner (1997), "Stronger Protection or Technological Revolution: What is Behind the Recent Surge in Patenting?" Working Paper 6204, National Bureau of Economic Research (NBER), Cambridge.
Nelson, R. R. (1990), "Capitalism as an Engine of Progress," *Research Policy*, 19: 193–214.
(1995), "Co-evolution of Industry Structure, Technology and Supporting Institutions, and the Making of Comparative Advantage," *International Journal of the Economics of Business*, 2: 171–184.
Nooteboom B. (1994), "Innovation and Diffusion in Small Firms," *Small Business Economics*, 6: 327–347.
OECD (1997), *Employment Outlook*, Paris: OECD.

2 Wages, firm size, and wage inequality: How much do exports matter?

Bee Yan Aw and Geeta Batra

1 Introduction

There has been a renewed interest in the role that international trade plays in a country's employment and wages. Much of this work to date has focussed on the effect of imports or, more generally, international trade in developed countries. From the perspective of the newly industrializing countries (NICs), where exports occupy a very large share of the gross domestic product and where rapid increases in real wages have been accompanied by little wage inequality, a natural question, but one that has not previously been examined systematically, is the relationship between exports, wages, and wage inequality.[1]

In order to accurately address the issue of whether exports matter in the wages that are paid to workers, many firm characteristics that are known to be highly correlated with wages need to be taken into account, the key characteristic being firm size. Employees in large firms earn higher wages than those in small firms. Brown and Medoff (1989) conclude that even after controlling for observable labor quality, working conditions, unionization, and product market power, "the size–wage differential appears to be both sizable and omnipresent." Given that the export activity tends to be dominated by large firms (Berry, 1992; Aw and Hwang, 1995; and Bernard and Jensen, 1995), the export–wage relationship at the industry level is likely to reflect the influence of firm size as well as other firm characteristics that are correlated with wages. Firm-level data are thus crucial in enabling us to more accurately portray the export–wage relationship.

---

[1] The first generation NICs in East Asia are made up of Hong Kong, Singapore, South Korea, and Taiwan. In the decade of the eighties, real wages in Hong Kong, Singapore, South Korea, and Taiwan rose at an average per year of 4.4 percent, 6.3 percent, 5.5 percent, and 7.6 percent respectively, compared to the corresponding figure of 2 percent in Japan and negative rates in the countries in Latin America.

14   Bee Yan Aw and Geeta Batra

Recent theoretical growth models by Romer (1990), Grossman and Helpman (1991), and others emphasize the importance of international trade in increasing the use of specialized inputs and in generating higher productivity. One implication of these models is that a wage premium will be associated with exports, one measure of international trade. However, empirical verification of this link at the micro-level in developing countries is very limited.[2]

In this chapter, we use microdata for 80,584 firms in ten manufacturing industries from the 1986 Taiwanese Census to examine the wage–firm size profile separately for both exporters and non-exporters. We are interested, first, in whether the strong, positive relation between wage and firm size that is observed in the developed countries, holds for Taiwan's manufacturing firms. Second, we are interested in whether, relative to firms that restrict their sales to the domestic market, exporting firms pay higher and/or more equal wages, once we have controlled for firm size and other observable firm characteristics. Finally, we estimate the extent of wage inequality between non-production and production workers and ask if the export status of firms is related to this skill premium.

Our results reveal several interesting features of the Taiwanese labor market. First, the strong positive wage–firm size profile found in numerous developed country studies holds only for non-production workers. Second, the employer size–wage profile of production workers is highly dependent on the firm's market-orientation (exporter or non-exporter). Exporters in the bulk of the industries studied have relatively flat wage–firm size profiles for their production workers.

Third, in contrast to the mixed results relating firm size and wages, the export status of firms has a clear and positive relationship with firm wages. For all ten industries studied, exporters pay higher wages than non-exporters to both their non-production and production labor. The average cross-industry export–wage premium, after controlling for other firm characteristics known to be correlated with higher wages, is almost 30 percent for non-production workers and 14 percent for production workers. In order to gauge the magnitude of these figures, we compare them with the wage premia associated with working in the largest firms (those with more than 100 employees). The size premia for non-production and production workers average at 43 percent and 6 percent respectively. Thus, for production workers, the magnitude of the wage

---

[2] Bernard and Jensen (1995) documents the role of exports in US manufacturing from 1976–1987. Their major finding is that exporting plants contribute heavily to the increases in high-skilled workers and wages at the industry level.

premium associated with exports is more than twice that linked with firm size.

Finally, our results indicate that, on average, the level of wage inequality is higher among exporters than non-exporters, although for firms in the very large size category, the opposite result holds in eight out of the ten industries.

Section 2 presents some descriptive statistics contrasting exporters and non-exporters in the ten two-digit industries considered. The empirical model and the data used for estimation is discussed in section 3. In section 4, we present the empirical results. The summary and conclusions are in section 5.

2 Features of exporting firms and the labor market in Taiwan

The ten two-digit industries that are in this study were chosen to represent a mix of traditional and modern manufacturing activities in Taiwan. Together they make up 67 percent of the total value of manufacturing output, 73 percent of total employment in the manufacturing sector, 72 percent of the total number of manufacturing plants, and 73 percent of total value of exports of manufactures in 1986. The electric/electronics, textiles, and plastics industries dominate the manufacturing sectors' output, employment, and exports.

In table 2.1, we present some average characteristics of firms broken down by market-orientation. In this chapter, exporters are defined as those with positive export value and non-exporters as those that limit their sales to the local market.[3] On average, exporters in all industries employ several times more workers, and pay higher wages to both their non-production and production labor, relative to non-exporters. In addition, the ratio of non-production to production employment (and wages) is higher among exporters. Given the well-documented size–wage premium relation in developed countries, part of the exporters' higher wage may be related to their larger size.[4] In our empirical analysis, we account for firm size when estimating the wage premium associated with exporting.

---

[3] The analysis is also carried out defining a firm as an exporter if exports account for more than 50 percent of its total sales and also for firms that have 100 percent of their sales in the export market. The qualitative nature of our results are not sensitive to these changes in the cut-offs in the definition of exporters.

[4] See Brown and Medoff (1989) for a discussion of the firm size–wage premium in the US. In developing countries, the employer size–wage effect is often limited to sample surveys of narrowly defined industries. Little (1987) summarizes studies of specific industries in Colombia and India. These papers generally confirm the positive relationship between wages and firm size found in developed countries although there is some evidence that

Table 2.1 *Mean characteristics by two-digit industries and market-orientation in the Taiwanese manufacturing sector, 1986*

Industry/market orientation	Number of firms	Average annual wage of non-production labor ('000 NT$)	Average annual wage of production labor[a] ('000 NT$)	Ratio of non-production to production labor	Percent of firms with R&D or training[c]	Percent of firms with foreign capital	Percent of multiplant firms	Age (years)	Average employment
Textiles									
Exporters[b]	1,596	185.52	136.33	0.46	21.55	2.94	31.14	10.68	131.20
Non-exporters	6,186	135.76	117.80	0.26	1.86	0.19	4.46	6.78	16.58
Clothing									
Exporters	1,004	165.18	123.37	0.46	19.42	2.49	22.71	7.93	106.24
Non-exporters	2,295	118.64	105.56	0.26	1.48	0.09	2.00	5.88	16.12
Paper/Publishing									
Exporters	402	175.69	137.32	0.60	15.42	3.48	15.92	10.45	78.45
Non-exporters	8,699	123.12	116.58	0.39	1.49	0.11	1.29	7.48	8.82
Chemicals									
Exporters	217	265.05	192.81	0.91	44.24	14.75	53.00	13.90	316.54
Non-exporters	830	151.93	134.39	0.46	5.30	1.20	12.77	8.40	20.71
Plastics									
Exporters	2,113	169.20	133.01	0.46	17.18	2.13	13.63	8.04	94.27
Non-exporters	8,314	122.85	112.79	0.26	1.52	0.08	1.62	5.87	11.16
Iron and Steel									
Exporters	362	199.56	173.72	0.62	20.72	3.87	30.39	11.21	111.39
Non-exporters	2,521	138.54	134.82	0.39	2.54	0.32	5.47	7.50	14.56

Fabricated Metals								
Exporters	2,033	158.39	133.34	0.37	12.94	2.66	10.58	7.85	40.13
Non-exporters	22,505	121.57	123.33	0.21	1.10	0.12	0.81	6.30	5.79
Machinery								
Exporters	1,209	162.90	146.91	0.46	20.68	2.81	11.66	9.98	39.56
Non-exporters	8,557	124.04	128.44	0.27	1.93	0.19	1.60	7.37	6.77
Electric/Electronics								
Exporters	2,411	177.25	118.44	0.45	31.27	9.62	20.95	8.71	151.36
Non-exporters	5,170	128.91	108.71	0.36	4.16	0.58	3.50	5.81	16.60
Transport Equipment								
Exporters	715	172.95	145.20	0.37	23.08	4.20	15.66	9.22	103.02
Non-exporters	3,445	134.02	122.85	0.30	3.02	0.70	4.38	7.53	13.79

Notes:

[a] The average annual wage of production (or non-production) labor is defined as the total salary of permanent production (or non-production) labor among exporters (or non-exporters) within an industry in 1986 divided by the number of permanent employees in exporting (or non-exporting) firms within the industry.

[b] Exporters are those firms with a positive export to total sales ratio.

[c] Percentage of firms with R&D or training is defined as the ratio of the number of firms that invest positive amounts in research and development, know-how or on-the-job training to the total number of firms.

However, firm size is but one dimension of an array of firm characteristics that are correlated with wages across firms. Technological change,
biased toward skilled workers, and the use of advanced technology have
been identified by many researchers as the most likely factors underlying
the higher return to skilled manufacturing wages and the wide gap in the
wages between skilled and unskilled workers in the US.[5] Higher investments by foreign firms, and multiplant status as well as age have been
found to be associated with higher wages.[6] Indeed, all the above
characteristics also appear to play a role in distinguishing exporters from
non-exporters, as is evident from examining table 2.1. It is clear that
Taiwanese exporters, in addition to being larger, are more likely to invest
in formal technology, have foreign capital, be multiplant firms, and are
older relative to those whose sales are confined primarily to the domestic
market.[7] Thus, in order to understand the export–wage relation, it is
important that the heterogeneity of firms along these dimensions are
controlled for.

In Taiwan, more than elsewhere, employment and wages reflect,
primarily, demand and supply of labor of varying qualities. Fields (1992)
provides some evidence to indicate that Taiwan's labor market is best
characterized as an integrated, well-functioning one where wages of the
different groups of labor are set largely by the interaction of supply and
demand for labor services rather than by government policy (with respect
to minimum wage legislation or multinational corporations) or union
pressure. As such, labor market segmentation, that in other countries has
significant wage effects, is likely to be less important. Similar conclusions
are voiced by Deyo (1989), Li (1989), and Wade (1990).

The openness of the economy implies that much of the demand for
labor, in turn, is driven by the demand for production in the export
market. If there is a distinction in worker or job characteristics between
exporting and non-exporting firms, then a wage differential will be

---

the relationship in developing countries is less uniform across size and occupational
groupings.
[5] See Bartel and Lichtenberg (1991), Davis and Haltiwanger (1991), Berman, Bound, and
Griliches (1994), Lawrence and Slaughter (1993), and Dunne and Schmitz (1995). In all
of these papers, skilled and unskilled labor are proxied by non-production and
production labor, respectively.
[6] See Little (1987).
[7] For a sample of Israeli firms, Bregman, Fuss, and Regev (1991) show that larger firms
are more technology intensive, employ more skilled workers, and are more export
oriented. Bernard and Jensen (1995) find that in the US manufacturing sector, exporters
tend to have higher employment and shipments, are more capital intensive, and employ
relatively more non-production workers than non-exporters. Similar patterns are
present in Taiwan.

associated with the export status of firms. To the extent that labor and product markets in Taiwan are competitive, as existing evidence suggests, wage differentials between exporters and non-exporters are likely to arise, not from institutional and other factors, but from the non-measured quality dimensions of labor.[8] While many of the labor market characteristics observed in Taiwan are suspected to be linked to the country's export orientation, we know of no empirical work that has confirmed such a link.

Research to date suggests that, compared to firms geared toward the domestic market, exporting firms in response to their exposure to the international market are more likely to hire higher-quality labor and thus pay more. This result is consistent with recent research on the marketing of exports of consumer goods made by local firms in developing countries for industrial markets. This research suggests that these exports are systematically different from the analogous products made for the domestic market (Keesing and Lall, 1992). In general, the bulk of exports from East Asia are products manufactured to the orders of buyers from industrial countries that satisfy specific standards of finish, styling, quality, reliability, and packaging. There is some scattered evidence in the literature that much of the relevant knowledge on quality control and design changes comes from these foreign buyers.[9] The type of technology most easily transmitted via exporters' foreign contacts is likely to be knowledge that is "standardized" and "non-proprietary" as is found in less-technology-intensive industries, such as clothing. Learning and assimilating this knowledge, which is crucial to success in exporting, is facilitated by the presence of a substantial core of labor with managerial abilities and education superior to those employed in producing for the local market (Pack, 1992b).

In addition to this potential link between wages and exports, Taiwan has often been cited as an example of a country where the benefits of growth have been relatively evenly spread among different groups of

[8] The predominance of a very large number of small firms within the manufacturing sector of Taiwan and the general openness of the economy has lead to intense competition within the country (Dahlman and Sananikone, 1990; Wade, 1990). This feature is also characteristic of the international market for many of Taiwan's exports. Riedel (1988, 1993) provides evidence that Hong Kong, Korea, and Taiwan are price takers in world markets for manufactures. Aw (1992) empirically tests for non-competitive conditions in the market for Taiwanese footwear exports and finds no evidence of price mark-ups.

[9] Westphal et al. (1984) find that a significant amount of knowledge of production engineering possessed by Korean firms came from their foreign purchasers. Pack (1992a) cites this as a potentially important channel of technology transfer for Taiwanese exporters.

workers. Pack (1992b) provides evidence indicating very low dispersion of wages in Taiwan relative to other LDCs, but comparable to those in the OECD countries. Others document that the gap in Taiwanese skilled and unskilled wages is modest relative to that in the countries in Latin America or even the US (Ranis, 1992; World Bank, 1993). These observations are made using aggregate economy-wide or industry-level data. In this chapter, firm-level information will be used to shed some light on the relationship between the export activity and the level of wage inequality.

3   The data and estimation

The data

The empirical work is based on a unique firm-level data set from Taiwan's 1986 Census of Manufacturing. While plant-level data are reported for the number of workers, information on all other variables is complete at the firm level. Our analysis is, thus, carried out at the firm level. We focus on ten of the country's major industries.

The data include the birth year and single or multiplant status of the firm. Output data include the total volume and value of production and sales, where each is broken down by domestic and export market. Data on foreign investment, expenditures on technology licenses, worker training, and research and development are also reported for each firm. Employment information is disaggregated into two broad categories: non-production and production labor. It is common in the literature for these occupational categories to be broadly classified as "skilled" and "unskilled" respectively.[10] Firms report total salaries and employment levels for each category.[11] Hours data are not collected. The firm's labor is also subdivided into temporary and permanent labor.

Employers in Taiwanese manufacturing rely on temporary labor to provide firms with an important means of short-term adjustments to fluctuations in both output and input markets. In the Taiwanese Census,

---

[10] Berman, Bound, and Griliches (1994) argue that occupation distinctions do provide a reasonable separation between the more skilled and the less skilled. Their conclusion is based on data assembled on the educational attainment by broad occupational groups in the US for 1973, 1979, and 1987.

[11] Unfortunately, information on fringe benefits is not disaggregated by skilled and unskilled labor categories. On average, the share of fringe benefits in total compensation is 7.5 percent, a figure that is significantly smaller than that in the US where fringe benefits account for as much as 50 percent of total compensation in some industries (Katz and Summers, 1989).

temporary workers are defined as those employed for a period of less than six months. This category includes short-term contract workers, piece-rate and on-call workers. In 1986, temporary labor averaged 8.5 percent of the total labor force in the ten industries under study.[12] The data from the Census of Manufactures only allow us to obtain a measure of the annual wage of each category of labor. Since temporary labor only work part of the year, their wage has to be lower than the permanent worker wage. As a result, in the analysis that follows, we focus on the wage–firm size profiles of permanent labor.

Total employment is used as a measure of firm size. The wage of non-production labor is measured by the ratio of the salary of non-production labor to total employment of non-production labor; the wage of production labor is measured by the ratio of the salary of production labor to the total employment of production labor.

The empirical model

Given the absence of a well-developed theory linking exports with wages, our goal here is to describe the pattern of the export–wage relation observed in the data. The technique that we have chosen for this purpose is based on semi-parametric regression models (Robinson, 1988). Unlike the more familiar linear regression techniques, these models contain parametric and non-parametric components and are at their best when large cross-sectional data sets are available. The techniques do not put a lot of a priori structure on the form of the relationship between wages and firm size. Moreover, the technique provides graphical descriptions of the data in a way that is transparent and informative about the distributional structure of the data.[13]

Given the important relationship observed between firm size and wages in the extant literature, we let the non-parametric variable in our model be firm size and the parametric component be other firm-specific characteristics that have been shown in the literature to be correlated with wages across firms. That is, we use the semi-parametric regression technique to relate firm size with the wages of permanent production and non-production workers, controlling for other observable

[12] In a survey of flexible staffing in enterprises, the corresponding figure in the same year among US firms surveyed is 1.4 percent (Abraham, 1988).

[13] Deaton (1989) discusses these and other advantages of non-parametric techniques over alternative, more familiar econometric techniques such as cross-tabulations which are not very flexible and do not convey information as transparently and linear regressions which tend to over-summarize, "rarely doing justice to the amount of information available."

firm-specific characteristics that are assumed to be linearly related to firm wages. This is done separately for exporting and non-exporting firms.

Given a data set $[(y_i, x_i, z_i), i = 1,...,n]$, the semi-parametric model takes the following form

$$y = x'\beta + \theta(z) + u \tag{1}$$

where y is an $n \times 1$ vector representing the dependent variable, log(wage); y is assumed to be a linear function of x, an $n \times k$ matrix of firm characteristics that comprise foreign investment, technology investment, firm age, and multiplant status.[14] These are characteristics that are available in the Census database and are also ones that are linked in the literature to wages paid by firms. The non-parametric component, firm size, is represented by a $n \times 1$ vector, z, measured as log (employment). We assume that u is distributed with mean zero and finite variance. In addition, $E(u/z, x) = 0$ and θ is an unknown function of z.

We adopt the following two-stage estimation. The first stage, following Robinson (1988), involves estimating equation (1) to obtain the parameter estimates for β. Taking the expected value of equation (1) yields

$$E(y/z) = E(x/z)'\beta + \theta(z). \tag{2}$$

Subtracting equation (2) from equation (1) gives

$$y - E(y/z) = (x - E(x/z))'\beta + u. \tag{3}$$

In equation (3), $E(y/z)$ and $E(x/z)$ are estimated without imposing any parametric relationships of x and y on z by using non-parametric estimation techniques.[15] Representing the kernel estimates of $E(y/z)$ and $E(x/z)$ by $E_N(y/z)$ and $E_N(x/z)$ respectively, equation (3) can be rewritten as

$$y - E_N(y/z) = (x - E_N(x/z))'\beta + u. \tag{4}$$

---

[14] Foreign investment is a dummy variable equal to unity if the firm has any foreign capital, and zero otherwise; multiplant is a dummy variable with a value of one if the firm has more than one plant, and zero otherwise; and technology investment is represented by a dummy variable with a value of one if the firm invests positive expenditures on R&D, know-how, or training, and zero otherwise.

[15] The estimation is done by kernel smoothing, where the main idea is to set a "bandwidth" parameter that determines how near observations have to be in order to contribute to the average at each point. Instead of assuming a fixed smoothing parameter, we use the optimal smoothing parameter (see appendix).

Ordinary least squares estimation is then applied to equation (4), to obtain β.

In the second stage, to obtain the relationship between wages and firm size, after controlling for firm characteristics, we perform the following non-parametric estimation

$$E(y - x'\hat{\beta}|z) = \theta(z). \tag{5}$$

y is again log(wage), z is firm size (log total employment), and $x'\hat{\beta}$ is a vector of predicted values using the first-stage estimates, $\hat{\beta}$. We estimate these equations separately for production and non-production workers as well as by the market orientation of each of these groups of workers.

4   The empirical results

In tables 2.2 and 2.3, we report, separately for exporters and non-exporters, the semi-parametric coefficient estimates of the four independent variables, firm age, multiplant status, foreign capital, and technology investment in the estimation of equation (1).

For both groups of labor, wages are significantly related to firm age and investments in technology. The wage effect of firm age is positive and highly significant across all industries and labor groupings and market orientation. This finding appears consistent with the Brown and Medoff (1989) conjecture that the size–wage premium in the US may be reflecting a relationship between employer age and wages. However, we find that the magnitude of this variable is quite small in the case of Taiwanese industries. In contrast, investments in technology are positively and significantly related to the wages of both groups of workers, with the largest marginal impact for non-production labor of non-exporting firms and the smallest for production labor hired by exporters. The average for all workers across all firm types is 14 percent. This result is very similar to the evidence found by Dunne and Schmitz (1995) of an average wage premium of 12 percent (8 percent for non-production and 16 percent for production workers) to working in US plants with the most machines (the proxy for advanced technology use). On average, foreign capital and multiplant status have positive and large effects on the wage of non-production labor among exporters and non-exporters. In contrast, the influences of foreign capital and multiplant status on the wage of production workers are more mixed regardless of the firms' export status.

The graphs in figures 2.1 to 2.10 summarize the wage–size relationship using the semi-parametric estimator. Panel A is for non-production

Table 2.2 *Semi-parametric regression estimates by industry and market orientation*
Dependent variable: log (wage) of permanent production labor

Market orientation/independent variable	Textiles	Clothing	Paper/publishing	Chemicals	Plastics	Iron and steel	Fabricated metals	Machinery	Electric/electronics	Transport equipment
Exporters										
Age	0.007[a]	0.007[a]	0.008[a]	0.008[b]	0.016[a]	0.011[a]	0.010[a]	0.008[a]	0.012[a]	0.008[a]
	(0.002)	(0.003)	(0.003)	(0.004)	(0.002)	(0.003)	(0.002)	(0.002)	(0.002)	(0.003)
Multiplant	0.083[a]	0.087[a]	0.191[a]	0.163[b]	0.022	0.001	0.002	0.064	0.045	−0.016
	(0.028)	(0.034)	(0.071)	(0.069)	(0.031)	(0.049)	(0.033)	(0.040)	(0.024)	(0.044)
Foreign capital	0.034	0.086	−0.008	0.155	0.025	0.194	0.229[a]	0.112	−0.046	0.080
	(0.066)	(0.085)	(0.119)	(0.079)	(0.071)	(0.106)	(0.060)	(0.078)	(0.034)	(0.074)
Technology	0.078[a]	0.036	0.136	0.170[a]	0.099[a]	0.046	0.103[a]	0.088[a]	0.084[a]	0.086[b]
	(0.030)	(0.037)	(0.071)	(0.058)	(0.028)	(0.056)	(0.030)	(0.032)	(0.022)	(0.039)
Non-exporters										
Age	0.011[a]	0.008[a]	0.010[a]	0.005	0.014[a]	0.014[a]	0.012[a]	0.011[a]	0.022[a]	0.009[a]
	(0.001)	(0.002)	(0.001)	(0.003)	(0.001)	(0.002)	(0.001)	(0.001)	(0.001)	(0.001)
Multiplant	0.156[a]	0.105	0.214[a]	0.087	0.154[a]	0.113[a]	0.109	0.074	0.066	0.183[a]
	(0.034)	(0.071)	(0.049)	(0.058)	(0.042)	(0.045)	(0.034)	(0.042)	(0.041)	(0.042)
Foreign capital	−0.036	0.233	0.247	0.164	0.020	0.061	0.391[a]	0.249[b]	0.133	0.222[b]
	(0.116)	(0.312)	(0.162)	(0.160)	(0.170)	(0.179)	(0.086)	(0.116)	(0.094)	(0.097)
Technology	0.190[a]	0.110	0.162[a]	0.147	0.113[a]	0.135[b]	0.130[a]	0.126[a]	0.172[a]	0.156[a]
	(0.044)	(0.082)	(0.040)	(0.075)	(0.042)	(0.063)	(0.028)	(0.035)	(0.035)	(0.046)

Notes:
[a] Significant at 1% level. [b] Significant at 5% level.
Numbers in parentheses are standard errors.

Table 2.3 *Semi-parametric regression estimates by industry and market orientation*
Dependent variable: log(wage) of permanent non-production labor

Market orientation/ independent variable	Textiles	Clothing	Paper/ publishing	Chemicals	Plastics	Iron and steel	Fabricated metals	Machinery	Electric/ electronics	Transport equipment
Exporters										
Age	0.010^a	0.009^a	0.007^b	0.014^a	0.013^a	0.009^b	0.009^a	0.007^a	0.007^a	0.010^a
	(0.002)	(0.003)	(0.003)	(0.005)	(0.002)	(0.004)	(0.002)	(0.002)	(0.002)	(0.003)
Multiplant	0.103^a	0.128^a	0.170^b	0.365^a	0.067^b	0.106	0.062	0.115^a	0.079^a	0.099^b
	(0.029)	(0.038)	(0.080)	(0.086)	(0.031)	(0.056)	(0.036)	(0.044)	(0.025)	(0.044)
Foreign capital	0.135	0.294^a	0.318^b	0.248^b	0.199^a	0.316^a	0.353^a	0.217^a	0.174^a	0.295^a
	(0.069)	(0.095)	(0.142)	(0.102)	(0.068)	(0.124)	(0.066)	(0.086)	(0.036)	(0.076)
Technology	0.099^a	0.134^a	0.070	0.186^b	0.118^a	0.133^b	0.121^a	0.082^b	0.126^a	0.116^a
	(0.031)	(0.041)	(0.080)	(0.075)	(0.029)	(0.065)	(0.033)	(0.036)	(0.023)	(0.039)
Non-Exporters										
Age	0.011^a	0.011^a	0.010^a	0.003	0.015^a	0.011^a	0.012^a	0.009^a	0.018^a	0.009^a
	(0.001)	(0.002)	(0.001)	(0.003)	(0.001)	(0.002)	(0.001)	(0.001)	(0.002)	(0.002)
Multiplant	0.243^a	0.225^a	0.271^a	0.189^a	0.133^a	0.171^a	0.048	0.196^a	0.141^a	0.306^a
	(0.036)	(0.072)	(0.050)	(0.062)	(0.047)	(0.045)	(0.038)	(0.045)	(0.045)	(0.043)
Foreign capital	−0.136	−0.313	0.284	0.289	0.504^b	0.452^b	0.356^a	0.219	0.456^a	0.366^a
	(0.133)	(0.473)	(0.150)	(0.170)	(0.203)	(0.187)	(0.098)	(0.129)	(0.101)	(0.100)
Technology	0.216^a	0.124	0.115^a	0.279^a	0.098^b	0.227^a	0.150^a	0.208^a	0.262^a	0.128^b
	(0.049)	(0.086)	(0.046)	(0.081)	(0.049)	(0.066)	(0.035)	(0.043)	(0.041)	(0.052)

Notes:
^{a} Significant at 1% level. ^{b} Significant at 5% level.
Numbers in parentheses are standard errors.

Panel A

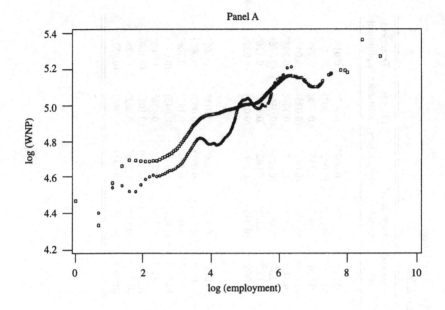

Panel B

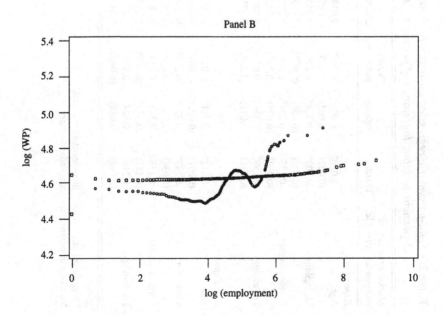

Panel C

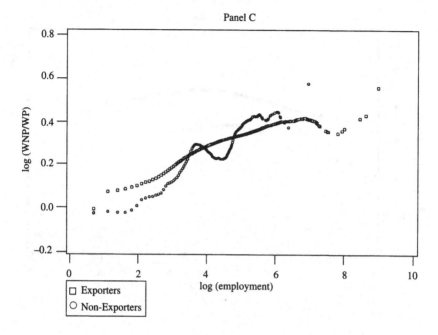

Figure 2.1   Industry: textiles

Notes: WNP – wage of non-production workers.

WP – wage of production workers.

The log values of 2, 4, 4, 5, 5, and 6 correspond to levels of 7, 55, 90, 148, and 403 respectively.

Units of measurement for wages is '000 NT$ and employment is number of workers.

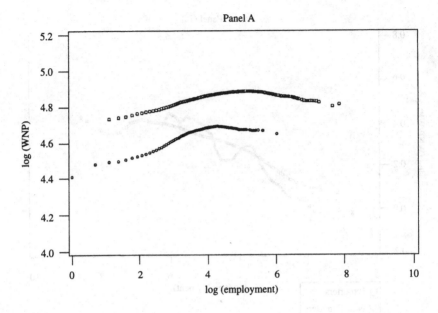

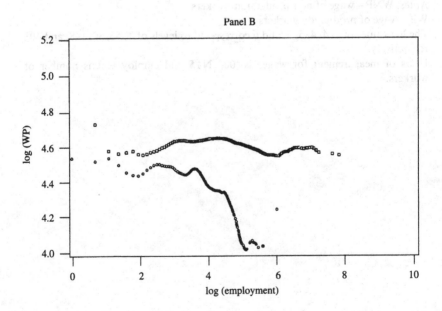

Panel C

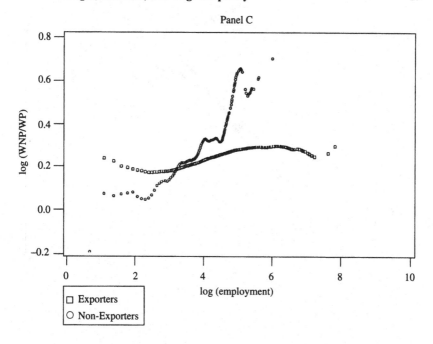

Figure 2.2   Industry: clothing
Notes: See figure 2.1.

Panel A

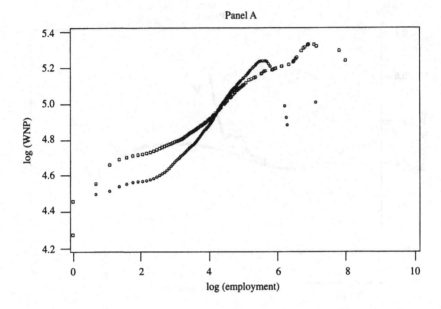

Panel B

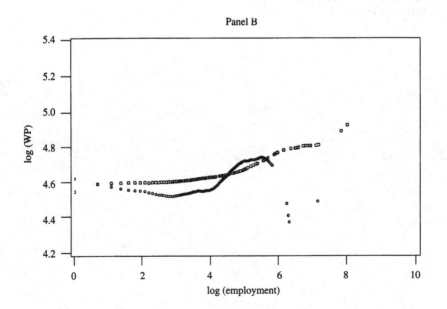

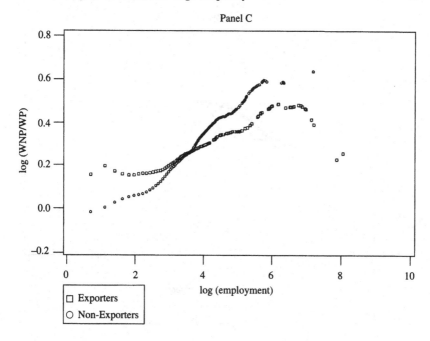

Figure 2.3 Industry: paper/publishing
Notes: See figure 2.1.

Panel A

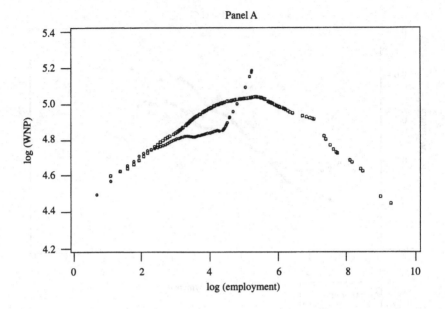

Panel B

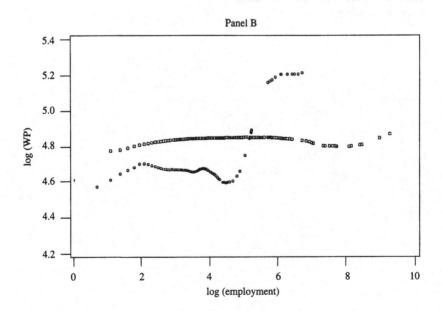

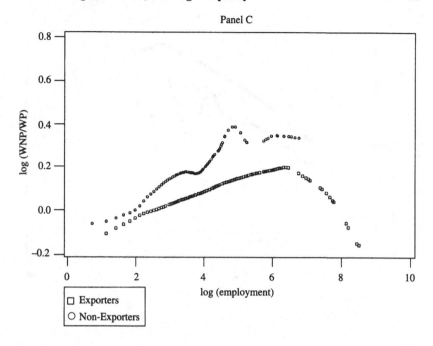

Figure 2.4 Industry: chemicals
Notes: See figure 2.1.

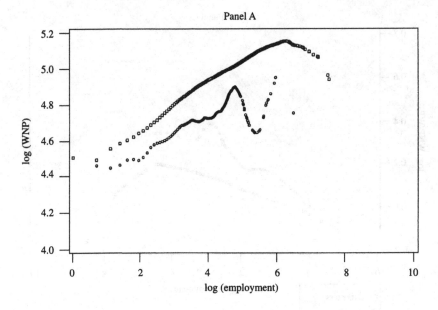

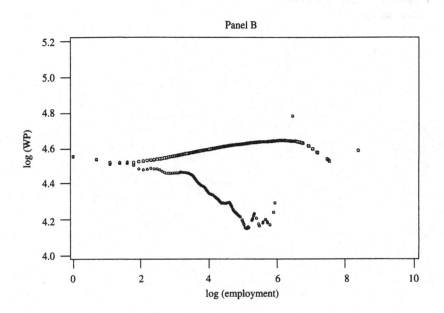

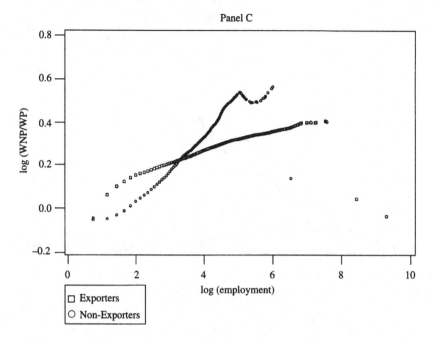

Figure 2.5   Industry: plastics
Notes: See figure 2.1.

Panel A

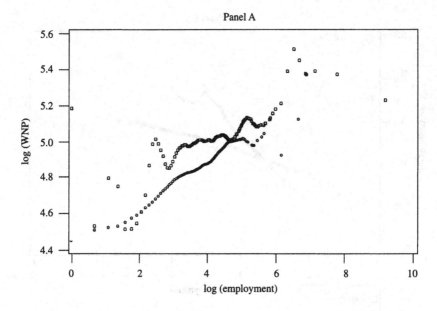

Panel A

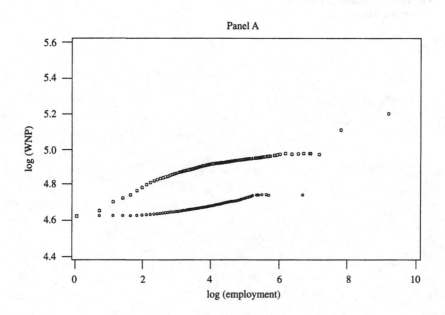

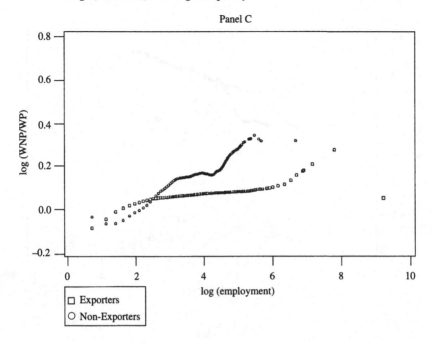

Figure 2.6 Industry: iron and steel
Notes: See figure 2.1.

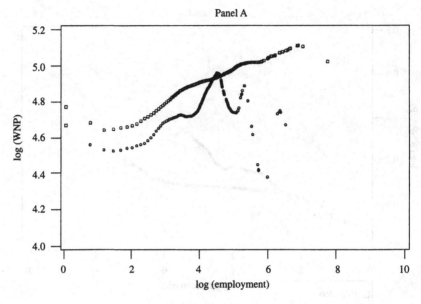

Panel A

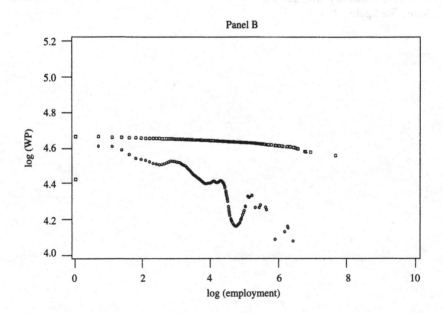

Panel B

Panel C

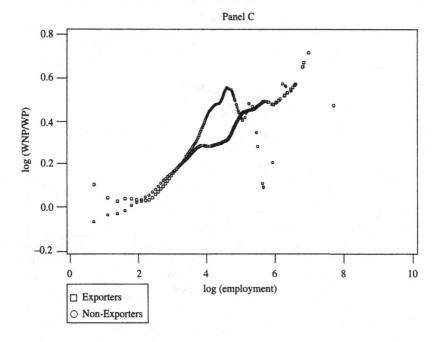

Figure 2.7   Industry: fabricated metals
Notes: See figure 2.1.

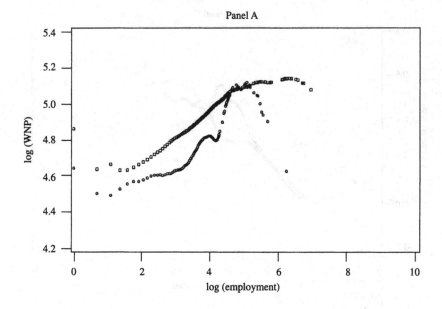

Panel A

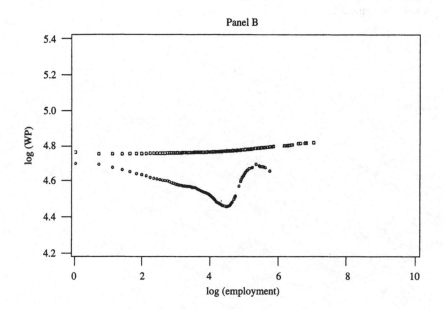

Panel B

Panel C

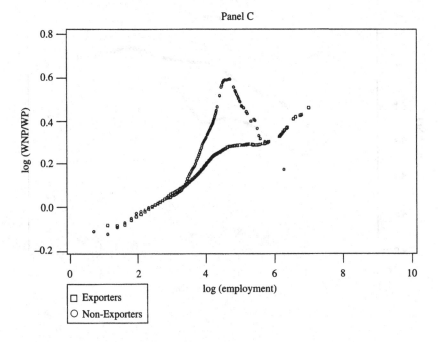

Figure 2.8   Industry: machinery
Notes: See figure 2.1.

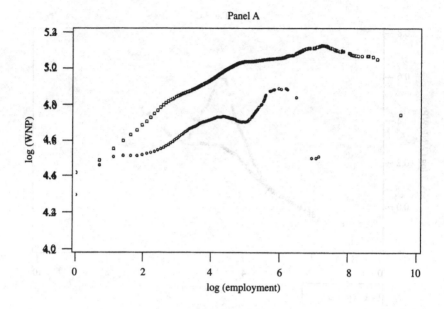

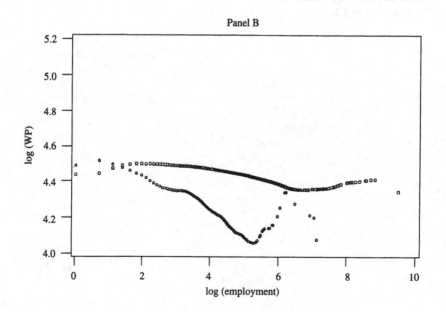

Panel C

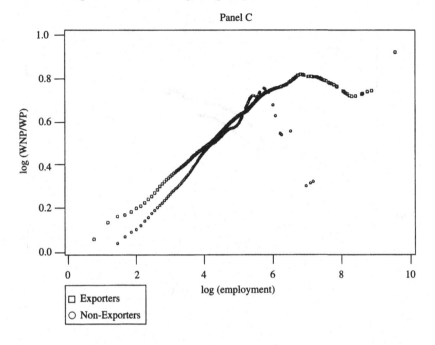

Figure 2.9 Industry: electric/electronics
Notes: See figure 2.1.

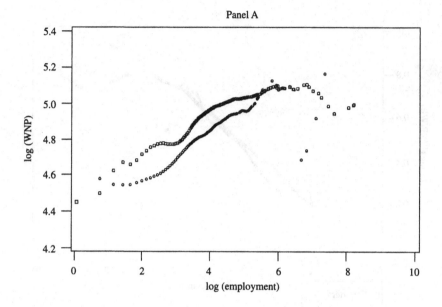

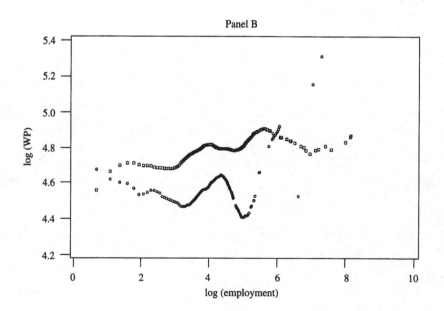

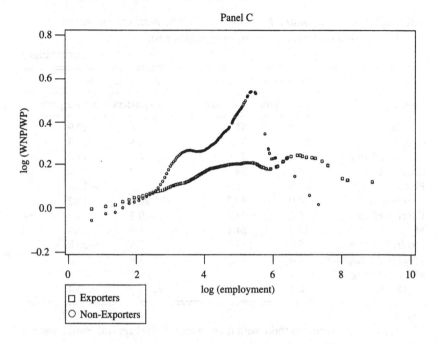

Figure 2.10   Industry: transport equipment
Notes: See figure 2.1.

Table 2.4 *The size-premium by labor type and by market-orientation*[a,b]
(based on semi-parametric regression results)

(percentage)

Industry	Non-production labor		Production labor	
	Exporters	Non-exporters	Exporters	Non-exporters
Textiles	42.8	55.7	5.8	10.9
Clothing	10.5	15.4	−0.4	−13.9
Paper/publishing	59.0	77.9	18.2	17.2
Chemicals	24.6	89.7	3.2	46.4
Plastics	36.6	34.6	7.5	−15.4
Iron and steel	34.0	47.7	26.0	14.2
Fabricated metals	35.1	23.4	−0.3	3.4
Machinery	48.9	64.1	1.9	6.2
Electric/electronics	35.0	22.3	−7.0	−20.8
Transport equipment	37.4	50.2	3.9	5.8
Manufacturing average	36.4	48.1	5.9	5.4

Notes:
[a] Large firms are defined as those with more than 100 workers and small firms are defined as those with 20 or less workers.
[b] The size-premium is calculated as the percentage difference between the average wage of large firms and the average wage of small firms.

worker wages, panel B for production worker wages, and panel C for the relative wage of non-production to production workers. Separate curves are plotted for exporters and non-exporters.[16]

Several key features stand out when we examine the separate panels of the graphs. Focusing on the panel for non-production labor (panel A in each graph), it is clear that firm size is strongly and positively correlated with non-production wages for both exporters and non-exporters. The results from the semi-parametric regression are used to tabulate the percentage difference in the wage of workers in large relative to small firms. These figures, reported in table 2.4, are broken down by the market orientation of firms. The difference in non-production wage between large (>100 workers) and small (≤20 workers) firms average at 36 percent and 48 percent for exporters and non-exporters respectively. For convenience, we will refer to this difference as the average size

---

[16] The magnitudes of 2, 3, 4, and 5 on a logarithmic scale correspond to actual levels of 7.3, 20, 55, and 148. The units of measurement for the X and Y axes of panels A and B of the graphs are employment levels and N.T. $'000 respectively.

premium.[17] The smallest size premium is among exporters in the clothing industry (10.5 percent) and the largest is found among non-exporters in the chemicals industry (89.7 percent).

The wage–firm size profile of production workers is quite different from the pattern observed above. This is clearly shown in panel B in the graphs and the average figures are reported in the last two columns of table 2.4. Among exporters, the wage–firm size profiles for eight of the ten industries (textiles, clothing, transport equipment, plastics, chemicals, fabricated metals, machinery, electric/electronics) are relatively flat. The ten-industry average size premium is only 5.9 percent.[18] This finding is particularly noteworthy given that significantly larger employer size–wage premia are typical in studies based in both developed and developing countries. For US firms, Dunne and Schmitz (1995), find that compared to the smallest plants, production workers in the largest plants earn a premium of 28 percent. In Peru, Schaffner (1994) found that, after controlling for worker characteristics, the wage of firms employing more than 100 workers average about 43 percent more than firms with less than ten workers.

In a separate exercise, we investigate the sensitivity of the above wage–firm size profiles to export levels. Exporters are divided into two groups: large exporters (firms with exports to total sales ratio exceeding 0.5) and small exporters (firms with exports to total sales ratio ranging from 0.01 to 0.5). Finer breakdowns are not possible since the generation of the graphs require a significant number of firms in each export category. For both production and non-production labor, the wage–firm size profiles are not sensitive to the two categories of export levels under consideration. In particular, the flat wage–firm size profiles of production workers among exporters in eight of the ten industries hold for both small and large exporters with the large exporters in the remaining two industries (paper/publishing and iron/steel) also assuming flat profiles.

---

[17] For US manufacturing firms examined by Bernard and Jensen (1995), the size–wage premium in 1987 for all workers in large (more than 250 employees) relative to small (less than 50 workers) is 7.2 percent for exporters and 24.3 percent for all plants in their sample. Brown and Medoff (1989) find that employees in large US manufacturing establishments can be expected to earn 6–15 percent more than their counterparts in smaller establishments. Size premiums in developing countries are generally found to be significantly higher. Little *et al.* (1987) summarize size premiums in the order of 100 percent for similar workers in India and Indonesia and lower corresponding figures in Korea, Malaysia, and Colombia (30–50 percent).

[18] Recall that for non-production workers the corresponding figure is 36.4 percent. This result suggests that any size differential in labor quality among production workers is small compared to non-production labor.

Table 2.5 *Export-premium by labor type and skill-premium by market-orientation*[a,b] *(based on semi-parametric regression results)*

(percentage)

Industry	Export premium		Skill premium	
	Non-production labor	Production labor	Exporters	Non-exporters
Textiles	29.8	11.6	25.5	7.9
Clothing	30.7	13.9	23.1	7.3
Paper/publishing	31.7	8.6	23.0	1.4
Chemicals	13.2	17.2	2.4	6.1
Plastics	32.7	10.2	25.9	4.5
Iron and steel	36.8	30.1	6.0	0.8
Fabricated metals	26.2	10.2	14.6	−4.7
Machinery	27.4	11.2	7.6	−6.5
Electric/electronics	40.4	10.5	45.6	14.7
Transport equipment	26.6	17.0	10.5	2.1
Manufacturing average	29.6	14.1	18.4	3.4

Notes:
[a] Export premium is measured as the difference between the average wage of exporters and non-exporters.
[b] Skill premium is measured as the difference between the average wage of non-production and production labor.

The wage–firm size profiles among production workers in non-exporting firms is much less uniform. Except for four of the ten industries (clothing, plastics, electric/electronics, and fabricated metals), wages generally rise with firm size. The non-uniformity of the profiles probably reflects the heterogeneity among the domestic firms in the hours worked by their permanent workers or the effect of female workers in these industries. Indeed our data indicate that large domestic-market-oriented firms in these industries, unlike the other industries, have a higher share of female workers than their smaller-sized domestic counterparts.[19] If female workers are also paid lower wages than male workers, the negative wage–firm size profile observed in several of the industries is less surprising than at first glance.

[19] Our data do not provide the breakup of female workers by production or non-production status. Our conjecture is that if these data were available, they would reinforce the pattern observed here.

While the existence of a positive employer size–wage profile is weaker and less pervasive in Taiwan than similar studies of developed countries suggest, trade status is an important dimension of firm characteristics that appears to be important across all industries, regardless of labor type and firm size. From table 2.5, we observe that on average, exporting firms pay on the order of 40 percent and 19 percent more than non-exporters to their non-production and production labor, respectively. After controlling for firm size and other firm characteristics known to be correlated with higher wages, the corresponding figures are still strikingly high at 30 percent and 14 percent.[20] These export premiums are obtained from the semi-parametric regression results and are reported for each of the ten industries in table 2.5. For non-production workers, the wage gap between exporters and non-exporters, or the export premium, ranges from 13.2 percent in the chemicals industry to 40 percent in electric/electronics. In the case of production workers, the wage differential between the same two groups of producers is smaller and ranges from 8.6 percent in paper/publishing to 30.1 percent in iron and steel.[21]

One possible source of the wage premia observed among exporters is the heterogeneity of skills and other unobserved or unmeasured labor quality characteristics among workers within each broad labor grouping.[22] In particular, if exporters hire workers with higher marginal products (for the reasons discussed in section 2) than non-exporters, then the higher wages paid by exporters simply reflects higher, unobserved labor quality. A related and more basic argument, and one that is consistent with recent studies, is that the technologies used by exporters may be quite different from those used by non-exporters either because the composition of products is distinctively different between the two groups or because exporters have more access to new and improved technology. If this technology relies heavily on standardization and teamwork and thus requires a homogeneous, high-quality workforce, then we are likely to observe exporters paying higher wages.[23]

---

[20] The only exception is that the wage of non-production workers among firms with more than 100 workers in the textiles, machinery, and paper/publishing industries are similar between exporters and non-exporters. These firms comprise less than 10 percent of the total number of firms in each of the three industries.

[21] For all ten industries under study, exporters pay significantly higher fringe benefits per worker than non-exporters. Thus, if we had included fringe benefits, the export–non-export wage differential would be reinforced.

[22] Among these unmeasured dimensions are managerial or entrepreneurial abilities among non-production (or skilled labor by our definition) workers.

[23] Coe and Helpman (1995) and Aw and Batra (1994) using cross-country and firm-level data, respectively, conclude that a country's trade appears to be an important mechanism for the worldwide transmission of innovation and technological progress.

An interesting pattern in the market for non-production labor, and to a smaller extent in the market for production workers, is that the separate curves representing exporters and non-exporters approach each other as firm size increases. This indicates that for the largest firms, wages are less correlated with the export activity of firms. This observation is consistent with the view in the literature that smaller firms have greater technological heterogeneity (Acs and Audretsch, 1990; Davis and Haltiwanger, 1992; and Dunne and Schmitz, 1995). To the extent that exports represent a good proxy for the level of informal technological activity among firms, the variable (exports) may do a better job in distinguishing among smaller rather than the largest ones.

The size-relative wage profile of exporters and non-exporters in each industry is graphed in panel C of each figure. The relative wage is calculated as the ratio of the wage of non-production labor to the wage of production labor. From the semi-parametric regression results, the average wage differentials between non-production and production labor by trade status of firms are reported in columns 4 and 5 of table 2.5. To the extent that non-production labor proxies skill and production labor proxies unskilled labor, a standard practice in the literature, we can refer to the relative wage measure as representing a skill premium.

Two features stand out on closer examination of these columns and Panel C. First, the graphs indicate that, in general, for both exporters and non-exporters alike, as firm size increases, the gap between the wage of non-production and production workers increases.[24] The range in wage inequality is highest in the electric/electronics industry, starting at around zero for the smallest firms to over 2.0 in the largest exporting firms. Second, in nine out of the ten industries, the magnitude of wage inequality, or skill premium, is higher for exporters than non-exporters. The highest wage differential between non-production and production wages are in the electric/electronics, plastics, and textiles, clearly the most export-oriented industries (see table 2.1). Thus, cross-sectional evidence indicating higher wage inequality among exporters relative to non-exporters appears consistent with time-series evidence in the US on the role of exports recently reported in Bernard and Jensen (1995). These authors find that exports account for almost all of the increase in the wage gap between non-production and production labor in the US. However, the graphs clearly illustrate that, for firms in the largest size category, the reverse pattern holds in eight of the ten industries. Thus,

[24] The unit of measurement on the vertical axis represents the logarithm of the ratio of the wage of non-production labor to that of production labor. The logarithm values of 0.2, 0.4, 0.6, and 0.8 correspond to actual ratios of 1.25, 1.5, 1.9, and 2.3 respectively.

increasing firm size appears to be associated with a leveling of relative wage magnitudes among exporting firms but a positive effect among non-exporting firms.

One possible explanation for the general pattern observed above is that for exporters, the size of the world market has a large positive effect on the level of demand for both types of workers, raising the absolute wages of both groups of workers, an effect not experienced by non-exporters. In addition, the system of apprenticeship and vocational training undertaken primarily by large export enterprises in Taiwan (Dahlman and Sananikone, 1990) may be a reason for the lower wage inequality observed among exporters. The trainees consist of junior high school graduates, who after two to three years go directly to production jobs in these enterprises. These workers are likely to command higher wages than the average production worker without apprenticeship training.[25]

5   Summary and conclusion

Semi-parametric and non-parametric regression techniques are used to study the relationship between exports, firm size, and the wages of production and non-production labor, by comparing the wage–firm size profiles of exporters versus non-exporters. The analysis is based on firm-level data from the Taiwanese Census of Manufactures in 1986.

Cross-sectional evidence on the pattern of wages among Taiwanese firms indicates that the strong and positive firm size–wage premium found in developed country studies does not hold for all workers in Taiwan. However, relative to non-exporters, exporting firms are always associated with higher wages for all workers. In fact, in the case of production workers, once we control for other observable firm characteristics, the employer size–wage premia disappears in many industries. In terms of magnitudes, the production wage premium associated with the export activity (14 percent) is more than twice that associated with working for the largest firms (6 percent). In the case of non-production labor, the export premium (30 percent) is about 70 percent of the premium associated with size (43 percent).

Our results also suggest that the wage gap between non-production and production labor is significantly higher for small exporters relative to non-exporters in the same size category. While this wage gap increases

---

[25] A similar explanation is given by Abraham and Houseman (1994) who attribute the falling earnings inequality in Germany since the mid 1970s to the high quality of training received by non-college-bound German youth.

with firm size for both exporters and non-exporters, the rate of increase across firms of different sizes appears to be lower for the exporters.

More generally, our findings reveal several distinctive differences in the labor market of Taiwan compared to the US. First, as far as Taiwanese production labor is concerned, average wage premiums associated with large firms are smaller than the corresponding figures in the US. Moreover, in the US, production labor wage premiums exceed the magnitude of those for non-production labor (Brown and Medoff, 1989; Dunne and Schmitz, 1995; Bernard and Jensen, 1995). The reverse pattern is true for Taiwan. To the extent that Taiwanese output and input markets are relatively more competitive than in the US, as suggested by existing literature, the difference in wage premium for production labor in the two countries may be a reflection of the difference in market competitiveness. In the same context, the higher wage premiums associated with Taiwanese non-production labor relative to production labor probably reflect the greater heterogeneity within the category of non-production labor due to unmeasured dimensions of labor quality.

Second, relative to magnitudes found in the US, exporting firms in Taiwan pay all groups of workers significantly higher wages than non-exporters. Exporters in the US pay a wage premium of 9 percent over non-exporters (Bernard and Jensen, 1995) while in Taiwan, exporter's wage premium is 14 percent for production labor and almost 30 percent for non-production labor. Thus, distinguishing exporters from other manufacturers in the examination of labor market issues is critical. This should not be surprising in a country where the share of direct exports in total manufactures is more than four times that in the US.

Appendix [26]

The relationship between economic variables is generally represented by means of conditional moments. Given that z represents an $n \times 1$ vector of independent variables and y is the $q \times 1$ vector of dependent variables and a known function of $g:R^q \to R$, one is interested in estimating the regression function

$$m(z) = E[g(y)/z = z]. \tag{1}$$

---

[26] The techniques described here are standard in the statistical literature. For a more detailed description of the kernel non-parametric regression technique, see Hardle (1990) and Delgado and Robinson (1992).

Typically, $m(z)$ is assumed to follow a particular parametric form, e.g., $m(z) = z'\beta$. Non-parametric regression estimates do not impose a rigid functional form on the regression function represented by (1).

Given the database $[(Y_i, Z_i)/i = 1,...,n]$, the non-parametric estimate of $m(z)$ is a weighted average of $g(Y_i)$, where the heavier weights are given to the observations with the z_i closest to z, that is $m(z)$ is estimated by

$$\hat{m}(z_j) = \sum_{i=1}^{n} g(Y_i) W(z, z_i) \tag{2}$$

where $[W(z,z_i), i = 1,...,n]$ is a sequence of weights which sum to one. W gives more weight to observations with the z_i close to z, the idea being that the observations $g(Y_i)$s, with z_i close to z, contain more information on $m(z)$ than observations far away from z.

The weights can be expressed in the following form

$$W(z, z_i) = (K(z - z_i)/h)/(\Sigma_i K(z - z_i)/h). \tag{3}$$

A weighting function as expressed in equation (3) will sum to one for all z_i. $K(z - z_i)/h$ is often referred to as a Kernel function given by $N \sim (z, h)$. h is a positive scalar bandwidth number or the smoothing parameter which determines the weights to be assigned to observations in the neighbourhood of z.

The choice of the smoothing parameter plays an important role in non-parametric regression as it affects the magnitude of the weights assigned to observations in the neighborhood of z. If h is too large, the observations far from z will have a large impact on $E(y/z)$, and vice-versa. It is common practice to assume an exogenous smoothing parameter. However, it is important that the smoothing parameter depends on the data, with a view to reflecting sample size and scale of measurement. In our analysis, the optimal smoothing parameter is selected using the Least Squares Cross Validation (LSCV) technique, which seeks to determine the optimal h that gives the best fit of the non-parametrically estimated regression curve to the actual data (Hardle, 1990).

References

Abraham, K. G. (1988), "Flexible Staffing Arrangements and Employers Short-term Adjustment Strategies," in R.A. Hart (ed.), *Employment, Unemployment and Hours of Work*, London: George Allen and Unwin.

Abraham, K. G. and S. N. Houseman (1994), "Earnings Inequality in Germany," W. E. Upjohn Institute for Employment Research Staff Working Paper, 94–24.

54   Bee Yan Aw and Geeta Batra

Acs, Z. J. and D. B. Audretsch (1990), *Innovation and Small firms*, Cambridge, Mass.: The MIT Press.

Aw, B. Y. (1992), "An Empirical Model of Mark-ups in a Quality Differentiated Export Market," *Journal of International Economics*, 33: 327–344.

Aw, B. Y. and G. Batra (1994), "Exports and Technical Efficiency: An Analysis at the Firm Level," Working Paper, The World Bank (PSD).

(forthcoming), "Technology Capability and Firm Eficiency," *World Bank Econmic Review*.

Aw, B. Y. and A. Hwang (1995), "Productivity and the Export Market: A Firm-Level Analysis," *Journal of Development Economics*, 47: 313–332.

Bartel A. P. and F. R. Lichtenberg (1991), "The Age of Technology and Its Impact on Employee Wages," *Economics of Innovation and New Technology*, 1 (2): 215–231.

Berman, E., J. Bound, and Z. Griliches (1994), "Changes in the Demand for Skilled Labor within US Manufacturing Industries: Evidence from the Annual Survey of Manufacturing," *Quarterly Journal of Economics*, 109: 367–398.

Bernard A. B. and J. B. Jensen (1995), "Exporters, Jobs, and Wages in US Manufacturing" *Brookings Papers on Economic Activity: Microeconomics*, Washington, DC, pp. 67–119.

Berry, R. A. (1992), "Firm (or plant) Size in the Analysis of Trade and Development," in G. Helleiner (ed.), *Trade Policy, Industrialization and Development: New Perspectives*. Oxford: Clarendon.

Bregman, A., M. Fuss, and H. Regev (1991), "High Tech and Productivity: Evidence from Israeli Industrial Firms," *European Economic Review*, 35: 1199–1221.

Brown, C. and J. Medoff (1989), "The Employer Size–Wage Effect," *Journal of Political Economy*, 97: 1027–1059.

Coe, D. T. and E. Helpman (1995), "International R&D Spillovers," *European Economic Review*, 39: 859–887.

Dahlman, C. and O. Sananikone (1990), "Technology Strategy in the Economy of Taiwan: Exploiting Foreign Linkages and Investing in Local Capability," World Bank, PSD Working Paper.

Davis, S. J. and J. Haltiwanger (1991), "Wage Dispersion Between and Within U.S. Manufacturing Plants, 1963–86," *Brookings Papers: Microeconomics*, pp. 115–200.

(1992), "Employer Size and the Wage Structure in US Manufacturing," unpublished mimeo, University of Chicago.

Deaton, A. (1989), "Rice Prices and Income Distribution in Thailand: A Non-Parametric Analysis," *Economic Journal*, 99: 1–37.

Delgado, M. A. and P. M. Robinson (1992), "Nonparametric and Semiparametric Methods for Economic Research," *Journal of Economic Survey*, 6, (3): 201–249.

Deyo, F. C. (1989), *Beneath the Miracle: Labor Subordination in the New Asian Industrialism*, Berkeley: University of California Press.

Dunne, T. and J. A. Schmitz, Jr. (1995), "Wages, Employment Structure and Employer Size–Wage Premia: Their Relationship to Advanced-Technology Usage at U.S. Manufacturing Establishments," *Economica*, 62: 89–107.

Fields, G. S. (1992), "Living Standard, Labor Markets and Human Resources in Taiwan," in G. Ranis (ed.), *Taiwan: From Developing to Mature Economy*, Westview Press, Inc.

Grossman, G. and E. Helpman (1991), *Innovation, and Growth in the Global Economy*, Cambridge, Mass.: MIT Press.

Hardle, W. (1990), *Applied Nonparametric Regression*, Cambridge University Press.

Katz, L. F. and L. H. Summers (1989), "Industry Rents: Evidence and Implications," *Brookings Papers: Microeconomics*, Washington, DC.

Keesing, D. and S. Lall (1992), "Marketing Manufactured Exports from Developing Countries: Learning Sequences and Public Support," in G. K. Helleiner (ed.), *Trade Policy, Industrialization, and Development: New Perspectives*, Oxford: Clarendon Press.

Lawrence, R. Z. and M. J. Slaughter (1993), "International Trade and American Wages in the 1980s: Giant Sucking Sound or Small Hiccup," *Brookings Papers: Microeconomics*, 2: 161–226.

Li, K. T. (1989), *The Evaluation of Policy Behind Taiwan's Development Success*, New Haven: Yale University Press.

Little, I. M. D. (1987), "Small Manufacturing Enterprises in Developing Countries," *The World Bank Economic Review*, 1: 203–235.

Pack, H. (1992a), "New Perspectives on Industrial Growth in Taiwan," in G. Ranis (ed.), *Taiwan: From Developing to Mature Economy*, Westview Press, Inc.

    (1992b), "Learning and Productivity Change in Developing Countries," in G. K. Helleiner (ed.), *Trade Policy, Industrialization, and Development: New Perspectives*, Oxford: Clarendon Press.

Ranis, G. (ed.) (1992), *Taiwan: From Developing to Mature Economy*, Westview Press, Inc.

Riedel, J. (1988), "Demand for LDC Exports of Manufactures: Estimates from Hong Kong," *Economic Journal*, 98: 138–148.

    (1993), "Explaining Economic Growth: Case Study of a Superstar," Working Paper, The Johns Hopkins University, SAIS.

Robinson, P. M. (1988), "Semiparametric Econometrics," *Journal of Applied Econometrics*, 3: 35–51.

Romer, P. M. (1990), "Endogenous Technological Change," *Journal of Political Economy*, 98: 71–102.

Schaffner, J. A. (1994), "Larger Employer Wage Premium in Peru," Working Paper, Department of Economics, Stanford University, Stanford, California.

Wade, R. (1990), *Governing the Market: Economic Theory and the Role of Government in East Asian Industrialization*, Princeton, NJ: Princeton University Press.

Westphal, L., W. Rhee, and G. Pursell (1984), "Sources of Technological

56   **Bee Yan Aw and Geeta Batra**

Capability in South Korea," in M. Fransman and K. King (eds.), *Technological Capability in the Third World*, London and Basingstoke: Macmillan.
World Bank (1993), *The East Asian Miracle: Economic Growth and Public Policy*, New York: Oxford University Press.

3 Trade, technology, and wage differentials in the Canadian manufacturing sector

John Baldwin and Mohammed Rafiquzzaman

1 Introduction

The 1980s and 1990s have seen a rising share of skilled labor in total employment. At the same time, the wage premium for skilled workers has increased, thereby widening the gap between skilled and unskilled workers (Freeman, 1995; Richardson, 1995; Katz and Murphy, 1992). Although the pattern of these changes is well documented, there is disagreement about the causes of these changes. Several hypotheses have been offered to explain them – increased international competition, changes in the relative supply of more-skilled versus less-skilled workers, and skill-augmenting technological change.

A. Wood (1994), D. Wood (1995), Batra (1993), and Leamer (1994) have suggested that the expansion of international trade is the main cause of the increased wage differential between skilled and unskilled workers. They argue that rising wage inequality is associated with increased imports of manufacturing goods from less-advanced countries.

An alternate explanation for the recent widening of the premium for skilled workers rests in the type of technological change that the computer-based revolution has wrought. Skill-augmenting technical progress also brings about relative shifts in labor demand and, thus, increases the wage differential between the skilled and unskilled, even without international trade pressures. Skill-augmenting technical change increases the marginal product of skilled labor, thereby shifting out its demand curve and increasing the relative wages of this group. Particularly, technological progress that is associated with the computer revolution and the introduction of advanced technologies is likely to raise the relative demand for more-skilled and flexible workers and reduce the demand for less-skilled labor. Since the production process and technical requirements differ across industries, the degree of labor-saving technical progress and the

58   John Baldwin and Mohammed Rafiquzzaman

relative demand for skilled workers is also likely to differ across industries.[1]

Empirical studies have investigated each of these explanations. Several studies use factor content calculations to examine the possible effect of trade on the decline of the relative wage of less-skilled workers during the 1980s and 1990s (e.g., Lawrence and Slaughter, 1993 and Sachs and Shatz, 1994). These studies find that changes in actual trade flows have not displaced that many low-skilled workers from manufacturing. Others disagree, arguing that standard factor-content analyses understate the effect of trade on employment (e.g., Wood, 1995).

On the other hand, a number of research studies have concluded that the shift toward more-skilled workers is caused partly or primarily by new technology (e.g., Lawrence and Slaughter, 1993; Krueger, 1993; Murphy and Welch, 1989; Katz and Murphy, 1992; Mincer, 1991; Berman, Bound, and Griliches, 1994; and Dunne and Schmitz, 1995). Berman, Bound, and Griliches (1994), for example, reach this conclusion by relying on evidence that changes in the wage share of non-production workers is related to the level of research and development intensity and to computer usage.

Most previous studies have investigated the effect of trade or new technology on skill differentials in the United States. This chapter examines the effects of both for Canada, which has an economy where trade is much larger relative to GNP and where large changes have occurred in trade intensity. Because of the dramatic changes in trade intensity, we might expect to be better able to see the effects of trade, if they exist. Moreover, in recent years, Canada's manufacturing industries have undergone important structural changes (e.g., Baldwin and Gorecki, 1990; and Baldwin and Rafiquzzaman, 1994). As part of this change, the composition of the manufacturing labor force has shifted toward more-skilled workers. A manifestation of this is the increase in the share of non-production workers in total employment. These are mainly white-collar supervisory personnel who are on average more highly paid than blue-collar production workers. As well, the share of non-production workers' remuneration in the total wage bill has increased. At the same time as the utilization of non-production workers relative to production workers has gone up, the yearly income of non-production relative to production workers has increased.

This chapter analyzes the nature and pattern of these shifts and the

---

[1]   Richardson (1995) observes that in a world of international trade, labor-enhancing technical progress can only serve to augment the wages of skilled labor if technical progress is felt unequally across industries.

extent to which they are related to both technology use and changing trade patterns. In an accompanying paper (Baldwin, Gray, and Johnson, 1996), we examine the effect of technology use on the structure of production worker wages. During the 1980s, the production worker wage structure has twisted – those working with advanced technologies have increasingly received higher wages than those not working with advanced technologies. In this chapter, we look at the differential between non-production and production workers and its relationship both to increased competition from trade and to technology use.

The following sections analyze changes in the composition of the manufacturing labor force between non-production and production workers from 1973 to 1993. The analysis has five parts. First, data sources and definitions of production workers and non-production workers are provided. Second, changes in the composition of manufacturing labor in favor of non-production workers are examined. Third, the chapter first uses plant-level data to investigate the relationship between technology use and the non-production worker wage premium. Fourth, it aggregates these plant-level data to the industry level, adds trade data and asks whether the effects of technology remain the same and, finally, whether changes in trade patterns are also related to changing patterns of wage differentials.

2   Data sources and definitions

The data used to investigate the relationship between technology and the wage structure are drawn from two sources – the 1989 Survey of Manufacturing Technology (SMT), which contains data on technology usage at the plant level, and the Census of Manufactures.

2.1   Non-production and production worker wages

The Census of Manufactures collects statistics on salaries and wages for non-production and production workers[2] as well as the number of non-production and production workers. Production workers consist of all non-supervisory workers (including working foremen) engaged in processing, assembling, inspecting, storing, handling, and packing; also workers engaged in maintenance, repair, and janitorial and watchman services

---

[2]   Salaries and wages refer to gross earnings of employees before deductions for income tax and employees' contributions to social services such as sickness, accident and unemployment insurance, pensions, etc. They include all salaries, wages, bonuses, profits shared with employees as well as any other allowance forming part of the worker's earnings.

(e.g., Statistics Canada, 1990). Non-production workers, defined by process of exclusion from the production-worker category, are those engaged in executive, administrative, and sales activities.

We use this classification of workers to examine trends in the wage differences between blue-collar (less-skilled) and white-collar (more-skilled) workers. For this analysis, the wage rate of production workers is calculated as the wages paid to production workers divided by the number of production workers employed; for salaried workers, the wage rate is calculated as the salaries paid divided by the number of salaried workers.

Non-production workers made up about 27 percent of total employment in manufacturing in 1980. The annual remuneration of non-production workers was about 27 percent higher than for production workers. Although the broad non-production/production worker categories aggregate a number of more detailed occupational groups together, the two categories can be fruitfully used to examine broad changes in relative skills in the workforce. Berman, Bound, and Griliches (1994) show that the ratio of non-production to production workers taken from the US Survey of Manufactures is much the same as the ratio of white-collar to blue-collar workers, where the latter are taken from the more detailed occupational data derived from the US Current Population Survey.

In order to examine changes in the proportion of non-production to production workers, only a subset of plants from the Canadian Census of Manufacturers is used here. This subset consists of those plants that report the actual numbers of production and non-production workers. These are plants that receive "long-forms."[3] Other plants receive "short-forms" and are only asked to list total employees. Since the latter do not divide total workers between non-production and production workers and these plants make up an increasing proportion of all plants, the trend in the ratio of non-production to production workers derived from the population of both long-form and short-form plants understates changes in the proportion of skilled workers to total employment. By choosing just those plants that are asked to report production and non-production workers, this problem is avoided.[4]

The second section of this chapter examines the relationship of wages to technology and trade. Since this chapter compares the wage structure

[3] These are the larger plants. However, a sample of smaller plants are also sent long-forms and thus differences between large and small plants can be investigated.
[4] Both operating establishments and head offices employ non-production workers. Both groups were used in this analysis.

of plants in 1989 and 1980, only those plants that can be linked to the technology survey that is described below and that continue throughout the decade are used in the analysis. The sample includes neither the deaths nor the births that occurred between 1980 and 1989. After births and deaths are excluded from the linked file, the total number of observations used in the calculations is 3,642.

2.2   Technologies

The second data source is the 1989 Canadian Survey of Manufacturing Technology (SMT),[5] which contains information on the use by establishments in the manufacturing sector of 22 separate advanced technologies. These technologies are used in design and engineering, fabrication and assembly, inspection and communications, automated materials handling, manufacturing information systems, and integration and control. The functional groups differ in terms of the degree to which they are directly involved in the production and assembly process or whether they serve to monitor it via diagnostics and quality control.

The technologies all emanate from the current technological revolution that is related to the computer, or more correctly to microchip use. The relatively cheap processing power of microchips has spawned the development of a host of *labor-saving* technologies. These technologies have permitted the replacement of costly labor with efficient, reliable, computer-controlled machinery. For example, robots provide an efficient and safe alternative to humans for repetitive jobs like spot welding or painting on the automobile assembly line. Automated guided vehicle systems replace delivery personnel.

In addition to labor-saving technologies, the new technological revolution has spawned a set of technologies that are described as *labor-enhancing* because they expand the tasks that workers can perform. The dramatic impact of labor-enhancing information technologies has been felt in many different parts of the production process. They have allowed management to receive, digest, and analyze unprecedented amounts of information. They have permitted designers to ponder problems that they did not have time to consider previously, and to shorten the design phase of projects. They have enhanced the ability of assembly-line workers to assemble made-to-order products.

---

[5]   The survey, conducted by mail, was based on a sample of all establishments in the Canadian manufacturing sector. The sample is stratified by size class, with a greater proportion of the larger plants being sampled than of smaller plants. Of the 4,200 establishments in the sample 3,952, or 94 percent, responded to the survey.

62   John Baldwin and Mohammed Rafiquzzaman

The effect of the information revolution has not been felt equally in all parts of the production process. The inspection and communications functional group (basically labor-enhancing technologies) has the highest adoption rate. Some 79 percent of shipments in 1989 come from establishments using technologies from this group. The high adoption rate here is due mainly to the use of automatic control devices – programmable controllers and stand-alone computers used for control on the factory floor. The inspection and communications group is followed by design and engineering (52.1 percent), and manufacturing information systems (51.2 percent). Fabrication, the traditional heart of the production process, is only fourth with 46.7 percent. While the computer-based revolution is often described in terms of its effects on labor-saving technologies in fabrication and assembly, its usage so far has been greatest in the area of the labor-enhancing technologies in inspection and communications as well as in design and engineering.

The integration of labor-saving and labor-enhancing technologies has created new manufacturing processes that are at the heart of what has been called "soft manufacturing." Bylinsky (1994) notes that "soft manufacturing" differs from traditional manufacturing in that software and computer networks are as important as production machines. These new technologies complement problem-solving skills in the workforce. The introduction of labor-enhancing technologies has been stimulated by the recognition that humans possess the invaluable kind of dexterity and judgment that has yet to be programmed into a robot. On the one hand, inspection and communications technologies permit skilled engineers to control a vast array of processes. On the other hand, they allow real time ordering and the production of products on demand, tailored to specific needs. Inspection and communications as well as integration and control technologies facilitate the rapid transmission of orders to the assembly process, the delivery of parts to the assembler, and the assembly of specialized products by a worker who is instructed by a computer as to what parts are needed for the particular product ordered and the nature of the assembly required. Instead of replacing workers with robots, these soft technologies have enhanced human skills. In this environment, robots are relegated to repetitive tasks, while computer technologies aid workers to assemble custom-designed products with the aid of computer-transmitted requests.

The introduction of both types of technologies is associated with skill upgrading. Baldwin, Gray, and Johnson (1995) report that plants that have introduced these technologies have found that their skill requirements increased, and responded by implementing internal training programs at a substantial increase in training costs.

This chapter asks whether the relative skill requirements associated with these technologies, as reflected in wage differentials, has changed. Labor-saving technologies do not impact just on production workers; similarly labor-enhancing technologies do not impact just on non-production workers. While advanced fabrication and technologies directly affect production workers, they may also affect the skills required of non-production workers. For example, the introduction of many of these technologies has led to a greater requirement for skilled supervisory personnel. Therefore, the use of labor-saving technologies may be associated with either an increase or decrease in the relative skills of non-production relative to production workers.

Similarly, the use of labor-enhancing advanced communications technologies affects the skills required of both production and non-production workers. They directly involve supervisory personnel but they may also increase the skill levels of production workers who may require greater cognitive skills as a result of the new technologies. The direction of the impact of both types of technologies on the relative skills and wage rates of each group is indeterminate, *a priori*.

Prior to examining the relationship between the use of these new technologies and relative wages, this chapter outlines the changes that have taken place in the relative quantities and wage rates of these two groups in the next section.

3.   Changes in employment and remuneration of non-production workers

3.1   Changes in the composition of employment

During the 1973–1992 period, the share of non-production workers in the manufacturing labor force increased from 27.9 percent to 30.5 percent (figure 3.1). This is 0.14 percentage points per year.[6] The 1970s experienced a larger increase (0.16 percentage points per year) than the 1980s (0.07 percentage points per year).The increase accelerated in the 1990s (0.30 percentage points per year). The Canadian trend is consistent with events in the US manufacturing sector (see Berman, Bound, and

[6]   A time trend regression of the form Ln (Share) = $a + bT$, where T is time, was run for the periods 1973–1992, 1973–1979, and 1979–1989. The results indicated that the share of non-production employment was growing at the rate of 0.4 percent per year for the period 1973–1992, 0.7 percent per year for the period 1973–1979, and 0.07 percent per year for the period 1979–1989.

Figure 3.1 Non-production workers' share in total employment

Griliches, 1994), though the magnitude of the increase is somewhat less in Canada.[7]

3.2   Changes in the share of non-production workers in the wage bill

Changes in the non-production worker share of total employment suggest that compositional shifts have been taking place in the manufacturing labor force. The wage share of non-production workers provides an alternate measure of compositional change. Wage share provides a measure of the importance of the shift in demand for non-production labor that is superior, in some instances, to the ratio of quantities demanded since the change in the latter is attenuated to some degree by relative wage changes (Berman, Bound, and Griliches, 1994).

The non-production workers' share in the total wage bill has increased since the beginning of the period (figure 3.2). It shows virtually no change during the mid 1970s and then an increase to sharply higher levels in the 1980s. The increase in the non-production workers' share of the wage bill is a phenomenon primarily of the early 1980s, around the time of the major recession. The dramatic change in wage share that occurs about the time of the early 1980s' recession, along with the increases in the relative non-production share during the 1990s' recession, point to the difficulty of abstracting trend from cycle. There is some evidence that

---

[7]   The magnitude of the increase in each period in US manufacturing is larger than Canadian manufacturing. In the US, the increase was 0.23 percentage points per year between 1973 and 1979, and 0.38 percentage points per year between 1979 and 1989 (e.g., Berman, Bound, and Griliches, 1994). Thus, the change accelerates in the 1980s in the US, but slows in Canada.

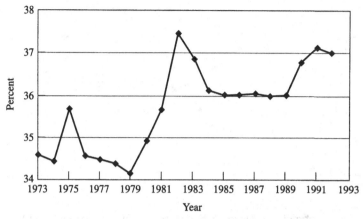

Figure 3.2 Non-production workers' share in the wage bill

long-term changes in the importance of non-production workers are occurring as ratchets at or just before the recessionary downturns.

3.3 Changes in wage differentials between production and non-production workers

The data presented in the preceding sections provide evidence of a shift in the composition of manufacturing employment toward non-production workers in Canada. Changes in the composition of labor can be caused both by shifts in demand or supply. While a number of researchers have focused on skill-augmenting technical change as the reason that demand for skilled workers may have increased, changes have also occurred in the supply of skilled labor over the last 20 years. This was the period when the proportion of college-educated labor increased dramatically. Moreover, this increase was somewhat greater in the 1970s than the 1980s (Freeman and Needels, 1991).

Examination of the relationship between changes in relative quantities and relative prices helps to discriminate between the relative importance of demand and supply factors.[8] An increase in the supply of non-production relative to production workers should be expected to affect the relative wages of the two types of workers in a fashion that is different from a shift in demand. If supply effects are the predominant cause of the changes that were taking place, relative prices and quantities

---

[8] It only helps to discriminate between these causes because quality may be changing within each category.

Figure 3.3 Ratio of non-production workers to production workers (NPW/PW), and wages of non-production workers relative to production workers (Wn?Wp)

should be inversely related. If demand factors predominate, relative quantities and relative prices should be positively related.

The time pattern of wage differentials – measured by the ratio of annual remuneration of non-production workers to production workers – is depicted in figure 3.3. It shows a decline until the end of the 1970s, then an increase until the end of the period.

In the 1970s, the ratio of the quantity of non-production to production workers increases while their relative wage falls. Explanations based on increases in relative supplies of skilled labor, or with a substitution away from skilled labor because of its high costs, are compatible with the trends observed in the 1970s.

The relative price decline of the 1970s is reversed in the 1980s. This may partially be the result of a decline in the rate of increase of skilled labor in the latter period (Freeman and Needels, 1991). However, based on the 1970s experience, the increasing non-production worker wage premium should have been accompanied by a decline in the ratio of non-production to production workers. This did not occur. Abstracting from the cyclical peak in the 1982 recession, there is little decline in the relative importance of non-production workers from 1979 to 1989. Indeed, the share of non-production workers in the wage bill moves to a higher level in the early 1980s and then remains relatively constant for the rest of the decade. Increasingly higher relative wages in the 1980s did not lead to a substitution of production workers for non-production workers, though it did lead to a slowing down in the rate of increase of the quantity of non-production labor being used.[9]

The asymmetry between the experience of the 1980s and the 1970s suggests that the demand for non-production workers increased in the second period relative to the first and accords with the argument that skill-based technical change became more important in the 1980s. The next two sections examine the extent to which the wage differentials depicted above relate to the use of advanced technology use. First, we use plant data to ask how these differentials are related to technology use. Then we use industry data to ask how changes in these differentials are related both to technology use and to changing trade patterns.

4   Wage rates and technology usage

Changes in the composition of the manufacturing labor force and the skill premium for non-production workers suggest that technological change has increased the demand for skilled workers. However, the effect has varied across industries, partially because the new technologies have not penetrated each sector equally. Moreover, even within industries, there are substantial differences in technology use across plants. It is, therefore, best to examine the connection between technology use and the wage structure at the plant rather than the industry level.

Other studies have emphasized the need for a microeconomic examination, since they have argued that most of the changes that are occurring in the ratio of non-production to production workers are occurring because of changes taking place within industries at the level of the plant. For example, Berman, Bound, and Griliches (1994) decompose the non-production worker share change that occurred in the United States into two components – that due to a shift in the importance of different industries and that due to change occurring within industries. Between 1973 and 1979, within-industry change accounted for some 63 percent of total change; between 1979 and 1987, the within-industry share is 70 percent. This is also the case for Canada, where the within-industry share accounted for 71 percent of total change over the period 1973–1990.[10]

---

[9] In order to investigate this further, time series correlations between the ratio of non-production workers to production workers and the ratio of wages of production to non-production workers were calculated. Correlation values were -0.71 for the period 1973–1979, $+0.20$ for the period 1979–1989, and $+0.31$ for the period 1989–1992.

[10] The US estimates use a four-digit industry breakdown; the Canadian estimate (Baldwin and Rafiquzzaman, 1994) uses a five-sector taxonomy.

While the debate over the causes of the growing skilled/unskilled wage differential attributes at least some of this to technological changes, technology itself is generally treated as a black box. Sometimes this technological change is attributed to computer use, but measures of advanced technology use are rarely employed to test this proposition – with several exceptions. After accounting for easily measurable worker characteristics, Krueger (1993) finds that a substantial wage premium of 10–15 percent exists for those workers having computer skills. However, simple measures of computer use do not capture in much detail the complicated way in which computers have affected the production process. Computers are embedded in machines used in different phases of the production process – design and engineering, fabrication and assembly, and inspection and communications. A full image of the importance of computer-driven technologies requires a more comprehensive measure.

Dunne and Schmitz (1995) approach this problem by employing measures of advanced technology use (i.e., computer numerically controlled machines) along with other plant characteristics to estimate the determinants of the wages of production workers in a cross-section of US manufacturing establishments. Production workers in plants using these advanced technologies receive higher wages. Doms, Dunne, and Troske (1997) investigate the differences in the non-production worker wage share and how it relates to advanced technology use by employing the same set of technologies.

This chapter also uses a direct measure of technology use – the number of technologies that are employed in different parts of the production process. It investigates the relationship between technology use and the non-production worker wage premium for Canada. Contrary to the American studies of Dunne and Schmitz (1995) and Doms, Dunne, and Troske (1997), which only cover five of the two-digit industries, this study employs data for all of the manufacturing sector. Since the five industries are quite unique – being the most advanced technology users – the Canadian data provide a broader overview of the effects of technology on the wage structure than is provided in the American studies. This study also incorporates trade data in addition to the technology data to see whether both are related to the non-production/production worker differentials.

4.1   Model

Wage differentials are the result of both demand and supply effects. Disentangling the relative importance of each is difficult. This section focuses on the demand side by primarily using data at the plant level. This permits the results of interplant differences in technology to be set against changes that are occurring in wage differentials and thus inferences to be made about the changing nature of demand.[11] The results do not imply that supply shocks are unimportant. But these supply shocks are presumed in this chapter to be more equally felt across the plant universe than the demand shocks arising from differences in changing trade patterns and differences in technology usage. Thus, the analysis here is used to isolate the nature of the changes that more aggregate analyses have had to infer from residual effects in their models. [12]

In order to examine the effects of technology use on plant wages and plant wage differentials between non-production and production workers, wage equations are estimated at the plant level. Plant wages are hypothesized to be a function of plant size, the relative quantity of other factors (capital and other types of labor), and several plant characteristics related to a plant's technological capabilities. There are a number of reasons that plant size is included. Larger plants have been observed to use higher-skilled workers. They also tend to be more profitable, and more unionized, which is likely to give rise to higher wages as a result of the bargaining process. Relative quantities of other factors (capital/ production workers, or non-production/production workers) are included because larger quantities of each may increase the marginal product of labor and thus increase the wage rate. A number of other plant characteristics that are posited to be related to the demand for skilled labor are also included. The most important are the variables that directly capture a plant's use of advanced technologies. Other variables like age, diversification, innovativeness, and nationality are included to capture aspects of sophistication that the technology variables cannot be expected to capture on their own.

Two different sets of specifications are used. First, the plant-level wages of production and non-production workers are examined by estimating separately the following two log-wage equations:[13]

$$\ln(W_P)_j = \alpha_0 + \alpha_1 \ln(K/L_P)_j + \alpha_2 \ln(NPR)_j + \alpha_3 \ln(PLANT\_SIZE)_j$$
$$+ \alpha_4 X_j + \alpha_5 (TECH_{kj}) + \varepsilon_j, \qquad (1)$$

---

[11] On this, see Hamermesh (1993: 352).

[12] For a discussion of this literature, see Levy and Murnane (1992).

[13] In a three-factor world – physical capital, production workers, and non-production workers, these wage equations may be derived by assuming that the production technology is Cobb–Douglas and the firm maximizes profits by selling in a perfectly competitive product market.

$$\ln(W_N)_j = \lambda_0 + \lambda_1\ln(K/L_N)_j + \lambda_2\ln(NPR)_j + \lambda_3\ln(PLANT\_SIZE)_j$$
$$+ \lambda_4 X_j + \lambda_5(TECH_{kj}) + \omega_j, \tag{2}$$

where P and N indicate production and non-production labor, respectively; j indexes plant; W_P and W_N represent the wages of production and non-production workers, respectively; NPR represents the use of non-production workers relative to production workers; K/L_P and K/L_N are capital intensities of production and non-production workers, respectively; $PLANT\_SIZE$ is plant size; X is a vector of other plant-specific characteristics; $TECH_k$ represents a vector of the type of technology use ($k = 1,2,...,6$); and ε_j and w_j are error terms.

Second, the effects of technology use, plant characteristics, and other relevant production-related variables on plant-level wage differentials are investigated by estimating the following wage inequality equation:[14]

$$(W_N/W_P)_j = \beta_0 + \beta_1(K/L)_j + \beta_2(NPR_j) + \beta_3(PLANT\_SIZE)_j$$
$$+ \beta_4 X_j + \beta_5(TECH_{kj}) + \upsilon_j, \tag{3}$$

where (W_N/W_P) is the ratio of wages of non-production workers to those of production workers and υ_j is an error term.

4.2   The variables

Production worker wage rates The average annual wage is calculated as the total wage bill for production workers divided by the total number of production workers.[15]

Non-production worker salary rates The average annual salary is calculated as the total salary bill for non-production workers divided by the total number of non-production workers.

Plant Size Plant size ($PLANT\_SIZE$) is measured as the log of plant employment. Plant employment is calculated as the average plant employment of production workers.

---

[14] This wage inequality equation may also be derived by considering the simplest CES technology with three factors – physical capital, production workers, and non-production workers.

[15] A two-year average (over 1988–1989 for 1989 and 1980–1981 for 1981) is used to smooth out random movements that reflect regression-to-the-mean effects. This is done for each of the wage rate, plant size, and capital–labor ratios.

Capital/labor ratio The capital/labor ratio (CLR) is proxied by profits in manufacturing divided by production workers. The ratio is calculated as total activity value-added minus the sum of the wage bills of production and non-production workers divided by the total number of workers in the wage inequality equation (3). The divisor becomes the total number of production workers in the wage equation of production workers in equation (1) and the number of non-production workers in equation (2).

Technology use Technology in use within the plant captures aspects of capital intensity that the dollar measure of capital does not. While the normal practice is to encapsulate all information on capital into one aggregate measure using dollars as the common numeraire, these measures cannot capture differences in the efficiency of machines. Some plants may have more of the latest equipment than others, even though investment levels are about the same. Specification of the capital stock in more detail, using information on the types of machines in use, potentially corrects for the shortcomings of dollar measures of capital.

Technology use is measured here for each of six functional categories. These functional groups are: design and engineering (*DESIGN*); fabrication and assembly (*FAB*); automated materials handling systems (*MATHAN*); inspection and communications technologies (*INSCOM*); manufacturing information systems (*MANINF*); and integration and control technologies (*INTCON*). A binary variable that captures the use of *any* technology within each group is used in the regression.

Other plant characteristics

A number of additional characteristics are included to capture other factors that have been found to be related to wage rates – age of plant, whether a plant is owned by a firm with more than one plant (Davis and Haltiwanger, 1991). Each of these characteristics is hypothesized to capture some aspect of differences in technologies not captured by the other variables and, therefore, to affect the dependent variables in the model. These variables are:

Age Older plants are those that have managed to survive and will have built up accumulated knowledge that allows them to apply the same machines in a more sophisticated manner. Therefore, it is postulated that plant age (*AGE*) should be related to worker skill levels and plant wages. A binary variable is used that takes on a value of 0 for those plants that existed in 1970 and 1 for those born since that date.

Diversification Making advanced technologies work requires a set of sophisticated organizational skills. These are more likely to be present in a multi-establishment enterprise where a wider range of experiences is mastered by the firm's production engineering team. Therefore, firms are hypothesized to have higher skill levels and wages when they are diversified. Diversification is captured here as a multiplant binary variable (*MULTI_PLANT*), which equals 1 if the firm operates more than one plant in the same four-digit SIC industry where the plant is located, and 0 otherwise.

Innovation Plants in some industries are likely to receive greater benefits from the use of advanced technologies and to require higher skills because these industries engage in more complex technological and innovative activities. In order to capture this effect, a binary variable (*INNOV_INDS*) classifying industries as either more or less innovative is included in the regression. The taxonomy is derived from Robson *et al.* (1988), who classify two-digit industries into three basic groups. The first two groups, defined here as the innovative industries, produce the majority of innovations. The more innovative industries consist of electrical and electronic products, chemicals and chemical products, machinery, refined petroleum and coal, transportation equipment, rubber products, non-metallic mineral products, plastics, fabricated metals, and primary metals. The less-innovative group is made up of the textiles, paper, wood, clothing, leather, beverages, food, furniture and fixtures, and printing and publishing industries.

Foreign control The nationality of a plant is included to capture other competencies that are hypothesized to require higher skill levels. Multinationals are the vehicle through which hard-to-transfer scientific knowledge is moved from one country to another (Caves, 1982). This may be either because of scale economies associated with their larger size or because of an inherent advantage associated with information that is uniquely held by these types of firms. To capture the effect of foreign-owned plants, a binary variable (*FOREIGN_OWNER*) is included that equals one if a manufacturing plant is foreign controlled, and zero otherwise.

In what follows, regressions for the production-worker wage, the salary of non-production workers, and the ratio of the annual remuneration of non-production to production workers are reported.[16] These regressions all use the unweighted sample derived from the survey. We briefly report on differences when the weighted sample is used.[17] The first and second regressions allow us to investigate how technology use affects the wages of non-production and production workers. The third regression allows us to examine whether technology use affects the relative wages of non-production and production workers.

4.3   1989 wage rates and wage rate differentials

There is strong evidence that advanced technologies are closely associated with the use of more highly skilled workers. For the manufacturing sector as a whole, advanced technologies are associated with higher production worker wage rates.

The production worker wage rate (table 3.1, column 1) depends both on the size of plant (*PLANT_SIZE*)[18] and the ratio of capital to labor (*CLR*).[19] After both the size of the plant and the capital–labor ratio are taken into account, the use of advanced technologies is positively related to the wage rate. The use of technologies from four functional groups – inspection and communications (*INSCOM*), integration and control (*INTCON*), design and engineering (*DESIGN*), and automated material handling systems (*MATHAN*) – have a positive and significant effect on the wage rate paid to production workers. The largest positive effects are associated with the two labor-enhancing categories – inspection and communications and integration and control. The smallest positive effect occurs for design and engineering technologies. Wages are no higher in plants using fabrication and assembly technologies (*FAB*) than in those not using these technologies.

Thus, the presence of labor-enhancing advanced technology is associated with a positive wage premium for production workers. The advanced technologies used in fabrication and assembly that most directly affect the plant floor have the least effect of all on production

---

[16] These regressions are all OLS using the unweighted sample derived from the survey. Various alternatives that used corrections for simultaneity found no significant differences on the technology attached to technology use. For some of these results, see Baldwin, Gray, and Johnson (1996).

[17] The weighted sample increases the importance given to small as opposed to larger plants.

[18] See also Brown and Medoff (1989).

[19] See also Davis and Haltiwanger (1991).

Table 3.1 *Multivariate analysis of wages of non-production workers* (W_N), *production workers* (W_P), *and wages of the former relative to the latter* (W_N/W_P): 1989

Variable	Production worker wage ln (W_P): column 1		Non-production worker wage ln (W_N): column 2		Relative wage (W_N/W_P): column 3	
	Parameter estimate	S.E.[a]	Parameter estimate	S.E.[a]	Parameter estimate	S.E.[a]
Intercept	9.7367***	0.0317	10.2112***	0.0369	1.8306***	0.0287
AGE	−0.0234*	0.0136	−0.0376**	0.0158	−0.0223	0.0359
FOREIGN_OWNER	0.0439***	0.0120	0.0307**	0.0139	−0.0924***	0.0319
INNOV_INDS	0.0992***	0.0112	0.0528***	0.0130	−0.0768***	0.0296
MULTI_PLANT	0.1173***	0.0109	−0.0195	0.0127	−0.2577***	0.0291
Technology use						
DESIGN	0.0223*	0.0125	0.0211	0.0146	−0.0195	0.0330
FAB	−0.0188	0.0126	0.0070	0.0147	0.0755**	0.0335
MATHAN	0.0624***	0.0134	0.0342**	0.0157	0.0036	0.0357
INSCOM	0.0621***	0.0130	0.0112	0.0151	−0.1476***	0.0339
MANINF	−0.0744***	0.0122	−0.0237*	0.0142	0.0674**	0.0323
INTCON	0.0460***	0.0156	0.0227	0.0182	−0.0590	0.0417
CLR[b]	0.0168***	0.0021	0.0059**	0.0024	−4.17E-07***	1.6E-07
PLANT_SIZE[b]	0.0429***	0.0055	0.0327***	0.0064	−3.83E-05	2.5E-05
NPR[b]	0.0522***	0.0063	−0.0411***	0.0073	0.1529***	0.0258
N[c]	2,847		2,847		2,847	
Adj R^2	0.234		0.051		0.078	
F	67.81		12.83		19.50	

Notes:
[a] Standard error. [b] They are in logarithmic form in the production and non-production worker wage equations. [c] Number of observations.
*** Significant at the 1% level. ** Significant at the 5% level. * Significant at the 10% level.

worker wage rates. It is the communications and control technologies that are at the heart of the soft manufacturing revolution that have the greatest effect on production worker wage rates. While these technologies have often been thought of as enhancing the abilities of management, their incidence of use is directly associated with higher wage levels for production workers.

Most of the hypotheses about the effect of other plant characteristics are confirmed. Plants that are older, more diversified, foreign-controlled, and are located in more-innovative industries also pay higher production worker wage rates. The coefficient on age (AGE), however, is statistically insignificant.

The salary of non-production workers is also related to size, to capital intensity of the plant, to the innovative environment, and to the technologies being employed. A regression of the 1989 salary rates similar to that for production worker wage rates (table 3.1, column 2) finds significant coefficients on many of the variables that affected the wage rate of production workers. In particular, the coefficients attached to *PLANT_SIZE*, *CLR*, *AGE*, and *INNOV_INDS* are significant. However, the coefficients attached to the technology variables are generally not significant, though they mainly have the same sign as in the production worker equation. Even when the coefficients on the technology variables have the same signs in both the production worker and non-production worker equations, the coefficients are smaller for non-production workers.

Fabrication and assembly (*FAB*) is the one technology variable that does not have the same sign for both production worker wages and the salary of non-production workers. Plants that use fabrication and assembly technologies pay higher salaries, while the reverse is true for production workers.

As a result of these differences in the relative strength of the technology variables in the two equations, the premium paid to non-production workers depends on the technologies that are being used in the plant (table 3.1, column 3). Non-production worker relative wages are significantly lower in plants that are using inspection and communications (*INSCOM*) as well as integration and control (*INTCON*) technologies. These are the technologies at the heart of the soft manufacturing revolution. In contrast, the premium paid to non-production workers is higher for plants using advanced fabrication and assembly (*FAB*) technologies. Thus, labor-enhancing technologies affect the skills required of production workers more than they do of non-production workers, while the reverse is true for labor-saving technologies.

Other plant characteristics that positively affected the production worker wage rate tend to negatively affect the premium paid to non-production workers. Being older, larger, owned by a foreign-controlled firm, belonging to a more diversified parent, or being located in an innovative industry leads to a lower non-production worker premium.[20] These are characteristics that lead to higher skill levels on the part of production workers but not *relatively* higher skill levels for non-production workers. This suggests that the technological change that all three variables proxy is being felt more in the blue-collar than the white-collar segment of the manufacturing workforce.

These results come from the unweighted sample of the technology survey – a sample that disproportionately represents larger plants. The establishment-weighted results (not reported here) are similar to the unweighted results, with two exceptions.[21] First, age emerges as significant in the establishment-weighted results whereas it is not significant in the unweighted results. Older plants, established before 1970, pay higher wages. Thus age does not significantly matter when primarily large plants (the unweighted results) are being considered, but it does matter in the population as a whole. Thus, among smaller plants, age is more closely related to maturity and sophistication when it comes to the adoption of advanced technologies. Second, the effect of technology use on wages is lessened in the establishment-weighted segment. This indicates that the wage effect associated with technology use is more important in larger than in smaller plants.

5   The Effects of Trade and Technology on Relative Wages

The previous section finds that the wage premium paid to non-production workers in 1989 is related to the technologies that are being used in the plant in that year. Here we ask what variables are related to changes in the premium in the 1980s. Both the technology being used in 1989 and changes in trade intensity in the 1980s may be posited to matter.

Changes in the premium over the 1980s could have been related to technology use if the factors that affected relative demand and that are caught in the 1989 cross-section were relatively slow to emerge over the

---

[20] The coefficients of almost all of these variables are highly significant. The exception is plant size, which becomes very significant if foreign control or innovation are removed.

[21] We also experimented with alternate specifications. A reduced form omitting relative quantities was used. Capital–labor ratios were replaced with capital–sales ratios. Relative quantities were used as the regressand rather than relative wages. None of the conclusions about the effect of technologies was affected.

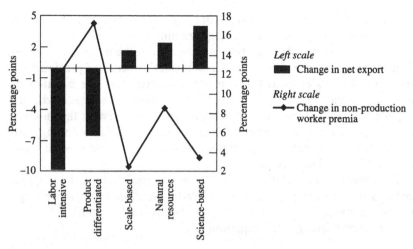

Figure 3.4 The relationship between changes in the non-production worker wage premia and changes in net export intensity, 1980–1981 and 1990–1991

decade. Changing trade patterns could also have played an important role in shifting demand in favor of more-skilled workers and as a consequence increased wage inequality during the decade. During the 1980s, the import and export intensity of the various manufacturing sectors increased steadily. Figure 3.4 depicts the changes for five sectors (the labor-intensive, natural-resource, scale-based, product differentiated, and science-based sectors) by plotting the percentage point change in net export intensity against the non-production/production worker premia. In the labor-intensive sector, imports increased faster than exports. In the high-tech science-based sector, exports increased faster than imports. The sectors where the non-production worker premia increased the most were those where net export intensity[22] increased the least (where net import intensity increased most).

While the increasing openness of the Canadian economy affected the non-production worker wage premium, those sectors where the non-production worker premium increased the most were also the sectors where the quantity of non-production workers increased rather than decreased (see Baldwin and Rafiquzzaman, 1998). As we might expect from the regressions reported in section 4, these were the sectors where the quantities of labor-saving technologies were large relative to the quantities of labor-enhancing technologies. Both the level of technology

[22] Net export intensity = (exports / total value of shipments minus imports / total value of shipments).

use and changes in trade intensity would, therefore, appear to be related to the changing non-production salary premium.

To investigate this, data are brought together at the industry level[23] on trade, wages, and technology use. The formulation reported previously at the plant level is estimated at the industry level with the addition of measures of trade intensity. Two questions are posed. The first is whether the effect of technology found at the plant level also exists at the industry level.[24] The second is whether both trade intensity and technology are related to the non-production/production worker wage ratio when trade intensity is added to the equation.

To determine the relative contributions of trade and technology to changes in the wage premium in the 1980s, we estimate a relative wage regression by pooling together the samples from 1981 and 1989. The basic relationship is given in equation (4).

$$(W_N/W_P)_j = \xi_0 + \xi_1(NETEXP_j) + \xi_2(NPR_j) + \xi_3(CLR_j) +$$
$$\xi_4(TECH_{ij}) + \xi_5 D_j + \xi_6(NETEXP_j)^* D_j + \xi_7(NPR_j)^* D_j +$$
$$\xi_8(CLR_j)^* D_j + \xi_9(TECH_{ij})^* D_j \qquad (4)$$

where N and P indicate non-production and production labor, respectively; j indexes industry; W_N and W_P represent the wages of non-production and production workers, respectively; $NETEXP$ is the net export intensity,[25] which is defined as the value of net exports divided by the total value of shipments; NPR represents the use of non-production workers relative to production workers; CLR is the capital–labor ratio; D is a dummy variable equal to 1 for observations in 1989 and 0 for observations in 1981; and $TECH_i$ represents a vector of the type of technology use ($i = 1,2,...,6$). The $TECH$ vector includes the use of six different technologies – design and engineering ($DESIGN$), fabrication and assembly (FAB), automated materials handling ($MATHAN$), inspection and communications ($INSCOM$), manufacturing information systems ($MANINF$), and integration and control ($INTCON$). Technology use is measured as the proportion of industry shipments in plants using the technologies.

The equation is estimated with interaction binary terms (D_j), both

---

[23] The technology data are available at the three-digit level.

[24] If the effect of technology is felt differently across industries and the number of plants varies by industry, then aggregation from the plant to the industry level changes the weights used to estimate average technology effects.

[25] Exports and imports were entered separately and were found to have coefficients whose absolute values were not significantly different from one another.

Table 3.2 *Trade and technology effects on wage differentials: pooled data*

Variable	Industry Level (1) Parameter estimate	S.E.[a]	Plant Level (2) Parameter estimate	S.E.[a]	Industry Level (3) Parameter estimate	S.E.[a]	Plant Level (4) Parameter estimate	S.E.[a]
Intercept	1.5979***	0.0460	2.2279***	0.0230	1.6290***	0.0479	2.2395***	0.0230
NETEXP	−0.0009***	0.0003			−0.0010***	0.0027		
DESIGN	−0.0035	0.0832	−0.0464*	0.0251	−0.0173	0.0826	−0.0482*	0.0252
FAB	−0.2060**	0.0833	0.0235	0.0255	−0.1926**	0.0827	0.0239	0.0254
MATHAN	0.2646**	0.1347	−0.0285	0.0273	0.2747**	0.1335	−0.0281	0.0273
INSCOM	−0.2661**	0.0809	−0.1960***	0.0258	−0.3257***	0.0849	−0.2203***	0.0272
MANINF	0.2588**	0.0875	0.0473*	0.0246	0.2429***	0.0870	0.0487**	0.0246
INTCON	−0.1143	0.1011	−0.0271	0.0316	−0.1172	0.1001	−0.0293	0.0316
CLR	−0.0021	0.0015	−0.0017***	0.00003	−0.0017	0.0015	−0.0017***	0.0003
NPR	−0.1732***	0.0539	−0.3492***	0.0167	−0.1707***	0.0533	−0.3472***	0.0167
D_CLR	0.0001	0.0015	0.0011***	0.00037	−0.0043*	0.0533	−0.0030	0.0016
D	0.1146**	0.0572	−0.4328***	0.0243	0.1575**	0.0572	−0.4173***	0.0253
D_CLRTECH					0.0044**	0.0021	0.0013***	0.0005
N[b]	190		5257		190		5257	
Adj R²	0.394		0.156		0.406		0.157	
F	12.25		98.00		11.81		89.91	

[a] Standard error. [b] Number of observations. *** Significant at the 1% level. ** Significant at the 5% level. * Significant at the 10% level.

separately for the intercept term and in conjunction with each of the exogenous variables. The interactive terms reveal the extent to which there is a different impact of a particular variable in 1989 as opposed to 1981.

Table 3.2 reports the results for the relative wage equation derived from industry data (column 1). For comparison, the same equation is estimated at the plant level without the trade variable (column 2). The capital–labor ratio (*CLR*), the relative use of non-production and production workers (*NPR*), and net export intensity (*NETEXP*) are, as expected, all significantly related to relative wages. Thus, the changes that occurred during the 1980s in net exports would have increased the skilled–unskilled wage gap in the Canadian manufacturing sector. Industries where imports increased faster than exports would have experienced a decline in production worker wages relative to non-production worker salaries.

The coefficients of *FAB* and *INSCOM* are significantly negative, while the coefficients of *MATHAN* and *MANINF* are positive and significant. The use of fabrication and assembly, as well as inspection and communications technologies decrease the wage differentials in the 1980s. On the other hand, the use of automated material handling and manufacturing information systems technologies contribute significantly to the wage differentials. In addition, the use of both design and engineering (*DESIGN*) and integration and control (*INTCON*) technologies decrease the wage differentials. However, the latter two coefficients are not statistically significant.

The pooled data at the plant level (column 2), which exclude the trade variable, produce very similar results to the industry-level data. Both the capital–labor ratio, its interaction term, and the ratio of non-production to production workers have the same signs as are reported in the industry equation and are highly significant. The use of inspection and communications (*INSCOM*) technologies has a negative and significant effect on the non-production worker wage premium, as it does at the industry level. The same is true of design and engineering (*DESIGN*) and integration and control (*INTCON*), though in this case, only the first is weakly significant. The main difference is the positive sign on fabrication and assembly (*FAB*) technologies in the plant equation and a significantly negative sign on the same technologies in the industry equation. The difference between the two suggests that the negative effect of this variable is larger in those industries where there are fewer plants.

The interaction term – *D_CLR* – is included in both the industry (columns 1 and 3) and the plant (columns 2 and 4) equations so as to determine whether the contribution of the capital–labor ratio differs between 1981 and 1989.[26] The negative coefficient of *D_CLR* indicates that the effect of the capital–labor ratio has changed between 1981 and 1989. However, the coefficient on the interaction term is not statistically significant. To further investigate this change, a variable was included to test whether this differential effect of capital was related to advanced technology use. Column 3 contains the same version as column 1 with the exception of an interaction term between the capital–labor ratio and the use of three groups of technologies (fabrication, inspection and communications, and design and engineering) – *D_CLRTECH* – that have a similar effect on the non-production worker premium. This coefficient is positive and significant. The non-production worker wage premium has increased where the capital–labor ratio is high and these technologies are being used.

The pooled plant data that include an interaction term between capital and technology use in the second period (*D_CLRTECH*) produce shifts (column 4) that are very similar to those produced by the industry equation (column 3). The non-production worker premium increases in 1989 relative to 1981 for those plants that are more capital intensive and that use inspection and communications technologies, design and engineering, and fabrication and assembly technologies.

It is useful to compare the effects of the trade and technology variables by contrasting their elasticities across five different industry sectors.[27] The elasticity of the net export intensity variable is 0.013.[28] The increase in the net balance of trade for five sectors – the natural resource, labor-intensive, scale-based, product-differentiated, and science-based sectors – is 39.5 percent, 55.3 percent, 13.6 percent, 11.9 percent, and −12.6 percent respectively (table 3.3, column 3). If it is assumed that the net export elasticity is 0.0013 across all sectors, the changes in the wage premium in the 1980s attributable to the changes in the net export intensity are given in table 3.3, column 4. Some 17 percent of the change in the wage premium in the labor-intensive sector is attributable to the changes in net export intensity.[29] Changes in the

---

[26] Exclusion of the other interaction terms does not change the other coefficients in any significant fashion.

[27] See Baldwin and Rafiquzzaman (1994) for a discussion of the characteristics of these five sectors.

[28] The net export elasticity (0.013) was estimated at the mean by using the coefficient of *NETEXP* from table 3.1. The mean ratio of wages of production and non-production workers and the mean new export intensity across three digit industries were 1.374 and 19.809, respectively. The value of the elasticity is positive because both the value of *NETEXP* and the coefficient of *NETEXP* are negative.

[29] The contribution of the changes in net export intensity is calculated as: (column 4/column 2) x 100.

82   John Baldwin and Mohammed Rafiquzzaman

Table 3.3 *Changes in wage differentials due to changes in net balance of trade*

Industry	Percentage change in wage premium (2)	Percentage change in net export intensity (3)	Change due to change in net export intensity (4)[a]
Natural resources	6.62	39.45	0.51
Labor intensive	4.25	55.29	0.72
Scale-based	2.46	13.62	0.18
Product-differentiated	12.37	11.90	0.15
Science-based	−0.06	−12.60	−0.16

[a] Column 3 x elasticity (= 0.013)

net trade balance contribute 7.8 percent, 7.2 percent, and 1.2 percent of the changes in the wage premium in the natural resources, scale-based, and product-differentiated sectors, respectively.

6   Conclusion

The past 20 years have seen a change in earnings inequality, both in the United States and Canada. The debate over the causes of increasing inequality has focused on whether it is changes in trade patterns or whether it is technological change that is at fault. This chapter has demonstrated that both are at work in Canada. As other authors (Wood, 1995) have indicated, there is good reason to believe that both trade and technology go hand in hand. This is indeed the finding of this chapter. Industries that have experienced the greatest increase in exports are also those where advanced manufacturing technologies are used most intensively. These are also the industries where the wages of production workers and the salaries of non-production workers are highest. Physical capital in the form of advanced technologies and human capital as evidenced by higher wage rates are complementary. Moreover, it is in these industries where wages and by inference human capital have been increasing the most. Industries that have experienced the greatest increase in imports are less likely to use advanced manufacturing technologies. They pay the lowest wage rates. Moreover, over the 1980s, they have fallen increasingly behind the other sectors in terms of their wages paid.

This chapter also shows that the effects of technology have not been felt equally in all segments of the labor market. In particular, the wages of non-production workers have gone up relative to production workers. Some of this is related to changing trade patterns. Increases in import intensity over the period contributed to the growing wage premium. But technology use is also related to the wage premium for non-production workers. The premium has increased over the 1980s where capital intensity and labor-enhancing technology use is highest.

The Canadian experience – that the changing wage premium is related to technology use – differs from that reported for the United States by Doms, Dunne, and Troske (1997). This probably results from the fact that the US results apply only to five of the some 20 two-digit industries that exist in manufacturing. These five industries, at least based on Canadian experience, are not representative of the population of all manufacturing industries.[30] These are the industries in Canada where non-production/production worker ratios are already high and where there was much less change in the 1980s.[31]

References

Baldwin, J.R. and P.K. Gorecki (1990), *Structural Change and the Adjustment Process: Perspectives on Firm Growth and Worker Turnover*, Ottawa, Ministry of Supply and Services Canada.

Baldwin, J., T. Gray, and J. Johnson (1995), "Advanced Technology Use and Training in Canadian Manufacturing," *Canadian Business Economics*, 5: 51–70.

Baldwin, J.R. and M. Rafiquzzaman (1994), "Structural Change in the Canadian Manufacturing Sector: 1970–1990," Research Paper No. 61, Analytical Studies Branch, Ottawa, Statistics Canada.

(1997), "The Effect of Technology and Trade on Wage Differentials Between Production and NonProduction Workers," Research Paper No. 98, Analytical Studies Branch, Ottawa, Statistics Canada.

Batra, R. (1993), *The Myth of Free Trade*, New York: Charles Scribner's Sons.

Berman, E., J. Bound, and Z. Griliches (1994), "Changes in the Demand for Skilled Labour within U.S. Manufacturing: Evidence from the Annual Survey of Manufactures," *Quarterly Journal of Economics*, 109 (May): 367–397.

[30] Another difference is that Doms, Dunne, and Troske (1997) use a wage share equations whereas we use relative quantities or prices. Relative share equations will hide the effect of demand shifts if the elasticity of substitution of non-production workers for production workers is less than one. Most of the studies reported in Hamermesh (1993) have an elasticity of less than one.

[31] See Baldwin and Rafiquzzaman (1998).

Brown, C. and J. Medoff (1989), "The Employer Size Wage Effect," *Journal of Political Economy*, 97: 1027–1059.

Bylinsky, G. (1994), "The Digital Factory," *Fortune*, November 14.

Caves, R.E. (1982), *Multinational Enterprise and Economic Analysis*, Cambridge: Cambridge University Press.

Davis, S. and J. Haltiwanger (1991), "Wage Dispersion between and within US Manufacturing Plants, 1963–86," *Brookings Papers on Economic Activity: Microeconomics*, 115–180.

Doms, M., T. Dunne, and K. Troske (1997), "Workers, Wages and Technology," *Quarterly Journal of Economics*, 113 (February): 253–290.

Dunne, T. and J.A. Schmitz (1995), "Wages, Employment Structure and Employer Size-Wage Premia: Their Relationship to Advanced-Technology Usage at US Manufacturing Establishments," *Economica*, 62 (February): 89–107.

Freeman, R.B. (1995), "Are Your Wages Set in Beijing?" *Journal of Economic Perspectives*, 9 (3, Summer): 15–32.

Freeman, R. and K. Needels (1991), "Skill Differentials in Canada in an Era of Rising Labor Market Inequality," NBER Working Paper No. 3827, Cambridge, Mass., National Bureau of Economic Research.

Hamermesh, D.S. (1993), *Labour Demand*, Princeton, NJ: Princeton University Press.

Katz, L.F. and K. M. Murphy (1992), "Changes in Relative Wages, 1963–1987: Supply and Demand Factors," *Quarterly Journal of Economics*, 107 (February): 35–78.

Krueger, A.B. (1993), "How Computers Have Changed the Wage Structure: Evidence from Microdata," *The Quarterly Journal of Economics*, 108 (February): 33–60.

Lawrence, R.Z. and M.J. Slaughter (1993), "Trade and American Wages in the 1980s: Giant Sucking Sound or Small Hiccup?" *Brookings Papers on Economic Activity: Microeconomics:* 161–226.

Leamer, E.E. (1994), "Trade, Wages and Revolving Door Ideas," NBER Working Paper No. 4716, Cambridge, Mass., National Bureau of Economic Research.

Levy, F. and R. J. Murnane (1992), "US Earnings Levels and Earnings Inequality: A Review of the Recent Trends and Proposed Explanations," *Journal of Economic Literature*, 30: 1333–1381.

Mellow, W. (1982), "Employer Size and Wages," *Review of Economics and Statistics*, 64: 495–501.

Mincer, J. (1991), "Human Capital, Technology, and the Wage Structure: What do Time Series Show?" NBER Working Paper No. 3581, Cambridge, Mass., National Bureau of Economic Research.

Murphy, K. M. and F. Welch (1989), "Wage Premiums for College Graduates: Recent Growth and Possible Explanations," *Educational Researcher*, 18 (May): 17–26.

Richardson, J. D. (1995), "Income Inequality and Trade: How to Think, What to Conclude," *Journal of Economic Perspectives*, 9 (3, Summer): 33–55.

Robson, M., J. Townsend, and K. Pavitt (1988), "Sectoral Patterns of Production and Use of Innovations in the UK: 1945–1983," *Research Policy*, 17: 1–14.

Sachs, J. D. and H.J. Shatz. (1994), "Trade and Jobs in US Manufacturing," *Brookings Papers on Economic Activity*, 1: 1–84.

Statistics Canada (1990), "Manufacturing Industries of Canada: National and Provincial Areas," Catalogue No. 31–203, Ottawa, Minister of Supply and Services Canada.

Wood, A. (1994), *North-South Trade, Employment and Inequality: Changing Fortunes in a Skill-Driven World*, Oxford: Clarendon Press.

Wood, D. (1995), "How Trade Hurts Unskilled Workers," *Journal of Economic Perspectives*, 9 (3, Summer): 57–80.

4 Industrial structure and economic growth

Martin Carree and Roy Thurik

1 Introduction

Several economists have claimed that economic activity moved away from large firms to small firms in the 1970s and 1980s. With this shift also the locus of economic activity moved away from larger, incumbent firms to smaller, predominantly young firms. Acs and Audretsch (1993) and Carlsson (1992) provide an overview of empirical evidence concerning manufacturing industries in countries in varying stages of economic development. Carlsson mentions two explanations for the shift. The first deals with fundamental changes occurring in the world economy from the 1970s onwards. These changes relate to the intensification of global competition, the increase in the degree of uncertainty, and the growth in market fragmentation. The second deals with important changes in the character of technological progress. He shows that flexible automation has various effects resulting in a shift from large to smaller firms.[1] Piore and Sabel (1984) also argue that increased market instability resulted in the demise of mass production and promoted flexible specialization. The change in the path of technological development led to the occurrence of important diseconomies of scale.

This shift away from large firms is documented predominantly for manufacturing industries but it is not completely confined to this sector. Brock and Evans (1989) show that this trend has been economy wide, at least for the United States. They suggest four more explanations for this shift: the increase in labor supply; changes in consumer tastes; relaxation of (entry) regulations; and the intensity of the creative destruction process. Loveman and Sengenberger (1991) stress the influence of two

---

[1] Meredith (1987) argues that small firms are just as well, or better, equipped to implement technological advances like CAD/CAM. Small business owners often can more clearly see the benefits and problems of their automation decisions as they are very selective in where they invest their capital and because they are close to the operational level.

trends of industrial restructuring: that of decentralization and vertical disintegration of large companies and that of the formation of new business communities. They also mention the role of public and private policies promoting the small business sector.[2]

The question whether this change of the size class structure of industries has influenced their economic performance is under researched. Here we are concerned with one of the most important questions in economics: Why do industries grow? The link between industrial organization and economic growth has always been the subject of considerable debate. Traditionally, the prevalent assumption was that giant companies are at the heart of the process of innovation and creation of welfare. This assumption is generally referred to as the Schumpeterian hypothesis. Recently, the debate centers around the question whether the process of decentralization and deconcentration, which virtually every industrialized country has experienced in the last two decades, has had positive welfare implications. Audretsch (1995) calls this shift in orientation of our social economic thinking "the new learning."

The question of the link between the shift in the industrial structure and subsequent growth can be answered in two ways. First, by investigating the many consequences of the shift in the locus of economic activity. For instance, one may study whether this shift has been favorable for the process of innovation and rejuvenation of industries. See Acs and Audretsch (1990), Audretsch (1995), and Cohen and Klepper (1996). Alternatively, one may zoom in on the discussion of the relation between the role of small firms and competition and industry dynamics. See Audretsch (1993,1995) and You (1995). Moreover, the role of small firms in the job creation process, usually treated as a controversial topic despite countless studies showing that small firms are a major engine in this process, may be dealt with. Davis *et al.* (1996) and Carree and Klomp (1996) provide a recent discussion. Lastly, the role of small firms as a vehicle for entrepreneurship may be the focal point of our attention.[3] Baumol (1990) amply deals with the role of entrepreneurial activities and their consequences for prosperity throughout history. Acs (1992) has been one of the first to bring it all together in a short descriptive manner and to survey some consequences of the shift of economic activity from large to smaller businesses. His claims are that small firms play an important role in the economy serving as agents of

---

[2] De Koning and Snijders (1992) provide a survey of the various public policies in countries of the European Union which have been introduced during the 1980s.

[3] Entrepreneurship is not necessarily confined to small firms. Large enterprises seek to promote entrepreneurship by creating largely independent business units. Burgelman (1994) discusses possibilities for large firm entrepreneurship.

change by their entrepreneurial activity, being the source of considerable
innovative activity, stimulating industry evolution, and creating an
important share of the newly generated jobs.[4] The evaluation of the
various consequences of this shift is difficult but necessary to establish
whether it is desirable and to be promoted by economic policy. It is
difficult because none of these consequences is, in fact, independent from
the other three and because the evaluation offers something of a series of
tradeoffs (see Audretsch and Thurik, 1997). For instance, small businesses may contribute to higher growth because of their contribution to
the selection process due to their variety. On the other hand, however,
their lower level of stability, inherent to the selection process, leads to
welfare losses. Or, while employment levels may rise as firm size declines,
the lower average wages small firms pay may at least offset the welfare
effect induced by the employment growth.

A second way to answer the question is to circumvent the intermediary
variables between the shift and growth, like technological change, entrepreneurship, competitiveness, and job generation. The focus is on a direct
link between the shift and performance measures, like growth or productivity. Some preliminary empirical results of the relation between changes
in firm size distribution and economic growth are presented in Thurik
(1995, 1996). The analysis shows a positive effect of an increase in the
economy-wide share of small firms on growth in GDP. The interpretation
of this result is somewhat difficult because it is not clear whether changes
in the economy-wide share of small firms result mainly from changes in
the sectoral composition or from downscaling in the specific industries.
Moreover, the papers lack a theoretical component. Schmitz (1989)
develops an endogenous growth model which relates entrepreneurial
activity and economic growth. He shows that an increase in the proportion of entrepreneurs in the working force leads to an increase in long-run
economic growth. His model also implies that the equilibrium fraction of
entrepreneurs is lower than the social optimal level, hence providing a
rationale for policies stimulating entrepreneurial activity. The size class
structure of an industry and the proportion of entrepreneurs in its
working force are strongly related. This paper lacks an empirical backup.[5]

[4] More recent contributions by Zoltan Acs (and others) on the relationship between small
     firms and economic growth include Acs (1996a, 1996b) and Acs et al. (1997).
[5] Recent studies on the relation between industry structure and performance are Nickell
     (1996) and Nickell et al. (1997) who present evidence that competition, as measured by
     increased number of competitors, has a positive effect on the rate of total factor
     productivity growth. Hay and Liu (1997) claim that firms have a higher incentive to
     improve their efficiency in competitive environments and provide empirical evidence for
     UK manufacturing industries.

The present chapter follows the second way. It investigates the link between smallness and growth bypassing the analysis of all the inter-mediary variables. It presents a new model linking performance and firm size distribution. The two mechanisms governing this link are ease of entry of new firms and ease of change of incumbent firms. Empirical tests are provided using a sample of 13 manufacturing industries in 12 European countries for the period 1990–1995. By dealing with data at a relatively low industry level the disturbing influence of changes in sectoral composition is eliminated. As a prelude to our formal model the relative virtues of large as well as small firms are dealt with in a new and descriptive way.

The contents of this chapter are as follows. A list of effects which stimulate the presence of either small or large firms are discussed in section 2. The empirical analyses in this chapter are preceded in section 3 by a tentative model of the effect of different market settings on industry structure and performance. The model is a pure selection model, in which entrepreneurs are assumed not to learn or innovate. Despite the simpli-city of the model assumptions the predicted relationship between the number of entrepreneurs and economic performance is far from simple. It depends upon the particular group of market participants. Section 4 discusses the data set of large firm presence in European manufacturing. Empirical results of the effect of the degree of large firm presence on growth of value added are provided in section 5. Section 6 provides some concluding remarks on the role of smallness in promoting economic growth in modern manufacturing industries.

2   Effects stimulating largeness and smallness

As long as there has been economics there has been a debate about the causes and consequences of firm size, about the meaning of average firm size, and about differences in firm sizes, say, about the firm size distribution (see Audretsch, 1993). Clearly, this has not been a conspic-uous debate, but it has been a continuous one. Until some 15 years ago its outcome was more or less unanimous: small firms would either disappear or be allowed to lead a marginal life. There have been isolated dissidents: Schumpeter accentuated the role of smallness in economic restructuring and Schumacher had the nerve to talk about the beauty of smallness in the darkest of the Galbraith times (see Schumacher, 1973). In his pioneering empirical study Birch claimed to have discovered that most new jobs emanated from small firms (see Birch, 1981). This finding contradicted the prevailing body of knowledge and intuition of that time. Mainstream economists, however, kept thinking that small firms would lead a fading life. It was not readily apparent how Birch's finding had to be reconciled with the empirical evidence displaying a level of concentration of economic activity which had been increasing for decades. Moreover, there are some theoretically powerful and empirically often corroborated mechanisms supporting the shift away from new and small firms and toward large and incumbent ones.

First, there is the effect of *scale*, usually interpreted as the fall of average costs with increasing volume of output. This mechanism occurs in many business functions from productive to administrative and on different levels of aggregation: in business units, in establishments, and in enterprises. The sources of scale economies are well known. One is that fixed set-up or threshold costs do not vary with the level of output. For instance, the costs of setting up a scientific gathering are fixed to a large extent. The costs of the organization and the preparation of the presentations and the presentations themselves become more effective if the number of attendants to the meeting increases.

Second, there is the effect of *scope*, usually observed as the fall of average costs of a product if the number of different products increases (see Teece, 1980 and Nooteboom, 1993). Its sources can range from the use of indivisible resources (the room where a scientific meeting is held can be used for various purposes), to complementarity (presentations at scientific meetings can also be used as material for prospective articles in journals) and interaction (discussion during and between the presentations).

Third, there is the effect of *experience*, defined as the decline of average costs with increasing production volume accumulated over time. The best documented examples of unit costs falling over time as a result of past experience are those of the Liberty freighters and B-29 bombers during World War II (see Scherer and Ross, 1990; Lucas, 1993; and Irwin and Klenow, 1994).

It is clear that these three cost effects are detrimental to the survival of small firms. Small firms may try to compensate for these cost disadvantages by creating networks or other interfirm relations. From Williamson's contribution to the economic sciences we know that the organizers of productive output can choose between two so-called governance structures: that of integration of input within the hierarchy of the firm and that of purchase of input on the market (see Williamson, 1975). The advantage of the latter structure lies in the economy of scale resulting from specialization. For example, the consultant gains from specialization, doing similar consultancy work for many firms for which it does not pay to employ a specialist for solving problems which only occur at intervals. The disadvantage lies in the occurrence of transaction costs.

Three stages of a transaction define three different sources of costs. The stage of contact involves search and marketing costs: search costs for the firm to be consulted and marketing costs for the firm supplying consultancy inputs. The stage of contract involves information, negotiation, and definition costs. The stage of control involves costs of monitoring, discussion, feedback, redesign, arbitration, etc. In a recent article Nooteboom (1993) argues that smaller firms face higher transaction costs per unit of transaction than larger ones.[6] First, there are threshold costs in all three stages of the transaction. The relative contribution of these threshold costs disappears the larger the transaction becomes. Second, small firms suffer more from the cost of acquiring and processing information. They are more sensitive to uncertainty, discontinuity, opportunism, and specificity. So, the fourth effect, the effect of *organization* defined as using outside production for one's inputs instead of inside production, boils down to the occurrence of more scale effects and to the appearance of transaction effects which are both damaging to the level of unit costs of small production kernels.

So far, the four effects would suggest an ever-decreasing share of small firms, which was the case until the 1970s (Chandler, 1990). Other effects are needed to explain the existence and success of small firms.

The first effect is the *transportation* effect. Production and organization costs discussed above are only part of the total cost structure. There is also the cost of delivering output to customers or bringing customers to the place where service is provided (see Scherer and Ross, 1990). Many studies predict and report significant scale economies in establishments in the retail industry (see Nooteboom, 1987a). Still there exists a considerable number of small retail stores. Prospective customers value their transportation costs when looking for supplies. This is why a geographic dispersion of demand goes together with a geographic dispersion of supply. And then smallness, at least at the establishment, plant, or, in the retail case, store level has a chance.

The second effect is that of the *market size*. Small markets require small firms. Markets exist where scale economies have no meaning because they cannot be obtained. For example, it is easy to check that all participants of some scientific gathering wear a different shirt. Variety is a significant customer requirement. The market for a singular piece of apparel is small when compared to the entire textiles market. There is no apparent bonus for large firms in markets which are fragmented in size.

---

[6] Jovanovic (1993) notes that recent advances in information technology have made market-based coordination cheaper relative to internal coordination partially causing the recent decline in the average size of firms.

The third effect is that of *adjustment*. There is a tradeoff between efficiency, lowest production costs, given some output level, and adjustability, the cost of adjusting a certain level of output. Large firms can produce at lower unit costs than small firms can. But small firms can adjust their output level at lower costs than large firms, because they are either more labor intensive or use different equipment.[7] It is the story of the two transportation firms: one firm using large lorries, thriving in a market with a persistant high demand for shipment, the other firm using small ones, thriving in a turbulent market with a varying demand for lorries. It is the story of many firms in the post-mass-consumption age: they produce exactly what the customer wants. They pay little attention to questions of whether anyone else wants the product, whether the firm has made the product before, or whether there will be follow-up demand for the product (see *The Economist*, March 5, 1994). It is also the story of the firms in the so-called industrial districts, competing and cooperating at the same time. There is no apparent bonus for large firms in markets which are fragmented in time.

The fourth effect is that of *effectiveness*. The essence of this effect is that different goods and services have different meanings for different people. A shirt that fits the average attendant of a scientific meeting is not the same good as a shirt tailored to fit a specific individual and bought for showing off at a specific occasion. A shirt factory can make shirts of the first type cheaper than a tailor can. But one receives more effective units of shirt from a tailor. At least the one who is sensitive to the satisfaction of knowing the uniqueness of his shirt or the gains of showing it off to others, will experience the effectiveness of a unique shirt. The rationale being that the existence of both the factory and the tailor in the shirt market can only be explained if output is measured in terms of effective units of shirts instead of just shirts. This not only explains the coexistence of clothing giants and tailors, but also that of supermarket chains and speciality stores, of the McDonald chain and three star restaurants.

Furthermore, there is the effect of *control*. Nooteboom (1987b) claims that this is the least documented of all effects. The discussion of what defines a small firm is probably as everlasting as the discussion of where small firms stem from. A challenging definition of a small firm is that of a firm where one person or a small group of persons is in control, or which

---

[7]   Mills and Schumann (1985) and Fiegenbaum and Karnani (1991) provide empirical evidence for small firms to benefit from variability of the environment. Camacho (1991) develops a theoretical model in which adaption costs rise with the size of the firm leading to optimal firm size to be negatively related to such variability.

bears the personal stamp of one person. Though ineffective and imprecise, this definition at least stimulates the investigation of behavioral advantages, like entrepreneurial energy, motivated and effective labor due to the mutual proximity of customers, suppliers, production floor, management, and ownership, etc. Entrepreneurial and organizational energy may flourish and be well controlled and guided in a small environment. The best evidence of this entrepreneurial energy is that many entrepreneurs convince themselves to work below the minimum wage and convince their employees to work below market prices, i.e., at a price lower than a large firm would offer for a similar job (see Brown and Medoff, 1989, Evans and Leighton, 1989, and Oosterbeek and Van Praag, 1995). This wage differential which continues to surprise many labor economists is partly explained by the higher levels of control, commitment, motivation, perseverance, and energy, if these levels are to prevail in small units. We think they do and that is why the effect of control can be presented as a fifth effect. It is straightforward that the effect of control is not futile in an environment where the effect of adjustment (and hence flexibility and maneuverability) plays a role. They reinforce each other in their struggle to outperform the advantages of scale.

A final effect we mention is that of *culture*. It is safe for any researcher in the social sciences to point at culture as a factor influencing any phenomenon demanding explanation. But since William Baumol's essay showed us that entrepreneurship can be productive as well as unproductive, and can even be destructive, we should start thinking of ways to grab the essence of Baumol's culture, using it for reinforcing or demolishing other effects like control, adjustment, or effectiveness. See Baumol (1990). Baumol's basic hypothesis is that, while the supply of entrepreneurship varies across societies, its productive contribution varies even more. The reason is that the societal perspective determines to what degree entrepreneurial activities are used for productive achievements, such as innovation, or unproductive ventures, such as rent seeking or organized crime. Murphy *et al.* (1991) provide some empirical evidence showing that countries with a relatively high number of graduates from law schools, educated mainly to redistribute income, grow slower, *ceteris paribus*, than countries which have a relatively high number of graduates in technical disciplines. The effect of culture may be beneficial to large or to small firms.

Like the effects stimulating largeness, those stimulating smallness are not independent in their influence. The effects of market size and adjustment are mutually reinforcing when explaining smallness in many markets of producer goods and services. The supplier producing a specific car part this year is likely to produce a different but equally specific part next year. This supplier operates in a market which is fragmented both in size and time. The effects of market size, adjustment, and effectiveness are mutually reinforcing when explaining smallness in many markets of consumer goods and services. The small firm producing a unique shirt this year is likely to produce a different unique shirt next year, particularly if the shirt has a high fashion value. This market is fragmented in size, in time, and in taste.

3   Competitive selection with differing rates of entry and adjustment

In the previous section we have discussed possible reasons for small firms outperforming large firms or vice versa. The variety of reasons does not allow for a model incorporating all elements. However, we think that recent developments in evolutionary economics may contribute to our understanding of the relation between the structure and performance of industries. More specifically, in this section we investigate two factors at the industry level which may strongly influence both the firm size distribution of firms and the performance of industries. These are the ease of entry and the ease of change of incumbent firms.

Evolutionary economists consider both structure and performance as endogenous and are usually interested in the long-term effects of market settings. They stress the importance of competitive selection (Jovanovic, 1982). Entry and exit which have barely any short effect on market structure in the short term may radically alter the market settings in the somewhat longer term. Eliasson (1995) shows that lack of entry may affect economic performance to a non-negligible extent only after a period of about 25 years. In this section we use a simple model to highlight the effects of lack of entry and lack of mobility in industries which progress through a process of competitive selection. It will be made clear that these effects depend on the precise group of market participants.

Consider a population of N persons who choose between being entrepreneurs and being employees. Each person has an "entrepreneurial ability" e_i which can be used in combination with L_i employees earning a wage w to produce an output of $e_i L_i^{\beta}$ with $0<\beta<1$.[8] Taking the price of the good to be unity, total profit will be $\pi_i = e_i L_i^{\beta} - wL_i$. From the first-order condition it is easy to find that the optimal level of labor input and profit are equal to

---

[8] Some other models in which heterogeneous ability is an essential feature are Lucas (1978), Gifford (1993), and Klepper (1996).

$$L_i^* = \left(\frac{\beta e_i}{w}\right)^{\frac{1}{1-\beta}} \qquad \pi_i^* = (1-\beta)e_i\left(\frac{\beta e_i}{w}\right)^{\frac{\beta}{1-\beta}}$$

Entrepreneurs exit the industry in case the optimal level of profit is below the wage level w. These entrepreneurs have no long-term prospect of their venture being profitable. That is, firms remain incumbent if

$$e_i > \frac{w}{\beta^\beta (1-\beta)^{1-\beta}}$$

The extent of entry and mobility are built into the model by having for each period every person receiving a constant probability p of (re-) entering the industry.[9] The amount of labor entrepreneurs use is assumed to adjust gradually to the optimal level

$$L_{it} = L_{i,t-1} + \lambda(L_{it}^* - L_{i,t-1})$$

The equilibrium wage level is derived from the condition that the demand and supply of labor are identical. Let M be the total number of entrepreneurs and $\ominus$ the set of entrepreneurs, then we have

$$N - M = \sum_{i \in \ominus} L_{it} \Leftrightarrow N - M = (1-\lambda)\sum_{i \in \ominus} L_{i,t-1} + \lambda \sum_{i \in \ominus} L_{it}^* \Leftrightarrow$$

$$w = \beta \left(\frac{\lambda \sum_{i \in \ominus} e_i^{\frac{1}{1-\beta}}}{N - M - (1-\lambda)\sum_{i \in \ominus} L_{i,t-1}}\right)^{1-\beta}$$

Competitive selection proceeds through entry, exit, and mobility of firms. The intensity of the competitive selection process in this model depends on the probability of entry, p, and the adjustment rate, λ. We use some simple simulations to show the effect of this intensity on the market performance, measured by total market output. We first introduce the market settings which are identical across the scenarios and then we discuss the specific assumptions about the particular group of market participants. The abilities are assumed to be distributed as a linear combination of two independent log-normally

---

[9] See Carree (1997) for scenarios in which the probabilities of persons entering the industry depend on their ability as p times the ratio of e_i over the mean of the abilities in the population. That is, entrepreneurs are assumed to be aware to some extent of their own chances of success in the market.

distributed variables X_1 and X_2 with the same mean and variance. The weighting factor is α_t. That is, $e_{it} = \alpha_t x_{1i} + (1 - \alpha_t) x_{2i}$ where x_{1i} and x_{2i} are the realizations of X_1 and X_2 for person i. Note that the mean of the abilities is independent of α_t while the variance is at a minimum when $\alpha_t = 0.5$ and at a maximum when α_t is either 0 or 1. The variables X_1 and X_2 stand for two "underlying" abilities which combine into the entrepreneurial ability necessary to be successful in the industry. Gifford (1993) also distinguishes between two kinds of ability: ability to *innovate* (also used in Klepper, 1996) and ability to *manage* (also used in Lucas, 1978).

In the rest of this section we will discuss some scenarios. In each scenario the mean and variance of the log-normal distribution are $e^{-0.5}$ and $(e^{0.25} - 1)/e$. In the first period there is a probability of 0.1 for each person to be one of the initial entrepreneurs. The value of β is taken as 0.8. Changing the value of β over time would certainly have an impact on the firm-size distribution. However, in this model we concentrate on selection instead of on changes in production technologies or organizational forms. The number of persons N is fixed at 10,000.

The scenarios

We will show three scenarios which are derived by choosing between two alternative assumptions. The first choice is between:
(a) Nobody enters or leaves the population.
(b) Each period 200 persons (2 percent) are removed from the sample and 200 new ones are added. The ordering in which this is executed is determined before the simulation.

We first choose between having the same group of market participants throughout the entire simulation period or having this group "refreshed" each period as some retire while others start their working career. The first option is viable only when the firm "inherits" the ability of the founder. Successive entrepreneurs leading the firm are then assumed to be influenced strongly by their predecessors (see also Cohen and Klepper, 1992b, and Klepper, 1996, who suggest that R&D-related capabilities are *firm specific*). The second choice is between:
(c) The weighting factor α_t is 0.75 and constant in time.
(d) The weighting factor α_t starts at 0.5, increases with constant steps to 0.9 50 periods later, then decreases again with the same steps to 0.1 100 periods later, etc.

Taking a constant α_t implies that entrepreneurial ability is also constant over time. Changes in the production process or market

Table 4.1 *Simulation results for three scenarios*

Scenario	λ	p	Number of entrepreneurs				Output index			
			$t=10$	$t=25$	$t=100$	$t=300$	$t=10$	$t=25$	$t=100$	$t=300$
(a)(c)	0.15	0.03	701	810	816	802	117	130	143	144
	0.15	0.01	429	494	567	624	111	119	138	145
	0.05	0.03	702	808	799	778	112	125	143	144
	0.05	0.01	409	479	544	611	109	117	137	145
(b)(c)	0.15	0.03	623	736	816	678	120	126	126	133
	0.15	0.01	387	445	489	388	110	112	111	115
	0.05	0.03	623	775	919	728	116	124	125	131
	0.05	0.01	393	465	556	405	108	111	110	113
(a)(d)	0.15	0.03	807	846	845	835	120	140	140	140
	0.15	0.01	523	539	586	557	115	129	133	137
	0.05	0.03	785	825	817	820	115	135	137	137
	0.05	0.01	487	536	579	556	112	126	131	135

Note: The total number of market participants is 10,000. The output index is 100 in the first year.

environment may shift the relevant abilities over time. In the second option α_t changes by 0.008 each period. It implies that the importance of X_1 and X_2 and therefore the set of individuals with the highest abilities also changes over time. The second alternative in both the first and second choice creates continuous incentives for *displacement* and *replacement*. Entrepreneurs who retire are replaced and entrepreneurs whose abilities decrease below a certain level due to a changing weighting factor are displaced. Table 4.1 shows the three scenarios for the adjustment rate equal to 0.15 and 0.05 and the probability of entry equal to 0.03 and 0.01.

The following conclusions can be drawn from these simulations. First, in case of an unstable environment, i.e., changing population and abilities, the performance is considerably better when the rate of mobility and entry are higher. This is a consequence of the constant need for selecting the most able entrepreneurs. In a stable environment the rate of entry may turn out to be inefficiently high after the selection process has done most of its work and the best entrepreneurs run the firms. The extent to which the number of entrepreneurs and economic performance are positively related depends therefore on the stability of the business environment. This is in line with the findings of Mills and Schumann (1985) and Das *et al.* (1993) who conclude that small firm presence is positively related to fluctuations in demand.

Table 4.2 *Simulation results for a period of creative destruction*

Scenario	λ	p	Number of entrepreneurs				Output index			
			t=300	t=305	t=310	t=325	t=300	t=305	t=310	t=325
(a)(c)	0.15	0.03	802	647	678	798	100	84	88	93
	0.15	0.01	624	407	434	478	100	84	86	89
	0.05	0.03	778	634	670	789	100	80	83	90
	0.05	0.01	611	400	423	466	100	80	83	87

Note: The total number of market participants is 10,000. The output index is 100 in the first year.

Second, a higher number of firms need not be positively correlated with market performance. The number of firms for the low-mobility scenarios is higher than that for high-mobility scenarios in the case when the population changes from period to period. The reverse is the case when the population does not alter over time. In the case of a changing population the optimal market structure is also constantly changing. An inefficiently large number of small firms survive in that market setting due to more able entrepreneurs not being capable of quick responses to a changing optimal firm size.

The conclusions show that there is not a simple relation between the number of firms and economic performance. However, it is likely that in a period of creative destruction a positive relation between these variables can be found. To test for this we simulate a period of creative destruction by abruptly changing the value of α_t from 0.75 to 0.25 in period 301 for one scenario. The results can be found in table 4.2.

The simulation results show that a fast recovery in the number of firms after the shake-out due to a sudden change in abilities is beneficial for the recovery process. This process can be seen to have been almost twice as fast in the case of $\lambda = 0.15$ and $p = 0.03$ when compared to that of $\lambda = 0.05$ and $p = 0.01$.

The simulation results which we have discussed above show that the qualitative assumptions about the "pool" of market participants may affect the evolution of market structure and performance considerably. It makes clear that an increase in the number of firms may be due to higher mobility barriers or to too high a level of entry and therefore possibly be negatively correlated with performance. It may of course be the reverse case: an increase in the number of firms may be due to lower mobility barriers or an increase in the rate of entry to more efficient levels. The question of which case is relevant in which industry and in which period remains an empirical one. The presented model of competitive selection is only tentative. Alternative analyses, also considering the role of technological learning, can be found in Eliasson (1984), Winter (1984), and Dosi *et al.* (1995).

4 Large-firm presence in European manufacturing

The most impressive and also the most cited example of changes in the size class distribution of firms is that of the 500 largest American firms, the so-called Fortune 500. Their employment share dropped from about 20 percent in 1970 to somewhat more than 10 percent now. Yearly summaries of the firm-size distribution of (potential) EU members at the two-digit level for the entire business sector are published by Eurostat. In this study we will use data from the third edition of this summary, entitled *Enterprises in Europe*.[10]

The share of small firms in most manufacturing industries has increased since the 1970s. This may have been the result of, for example, down sizing of large firms, entry of new firms using advanced technologies and introducing new products, and of flexible specialization of small firms. The speed and intensity of these developments have not been equal across industries and across countries as demonstrated in OECD (1994). Prominent examples of down sizing are IBM which has been reported to have reduced its workforce from about 400,000 employees in 1987 to about 200,000 employees in 1995, and General Motors which cut employment from about 800,000 in 1979 to about 450,000 in the early 1990s (*The Economist*, December 21, 1996).

Smaller firms gaining market share can be positively related to economic performance in two ways. First, a decrease in market concentration may lead to more competition and hence an improved performance. Second, the increase in the market share of small firms may point at a fast and intensive process of introducing new products and technologies.[11] It may be interpreted as a measure of industry flexibility which is likely to be positively related to economic performance.

In the next section we investigate the effect of differences in the size class structure of firms on the growth of industrial value added. This will

[10] The efforts of Eurostat are currently being supplemented by the European Network of SME Research (ENSR), a cooperation of 16 European institutes. This organization publishes a yearly report of the structure and the developments of the small business sectors in the countries of the European Union (see EIM, 1996).

[11] Prusa and Schmitz (1991) provide evidence for the PC software industry that new small firms are an important source of innovation.

be done for a sample of 13 manufacturing industries in 12 European countries for a recent period (1990–1995). A related analysis was pursued in Carree and Thurik (1998). In that paper the dependent variable is the growth of industrial output and both the number of manufacturing industries and the number of countries is one larger while the period is one year shorter, i.e., 1990–1994. The share of large firms is calculated from Eurostat (1994). Not all data of industries and countries in this Eurostat report are used. Some countries are not incorporated because they provide establishment data instead of enterprise data. We also do not take industries into consideration where the total number of employees is below 10,000. Finally, Eurostat sometimes does not provide employment data due to reasons of confidentiality. We define the share of large firms as the employment share of enterprises with 100 or more employees, Large Firm Presence (LFP for short). For this variable there is a total of 126 observations. Growth in total value added from 1990 to 1993, 1994, and to 1995 is measured by the ratio of total real value added of the industry in 1993, 1994, and 1995 with base year 1990. The source for the indices is OECD STAN Database (1996). We note that the purchasing power parities used in this database to adjust the nominal figures are neither industry specific nor do they reflect relative producer prices. Additionally, some of the data points are estimated by the OECD Secretariat.

Data are available for 12 countries: Belgium, Denmark, Finland, France, Germany, Italy, The Netherlands, Norway, Portugal, Spain, Sweden, and the United Kingdom. All data on large-firm presence refer to the year 1990 except for Italy (1989). The five countries with total employment in the industries incorporated above one million persons are Germany (6.5 million), United Kingdom (4.1 million), Italy (3.8 million), France (3.7 million), and Spain (2.3 million). Total employment in the 126 industries equals 23.9 million persons. The fourth column of table 4.3 shows how these are distributed over the 13 two-digit-level manufacturing industries. The next two columns of the table show the average value added indices in 1995 (1990=1) and the average large firm presence, LFP. The right-hand column shows the correlation between LFP and the value added indices in 1995. The non-weighted average of these correlations is −0.25. On average large-firm presence and growth of value added appear to be negatively related, but the differences across industries are large. The correlations range from −0.80 to +0.16. In the rest of this chapter we focus on the average effect of LFP on growth of production. The large range in correlations indicates that the effect may differ quite strongly from one specific industry to another.

Table 4.3 *Summary statistics for the 13 industries*

Sector	Description	N	Empl	VA95	LFP	Corr
21/22	Basic metals	8	907	1.037	0.870	−0.40
24	Non-metallic mineral products	9	1,056	0.998	0.566	−0.40
25/26	Chemicals	11	1,975	1.120	0.812	+0.16
31	Metal articles	9	2,972	0.987	0.391	−0.80
34	Electrical engineering	11	3,011	1.226	0.752	+0.02
35	Motor vehicles	6	1,807	1.023	0.903	−0.52
37	Instrument engineering	7	492	1.129	0.542	−0.20
41/42	Food, drink and tobacco	12	3,114	1.046	0.576	+0.13
43	Textiles	9	1,388	0.919	0.604	−0.77
45	Footwear and clothing	10	1,853	0.860	0.371	−0.48
46	Wood and wooden products	12	1,698	1.010	0.286	−0.10
47	Paper, publishing and printing	12	2,419	1.058	0.561	−0.02
48	Rubber and plastics	10	1,245	1.109	0.569	−0.38
	Total / Average	126	23,937	1.040	0.600	−0.25

Note: N is the number of countries for which the value added and large firm presence data are available. *Empl* stands for the total number of employees (in 1,000s). *VA95* is the value added index in 1995 (1990 = 1). *LFP* is the share of firms with 100 or more employees in total employment. *Corr* is the correlation coefficient between *VA95* and *LFP* for the specific industry.

5 Empirical results

To test for the effect of the share of large firms on growth of value added we consider the following equations

$$VA_{ijt} = a_i + b_1 LFP_{ij} + \eta_{1ijt}, \ t = 1993, \ 1994, \ 1995$$
$$VA_{ijt} = a_i + b_1 LFP_{ij} + b_2 LFP_{ij} * Y_{ij} + \eta_{2ijt}, \ t = 1993, \ 1994, \ 1995$$

where i refers to industry and j to country. The variable VA_{ijt} is the value added index of industry i in country j and year t (1990 = 1). The variables a_i are industry dummies. The variable Y_{ij} is a proportional GDP per capita index (for 1990) ranging from 0.57 for Portugal to 1 for Germany. This variable is taken as a proxy for the stage of economic development. The variables η_{1ij} and η_{2ij} are residuals assumed to be independent and identically distributed (i.i.d.). It is necessary to incorporate industry dummies because a certain level of large-firm presence considered relatively high in one industry may be considered relatively low in another.

The effect of industrial structure on economic progress may depend upon the stage of economic development of a country, as we test by incorporating $LFP*Y$. First, the introduction of new products and production techniques is especially important for the group of highly developed countries. Small innovative firms may play an even more important role in these countries than in countries which lag behind in terms of economic development. Second, the stage of ousting of inefficient (craft) firms may not have been completed in industries of less-developed countries. A large share of small firms in these countries may still have a mom-and-pop character. Economic progress is not promoted to a considerable extent by these non-innovative firms. Third, the success of small firm networks is highly dependent upon the quality of regional infrastructure. Countries which are highly developed in economic terms generally have a well-developed infrastructure.

Choosing a specific period over which to evaluate economic growth is an important decision. If the period is too long then the size class structure of the industry may change considerably during the period of observation. If the period is too short then the effect of the size class structure may be overshadowed by the business cycle influence on industry output. We consider three periods, 1990–1993, 1990–1994 and 1990–1995. In 1993 most European manufacturing industries experienced a period of recession. The average value added index in our sample in that year was 4% below that in 1990. The years 1994 and 1995 disclosed a strong recovery for most industries and the average value added index rose to 4% higher than that in 1990. Summary statistics for the variables can be found in table 4.4.

In this section we determine the estimates of b_1 and b_2 by performing least squares regressions on the equations presented above in deviation of the industry-specific average of each variable:

$$VA_{ijt} - \overline{VA_{it}} = b_1(LFP_{ij} - \overline{LFP_i}) + e_{1ijt} \tag{1}$$

$$VA_{ijt} - \overline{VA_{it}} = b_1(LFP_{ij} - \overline{LFP_i}) + b_2(LFP_{ij} * Y_{ij} - \overline{(LFP * Y)_i}) + e_{2ijt} \tag{2}$$

In table 4.5 we present least squares estimation results of equations (1) and (2). We have considered four different least squares techniques. The first is ordinary least squares (OLS). The results of this technique suggested one particularly strong outlier, viz. the electrical engineering industry in Sweden (NACE 34). The second technique, therefore, is OLS without this one observation. A more general way to deal with (possible) outliers was suggested by Rousseeuw (1984). His robust regression

Table 4.4 *Summary statistics for dependent and independent variables*

Variable	Description	Mean	Stdev	Max	Min
$VA93$	Value added index 1993	0.955	0.096	1.230	0.624
$VA94$	Value added index 1994	1.005	0.116	1.591	0.677
$VA95$	Value added index 1995	1.042	0.166	2.106	0.581
LFP	Large-firm presence	0.586	0.218	0.971	0.073
$LFP*Y$	LFP times GDP per cap. index	0.509	0.214	0.971	0.048

Note: The mean, standard deviation (Stdev), maximum (Max) and minimum (Min) are computed on the basis of 126 observations of available country-industry pairs.

procedure is programmed in PROGRESS.[12] The robust regression is a two-step procedure of least median squares (LMS) followed by reweighted least squares (RLS). This procedure proposed by Rousseeuw to cope with (multivariate) outliers is the third technique. The fourth least squares technique is to weight each observation by employment (WLS). This implies that countries and/or industries with a large number of employees have a stronger impact on the regression results. The interpretation of the coefficients in the table is straightforward. For example, the ordinary least squares results in the third column of table 4.5 imply that an increase in LFP by 0.1 leads to a decrease in growth of value added by 1 percent for the 1990–1993 period, 1.5 percent for the 1990–1994 period, and 2.25 percent for the 1990–1995 period.

We first discuss the estimation results of equation (1). The estimated value of b_1 is negative as expected and in most cases it is significantly different from zero at the 5 percent significance level. The two exceptions are the estimates using the reweighted and weighted least squares techniques for 1993. For each of the four techniques the effect of large-firm presence on the value added index becomes stronger when going from the period 1990–1993 to the period 1990–1995. That is, industries not only appear to have been more affected by the recession in the case when large firms had a larger employment share, they also tend to have recovered slower from this recession.

The results of equation (2) are somewhat less straightforward to interpret. Multicollinearity is caused by incorporating both *LFP* and *LFP*Y* into the regression equation. The GDP per capita variable *Y* has only limited spread across countries causing the two variables to

---

[12] A description of the PROGRESS program can be found in Rousseeuw and Leroy (1987). See also Wagner (1994) for an application of the procedure.

be highly correlated. The OLS results show clearly the multicollinearity problem. Whereas the estimate of b_1 is significant in equation
(1), both the estimates of b_1 and b_2 are insignificantly different from
zero in equation (2). The reweighted and weighted least squares
techniques both have a positive value for b_1 and a negative value for
b_2. These results clearly suggest that less-developed countries may
have benefitted from relatively high large-firm presence during the
early 1990s, while the reverse has been the case for the more highly
developed countries. This corresponds to the results presented in
Carree and Thurik (1998) who find that for the two countries in the
data set with lowest GDP per capita, viz. Portugal and Spain, there is
a different effect, on average, of large-firm presence on growth of
production than for the other European countries. If we consider the
RLS and WLS results for the 1990–1995 period, the critical point of
economic development is around 0.6. That is, European countries
with GDP per capita above 60 percent of the highest GDP per capita
(e.g. that of Germany) have tended to benefit, on average, from a
higher presence of small firms in manufacturing industries in the early
1990s. It is not unlikely that many firms in the less-developed
Portuguese and Spanish manufacturing sectors have a suboptimal
scale. Small firm presence may only have a positive effect on economic
growth in a certain stage of organizational and technological development in which scale economies have become less important. Spain and
Portugal which joined the European Union only recently, may not
have reached this stage yet.

We note that the precise reason for the relationship between large-
firm presence (industry structure) and change of value added (economic
growth) is left somewhat unclear. An increase in the share of small firms
may, for example, be due to the entry of new small firms, to downsizing
of large firms, or to spin-offs. This entails some research questions
which we will leave unanswered in this chapter. Despite the general
conclusion of a positive effect, on average, of small-firm presence in
European two-digit manufacturing industries on growth of value added,
there are some issues to be resolved in future research. First, the effect
appears to differ across industries (see table 4.3) and to depend upon
the stage of economic development of countries (and, as a result,
industries in these countries). Second, the empirical results presented are
based upon data at a level of aggregation which is still relatively high.
Research at a lower aggregation level is to be recommended. However,
these and other research topics are highly dependent upon the increasing supply of rich and broad data sets on industry structure and its
changes over time.

Table 4.5 Estimation results

Year	Par	OLS	OLS*	RLS	WLS	OLS	OLS*	RLS	WLS
1993	b1	−0.116	−0.126	−0.063	−0.049	−0.030	−0.022	0.115	0.151
		(2.1)	(2.4)	(1.6)	(1.5)	(0.3)	(0.2)	(1.3)	(1.7)
	b2					−0.080	−0.097	−0.200	−0.191
						(0.8)	(1.0)	(2.7)	(2.4)
1994	b1	−0.146	−0.170	−0.139	−0.164	0.018	0.036	0.064	0.283
		(2.2)	(2.8)	(2.6)	(3.7)	(0.1)	(0.3)	(0.6)	(2.4)
	b2					−0.153	−0.193	−0.208	−0.427
						(1.3)	(1.8)	(2.2)	(4.1)
1995	b1	−0.229	−0.272	−0.190	−0.307	0.000	0.033	0.263	0.353
		(2.3)	(3.4)	(3.1)	(5.1)	(0.0)	(0.2)	(2.1)	(2.3)
	b2					−0.214	−0.285	−0.403	−0.631
						(1.2)	(2.0)	(3.8)	(4.5)

Note: OLS is Ordinary Least Squares. OLS* is OLS without the outlying observation Sweden NACE 34. RLS is reweighted least squares (after LMS) developed by Rousseeuw (1984). WLS is weighted least squares with total industry employment as weighting variable. *Par* stands for the estimated parameter.

6   Conclusion

The consequences of the shift in economic activity from large to small firms have recently attracted the attention of "small business economists." In the present contribution we supplement the work of the pioneers in this field by investigating whether a higher share of small businesses at the start of the 1990s has led to higher growth of value added in the subsequent three to five years in European manufacturing. Our results indicate that an industry with a low large firm presence relative to the same industries in other countries has performed better, on average, in terms of growth of value added. This suggests that lagging behind in the industrial restructuring process of the 1980s has come at a cost of lower economic growth. Countries which have been most active in improving the business environment for the small business sector in the 1980s may very well have reaped the fruits of this policy. However, the results also suggest that promoting the small business sector may be counter-productive in some parts of the manufacturing sector and in less-developed economies. The findings are in line with our earlier results (Carree and Thurik, 1998) for output growth using a slightly different sample.

European politicians and representatives of social and institutional groups fear for a further rise of the already unacceptably high level of unemployment caused by the sheer endless series of efficiency and cost-cutting operations of the public and large business sectors. They hope that unemployment can be fought by stimulating smallness. There are several reasons which may support their hopes. Firstly, stimulating smallness lifts the dependency on possibly sluggish and transient resources like scale, scope, and experience, and intensifies the dependency on resources like adjustment and effectiveness. The latter resources are likely to be more robust against uncertainty and change than the former. Secondly, stimulation of smallness means stimulation of labor intensity and hence employment by definition (see Loveman and Sengenberger, 1991). Thirdly, stimulation of smallness implies an increase in the variety of the range of products and services offered. This not only paves the way for a competitive selection process, and a process with different innovative approaches (Cohen and Klepper, 1992a) but may also satisfy a fragmented and differentiated demand. Finally, Murphy *et al.* (1991) argue that stimulating talented people to become entrepreneurs instead of rent-seekers will benefit growth. In many Western countries, rent seeking has rewarded talent more than entrepreneurship has done, resulting in stagnation.

Throughout Europe, job layoffs and downsizing of large firms, often in moderate-technology industries, have been common phenomena. Meanwhile, small firms replaced large firms in the United States not just in terms of generating almost all of the 18 million new jobs created in the 1980s, but also in terms of much of the innovative activity that has driven the rise of new industries and renewed international competitiveness. The empirical results in this study suggest that a policy of stimulating small firms, or more generally entrepreneurship, may be an effective way of combatting the current decrease in competitiveness of European industry. However, the results also show that the effectiveness of such a policy may differ significantly across industries and between different stages of economic development.

References

Acs, Z.J. (1992), "Small Business Economics: A Global Perspective," *Challenge*, 35 (November/ December): 38–44.

(1996a), "Small Firms and Economic Growth," in P.H. Admiraal (ed.), *Small Business in the Modern Economy, De Vries Lectures in Economics*, Oxford: Blackwell Publishers.

(1996b), *Small Firms and Economic Growth, Vols. I and II*, The International

Library of Critical Writings in Economics, No. 61, Cheltenham: Edward Elgar.

Acs, Z.J. and D.B. Audretsch (1990), *Innovation and Small Firms*, Cambridge, Mass.: MIT Press.

(1993), "Conclusion," in Z.J. Acs and D.B. Audretsch (eds.), *Small Firms and Entrepreneurship: An East–West Perspective*, Cambridge: Cambridge University Press.

Acs, Z.J., R. Morck, J.M. Shaver, and B. Yeung (1997), "The Internationalization of Small and Medium-Sized Enterprises: A Policy Perspective," *Small Business Economics*, 9: 7–20.

Audretsch, D.B. (1993), "Kleinunternehmen in der Industrieökonomiek: Ein neuer Ansatz," Discussion Paper FS IV 93–26, Wissenschaftszentrum, Berlin.

(1995), *Innovation and Industry Evolution*, Cambridge, Mass.: MIT Press.

Audretsch, D.B. and A.R. Thurik (1997), "Sources of Growth: The Entrepreneurial Versus the Managed Economy," Discussion Paper 97–109/3, Tinbergen Institute, Rotterdam.

Baumol, W.J. (1990), "Entrepreneurship: Productive, Unproductive and Destructive," *Journal of Political Economy*, 98: 893–921.

Birch, D.L. (1981), "Who Creates Jobs?" *Public Interest*, 65: 3–14.

Brock, W.A. and D.S. Evans (1989), "Small Business Economics," *Small Business Economics*, 1: 7–20.

Brown, C. and J. Medoff (1989), "The Employer Size-Wage Effect," *Journal of Political Economy*, 97: 1027–1059.

Burgelman, R.A. (1994), "Fading Memories: A Process Theory of Strategic Business Exit in Dynamic Environments," *Administrative Science Quarterly*, 39: 24–56.

Camacho, A. (1991), "Adaption Costs, Coordination Costs and Optimal Firm Size," *Journal of Economic Behavior and Organization*, 15: 137–149.

Carlsson, B. (1992), "The Rise of Small Business: Causes and Consequences," in W.J. Adams (ed.), *Singular Europe, Economy and Policy of the European Community After 1992*, Ann Arbor, MI: University of Michigan Press.

Carree, M.A. (1997), "Market Dynamics, Evolution and Smallness," Ph.D. thesis, Tinbergen Institute Research Series No. 169, Rotterdam.

Carree, M.A. and L. Klomp (1996), "Small Business and Job Creation: A Comment," *Small Business Economics*, 8: 317–322.

Carree, M.A. and A.R. Thurik (1997), "Small Firms and Economic Growth," OCFEB Research Memorandum 9708.

(1998), "Small Firms and Economic Growth in Europe," *Atlantic Economic Journal*, 26(2): 137–146.

Chandler, A.D., Jr. (1990), *Scale and Scope: The Dynamics of Industrial Capitalism*, Cambridge, Mass.: Harvard University Press.

Cohen, W.M. and S. Klepper (1992a), "The Trade-Off Between Firm Size and Diversity in the Pursuit of Technological Progress," *Small Business Economics*, 4: 1–14.

Cohen, W.M. and S. Klepper (1992b), "The Anatomy of Industry R&D Intensity Distributions," *American Economic Review*, 82: 773–799.

—— (1996), "A Reprise of Size and R&D," *Economic Journal*, 106: 925–951.

Das, B.J., W.F. Chappell and W.F. Shughart II (1993), "Demand Fluctuations and Firm Heterogeneity," *Journal of Industrial Economics*, 41: 51–60.

Davis, S.J., J. Haltiwanger and S. Schuh (1996), "Small Business and Job Creation: Dissecting the Myth and Reassessing the Facts," *Small Business Economics*, 8: 297–315.

Dosi, G., O. Marsili, L. Orsenigo and R. Salvatore (1995), "Learning, Market Selection and the Evolution of Industrial Structures," *Small Business Economics*, 7: 411–436.

The Economist (1994), "Between Two Worlds: A Survey of Manufacturing Technology," (March 5).

—— (1996), "Making Companies Efficient. The Year Downsizing Grew Up," 341 (December 21): 113–115.

EIM (1996), The European Observatory for SMEs, Fourth Annual Report, Zoetermeer.

Eliasson, G. (1984), "Micro Heterogeneity of Firms and the Stability of Industrial Growth," *Journal of Economic Behavior and Organization*, 5: 249–274.

—— (1995), "Economic Growth Through Competitive Selection," Paper presented at the 22nd Annual EARIE Conference, Juan les Pins, 3–6 September.

Eurostat (1994), *Enterprises in Europe*, 3rd edn, Luxembourg.

Evans, D.S. and L.S. Leighton (1989), "Why Do Smaller Firms Pay Less?" *Journal of Human Resources*, 24: 299–318.

Fiegenbaum, A. and A. Karnani (1991), "Output Flexibility – A Competitive Advantage for Small Firms," *Strategic Management Journal*, 12: 101–114.

Galbraith, J.K. (1956), *American Capitalism: The Concept of Countervailing Power*, Boston: Houghton Mifflin.

Gifford, S. (1993), "Heterogeneous Ability, Career Choice and Firm Size," *Small Business Economics*, 5: 249–259.

Hay, D.A. and G.S. Liu (1997), "The Efficiency of Firms: What Difference Does Competition Make?" *Economic Journal*, 107: 597–617.

Irwin, D.A. and P.J. Klenow (1994), "Learning-by-Doing Spillovers in the Semiconductor Industry," *Journal of Political Economy*, 102: 1200–1227.

Jovanovic, B. (1982), "Selection and Evolution of Industry," *Econometrica*, 50: 649–670.

—— (1993), "The Diversification of Production," *Brookings Papers: Micro-Economics*, 197–235.

Klepper, S. (1996), "Entry, Exit, Growth, and Innovation over the Product Life Cycle," *American Economic Review*, 86: 562–583.

Koning, A. de and J. Snijders (1992), "Policy on Small and Medium-Sized Enterprises in Countries of the European Community," *International Small Business Journal*, 10: 25–39.

Loveman, G. and W. Sengenberger (1991), "The Re-emergence of Small-Scale

Production: An International Comparison," *Small Business Economics*, 3: 1–37.

Lucas, R.E. (1978), "On the Size Distribution of Business Firms," *BELL Journal of Economics*, 9: 508–523.

(1993), "Making a Miracle," *Econometrica*, 61: 251–272.

Meredith, J. (1987), "The Strategic Advantages of New Manufacturing Technologies for Small Firms," *Strategic Management Journal*, 8: 249–258.

Mills, D.E. and L. Schumann (1985), "Industry Structure with Fluctuating Demand," *American Economic Review*, 75: 758–767.

Murphy, K.M., A. Shleifer and R.W. Vishny (1991), "The Allocation of Talent: Implications for Growth," *Quarterly Journal of Economics*, 106: 503–530.

Nickell, S.J. (1996), "Competition and Corporate Performance," *Journal of Political Economy*, 104: 724–746.

Nickell, S., P. Nicolitsas and N. Dryden (1997), "What Makes Firms Perform Well?" *European Economic Review*, 41: 783–796.

Nooteboom, B. (1987a), "Threshold Costs in Service Industries," *Service Industries Journal*, 6: 65–76.

(1987b), "Doen en Laten van het MKB," in *Op Maat van het Midden- en Kleinbedrijf*, Wetenschappelijke Raad voor het Regeringsbeleid, Den Haag.

(1993), "Firm Size Effects on Transaction Costs," *Small Business Economics*, 5: 283–295.

OECD (1994), *Economic Outlook*, (July), Paris.

(1996), *The OECD STAN Database 1970–1995*, Economic Analysis and Statistics Division, Paris.

Oosterbeek, H. and C.M. van Praag (1995), "Firm Size Wage Differentials in the Netherlands," *Small Business Economics*, 7: 173–182.

Piore, M.J. and C.F. Sabel (1984), *The Second Industrial Divide: Possibilities for Prosperity*, New York: Basic Books.

Prusa, T.J. and J.A. Schmitz, Jr. (1991), "Are New Firms an Important Source of Innovation? Evidence from the PC Software Industry," *Economics Letters*, 35: 339–342.

Rousseeuw, P.J. (1984), "Least Median of Squares Regression," *Journal of the American Statistical Association*, 79: 871–880.

Rousseeuw, P.J. and A.M. Leroy (1987), *Robust Regression and Outlier Detection*, New York: Wiley-Interscience.

Scherer, F.M. and D. Ross (1990), *Industrial Market Structure and Economic Performance*, Boston: Houghton Mifflin Company.

Schmitz, Jr., J.A. (1989), "Imitation, Entrepreneurship, and Long-Run Growth," *Journal of Political Economy*, 97: 721–739.

Schumacher, E.F. (1973), *Small is Beautiful*, New York: Harper and Row.

Teece, D.J. (1980), "Economies of Scope and the Scope of the Enterprise," *Journal of Economic Behavior and Organization*, 1: 223–247.

Thurik, A.R. (1993), "Recent Developments in the Firm-Size Distribution and Economics of Scale in Dutch Manufacturing," in Z. Acs and D. Audretsch

110   Martin Carree and Roy Thurik

(eds.), *Small Firms and Entrepreneurship: An East–West Perspective*, Cambridge: Cambridge University Press.

(1995), "Small Firms, Large Firms and Economic Growth, Paper presented at the OECD Conference on SMEs: employment, innovation and growth," Washington, June 16–17.

(1996), "Small Firms, Entrepreneurship and Economic Growth," in P.H. Admiraal (ed.), *Small Business in the Modern Economy*, De Vries Lectures in Economics, Oxford: Blackwell Publishers.

Wagner, J. (1994), "Small Firm Entry in Manufacturing Industries: Lower Saxony, 1979–1989," *Small Business Economics*, 6: 211–223.

Williamson, O.E. (1975), *Markets and Hierarchies: Analysis and Antitrust Implications*, London: Free Press.

Winter, S.G. (1984), "Schumpeterian Competition in Alternative Technological Regimes," *Journal of Economic Behavior and Organization*, 5: 287–320.

You, J.I. (1995), "Small Firms in Economic Theory," *Cambridge Journal of Economics*, 19: 441–462.

5 The impact of competition on productivity in Dutch manufacturing

Marcel Lever and Henry Nieuwenhuijsen

1 Introduction

Competition is generally believed to improve both static and dynamic efficiency of the production process. In other words, it is supposed to increase both the level and the growth rate of factor productivity. If an increase of competitive pressure reduces X-inefficiency of the production process, it increases the level of factor productivity. If competition improves the rate of product and process innovations, it increases the growth rate of factor productivity. Despite the acceptance of the intuition that competition improves productivity (growth), it is unclear through which channels this occurs. Competition may improve the level of productivity, for example, by increasing effort of managers and employees. Competition may improve productivity growth, for example, by stimulating the intensity of research and development (R&D)[1] or by letting only the fittest firms survive.

The argument that competition enhances the level of productivity by improving effort of managers and workers has been brought forward by Hölmstrom (1982) and Vickers (1992). They present a model which shows that an increase in the number of competitors enables the owners of the firm to determine more precisely its relative performance. The

The computations for this study were performed at Statistics Netherlands. The authors acknowledge useful comments on a previous draft from B.M. Balk, M.A. Carree, A.R.M. Wennekers, C. Zeelenberg and participants of the conference "The impact of technological change on firm and industry performance," 29–30 August 1997, Tinbergen Institute, Erasmus University Rotterdam.

[1] Empirical evidence for the impact of R&D on productivity is provided by Hall and Mairesse (1995) and Bartelsman *et al.* (1996).

reduction of the asymmetry of information between managers and owners provides an incentive for managerial effort.

The question of what market structures are most favorable to technological change and hence economic growth was brought into the main stream of economic discourse by Schumpeter (1942). Fifty years later, Scherer (1992) concludes that theoretically the links between market structure, innovation, and economic welfare are extremely complex. Most models support Schumpeter's conjecture that the incentives for innovation are probably inadequate in a world of atomistically competitive markets. However, it remains unclear, a priori, where technological progress is most vigorous: with loose oligopoly, tight oligopoly or pure monopoly, with or without impeded entry. In their surveys of the empirical literature, both Cohen and Levin (1989) and Scherer (1992) conclude that the effects of firm size and concentration on innovation, if they exist at all, do not appear to be important. More recently, Cohen and Klepper (1996) argue that large firms have an advantage in R&D as they are able to spread its costs over more output. Their empirical evidence supports this hypothesis.

Case studies provide some support for the conjecture that there is a positive relationship between competition and either levels or growth rates of productivity. Porter (1990) provides some examples which suggest that domestic rivalry improves international competitiveness: pharmaceutical industry in Switzerland, car and truck industry in Sweden, chemical industry in Germany and computer and software industry in the US. Gersbach and Baily (1996), comparing the performance of nine sectors in the US, Japan, and Germany find that productivity growth rates are higher in exposed than in sheltered sectors.

Only recently, the relationship between competition and productivity has been subject to sound empirical testing. Using panel data of 700 manufacturing companies in the UK (1972–1986), Nickell *et al.* (1992) and Nickell (1996) find that competition increases both the level and the growth rate of factor productivity. In his study, the impact of competition on the level of productivity is measured by the firm's market share, whereas the impact on productivity growth is investigated using profitability, a dummy variable for the presence or absence of more than five competitors, the import share, and firm size. The conclusion of his study that competition improves productivity growth is mainly based on the observed negative impact of profitability and the positive impact of the presence of more than five competitors on output. On the interpretation of the impact of profitability besides the impact of variables describing market structure and market contestability, we will return later. Blanchflower and Machin (1996), on the other hand, find no impact of product market competition on labor productivity in British work places, whilst they only find evidence of the expected positive impact in manufacturing work places in Australia. OECD (1996) reports that both export intensity and entry rates have a significant positive impact on labor productivity in the manufacturing industries in the G-7 countries.

The purpose of this chapter is to investigate whether competition in the product market affects the level and/or the growth rate of factor productivity. The methodology is to estimate an output equation which includes besides factor inputs several measures of competition. The output equation is estimated on a panel of nearly 2,000 firms in Dutch manufacturing for the years 1978 up to and including 1993. A limitation of this reduced-form approach is that it does not provide any insight into the channels through which competition improves productivity. The main reason to adopt this approach is that the most important candidates for intermediate variables, e.g. innovation and effort, are difficult to observe. As our panel includes only surviving firms, any impact of selection effects on productivity growth is excluded.[2]

The structure of the paper is as follows. Section 2 presents the model which is used to investigate the impact of competition on productivity (growth). The data are described in section 3. The empirical results are to be found in section 4, and the implications in section 5. Section 6 provides the conclusions.

2   Model

The output equation which is used to investigate the impact of competition on the level and the growth rate of factor productivity is based on a Cobb–Douglas production function. Besides factor inputs the equation includes several variables measuring competition. The basic equation is

$$q_{i,t} = \alpha_{1,i} + \alpha_{2,t} + \alpha_3 m_{i,t} + \alpha_4 n_{i,t} + \alpha_5 k_{i,t} + \alpha_6 ur_{i,t} + \alpha_7 c_{i,t} + \alpha_8 c_i t + \varepsilon_{i,t},$$
$$\alpha_3 + \alpha_4 + \alpha_5 = 1(?), \quad \alpha_6, \alpha_7, \alpha_8 > 0 \tag{1}$$

where $q_{i,t}$ denotes the volume of sales, $m_{i,t}$ the volume of materials, $n_{i,t}$ the employment level, $k_{i,t}$ the capital stock (all four variables are in logarithms), $ur_{i,t}$ the utilization rate of the capital stock, $c_{i,t}$ and c_i the

---

[2] An analysis for Dutch manufacturing (1980–1991) reveals that labor productivity growth in the subsample of continuing firms (2.9 percent per year) is nearly the same as labor productivity growth in the manufacturing sector as a whole (3.0 percent per year); see Bartelsman et al. (1995).

degree of competition (to be defined later), and t a time trend. With respect to the production technology, the constant-returns-to-scale assumption is not imposed a priori, but will be tested for. As our measure of the capital stock may be not proportional to capital services, the utilization rate is included as well. It is supposed to have a positive impact on output. The most interesting variables are those measuring competition. A significant positive estimate for α_7 implies that competition enhances the level of factor productivity; a significant positive estimate for α_8 implies that competition enhances the growth rate of factor productivity.

The impact of competition on the level of productivity ($c_{i,t}$) is measured by the market share, which determines the extent to which the firm can control sectoral output. The measurement of the market share is not perfect, because the denominator is sectoral output instead of market size. Obviously, sectoral output underestimates market size, as the export share and the competing-import share of Dutch manufacturing (1978–1993) are around 47 and 45 percent, respectively. As the ratio of domestic output to market size differs between industries, market share cannot be used as a cross-section variable. The measurement problem is less serious if the variable is used as a time series variable. Due to the inclusion of firm-specific constants it is actually used to investigate the impact of changes over time. As the market share is an inverse measure of competition, we expect that its impact on factor productivity is negative.

The impact of competition on the growth rate of factor productivity (c_i) is measured by three variables describing market concentration: the sectoral Herfindahl index, the firm's export share, and the sectoral share of competing imports. The Herfindahl index, the sum of squared market shares, is limited to domestic producers. The export share and the import share indicate the exposure to foreign competition at foreign and domestic markets, respectively. We expect the Herfindahl index to have a negative coefficient and the export and the import share a positive one. As we concentrate on structural productivity growth differences between industries, the Herfindahl index, the import share, and the export share are averaged over time.

In our opinion the impact of market structure on competition is better measured by relative firm size (i.e., market share, Herfindahl index) than by absolute firm size. However, the estimates of the impact of variables measuring relative firm size could be biased if absolute firm size matters and absolute and relative firm size are correlated. Therefore, firm size (in logs) is included as determinant of productivity growth. As we are interested in structural effects, firm size is averaged over time. If the argument that large firms have an advantage in spreading the costs of R&D is correct, its coefficient should be positive.

Market contestability is measured by the net entry rate, i.e., the relative change in the number of firms. Actually, we would have preferred to use the sum of the entry and exit rates, also called turbulence, instead of their difference. Unfortunately, this variable was not available for the major part of the time period. We expect net entry to have a positive impact on productivity growth.

Besides including determinants of competition, we also include an outcome of competition, viz. profitability. Two measures of profitability are available, viz. net results (results before taxes) and cash flow (net results and depreciation), both scaled on value added. As we are interested in structural effects, profitability is averaged over time. The rationale for including profitability is that our measures for competition may imperfectly measure market contestability and do not include behavior, which is difficult to observe. It should be noted, however, that firms' profitability is not determined by industrial competition only, but also by firm-specific factors like capability of management, worker effort, and success of R&D projects. So, profitability is at best a noisy signal of competition.

As profitability is inversely related to competition and if competition enhances productivity growth, one could expect that profitability has a negative impact on productivity growth. There are also reasons to suppose that there is a positive relationship between profitability and productivity growth, however. Firstly, as capital markets are imperfect, profits are conducive to finance R&D which increases productivity. Secondly, firms which are able to raise their productivity growth rate above the industrial growth rate may increase price mark-ups and profitability. The latter effect, which is based on reverse causality, is not what we are looking for. This reverse effect cannot easily be excluded, as it is difficult to find suitable instruments for cross-sectional (averages over time) variables. The relationships between profitability and productivity growth are illustrated in figure 5.1.

The upshot of this discussion is the following. If we find a negative impact of profitability on productivity growth, it is likely due to competition effects not captured by the other competition variables. If we find a positive impact, however, it does not reject our hypothesis that competition enhances productivity growth. This hypothesis is tested by investigating the impact of market concentration and market contestability on productivity growth.

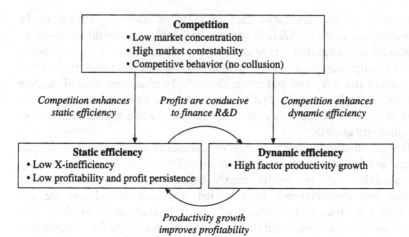

Figure 5.1 The relationship between competition, profitability, and productivity growth

After including two-digit industry dummies to capture the impact of omitted variables, the equation to be estimated becomes

$$q_{i,t} = \alpha_{1,i} + \alpha_{2,t} + \alpha_3 m_{i,t} + \alpha_4 n_{i,t} + \alpha_5 k_{i,t} + \alpha_6 ur_{j,t} + \alpha_7 ms_{i,t} +$$

$$\left(\sum_j \alpha_{80,j} d_j + \alpha_{81} hf_j + \alpha_{82} x_i + \alpha_{83} cm_i + \alpha_{84} rt_i + \alpha_{85} fs_i + \alpha_{86} ne_j \right) t + \varepsilon_{i,t},$$

$$\alpha_3 + \alpha_4 + \alpha_5 = 1(?), \quad \alpha_6 > 0, \quad \alpha_7, \alpha_{81} < 0, \quad \alpha_{82}, \alpha_{83} > 0,$$

$$\alpha_{84} < 0(?), \quad \alpha_{85} > 0(?), \quad \alpha_{86} > 0 \tag{2}$$

where ms denotes market share, hf Herfindahl index, x and cm export share and competing import share, respectively, rt profitability, fs firm size, and ne net entry rate. The subscript i indicates that the variable is measured at firm level, the subscript j that it is measured at sector level.

The equation to be estimated is essentially the same as in Nickell (1996). The differences are the following:

1   we include materials as explanatory variable, whereas Nickell does not (even if sales is used as variable to be explained);
2   a Herfindahl index is used instead of a five-firm concentration ratio;
3   unlike Nickell we include, besides the import share, the firms' export share to measure the exposure to foreign competition;
4   unlike Nickell we include the net entry rate to measure market contestability;
5   no dummy is included indicating whether there are more than five competitors in the market for their products.

Table 5.1 *Coverage of panel with respect to population (firms with 20 or more employees)*

	Population	Panel	Coverage (%)
Number of employees 1978	828,619	337,271	41
Number of employees 1985	732,890	312,729	43
Number of employees 1993	711,092	290,341	41
Value added (factor costs) 1978 (*1,000,000)	43,752	19,101	44
Value added (factor costs) 1985 (*1,000,000)	62,373	26,489	42
Value added (factor costs) 1993 (*1,000,000)	77,450	32,399	42
Number of firms 1978	6,091	1,932	33
Number of firms 1985	5,533	1,932	37
Number of firms 1993	6,574	1,932	31

3   Data

The output equation is estimated on a panel of yearly observations for 1,932 firms in Dutch manufacturing for the years 1978 up to and including 1993. Unfortunately, data on the capital stock are not available. This variable can be approximated by either depreciation or electricity usage, which are assumed to be proportional to the capital stock. Some of the variables are measured at firm level, others at sector level. Variables which are measured at firm level are: sales, materials, employment, capital (measured by depreciation or electricity usage), export share, net results, cash flow, and market share. Variables measured at sector level are: utilization rate, Herfindahl index, producer price indices, and share of competing imports.

The data are obtained from the following four data bases from Statistics Netherlands (CBS): Production Statistics, National Accounts, Producer Price Statistics, and the Business Cycle Survey. The Production Statistics, which provide information on exploitation and employment for firms with 20 or more employees, are collected at the level of the so-called "kind of activity unit." This unit is defined as an enterprise (or part of an enterprise) that operates independently and is active in one (or mainly one) economic activity. Enterprises are divided into groups according to their activity by using the standard industrial classification (SIC). The classification at the three-digit level involves more than 100 activity groups.

118   Marcel Lever and Henry Nieuwenhuijsen

Table 5.2 *Characteristics of panel and population*[a]

	Population	Panel
Electricity (kWh) per employee 1978	12,004	9,667
Electricity (kWh) per employee 1985	14,706	12,416
Electricity (kWh) per employee 1993	17,095	15,999
Value added (factor costs) per employee 1978	48,730	51,694
Value added (factor costs) per employee 1985	70,867	72,476
Value added (factor costs) per employee 1993	89,677	91,608
Cash flow/sales 1978 (*100)	11.65	9.53
Cash flow/sales 1985 (*100)	5.50	9.69
Cash flow/sales 1993 (*100)	3.99	8.21

Note: [a] Unweighted means are presented.

The panel of micro data is constructed by linking the Production Statistics at firm level. In terms of number of employees, value added, and number of firms, the panel covers around 40 percent of the total industrial population of firms with 20 or more employees; see table 5.1.

Table 5.2 presents some characteristics of both the panel and the total population. The panel group has (on average) higher labor productivity and cash flows (scaled on sales) than the total population, while electricity usage is lower in the panel group. Finally, the panel firms demonstrate some higher performance.

Competition in Dutch manufacturing has increased

The Herfindahl index, export share, share of competing imports are presented for the period 1978–1993 at the manufacturing level in table 5.3. The decrease of the Herfindahl index and the increase of both the export share and the import share suggest that competition in Dutch manufacturing has increased. This impression is corroborated by survey evidence among Dutch entrepreneurs; see Amse *et al.* (1997).

4   Empirical results

In order to investigate the robustness of the results, the coefficients of the output equation (2) are estimated by both fixed effects and GMM. The fixed effects or within estimates are obtained by TSP, the GMM estimates by DPD, a computer package written by Arellano and Bond (1988). The GMM estimates are preferred, as this method allows both the usage of instrumental variables for explanatory variables which are

Table 5.3 *Competition indicators in Dutch manufacturing, 1978–1993*

Year	Herfindahl index	Export share	Import share
1978	0.180	0.395	0.389
1979	0.183	0.423	0.412
1980	0.179	0.437	0.418
1981	0.181	0.467	0.432
1982	0.181	0.472	0.430
1983	0.174	0.476	0.434
1984	0.180	0.497	0.445
1985	0.177	0.510	0.474
1986	0.173	0.473	0.459
1987	0.159	0.474	0.469
1988	0.160	0.485	0.473
1989	0.158	0.501	0.484
1990	0.152	0.498	0.481
1991	0.147	0.495	0.486
1992	0.142	0.488	0.481
1993	0.139	0.481	0.471

not strictly exogenous and the inclusion of a lagged dependent variable to capture adjustment lags. The validity of the instruments used is tested by the Sargan test, which is χ^2-distributed. A basic requirement of GMM is that the disturbances of the undifferenced equation are serially uncorrelated. This is tested by a test for second-order serial correlation of the disturbances of the differenced equation, which has a standard-normal distribution.

The empirical results are summarized in table 5.4.[3] We experimented with including a lagged dependent variable. As its coefficient was quite small and insignificant, this variable was not included. The coefficient of the relative change in the number of firms appeared quite insignificant and was omitted. With respect to the estimates obtained by GMM, there is clearly no second-order serial correlation of the disturbances of the differenced equation. The instrumental variables appear to be acceptable as well.

[3] The reported GMM estimates are two-step estimates. These are quite similar to the one-step estimates. There is some Monte Carlo evidence that the standard errors of the two-step estimates are underestimated, the t-statistics are thus overestimated; see Arellano and Bond (1991). In this study, the difference between the one-step and two-step t-statistics appears to be relatively small. There is no case where the two-step estimate is significantly different from zero, whereas the one-step estimate is not.

If the output equation is estimated unrestricted, the sum of the parameters of the production factors materials, labor, and capital is somewhat below unity.[4] This suggests that the firms experience decreasing returns to scale. This result is somewhat unlikely: if production facilities can be duplicated, firms must be able to realize at least constant returns to scale. The result of decreasing returns to scale may be due to the small coefficient of capital. As this may be caused by measurement errors, we replaced depreciation by electricity usage to approximate the capital stock. This produced similar coefficients, however. As the imposition of the constant-returns-to-scale assumption does not affect the coefficients of most other variables, we do not bother too much about this result. The coefficient of the utilization rate is significantly positive, as expected.

The most interesting results are the coefficients of the variables measuring competition. Firstly, a decrease of the firm's market share increases its level of productivity. Secondly, industries with relatively low market concentration, high export share, and high import share, display above average productivity growth. Firm size has a positive impact on productivity growth as well, although the effect is generally insignificant. Profitability appears to have a significantly positive impact on productivity growth, irrespective of whether it is measured by net results or cash flow divided by value added. As discussed before, we are reluctant to interpret this result as a rejection of the hypothesis that competition enhances productivity growth. Rather, it suggests that firms which are able to realize a high profitability are able to finance R&D to boost productivity relative to the sector, which enables them to realize a high profitability, etc. Overall, the estimates imply that competition improves both the level and the growth rate of factor productivity.

For those who are skeptical about multivariate techniques, figure 5.2 clearly demonstrates that the growth of sales per worker is higher in firms with a high export share than in firms with a low export share. The firms are classified as having a high respectively a low export share if their export share during 1978 up to and including 1993 is on average above respectively below the median (9.8 percent). The growth of sales per worker during this period is on average 1.8 percent in the firms with a high export share, as opposed to 1.0 percent in the firms with a low export share.[5]

[4]   The constant-returns-to-scale restriction is accepted according to the one-step estimates ($t=1.88$), but rejected according to the two-step estimates ($t=2.24$).
[5]   The growth of sales per worker is the unweighted average of the growth of sales per worker in the firms with an export share above and below the median.

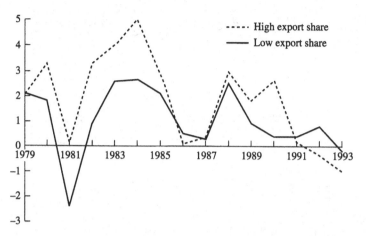

Figure 5.2   Growth of sales per worker in Dutch manufacturing firms, 1979–1993 (in percent)

5   Implications

The empirical results reported in the previous section have some interesting policy implications. The estimated coefficients of the output equation can be used to compute sectoral differences in factor productivity growth due to differences in competitive pressure. Competitive pressure is measured by the Herfindahl index, the export share, and the import share. The implied productivity growth differential for sector j can be computed by

$$\hat{\alpha}_{81}(hf_j - hf_r) + \hat{\alpha}_{82}(x_j - x_r) + \hat{\alpha}_{83}(cm_j - cm_r) \tag{3}$$

where the subscript r indicates some reference value. Assuming the explanatory variables are non-stochastic, its variance is equal to

$$\begin{aligned}
&\mathrm{var}(\hat{\alpha}_{81})(hf_j - hf_r)^2 + \mathrm{var}(\hat{\alpha}_{82})(x_j - x_r)^2 + \mathrm{var}(\hat{\alpha}_{83})(cm_j - cm_r)^2 \\
&+ 2\mathrm{cov}(\hat{\alpha}_{81}, \hat{\alpha}_{82})(hf_j - hf_r)(x_j - x_r) + 2\mathrm{cov}(\hat{\alpha}_{81}, \hat{\alpha}_{83})(hf_j - hf_r)(cm_j - cm_r) \\
&+ 2\mathrm{cov}(\hat{\alpha}_{82}, \hat{\alpha}_{83})(x_j - x_r)(cm_j - cm_r) \tag{4}
\end{aligned}$$

where var and cov denote the estimated variance and covariance, respectively. The estimates are taken from the regression results reported in the first column of table 5.4.

A decrease of the Herfindahl index and an increase of both the export share and the import share by 0.1 together result in an increase of productivity growth by 0.24 percentage points per year. Half of this

Table 5.4 *Estimation results for output equation based on a panel of firms in Dutch manufacturing (1978–1993)*

Specification	Basic equation	Capital stock approximated by electricity usage	Profitability measured by cash flow / value added	Constant returns to scale	Market share three years lagged	
Estimation method	GMM	GMM	GMM	GMM	FE	Constant returns to scale FE
Materials	0.685	0.691	0.704	0.679	0.658	0.672
	(24.10)	(24.28)	(25.24)	(23.50)	(199.57)	(207.72)
Employment	0.238	0.236	0.223	0.305	0.232	0.286
	(5.84)	(5.81)	(5.43)	(10.62)	(51.86)	(82.15)
Capital stock (depreciation or electricity usage)	0.021	0.008	0.020	0.017	0.038	0.042
	(5.82)	(2.18)	(5.75)	(–)	(19.76)	(–)
Utilization rate	0.490	0.494	0.490	0.468	0.138	0.131
	(2.84)	(2.87)	(2.84)	(2.65)	(3.92)	(3.70)
Market share (2 or 3 years lagged)	−1.174	−1.048	−1.121	−1.496	0.080	−0.148
	(2.73)	(2.42)	(2.60)	(3.52)	(1.08)	(2.02)
Average profitability * t (net results or cash flow, scaled on value added)	0.017	0.018	0.021	0.014	0.017	0.013
	(5.01)	(5.33)	(5.83)	(4.32)	(12.04)	(9.03)
Average Herfindahl * t	−0.0056	−0.0060	−0.0077	−0.0032	−0.0073	−0.0043
	(1.02)	(1.08)	(1.40)	(0.56)	(2.78)	(1.63)
Average export share * t	0.0059	0.0060	0.0057	0.0060	0.0056	0.0059
	(3.39)	(3.40)	(3.27)	(3.36)	(7.15)	(7.50)
Average import share * t	0.012	0.013	0.011	0.013	0.0085	0.0087
	(2.15)	(2.26)	(2.00)	(2.16)	(3.35)	(3.41)

Average firm size * t	0.0003	0.0002	0.0002	0.0007	0.0002	0.0006
	(0.55)	(0.50)	(0.45)	(1.38)	(0.80)	(2.55)
Two-digit industry dummies * t	yes	yes	yes	yes	yes	yes
time dummies	yes	yes	yes	yes	yes	yes
Sargan test for instrument validity, χ^2	125.9	123.5	126.3	125.7		
(degrees of freedom)	(102)	(102)	(102)	(103)		
Test for second-order serial correlation, $N(0,1)$	0.246	0.246	0.239	0.260		
Number of firms	1,932	1,932	1,932	1,932	1,932	1,932
Number of years	12	12	12	12	13	13
Number of observations	23,184	23,184	23,184	23,184	25,116	25,116

Notes: t-statistics are given between brackets. With respect to the GMM estimates, the variables materials, employment and utilization rate are assumed to be endogenous and instrumented by their three-year lags. Lagged values of output (two years or more) are included as instruments as well.

124   Marcel Lever and Henry Nieuwenhuijsen

Table 5.5 *Productivity growth differentials due to competitive pressure (in percent per year)*

SBI code (2 digit)	Sector	Growth differential	Absolute t-value
20, 21	Food processing	−0.29	2.19
22	Textile	0.42	2.63
23	Clothing	0.43	2.37
24	Leather	0.48	2.54
25	Wood and furniture	−0.06	0.68
26	Paper	0.19	2.22
27	Printing	−0.58	2.59
29, 30, 31	Chemical and rubber	0.25	3.77
32	Construction material	−0.22	3.15
33, 34, 36, 39	Metal, electrical, and miscellaneous	−0.02	0.18
35	Machine	0.22	2.67
37	Transport means	0.37	2.62

effect is due to the increased pressure from imports, the other half equally to the effects of the Herfindahl index and exports.

The differences in productivity growth between two-digit sectors and the manufacturing sector as a whole which are due to differences in competitive pressure are reported in table 5.5 and illustrated in figure 5.3. Productivity growth in textile, clothing, leather, paper, chemical and rubber, machine, and transport means industries is significantly above average due to high competitive pressure, whereas in food processing, printing, and construction material industries it is below average due to low competitive pressure. Productivity growth in highly competitive sectors is about 0.5 percent above average, whereas in low competitive sectors about 0.5 percent below average.

6   Conclusion

The purpose of this chapter is to investigate the impact of product market competition on the level and the growth rate of factor productivity. Estimates based on a sample of nearly 2,000 firms in Dutch manufacturing for the years 1978 up to and including 1993 show that:

  a decrease of the market share enhances the level of productivity;
  a competitive market structure, as indicated by either a low market concentration, a high export share or a high import share, enhances the rate of factor productivity growth;

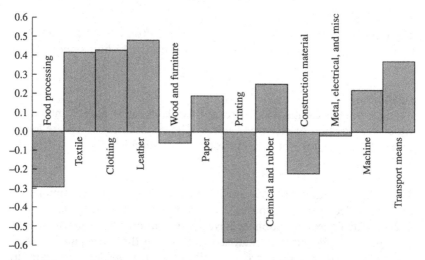

Figure 5.3   Productivity growth differentials due to competitive pressure (in percent per year)

the impact of firm size on productivity growth is generally insignificant;

profitability is conducive to factor productivity growth.

We do not interpret the latter result as counter evidence for the hypothesis that competition enhances productivity growth. Rather, it suggests that firms which are able to realize a high profitability are able to finance R&D to boost productivity relative to the sector, which in turn enables them to realize a high profitability, etc.

Data appendix

Sales
The volume of sales is obtained by deflating sales by a price index. The price index is a weighted average of the three-digit industry price indices for domestic and foreign sales. As export shares are available at firm level, a firm-specific deflator for sales can be constructed. The price indices for domestic and foreign sales are obtained from the Producer Price Statistics.

Materials
The volume of materials is obtained by deflating the firm-specific value of materials by the sectoral price index for materials. The value of materials is obtained from the Production Statistics.

Employment
The number of employees is obtained from the Production Statistics. The number of employees is restricted to those working 15 hours per week or more.

Capital stock
As data on the capital stock are not available, it is approximated by either depreciation or electricity usage. These variables, which are available at firm level, are obtained from the Production Statistics.

Capacity utilization
The utilization rate, which is available at SIC two-digit level (manufacturing divided into 17 groups), is obtained from the Business Cycle Survey. The figures are published every three months. The quarter scores have been aggregated in annual scores by using the unweighted means. The annual industry rates are normalized on their means over time, in order to eliminate any differences in level between industries.

Market share
The market shares are computed as firms' sales divided by sales of all firms in the relevant three-digit industry with 20 or more employees. They are obtained from the Production Statistics.

Herfindahl index
The Herfindahl index is used to measure the industrial concentration rate. The index (H) is calculated at three-digit level SIC:

$$h_j = \sum_{i=1}^{Fj}(Q_i/Q_j)^2,$$

where Q denotes sales, the subscripts i and j denote firm and industry, respectively, and F_j the number of firms in industry j. The data are obtained from the Production Statistics.

Export share
The export share is defined as foreign sales divided by total sales. This variable, which is measured at firm level, is obtained from the Production Statistics.

Import share
Import share is defined as competing imports divided by the sum of domestic sales and competing imports. The figures, which are available

for 32 manufacturing industries (between SIC two- and three-digit classification), are obtained from the National Accounts.

Firm size
Firm size is measured by the log of the average employment level of the firm during the observation period. The data, which are available at firm level, are obtained from the Production Statistics.

Profitability
Two alternative measures for profitability are employed. Profitability is measured by either result before taxes or cash flow, both divided by value added at factor costs. The data are obtained from the Production Statistics.

Net entry rate
Net entry is measured by the relative change in the number of firms with 20 or more employees. The rate is calculated at three-digit level SIC. The data are obtained from the Production Statistics.

References

Amse, A.K., R. Depoutot, B. van der Eijken, and H.R. Nieuwenhuijsen (1997), "Increased Competition in Europe: What European Enterprises think of the Impact of the Single Market Program," *Netherlands Official Statistics*, (Summer): 40–45.

Arellano, M. and S. Bond (1988), "Dynamic Panel Data Estimation Using DPD: A Guide for Users," Working Paper 88/15, Institute for Fiscal Studies, London.

Arellano, M. and S. Bond (1991), "Some Tests of Specification for Panel Data: Monte Carlo Evidence and an Application to Employment Equations," *Review of Economic Studies*, 58: 277–297.

Bartelsman, E.J., G. van Leeuwen, and H.R. Nieuwenhuijsen (1995), "Downsizing and Productivity Growth: Myth or Reality?," *Netherlands Official Statistics* (Autumn): 23–28.

Bartelsman, E.J., G. van Leeuwen, H.R. Nieuwenhuijsen, and C. Zeelenberg (1996), "R&D and Productivity Growth: Evidence from Firm-Level Data for The Netherlands," *Netherlands Official Statistics* (Autumn): 52–69.

Blanchflower, D.G. and S. Machin (1996), "Product Market Competition, Wages and Productivity: International Evidence from Establishment-level Data," Discussion Paper 286, Centre for Economic Performance, London School of Economics, London.

Cohen, W.M. and S. Klepper (1996), "A Reprise of Size and R&D," *Economic Journal*, 106 (437): 925–951.

128   Marcel Lever and Henry Nieuwenhuijsen

Cohen, W.M. and R.C. Levin (1989), "Empirical Studies of Innovation and Market Structure," in R. Schmalensee and R.D. Willig (eds.), *Handbook of Industrial Organization*, Amsterdam: North-Holland.

Gersbach H. and M.N. Baily (1996), "Explanations of International Productivity Differences: Lessons from Manufacturing," in K. Wagner and B. van Ark, *International Productivity Differences: Measurement and Explanations: Contributions to Economic Analysis*, 233, Amsterdam: Elsevier.

Hall, B.H. and J. Mairesse (1995), "Exploring the Relationship between R&D and Productivity in French Manufacturing Firms," *Journal of Econometrics*, pp. 263–293.

Hölmstrom, B. (1982), "Managerial Incentive Problems – A Dynamic Perspective," *Essays in Economics and Management in Honor of Lars Wahlbeck*, Swedish School of Economics, Helsinki.

Nickell, S.J. (1996), "Competition and Corporate Performance," *Journal of Political Economy*, 104 (4): 724–747.

Nickell, S.J., S. Wadhwani and M. Wall (1992), "Productivity Growth in U.K. Companies, 1975–86," *European Economic Review*, 36: 1055–1091.

OECD (1996), "Competition, Wages and Productivity," Working Party No. 1 on Macroeconomic and Structural Policy Analysis, Economic Policy Committee, Paris.

Porter, M.E. (1990), *The Competitive Advantage of Nations*, London: MacMillan.

Scherer, F.M. (1992), "Schumpeter and Plausible Capitalism," *Journal of Economic Literature*, 30: 1416–1433.

Schumpeter, J.A. (1942), *Capitalism, Socialism and Democracy*, New York: Harper.

Vickers, J. (1992), "Competition and Implicit Incentives," mimeo., Institute of Economics and Statistics, University of Oxford, Oxford.

6 Does cash flow cause investment and R&D? An exploration using panel data for French, Japanese, and United States scientific firms

Jacques Mairesse, Bronwyn Hall, Lee Branstetter, and Bruno Crepon

1 Introduction

It is a widely held view that the capital market and corporate governance systems of such countries as France, Germany, and Japan differ in important ways from those of the so-called "Anglo-Saxon" countries, the United States, the United Kingdom, and possibly Canada. Those who hold this view argue that features such as interlocking directorates, large-scale share holding by banks, restrictions on and the absence of hostile takeover activity, relatively less active share markets, and a general tendency to rely on voice rather than exit lead to more extensive monitoring by large institutional shareholders and possibly to a greater willingness on the part of firms to undertake long-term risky investments than exists in the more actively traded capital markets of the United States and the United Kingdom.[1]

If this view is accurate, it is natural to ask whether one can see its effects in the investment patterns of firms in these countries, and in their relationship to such indicators of financial performance as sales and cash flow. We think that looking at the dynamic relationships of output measures such as deflated sales and cash flow with investment inputs (both tangible and intangible) in similar samples of firms in a comparison group of countries is one way to investigate whether the institutional difference in these countries, which undoubtedly exist, have consequences

The first author thanks Stephen Bond for very helpful conversations and INSEE-CREST, Paris, Nuffield College, Oxford, and the Institute for Fiscal Studies, London for hospitality while the paper was being written.

[1] Among others, see Franks and Mayer (1990) [France, Germany, and the UK], Kester (1992) [Japan and Germany], Mayer and Alexander (1990) [Germany and UK], and Hoshi, Kashyap, and Scharfstein (1990) [Japan], Hall (1994) [US plus some international comparisons], and Soskice (1995) [Germany, Japan, US, UK, and France] for evidence on this topic.

for the real behavior of firms. If we cannot see evidence of differences at this level, then it seems unlikely that the contrasting institutional features can be having much of an impact on the firms' actual performance.

In Mairesse and Hall (1996), two of us explored the simultaneity between output (sales) and inputs (capital stock, labor, and R&D capital) while estimating production functions for the United States and France. During the course of this exploration, we found evidence that investment in both research and development and in physical capital were more sensitive to sales growth in the United States than in France, suggesting that either demand shocks or liquidity constraints play a more important role in determining investment in the former country than the latter. In work closely related to ours, Bond, Elston, Mairesse, and Mulkay (1997) found that investment spending in UK firms was more sensitive to cash flow or profits than investment spending in French, German, or Belgian firms; their finding was robust to changes in specification of the investment equation. They did not consider R&D investment in their work.

The current chapter explores the finding in the earlier work of Mairesse and Hall and extends it by including cash flow as a variable in addition to sales, employment, and investment of both kinds (tangible and R&D), and by augmenting the data samples with data on another country whose institutions differ from both those in the United States and France, that is, Japan. For data reasons, and because we are particularly interested in the role played by country environments in the encouragement of industrial innovation and technical change, we restrict our sample in this chapter to firms in the scientific or high technology sectors in these countries, that is, chemicals, pharmaceuticals, electrical machinery, computing equipment, electronics, and scientific instruments.[2]

Our second motivation in undertaking this study is an interest in exploring further the use of efficient generalized method of moments estimation on panel data where we allow for the presence of both correlated effects and lagged dependent variables. In this, our immediate inspiration was Holtz-Eakin, Newey, and Rosen (1988), although we have also made use of ideas in Arellano and Bond (1991), Arellano and Bover (1991), and Blundell and Bond (1998). An appendix to this chapter chronicles some of our simulation experience with the problem of distinguishing a model with correlated effects from one in which there

---

[2] We have excluded aircraft and aerospace because of the large share of federal government spending on investment in these industries, and the role of the federal government as the primary customer for the output, which means that these industries behave quite differently in these three countries, for reasons largely unrelated to our central interest.

are no effects, but where each firm's data follow an autoregressive process with a unit root in short panels. Our conclusions are twofold: First, we find that it is frequently difficult to distinguish the two when the lag length is unknown. Second, instrumental variable estimation (GMM) of models with correlated effects is subject to substantial finite sample bias, even in fairly good-sized sample sizes (approximately 300–400 firms) when the number of time periods available is fairly large (12 years, in our case) and the efficient estimator is used.[3] Because of this, we use a slightly less efficient estimator in the body of the chapter (one with fewer instruments and therefore fewer orthogonality conditions) that is somewhat better behaved.

We begin with a discussion of the issues raised by comparative corporate governance studies, most of which are fairly qualitative, for the examination of firm-level behavior across G-7 countries. Then we describe our datasets, and how we attempt to make them as comparable as possible across the three countries we consider. We present some basic descriptive data in order to illustrate the similarities and differences. In a related paper (Hall and Mairesse, 1998), we explore the question of whether the univariate time series properties of our basic variable set (deflated sales, R&D investment, ordinary investment, number of employees, and cash flow before investment and taxes) suggest the presence of correlated firm effects or whether they display unit root behavior. Our conclusion here is that it is extremely difficult to distinguish the two in these data because of the short length of the time period and the fact that the instruments available for differenced estimation are weak if the data are close to a random walk. We have included permanent firm effects in all the models in the subsequent section, although it is probable that investment is the only stationary process in these data.[4]

Section 4 contains the meat of the paper: the results of bivariate causality testing between our two output measures (deflated sales and cash flow) and our two investment measures (R&D and ordinary investment). In future work, we plan to expand the bivariate model to control for other variables, but we believe that the current results are worth reporting even in the absence of such controls.

---

[3] In the case here, where we have lagged predetermined variables as regressors (not strictly exogenous) and fixed firm effects, the number of orthogonality conditions in the efficient GMM estimator increases at the rate T^2 in general.

[4] It is clear that all of the series are either nonstationary OR have a fixed firm effect. It is distinguishing these two possibilities in the presence of serially correlated disturbances that is the difficulty.

2   Corporate governance and the market for corporate capital

In the recent past, many economists and other researchers have attempted to characterize the contrasting styles of corporate governance in the major industrial economies. This research has been spurred by a general increase in global competition during the 1980s: this increased competition simultaneously revealed the comparative strength of economies like Germany and Japan, especially in manufacturing, and caused substantial turbulence in the United States and United Kingdom, turbulence driven partly by a perceived need to restructure and shrink industries in the face of increasing foreign competition. Although the particular set of considerations that focused attention on these issues may have lost importance in the most recent past, the question of whether institutions "matter" for the performance of the industrial sector of an economy is still an interesting and important one.

The fact that corporate governance and financing institutions differ across the three countries considered here (the United States, France, and Japan) is not in question. The issue is whether selection operates in such a way as to undo the possible negative effects that each set of institutions might have as the institutions evolve, causing the actual observed behavior of firms in these countries to be closer than implied by the caricatures of the corporate governance literature. As Gilson (1995) points out, institutions can differ at first, but if they do not function effectively, they will either be selected out, or they may evolve some of the characteristics of successful institutions. As an example of the forces that push institutions to evolve, consider the rise of EASDAQ in Europe and the attempts to create a successful capital market for new firms and startups in France. In this chapter, we focus on the consequences of institutional differences across the three countries for the investment behavior of individual technology firms.

Table 6.1 presents a stylized view of the corporate governance structures in the US, France, and Japan (due to David Soskice (1995)); one can find similar discussions in other places, see Charkham (1994), for example. This table focuses on a set of relationships between an industrial company and its owners: who the owners are, how they monitor the behavior of the firm, what happens when restructuring is necessary, and the incentives faced by the Chief Executive Officer. The major contrast is between Japan and the US: in the former country, even when ownership is dispersed, the management of the shares tends to be delegated to large shareholders (like banks), and monitoring and restructuring tends to be done by the main bank or major shareholder in the firm. Public financial markets place relatively little pressure on the firm.

Table 6.1 *A stylized view of corporate governance structures in the 1980s*

Company-Owner Relationship	US	France	Japan
Ownership	dispersed	delegated monitoring	delegated monitoring
Monitoring	public data	unsystematic; evolving	direct; product market
Restructuring	takeovers	decisions within an elite network	main bank
CEO's incentives	high powered; market-oriented	public–private network for promotion	low power; company men
Length of financial commitment	SHORT	LONG?	LONG

Source: David Soskice, presentation to WZB, June 22, 1995.

In the latter country, the opposite picture prevails: ownership is dispersed, and the monitoring and restructuring of the firm take place in public. Because considerable data on the firm's activities are publicly available, monitoring by outsiders and shareholders is somewhat easier (although incentives to monitor are low for small shareholders, of course). And restructuring is often achieved via hostile takeover or acquisition by outsiders rather than quietly within the firm or its keiretsu.

The situation in France is somewhere inbetween the other two, possibly leaning toward the Japanese system. There are more large block shareholders, and many small shareholders hold "bearer" shares, which imply that there is no way a firm can supply information directly to these shareholders, even if it wanted to. Therefore monitoring tends to be done by a few shareholders, banks, or even the government in the case of firms that are wholly or partially government owned. Restructuring tends to be managed within a fairly elite network of private/public managers and holding companies, and is not often hostile as it is in the United States.

Based on these comparisons of owner–manager relationships, many have suggested that company owners in the United States will tend to have a much shorter-term commitment to the firms in which they hold shares, whether or not they actually trade them more often. In fact, financial markets in the United States are quite accommodating to this kind of shareholder, as they are very thick and active. Thus "exit" is viewed as a viable option by an unhappy shareholder in the US, while less so in the other two countries, where "voice" is more likely to be used.

That is, shareholders in different countries are somewhat self-selected in response to the institutional differences, with greater concentration and/ or a willingness to hold shares for a longer period in France and Japan than in the United States.

The conclusion of this kind of argument is the suggestion that firms in the United States may try harder to satisfy shareholders in the short run, rather than taking a long-term view.[5] Thus, an implication of this world view is that firms in Japan and France may find it easier to undertake longer-term investments. A second implication is that because they do not have to go to the external capital markets to finance new investment, but can potentially rely on agents that are not in the public market (either their main bank or another firm in the group in Japan, and an informal network or the government in France), firms in these two countries may be less subject to "liquidity constraints" when undertaking investment. It is this possibility that we explore in this chapter, where we compare the bivariate relationship of cash indicators such as sales and cash flow with investment and R&D across the three countries. We ask two questions: First, what does conventional causality testing have to say about the relationship? Does our cash proxy cause investment or the other way around? Second, what is the size of the impact of lagged cash on investment or R&D? Does it vary across countries?

3   Data and descriptive statistics

Our goal is to produce similar samples of high-technology manufacturing firms for each of our countries: France, the United States, and Japan. However, our sources of data are quite different and this means that the samples will never be exactly comparable, although they are quite representative. Table 6.2 gives the sources of our data, our deflators, and some indication of the number of observations available to us, both before and after cleaning. The primary difference in the data sources is between France and the other two countries: in France, we have access to a Census of Manufactures-type sample with R&D data collected in survey form by the government for the Ministère de la Recherche. This means the data tend to be at a level somewhat lower than that of

---

[5] Obviously perfect capital markets would overturn this result easily; in markets that correctly value the expected present discounted value of the future returns to investment, it makes no difference what the horizon of an individual investor is. But there is some empirical evidence that this theoretical prediction is not always true, and the apparent persistence of the belief on the part of firms that they must manage their stock price quarterly suggests that we cannot ignore the possibility that short-termism in ownership may lead to some short termism in investment.

Table 6.2 *Dataset characteristics*

	France	United States	Japan
Source	Annual Survey of Industrial Research and Development Spending; Annual Survey of Enterprises	Standard and Poor's Compustat Data – annual industrial and OTC, based on 10-K filings to SEC	Needs data; data from JDB (R&D data from Toyo Keizai survey)
Scientific sector*	1978–89, good R&D	1978–89, good R&D	1978–89, good R&D
firms	953	863	424
observations	5,842	6,417	5,088
Cleaned (No. of obs.)	5,139	5,721	4,260
No jumps (No. of obs.)	5,108	5,312	4,215
Balanced 1978–89			
(No. of obs.)	1,872	2,448	2,652
(No. of firms)	156	204	221
Positive cash flow			
(No. of firms)	104	174	200

Note: * This sector consists of firms in chemicals, pharmaceuticals, electrical machinery, computing equipment, electronics, and scientific instruments.

consolidated accounts (the "group" level), and that it is not confined to publicly traded firms.[6] For the other two countries, we have data based

---

[6] In this, our problem is similar to that of Bond *et al.* (1997), who had consolidated data for the UK and not for France, Germany, and Belgium. This feature of our data makes things particularly difficult, since it is driven fundamentally by the same institutional differences on which we have focused our interest. That is, the existence of an active public equity market means that data are publicly available at the level of the consolidated firm or at the level at which the shares trade. Absent this market, one is forced to use government or Central Bank data (as in France, Germany, and Japan), and such data tend to be unconsolidated. This may have implications for the "softness" of the budget constraint faced by the firm, but it is exactly that difference in which we are interested. The ideal exercise would be to compare estimates at different levels of consolidation. Bond *et al.* (1997) have begun such an exploration.

on the filings of publicly traded firms with agencies charged with monitoring the financial markets. Although the Japanese data are somewhat less consolidated than those for the United States, in the sense that they are not at the "group" level, they are consolidated to a level roughly comparable to that in the United States. Also in the case of Japan, the R&D data have been augmented with data from another survey, because the quality of publicly reported R&D data is very uneven.[7]

The deflators also differ somewhat across countries. In all cases, we deflate R&D, investment, and cash flow by a deflator that is common across all industries.[8] On the other hand, we have attempted to varying degrees to construct real output measures rather than sales by deflating our sales figures by at least a two-digit-level deflator. In the United States, we are using deflators aggregated up to the two-digit level from the NBER Productivity Database, which is at the four-digit level (Bartelsman and Gray, 1994). In France, we are using the N40 industry-level deflator (approximately two-digit), which do not contain very much of the type of hedonic quality adjustment that is used in the United States. In Japan, we have constructed "firm-level" deflators based on the four-digit industry composition of the firm's output.

Our choice of years (1978–1989) reflects data availability, as well as a desire to have a fairly long time series available for each variable for use in instrumental variables estimation. Because these datasets are large, and in some cases fairly dirty, and because we want to focus on the common time series properties across firms, rather than isolated reorganizations and other specific disturbances, we apply cleaning rules to all the variables: First, we require their growth rates to be between −90 percent and 900 percent. Second, in order to remove erroneous data values that might produce misleading autoregressive estimates, we remove firms that have sequential growth rates that are large and alternate in sign. For sales and employment, large is defined as below −50 percent or above 100 percent; for R&D, it is −67 percent, 200 percent; for investment and cash flow, it is −80 percent, 400 percent. Finally, we work with the logarithms of all the variables, in order to minimize heteroskedasticity and problems with influential outliers.

After cleaning, and requiring a full 12 years of data for each firm, we are left with 204 firms for the United States, 156 for France, and 221 for

---

[7] See Griliches and Mairesse (1990) for further discussion of this point.

[8] Thus we are implicitly assuming that the market for capital goods, and the market for R&D are common across all our firms, so they face the same prices. In fact, even when measured carefully, there is little variation in the relative price of investment goods across industries, so our procedure is unlikely to produce much bias.

Table 6.3a *Sample comparison*
The median firm (national currency)

Variable	United States ($M 1987)	France (M FF 1987)	Japan (100M yen 1987)
Sales	249.0	465.6	570.6
R&D	9.8	16.2	15.1
Investment	14.0	15.3	42.4
Cash flow	43.9	59.7	62.1
Employment (numbers)	2,762	604	1,732

Table 6.3b *The median firm (at PPP exchange rates in $M 1987)*

Variable	United States	France	Japan
Sales	249.0	67.3	283.5
R&D	9.8	2.4	7.6
Investment	14.0	2.1	21.1
Cash flow	43.9	8.4	30.0
1989 GDP ($N87)*	4,730	758	1,885
Sample sales/GDP	10.1%	5.4%	17.1%
1989 BERD ($B87)**	93.9	12.0	40.9
Sample share of BERD	29.9%	21.0%	41.2%

Notes: * GDP in 1989$ at PPP exchange rates is from OECD (1991a), converted to 1987$.
** BERD is Business Enterprise R&D, from OECD (1991b) in 1989$ at PPP exchange rates (approximately 7 francs per $ and 200 yen per $).

Japan. Table 6.3 gives some indication of the typical size of these firms, and their importance in their national economies. Each sample is a small but not insignificant portion of its economy, and a larger fraction of that economy's private R&D activity. The Japanese sample has the largest coverage of both GDP and BERD (Business Enterprise R&D) and the French sample the smallest. Although the national R&D intensities are ranked Japan (2.2 percent), the US (2.0 percent), and France (1.6 percent), the typical firm in these samples is more R&D intensive in the US (with an R&D to sales ratio of 4.0 percent), followed by France (3.6 percent), and then Japan (2.8 percent). This perhaps reflects the some-what greater selectivity of the US and French samples, and the large integrated firm structure typical of Japan. Because of this vertical integration, we suspect that our Japanese firms are slightly less

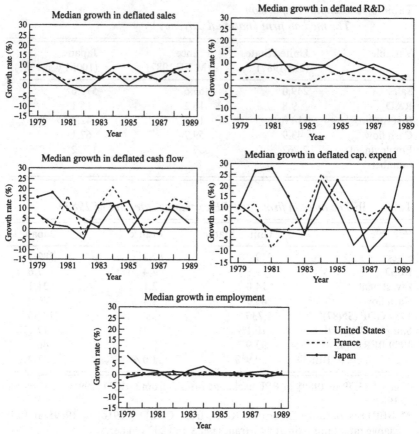

Figure 6.1   Growth rates for the median firm in the sample

concentrated in the high-technology sector than the sample of firms from the other two countries.

Figures 6.1 and 6.2 display the trends in the median growth rates and interquartile ranges for the three samples. The first thing to note in these figures is that there is more difference in the patterns among the variables than among the countries, with cash flow and ordinary investment fluctuating much more over the cycle than sales, R&D, and employment. The dispersion of growth rates in all three countries (measured by the interquartile range within each year) is also quite similar across the variables, except for the rather anomalous cash flow range in France. It is perhaps worth noting also that the fluctuations of the median and interquartile dispersion of employment growth rates are somewhat higher in the United States, although relatively low in all three countries.

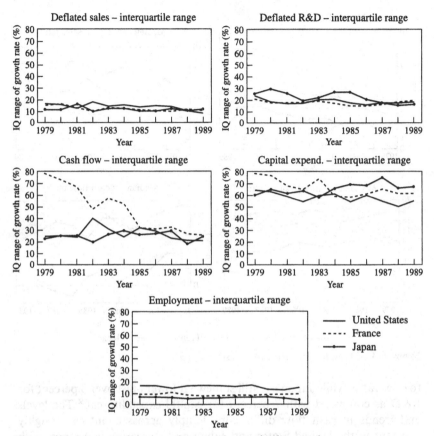

Figure 6.2 Interquartile ranges for growth rates in the sample

In other words, over the business cycle large manufacturing firms tend to increase and decrease employment more in the United States than in Japan and France, and the variance across firms of this behavior is also higher, facts that are consistent with the oft-cited flexibility of the US labor market.

Figure 6.3 shows the trends in three ratios over the three countries: the median R&D intensity (measured as R&D to sales), the median investment to sales ratio, and the median cash flow to sales ratio. The R&D to sales ratio is flat in France, while it increases during the period in both the US and Japan. The Japanese capital expenditure rate is higher than the US and the French rate throughout the 1980s. By the end of the period, both the US and France have R&D intensities for these samples of firms that are within one percentage point of the investment

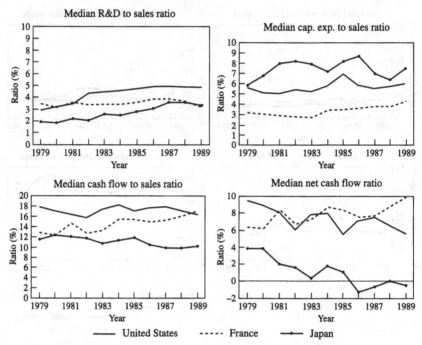

Figure 6.3   Median ratios for firms in the sample

to sales ratio, while Japan's is still somewhat lower (just over 3 percent for R&D as compared with 7 percent for capital expenditures).[9] The levels and trends in cash flow differ considerably across countries: roughly constant in the United States and Japan and increasing in France, with the rate much higher overall in the United States. This cash flow measure is approximately equal to revenues less labor and material costs in all three countries: that is, it should be a measure of cash available for both kinds of investment, as well as for payments to shareholders, possibly bondholders, and the government. The final panel of figure 6.3 shows the cash flow to sales ratio net of these two investment streams: by the end of the 1980s, the cash flow available for shareholder payments is approximately zero for Japan, while it is still quite positive and of roughly the same order of magnitude for France and the United States.

As a final summary of the data relationships in our three samples, we present the simple correlations of the growth rates of our five key variables in table 6.4. With the exception of the correlation of R&D

[9]   As mentioned earlier, this difference probably reflects the level of vertical integration in the Japanese firms.

Table 6.4 *Correlation of deflated growth rates, 1978–1989*

	Sales	R&D	Investment	Employment
R&D	0.324, 0.138, 0.208			
Investment	0.314, 0.231, 0.258	0.181, 0.146, 0.095		
Employment	0.609, 0.551, 0.197	0.271, 0.170, 0.118	0.376, 0.262, 0.172	
Cash flow	0.561, 0.142, 0.531	0.130, 0.100 0.212	0.165, 0.061, 0.166	0.294, 0.059, 0.048

growth and cash flow growth (which may be related to the way the data were constructed), in all cases the correlations are highest for the United States.

The order of the correlations in each cell of table 6.4 is US, France, and Japan. The number of firms is 204, 156, and 221 respectively, except for the cash flow correlations, where the numbers are 174, 104, and 200 (see table 6.2 for details on the sample).

From this survey of the main features of our samples, we conclude that there are no real surprises in the data: as expected, the United States generally exhibits higher correlations of most variables with cash flow, and United States employment fluctuates more over the cycle. In addition, the Japanese tangible investment rate is quite high, and there is a tendency to invest at a much higher rate out of profits in Japan. However, we also found some evidence that the samples may not be completely comparable, in that the vertical integration in the Japanese firms seems to be greater, leading to a sample that is less concentrated in the particular sector on which we are focusing our attention. Of course, this fact is yet another reflection of the differences in corporate institutions across the three economies, and not an "error" in constructing the samples.

4   Bivariate causality testing

As we discussed earlier, the central goal of this chapter is to describe the differences in the "causal" relationship or dynamics between R&D and investment, on the one hand, and sales and cash flow, on the other, across three economies that have different institutional structures for corporate governance and finance. In this section of the chapter, we perform this exercise using conventional Granger-causality testing. That is, we ask questions like the following: "Conditional on past R&D behavior and on average R&D behavior over the sample, does cash flow help to determine future R&D in the firm?" To perform these tests, we use a methodology similar to that of Holtz-Eakin, Newey, and Rosen (1988).

In Hall and Mairesse (1998), we present a series of investigations into the univariate time series processes that describe our data and reach the following conclusions: (1) Tests for the absence of correlated firm effects are somewhat inconclusive, and (2) because the first differenced series often display near random walk behavior, the small sample bias of instrumental variable estimation persists even when the sample is fairly good-sized. For these two reasons, we specify our two-variable model for causality testing with a permanent firm effect, and we estimate our model using GMM with a restricted set of lagged-level variables as instruments. Our maintained model is the following:

$$y_{it} = \alpha_i + \delta_t + \sum_{s=1} \beta_s y_{it-s} + \sum_{s=1} \gamma_s x_{it-s} + \varepsilon_{it} \qquad (1)$$

$$i = 1, ..., N \; firms \qquad t = 1, ..., T \; years(T = 12)$$

α_i is a correlated firm effect and δ_t are year dummies. ε_{it} is a serially uncorrelated disturbance (when m is large enough).

After differencing, the appropriate orthogonality conditions for GMM use lagged xs and ys as instruments. We use a maximum of five lags, based on our experience with finite sample bias in GMM when the full set of orthogonality conditions is used. Our assumptions imply the following set of orthogonality conditions:

$$E[z_{ir}\Delta u_{it}] = 0; \qquad t = m + 2, ..., T; \qquad r = \max(1, t - 6), ..., t - 2 \qquad (2)$$

where $\Delta u_{it} = \Delta y_{it} - \Delta\delta_t - \sum_{s=1}^{m} \beta_s y_{it-s} - \sum_{s=1}^{m} \gamma_s x_{it-s}$ and $z_{ir} = [x_{ir} \; y_{ir}]$. For example, there are $2 \cdot 5 \cdot (T - m - 1)$ orthogonality conditions in (2) when $m = 5$ plus $T - m - 1$ for the year dummies for a total of $11 \cdot (12 - 6) = 66$.[10]

Using (2) as our basic specification, we conduct the following tests: First, Arellano and Bover (1994) suggested that lagged Δxs and Δys can

---

[10] Computing the number of OCs is somewhat more complicated when $m < 5$. For example, suppose $T = 12$ and $m = 3$. Then the periods used for estimation are 5 through 12, and the instruments for Δu_{i5} are $(x_{i1}, x_{i2}, y_{i1}, y_{i2})$; those for Δu_{i6} are $(x_{i1}, x_{i2}, x_{i3}, y_{i1}, y_{i2}, y_{i3})$; those for Δu_{i8} are $(x_{i1}, x_{i2}, x_{i3}, x_{i4}, x_{i5}, y_{i1}, y_{i2}, y_{i3}, y_{i4}, y_{i5})$, and those for Δu_{i12} are $(x_{i5}, x_{i6}, x_{i7}, x_{i8}, x_{i9}, y_{i5}, y_{i6}, y_{i7}, y_{i8}, y_{i9})$. This yields a total of $2(2 + 3 + 4 + 5 \times 5) = 68$ OCs plus the 8 for the intercept (year dummies) for 76 in all.

Table 6.5 *Causality testing*

	United States	France	Japan
Number of firms	174	104	200
Does CF cause I?	111.3 (4)**	12.6 (5)*	71.4 (4)**
Does CF cause R?	235.2 (4)**	67.3 (3)**	16.3 (3)**
Does I cause CF?	40.7 (3)**	26.7 (5)**	25.5 (4)**
Does R cause CF?	42.0 (3)**	116.9 (4)**	25.6 (3)**
Number of firms	204	156	221
Does S cause I?	84.8 (3)**	6.6 (4)	77.6 (4)**
Does S cause R?	200.7 (4)**	133.0 (4)**	57.2 (3)**
Does I cause S	35.0 (5)**	14.0 (4)**	8.0 (5)
Does R cause S?	39.5 (4)**	13.7 (3)**	38.0 (4)**

Note: In each case, the statistic shown is a chi-squared (degrees of freedom) for the hypothesis that the lagged "causal" variables do not enter the equation once the appropriate lags of the dependent variable are included. That is, the statistic 111.3 (4) is the joint significance of the first four lags of the logarithm of cash flow in an equation with the logarithm of investment as the dependent variable and four lags of the logarithms of cash flow and investment as the independent variables. ** denotes significance at the 1% level and * at the 5% level.

be used as instruments for equation (1) in levels. Blundell and Bond (1998) show that this is valid if the initial deviation ε_{i1} is not correlated with the initial level of y, which is proportional to the firm effect α_i. We test for the validity of this restriction (notated AB in the tables) by adding equation (3) to our estimation and usually accept the restriction:

$$E[\Delta z_{it-1} u_{it}] = 0 \quad t = m+2, ..., T$$
$$(2(T - m - 1) \text{ additional restrictions}) \tag{3}$$

Second, conditional on the results of our test of Arellano and Bover's restriction, we choose the length of the lag from $m = 2, 3, 4,$ or 5. At the chosen length, we check that the AB restriction still holds. Once we have a preferred specification, we test for causality with a joint test of the significance of the γs . If we accept zero γs, then x does not cause y. If we reject, x causes y or a third variable causes y (or both). The results of this procedure for the sales, cash flow, R&D, and investment variables are shown in appendix A and summarized in tables 6.5 and 6.6.

Table 6.6 *Sums of the estimated lag coefficients: bivariate regressions*

Dep. Var.	Lag indep. vars.	United States	France	Japan
Investment and R&D with cash flow				
Investment	Investment	−0.111 (0.074)	−0.607 (0.053)	−0.007 (0.066)
	Cash flow	0.825 (0.086)	0.081 (0.099)	0.411 (0.075)
R&D	R&D	0.316 (0.038)	−0.124 (0.019)	−0.066 (0.037)
	Cash flow	0.431 (0.031)	0.124 (0.020)	0.042 (0.059)
Cash flow	Cash flow	0.101 (0.043)	−0.578 (0.052)	−0.372 (0.054)
	Investment	0.075 (0.038)	−0.170 (0.080)	0.039 (0.049)
Cash flow	Cash flow	−0.235 (0.046)	−0.303 (0.050)	−0.413 (0.047)
	R&D	0.226 (0.060)	0.345 (0.053)	0.023 (0.028)
Investment and R&D with sales				
Investment	Investment	−0.008 (0.050)	−0.192 (0.099)	−0.183 (0.086)
	Sales	0.608 (0.073)	−0.181 (0.197)	0.171 (0.137)
R&D	R&D	−0.055 (0.053)	0.142 (0.053)	0.167 (0.022)
	Sales	0.628 (0.053)	0.536 (0.071)	0.408 (0.057)
Sales	Sales	0.562 (0.061)	0.006 (0.068)	0.362 (0.066)
	Investment	−0.127 (0.047)	0.013 (0.025)	0.038 (0.039)
Sales	Sales	0.170 (0.062)	0.086 (0.052)	0.705 (0.029)
	R&D	0.092 (0.045)	−0.056 (0.028)	−0.004 (0.016)

Note: The table shows the sum of the estimated lag coefficients together with their standard errors in parentheses for the 8 bivariate regressions reported in table 6.5, one set for each country.

The tables in appendix A are organized in the following way: The top panels show the length of lag m that was chosen, together with the results of the causality tests with and without the AB restriction imposed. The bottom panels show the actual coefficient estimates at the chosen lag length; the sums of the estimated coefficients are shown in table 6.6. We also show the results of the test for the validity of this restriction, which is accepted easily in most cases. The exceptions are the relationship between cash flow and both investment and R&D in Japan, and more weakly, between investment and sales in France and Japan. This implies that in general the random year-to-year disturbances in sales, cash flow, and R&D are not correlated with the initial levels of these variables. In some, but not all, cases, adding the orthogonality conditions implied by AB reduces the standard errors substantially.

Table 6.5 summarizes the results of the causality testing, choosing the test that is based on the estimates with AB imposed where that restriction is accepted at the 1 percent level, and the other test if it is rejected. The causality tests themselves are not very meaningful in an accept–reject sense, since they almost all reject non-causality; that is, the second (x) variable helps to predict the first (y) variable even in the presence of ys own lags. The only cases where we can accept non-causality is in France, where sales does not cause investment and Japan, where investment does not cause sales. However, the magnitude of the test statistic and the sum of the lag coefficients on the variables display a large amount of rather systematic variation and are quite informative.

The bottom panels of the tables in appendix A give the full set of estimated lag coefficients for each bivariate regression, again with and without AB imposed. We summarize these results in table 6.6, which shows the sums of the lag coefficients for the chosen regressions, for each pair of variables, and for each country, 24 regressions in all.

From the perspective of the question we posed at the beginning, the results in table 6.6 are very striking: the US data display a high predictive power of cash flow for both R&D and investment, particularly when contrasted with France and Japan. The coefficients of cash flow in both the R&D and investment regressions are strongly positive in the United States, and very small in the other countries, except for investment in Japan, whose coefficient is half the level of that in the United States. For whatever reason, liquidity or flexibility in the face of demand shocks, large US scientific sector firms seem to be more sensitive to cash flow changes. The results for sales are quite similar, although the contrast between the countries is somewhat weaker in the case of R&D.

At the same time, the role of investment in generating future cash flow appears to be somewhat weaker, possibly zero in Japan and negative in France. The impact of R&D investment on future cash flow in Japan is also zero, but in the US and France, it is much higher than the impact of ordinary investment.

The sales regressions display the same kind of results, but much weaker: in this case sales growth clearly predicts R&D growth in all three countries, although somewhat more strongly in the United States. The converse is that R&D does not appear to cause future sales growth, except in the United States, and even here the coefficient is small (of the order of 0.09).[11] Investment appears unrelated to future sales in all three countries.

[11] It is worth noting that the magnitude of this coefficient is approximately equal to the estimate obtained using production function estimation with sales growth as the dependent variable and the growth in capital, labor, and R&D capital as the independent variables (see Mairesse and Hall, 1996). Thus our estimates here are consistent with the traditional TFP regression approach, but they highlight the fact that

5   Conclusion

We view these results as rather preliminary, but highly suggestive. The oft-told story of a softer budget constraint on investment in the major continental countries and Japan when compared to the United States is clearly supported by our analysis. However we would be extremely cautious about drawing strong conclusions from these data yet, for two quite different sets of reasons. First, findings like those here do not automatically imply that liquidity constraints are at the root of the differences: what we may be seeing is a greater flexibility of firms in the United States in all dimensions when faced with demand shocks; consider the evidence of the employment fluctuations. In addition, we have not fully explored the question of whether the "softer" budget constraint that may exist in the absence of active public financial market discipline means more or less productive investment, although the evidence of the reverse regressions is slightly daunting in this regard; in many cases we see no positive impact on sales and cash flow from investments as long as four years after they are undertaken.

The other reason for caution is the limited nature of our analysis thus far. First, bivariate regressions may not control properly for changes in other closely related factors; for example, it is more natural to include capital and labor when regressing sales on R&D, and surely investment and R&D are related in their impacts on cash flow. Extensions to this chapter will conduct the causality testing in a multivariate setting. Second, we found in appendix A that many of our univariate time series displayed random walk behavior. This suggests that a fruitful avenue of exploration might be to look for cointegration between our main variables in the spirit of recent work by Pesaran, Shin, and Smith (1997), where they allow short-run dynamics to vary across units but impose a constant relationship in the long run.

In spite of these caveats, the results in this paper are highly suggestive, especially when compared with those of Bond *et al* (1997) on investment and cash flow in UK, Belgian, French, and German firms, which show much higher sensitivity of investment to cash flow in the UK than in the other three countries. Our work confirms a similar stylized fact for both investment and R&D, contrasting the cash flow sensitivity of US firms with lack of the same in France and Japan. Given the gross similarity of the governance structures in the US and UK and their differences from

---

the simultaneity that we observed in the relationship between the inputs and outputs of the production process may be much more important running from output to input than from input to output.

continental economies and Japan, our view is that the similarity of our results to those of Bond *et al.* is not an accident: for whatever reason, either quicker responsiveness to market demand signals or higher costs of external capital, the Anglo-American environment is one in which there is a tighter correspondence between cash flow, profits, and sales on the one hand, and investment expenditures on the other.

Appendix   Bivariate causality regressions

Table A.1a *Does cash flow cause investment?*

Country	m	Causality w/o AB	Test for AB	Causality with AB
US (174)	4 or 5	32.0 (5)**	9.9 (13)	111.3 (4)**
France (104)	5	5.9 (5)	11.8 (11)	12.6 (5)*
Japan (200)	4	34.6 (4)**	9.6 (13)	71.4 (4)**

Notes: Chi-squared tests with degrees of freedom in parentheses. ** denotes significance at the 1% level and * at the 5% level.

Estimated coefficients of the lag variables (dep. var. is investment)

Country	Without AB			With AB	
	Investment	Cash flow	Lag	Investment	Cash flow
US	−0.110 (0.057)	0.333 (0.107)	1	0.183 (0.033)	0.434 (0.046)
	−0.287 (0.031)	0.158 (0.040)	2	−0.211 (0.021)	0.070 (0.025)
	−0.121 (0.038)	0.185 (0.040)	3	0.009 (0.028)	0.153 (0.033)
	−0.085 (0.032)	0.220 (0.048)	4	−0.093 (0.018)	0.168 (0.025)
	−0.085 (0.023)	0.090 (0.037)	5	—	—
	−0.688 (0.144)	1.006 (0.198)	Sum	−0.111 (0.074)	0.825 (0.086)
France	−0.162 (0.051)	0.027 (0.089)	1	0.006 (0.043)	−0.011 (0.053)
	−0.309 (0.037)	0.024 (0.028)	2	−0.373 (0.031)	−0.009 (0.033)
	−0.185 (0.028)	0.049 (0.024)	3	−0.136 (0.022)	0.046 (0.019)
	−0.116 (0.026)	0.050 (0.020)	4	−0.062 (0.026)	0.032 (0.025)
	−0.081 (0.025)	0.032 (0.020)	5	−0.106 (0.025)	0.022 (0.018)
	−0.853 (0.126)	0.182 (0.149)	Sum	−0.607 (0.053)	0.081 (0.099)
Japan	−0.077 (0.051)	0.279 (0.080)	1	0.172 (0.034)	0.346 (0.057)
	−0.206 (0.032)	0.034 (0.041)	2	−0.097 (0.024)	−0.025 (0.035)
	−0.095 (0.023)	−0.017 (0.037)	3	−0.035 (0.020)	−0.060 (0.033)
	−0.088 (0.020)	0.178 (0.038)	4	−0.046 (0.019)	0.150 (0.032)
	−0.467 (0.104)	0.474 (0.124)	Sum	−0.007 (0.066)	0.411 (0.075)

Table A.1b *Does cash flow cause R&D?*

Country	m	Causality w/o AB	Test for AB	Causality with AB
US (174)	4	1272.4 (4)**	8.6 (13)	235.2 (4)**
France (104)	3 or 4	18.7 (4)**	14.1 (15)	67.1 (3)**
Japan (200)	2 or 3	16.3 (3)**	26.1 (15)*	21.6 (2)**

Notes: Chi-squared tests with degrees of freedom in parentheses. ** denotes significance at the 1% level and * at the 5% level.

Estimated coefficients of the lag variables (dep. var. is R&D)

Country	Without AB		Lag	With AB	
	R&D	Cash Flow		R&D	Cash Flow
US	0.216 (0.049)	0.182 (0.022)	1	0.304 (0.060)	0.240 (0.020)
	−0.057 (0.019)	0.083 (0.012)	2	−0.100 (0.022)	0.059 (0.017)
	0.042 (0.013)	0.058 (0.010)	3	−0.054 (0.016)	0.087 (0.012)
	0.023 (0.012)	0.094 (0.010)	4	0.111 (0.049)	0.158 (0.016)
	0.224 (0.045)	0.416 (0.040)	Sum	0.316 (0.038)	0.431 (0.031)
France	−0.141 (0.034)	0.089 (0.016)	1	−0.128 (0.015)	0.081 (0.012)
	−0.025 (0.011)	0.022 (0.011)	2	−0.013 (0.005)	0.025 (0.007)
	0.008 (0.011)	−0.004 (0.008)	3	0.016 (0.005)	0.018 (0.005)
	0.002 (0.008)	0.009 (0.005)	4		
	−0.126 (0.054)	0.125 (0.037)	Sum	−0.124 (0.019)	0.124 (0.020)
Japan	0.028 (0.025)	−0.022 (0.037)	1	0.216 (0.017)	0.055 (0.025)
	−0.035 (0.014)	0.058 (0.017)	2	−0.014 (0.012)	0.069 (0.015)
	−0.058 (0.012)	0.005 (0.017)	3		
			4		
	−0.066 (0.037)	0.042 (0.059)	Sum	0.202 (0.015)	0.124 (0.020)

Table A.2a *Does investment cause cash flow?*

Country	m	Causality w/o AB	Test for AB	Causality with AB
US (174)	3	20.4 (3)**	9.8 (15)	40.7 (3)**
France (104)	5	19.2 (5)**	6.5 (11)	26.7 (5)**
Japan (200)	4	25.5 (4)**	30.1 (13)**	25.5 (4)**

Notes: Chi-squared tests with degrees of freedom in parentheses. ** denotes significance at the 1% level and * at the 5% level.

Estimated coefficients of the lag variables (dep. var. is cash flow)

Country	Without AB Cash Flow	Without AB Investment	Lag	With AB Cash Flow	With AB Investment
US	0.067 (0.038)	0.008 (0.028)	1	0.203 (0.030)	0.005 (0.023)
	−0.091 (0.017)	−0.001 (0.014)	2	−0.104 (0.015)	0.002 (0.013)
	−0.019 (0.015)	0.050 (0.013)	3	0.002 (0.013)	0.068 (0.011)
	−0.043 (0.056)	0.057 (0.046)	Sum	0.101 (0.043)	0.075 (0.038)
France	−0.275 (0.054)	0.010 (0.024)	1	−0.261 (0.043)	−0.018 (0.036)
	−0.152 (0.031)	0.019 (0.008)	2	−0.117 (0.025)	−0.015 (0.019)
	−0.106 (0.020)	−0.012 (0.005)	3	−0.104 (0.017)	−0.054 (0.020)
	−0.072 (0.014)	−0.035 (0.016)	4	−0.077 (0.012)	−0.053 (0.014)
	−0.065 (0.013)	−0.026 (0.011)	5	−0.069 (0.012)	−0.030 (0.009)
	−0.670 (0.096)	−0.044 (0.090)	Sum	−0.578 (0.052)	−0.170 (0.080)
Japan	−0.057 (0.035)	−0.023 (0.025)	1	0.050 (0.033)	−0.031 (0.025)
	−0.237 (0.029)	0.011 (0.012)	2	−0.230 (0.017)	−0.003 (0.013)
	−0.082 (0.018)	0.013 (0.012)	3	−0.067 (0.017)	−0.013 (0.011)
	0.004 (0.018)	0.040 (0.009)	4	0.052 (0.017)	0.031 (0.009)
	−0.372 (0.054)	0.039 (0.049)	Sum	−0.195 (0.052)	−0.015 (0.049)

Table A.2b *Does R&D cause cash flow?*

Country	m	Causality w/o AB	Test for AB	Causality with AB
US (174)	3	49.5 (2)**	13.9 (13)	42.0 (3)**
France (104)	4	60.2 (4)**	12.2 (13)	116.9 (4)**
Japan (200)	3	25.6 (3)**	31.0 (15)**	32.5 (3)**

Notes: Chi-squared tests with degrees of freedom in parentheses. ** denotes significance at the 1% level and * at the 5% level.

Estimated coefficients of the lag variables (dep. var. is cash flow)

Country	Without AB		Lag	With AB	
	Cash Flow	R&D		Cash Flow	R&D
US	−0.154 (0.029)	0.137 (0.068)	1	−0.124 (0.028)	0.170 (0.092)
	−0.086 (0.019)	0.083 (0.022)	2	−0.075 (0.017)	0.092 (0.020)
	−0.033 (0.013)	−0.008 (0.019)	3	−0.037 (0.010)	−0.036 (0.015)
			4		
	−0.273 (0.058)	0.211 (0.075)	Sum	−0.235 (0.046)	0.226 (0.060)
France	−0.143 (0.041)	0.361 (0.068)	1	−0.103 (0.032)	0.416 (0.049)
	−0.161 (0.018)	0.047 (0.023)	2	−0.174 (0.013)	0.028 (0.016)
	−0.065 (0.012)	−0.023 (0.022)	3	−0.053 (0.010)	−0.020 (0.014)
	0.002 (0.010)	−0.091 (0.017)	4	0.029 (0.009)	−0.079 (0.012)
	−0.366 (0.054)	0.294 (0.077)	Sum	−0.303 (0.050)	0.345 (0.053)
Japan	−0.093 (0.030)	−0.023 (0.020)	1	−0.107 (0.071)	−0.014 (0.016)
	−0.201 (0.017)	0.050 (0.010)	2	−0.210 (0.034)	0.049 (0.009)
	−0.119 (0.016)	−0.003 (0.009)	3	−0.122 (0.028)	0.010 (0.009)
			4		
	−0.413 (0.047)	0.023 (0.028)	Sum	−0.438 (0.042)	0.044 (0.023)

Table A.3a *Does sales cause investment?*

Country	m	Causality w/o AB	Test for AB	Causality with AB
US (204)	3	37.8 (3)**	12.8 (15)	84.8 (3)**
France (156)	4	7.2 (4)	7.7 (13)	6.6 (4)
Japan (221)	4	33.2 (4)**	13.9 (13)	77.6 (4)**

Notes: Chi-squared tests with degrees of freedom in parentheses. ** denotes significance at the 1% level and * at the 5% level.

Estimated coefficients of the lag variables (dep. var. is investment)

Country	Without AB Investment	Without AB Sales	Lag	With AB Investment	With AB Sales
US	−0.057 (0.043)	0.619 (0.137)	1	0.159 (0.030)	0.636 (0.070)
	−0.239 (0.022)	0.112 (0.054)	2	−0.141 (0.015)	−0.048 (0.047)
	−0.072 (0.018)	0.013 (0.043)	3	−0.025 (0.017)	0.020 (0.037)
	−0.368 (0.071)	0.743 (0.136)	Sum	−0.008 (0.050)	0.608 (0.073)
France	−0.010 (0.060)	−0.181 (0.265)	1	0.172 (0.050)	−0.093 (0.215)
	−0.230 (0.032)	0.056 (0.085)	2	−0.197 (0.027)	−0.065 (0.077)
	−0.129 (0.024)	0.135 (0.065)	3	−0.095 (0.020)	0.094 (0.059)
	−0.088 (0.026)	−0.124 (0.073)	4	−0.072 (0.024)	−0.117 (0.066)
	−0.458 (0.119)	−0.115 (0.247)	Sum	−0.192 (0.099)	−0.181 (0.197)
Japan	−0.184 (0.059)	0.392 (0.222)	1	0.053 (0.044)	0.430 (0.149)
	−0.211 (0.034)	−0.458 (0.117)	2	−0.111 (0.026)	−0.698 (0.089)
	−0.127 (0.024)	0.089 (0.087)	3	−0.055 (0.021)	0.196 (0.079)
	−0.080 (0.020)	0.308 (0.083)	4	−0.070 (0.020)	0.243 (0.083)
	−0.603 (0.033)	0.330 (0.229)	Sum	−0.183 (0.086)	0.171 (0.137)

152   **Jacques Mairesse, Bronwyn Hall, Lee Branstetter, and Bruno Crepon**

Table A.3b *Does sales cause R&D?*

Country	m	Causality w/o AB	Test for AB	Causality with AB
US (204)	4	86.4 (4)**	16.8 (13)	200.7 (4)**
France (156)	4	80.2 (4)**	18.2 (13)	133.0 (4)**
Japan (221)	3	25.1 (3)**	13.2 (15)	57.2 (3)**

Notes: Chi-squared tests with degrees of freedom in parentheses. ** denotes significance at the 1% level and * at the 5% level.

Estimated coefficients of the lag variables (dep. var. is R&D)

Country	Without AB		Lag	With AB	
	R&D	Sales		R&D	Sales
US	−0.081 (0.042)	0.233 (0.067)	1	−0.087 (0.036)	0.287 (0.047)
	0.001 (0.011)	0.111 (0.023)	2	−0.005 (0.011)	0.137 (0.018)
	−0.007 (0.015)	0.146 (0.025)	3	−0.003 (0.012)	0.108 (0.021)
	0.030 (0.014)	0.064 (0.024)	4	0.040 (0.011)	0.097 (0.022)
	−0.056 (0.049)	0.555 (0.081)	Sum	−0.055 (0.053)	0.628 (0.053)
France	0.081 (0.047)	0.313 (0.089)	1	0.188 (0.041)	0.352 (0.075)
	−0.049 (0.014)	−0.029 (0.028)	2	−0.060 (0.012)	−0.063 (0.026)
	0.011 (0.012)	0.069 (0.024)	3	0.038 (0.010)	0.063 (0.020)
	−0.019 (0.017)	0.178 (0.020)	4	−0.024 (0.013)	0.184 (0.022)
	0.024 (0.059)	0.531 (0.087)	Sum	0.142 (0.053)	0.536 (0.071)
Japan	0.042 (0.024)	0.224 (0.106)	1	0.179 (0.017)	0.290 (0.060)
	−0.047 (0.013)	0.083 (0.040)	2	−0.019 (0.012)	0.048 (0.029)
	−0.036 (0.013)	0.099 (0.036)	3	0.006 (0.009)	0.070 (0.026)
			4		
	−0.041 (0.033)	0.406 (0.105)	Sum	0.167 (0.022)	0.408 (0.057)

Table A.4a *Does investment cause sales?*

Country	m	Causality w/o AB	Test for AB	Causality with AB
US (204)	5	23.0 (5)**	9.1 (11)	35.0 (5)**
France (156)	4 or 5	14.0 (4)**	20.0 (11)*	18.57 (5)**
Japan (221)	5	8.0 (5)	21.0 (11)*	23.0 (5)**

Notes: Chi-squared tests with degrees of freedom in parentheses. ** denotes significance at the 1% level and * at the 5% level.

Estimated coefficients of the lag variables (dep. var. is sales)

Country	Without AB Sales	Without AB Investment	Lag	With AB Sales	With AB Investment
US	0.236 (0.049)	−0.016 (0.019)	1	0.213 (0.042)	−0.026 (0.019)
	0.072 (0.024)	−0.028 (0.011)	2	0.124 (0.023)	−0.032 (0.011)
	0.040 (0.022)	−0.015 (0.011)	3	0.078 (0.021)	−0.024 (0.011)
	0.098 (0.020)	−0.008 (0.007)	4	0.093 (0.019)	−0.010 (0.007)
	0.042 (0.020)	−0.028 (0.008)	5	0.054 (0.019)	−0.035 (0.007)
	0.488 (0.067)	−0.096 (0.048)	Sum	0.562 (0.061)	−0.127 (0.047)
France	−0.021 (0.061)	0.002 (0.012)	1	−0.070 (0.069)	−0.019 (0.017)
	−0.053 (0.019)	0.008 (0.007)	2	0.056 (0.020)	0.004 (0.009)
	0.020 (0.015)	0.008 (0.005)	3	0.072 (0.017)	−0.004 (0.008)
	0.061 (0.021)	−0.006 (0.004)	4	0.072 (0.024)	−0.008 (0.007)
	—	—	5	−0.035 (0.024)	−0.013 (0.005)
	0.006 (0.068)	0.013 (0.025)	Sum	−0.016 (0.077)	−0.039 (0.040)
Japan	0.074 (0.069)	0.009 (0.013)	1	0.017 (0.064)	0.011 (0.012)
	−0.104 (0.034)	0.001 (0.009)	2	−0.090 (0.031)	−0.006 (0.009)
	0.091 (0.025)	0.015 (0.008)	3	0.166 (0.024)	0.015 (0.007)
	0.134 (0.026)	0.005 (0.008)	4	0.126 (0.026)	0.003 (0.007)
	0.166 (0.026)	0.008 (0.006)	5	0.178 (0.024)	0.012 (0.006)
	0.362 (0.066)	0.038 (0.039)	Sum	0.398 (0.060)	0.035 (0.036)

154   Jacques Mairesse, Bronwyn Hall, Lee Branstetter, and Bruno Crepon

Table A.4b *Does R&D cause sales?*

Country	m	Causality w/o AB	Test for AB	Causality with AB
US (204)	4	27.2 (4)**	7.7 (13)	39.5 (4)**
France (156)	3	3.8 (3)	22.7 (15)	13.7 (3)**
Japan (221)	4	10.2 (4)*	13.0 (13)	38.0 (4)**

Notes: Chi-squared tests with degrees of freedom in parentheses. ** denotes significance at the 1% level and * at the 5% level.

Estimated coefficients of the lag variables (dep. var. is sales)

Country	Without AB		Lag	With AB	
	Sales	R&D		Sales	R&D
US	0.161 (0.048)	−0.006 (0.035)	1	0.128 (0.043)	−0.023 (0.034)
	−0.064 (0.018)	0.047 (0.011)	2	−0.042 (0.018)	0.047 (0.011)
	0.012 (0.020)	0.022 (0.011)	2	0.040 (0.019)	0.036 (0.010)
	0.056 (0.019)	0.026 (0.009)	4	0.044 (0.018)	0.032 (0.009)
	0.165 (0.064)	0.089 (0.046)	Sum	0.170 (0.062)	0.092 (0.045)
France	−0.015 (0.044)	−0.019 (0.024)	1	−0.063 (0.043)	−0.060 (0.024)
	0.043 (0.009)	0.004 (0.008)	2	0.074 (0.016)	−0.007 (0.006)
	0.046 (0.013)	0.010 (0.005)	3	0.075 (0.011)	0.011 (0.005)
			4		
	0.073 (0.054)	−0.005 (0.029)	Sum	0.086 (0.052)	−0.056 (0.028)
Japan	0.473 (0.043)	−0.003 (0.015)	1	0.679 (0.036)	0.009 (0.012)
	−0.122 (0.026)	−0.007 (0.005)	2	−0.163 (0.026)	−0.015 (0.004)
	0.040 (0.023)	0.006 (0.004)	3	0.075 (0.025)	0.018 (0.005)
	0.138 (0.022)	−0.013 (0.007)	4	0.113 (0.018)	−0.016 (0.004)
	0.533 (0.040)	−0.016 (0.020)	Sum	0.705 (0.029)	−0.004 (0.016)

References

Arellano, Manuel (1988), "An Alternative Transformation for Fixed Effects Models with Predetermined Variables," Oxford University Applied Discussion Paper No. 57, Institute of Economics and Statistics, Oxford University.

Arellano, Manuel and Stephen Bond (1991), "Some Tests of Specification for Panel Data: Monte Carlo Evidence and an Application to Employment Equations," *Review of Economic Studies*, 58: 277–297.

Arellano, Manuel and Olympia Bover (1991), "Another Look at the Instrumental-Variable Estimation of Error-components Models," *Journal of Econometrics*, 68: 29–52.

Bartelsman, Eric and Wayne Gray (1994), "TFP: The Productivity Database," Cambridge, Mass.: National Bureau of Economic Research. Diskette. *http://www.nber.org*.

Blundell, Richard S. and Stephen R. Bond (1998), "Initial Conditions and Moment Restrictions in Dynamic Panel Data Models," *Journal of Econometrics*, 287: 115–173.

Blundell, Richard S., Stephen Bond, Michael Devereux, and Fabio Schiantarelli (1992), "Investment and Tobin's Q," *Journal of Econometrics*, 51: 233–257.

Bond, Stephen, Julie Ann Elston, Jacques Mairesse, and Benoit Mulkay (1997), "A Comparison of Empirical Investment Equations Using Company Panel Data for France, Germany, Belgium, and the UK," Cambridge, Mass.: NEER Working Paper No. 5900 (January 1997).

Charkham, Jonathan (1994), *Keeping Good Company: A Study of Corporate Governance in Five Countries*, Oxford: Clarendon Press.

Crepon, Bruno, Francis Kramarz, and Alain Trognon (1998), "Parameter of Interest, Nuisance Parameter, and Orthogonality Conditions: An Application to Autoregressive Error Components Models," *Journal of Econometrics* (forthcoming).

Franks, Julian and Colin Mayer (1990), "Capital Markets and Corporate Control: A Study of France, Germany, and the UK," *Economic Policy*, 10: 189–232.

Gilson, Ronald J. (1995), "Corporate Governance and Economic Efficiency: When Do Institutions Matter?" Stanford, California: Stanford Law School John M. Olin Program in Law and Economics Working Paper Series No. 121 (July 1995).

Griliches, Zvi and Jacques Mairesse (1983), "Comparing Productivity Growth: An Exploration of French and U.S. Industrial and Firm Data," *European Economic Review*, 21: 89–119.

(1990), "R&D and Productivity Growth: Comparing Japanese and U.S. Manufacturing Firms," in Charles R. Hulten (ed.), *Productivity Growth in Japan and the United States*, Chicago, Illinois: University of Chicago Press.

Hall, Bronwyn H. (1990), "The Manufacturing Sector Master File: 1959–1987," Cambridge, Mass.: National Bureau of Economic Research Working Paper No. 3366.

(1992), "R&D Investment at the Firm Level: Does the Source of Financing Matter?" National Bureau of Economic Research Working Paper No. 4096 (June).

(1994), "Corporate Restructuring and Investment Horizons in the United States, 1976–1987," *Business History Review* 68: 110–143.

Hall, Bronwyn H. and Jacques Mairesse (1995), "Exploring the Relationship between R&D and Productivity in French Manufacturing Firms," *Journal of Econometrics*, 65: 263–293.

(1998), "Univariate Panel Data Models and GMM Estimators: An Exploration Using Real and Simulated Data," UC Berkeley, Nuffield College, Oxford University, INSEE-CREST, and NBER (Photocopied).

Holtz-Eakin, Douglas, Whitney Newey, and Harvey Rosen (1988), "Estimating Vector Autoregressions with Panel Data," *Econometrica*, 56: 1371–1395.

Hoshi, Takeo, Anil Kashyap, and David Scharfstein (1990), "The Role of Banks in Reducing Costs of Financial Distress in Japan," National Bureau of Economic Research Working Paper No. 3435.

Keane, Michael P. and David E. Runkle (1992), "On the Estimation of Panel Data Models with Serial Correlation When Instruments are not Strictly Exogenous," *Journal of Business and Economic Statistics*, 10: 1–29.

Kester, W. Carl (1992), "Governance, Contracting, and Investment Horizons: A Look at Japan and Germany," *Journal of Applied Corporate Finance*, 5: 83–98.

Mairesse, Jacques and Bronwyn H. Hall (1996), "Estimating the Productivity of Research and Development in French and United States Manufacturing Firms: An Exploration of Simultaneity Issues with GMM," in Bart van Ark, and Karin Wagner (eds.), *International Productivity Differences, Measurement, and Explanations*. Amsterdam: Elsevier – North-Holland.

Mairesse, Jacques and Alan Siu (1984), "An Extended Accelerator Model of R&D and Physical Investment," in Zvi Griliches (ed.), *R&D, Patents, and Productivity*, Chicago: Chicago University Press.

Mayer, Colin and Ian Alexander (1990), "Banks and Securities Markets: Corporate Financing in Germany and the UK," London: CEPR Working Paper No. 433.

OECD (1991a), *Economic Outlook: Historical Statistics, 1960–1989*, Paris: OECD.

(1991b), *Basic Science and Technology Statistics*, Paris: OECD.

Pesaran, M. H., Y. Shin, and R. P. Smith (1997), "Pooled Estimation of Long-Run Relationships in Dynamic Heterogeneous Panels," University of Cambridge, Cambridge (Photocopied).

Soskice, David (1995), "Complementarities between Product Manufacturing Strategies, Company Organisational Structures and Owner–Company Relations: Patterns across Advanced Economies," Presentation to the WZB Conference on Bank–Firm Relationships, Berlin, Germany, June 21–23, 1995.

World Bank (1993), *World Tables 1993*, Baltimore, Maryland: Johns Hopkins University Press.

7 Innovation, cooperation, and the region

Michael Fritsch and Rolf Lukas

1 Introduction

Recent empirical work shows that innovation activities tend to be clustered in space (Audretsch and Feldman, 1996; Feldman, 1994). This suggests that there are significant agglomeration economies at work and that the regional environment may be of relevance for innovation activities. Cooperative relationships between organizations (e.g., private firms, publicly funded research institutions) with regard to research and development (R&D) could be an important vehicle for such agglomeration economies. However, only little is known about the importance of location and spatial proximity for R&D-cooperation. If space really matters for cooperation on R&D, this may have considerable implications for the performance of regional innovation systems and for respective policy measures.

In this contribution, we will investigate the relationship between innovation activities of manufacturing establishments and their R&D cooperation with other organizations. We will particularly consider the regional structure of these cooperative relationships and argue that the regional context matters for innovation and should be accounted for in the analysis of innovation processes. We start with a sketch of some basic hypotheses concerning the relationship between innovation and cooperation (section 2) and then consider the importance of the regional context for cooperation (section 3). Section 4 gives some information on the data base of our empirical analysis and in section 5 we show to what extent the establishments of our sample maintain different kinds of cooperative relationships. In order to detect differences in the propensity to cooperate

Revised version of a paper presented at the conference 'The impact of technological change on firm and industry performance', 29–30 August 1997, Tinbergen Institute, Erasmus University Rotterdam.

between regions, multivariate analyses accounting for the characteristics of establishments with different kinds cooperative relationships are conducted (section 6). In section 7 we inspect the regional distribution of the cooperation partners and section 8 draws some conclusions.

2   Cooperation and innovation

Like production processes, most innovation activities are characterized by a significant division of labor between organizations (cf. Jewkes, Sawers, and Stillerman, 1969). There are, however, at least two indications that suggest differences between the division of labor for routine production activities and innovation processes:

First, in innovation processes the final product is often more or less unknown so that there may be considerable uncertainty with regard to what will be needed for a satisfactory outcome.

Second, a key issue in the division of innovative labor is the transfer of information. However, there are kinds of information that cannot be as easily purchased as normal product parts from a supplier. The exchange of information may require some degree of trust between the partners and may need special arrangements that include more than just "spot-market" types of relationships.

For these reasons, many relationships in the division of innovative labor between organizations may be characterized as a cooperation in a relatively wide definition of the term.[1] According to such a wide definition, every relationship between actors that involves more than just a spot-market exchange but which is not due to complete hierarchical control may be considered a cooperation.

The literature provides a number of arguments on the advantages of cooperative relationships over spot-market interaction. Many of these arguments relate to the transfer of information within a cooperation. In this respect it is argued that:[2]

If economic success of the partners in a cooperative arrangement is positively related, this may motivate both open communication and the supply of relevant information to each other.

Members of a cooperative relationship are better able to supply "good" and appropriate information to each other because they have better knowledge of the needs of their partner than is the case

[1]   It is quiet remarkable that many studies of cooperation between organizations leave the exact definition of a cooperative relationship more or less open. The above definition is in accordance with the way the term is used in most of the literature on cooperation.
[2]   See for example Axelsson (1992), Lundvall (1993), and Powell (1990).

in spot-market relationships. This better knowledge of information requirements also enables them to filter the information relevant for their partner.

As far as cooperation is associated with reputation and trust, the quality of information received can be much easier assessed than in spot-market relationships.

Due to a relatively high degree of inter-organizational adaptation and established interfaces between cooperation partners, information exchange within cooperative relationships may be faster and less exposed to errors than is the case in spot-market relationships.

If cooperation involves some knowledge about the respective partner or trust this may also result in a reduction of uncertainty with regard to the partner's future behavior (Thorelli, 1986; Galaskiewicz, 1985). Due to the transaction costs necessary to establish a cooperation, one can expect that actors tend to prefer the "voice" option over "exit" because abandoning the relationship would imply that these transaction costs become "sunk."

A relatively high degree of openness and richness of information exchange within cooperative relationships may particularly include kinds of information that are conducive to innovation and lead to mutual learning (Saxenian, 1994; Storper, 1992). It can therefore stimulate a relatively early adoption of process innovations and ideas as well as the generation of new ideas with regard to improvements of products and processes. For this reason, it is not only argued that cooperation may provide necessary inputs for a firm to successfully generate innovation (innovation needs or causes cooperation),[3] but that cooperation may also induce or stimulate attempts to innovate (cooperation causes innovation).[4]

3   The regional context

There is an emerging literature on the importance of the regional dimension for innovation. However, much of this literature is on a case study basis and remains rather speculative. One key result of recent empirical research is that in a number of countries innovation of a certain kind or in a certain sector is concentrated in specific locations or regions (Audretsch and Feldman, 1996; Feldman, 1994). The general

[3] Cf., for example, Dertouz, Lester, and Solow (1989), Teece (1992), Spencer and Grindley (1993).

[4] This is a main topic in the literature on innovation networks and "innovative milieux." See, for example, Maillat, Crevoisier, and Lecoq (1994) and the contributions in Aydalot and Keeble (1988) and in Camagni (1991).

explanation for this finding is the existence of spillovers or external effects of innovation activities which need spatial proximity in order to become effective. One important channel by which these spillovers may work is cooperative relationships between organizations like information trading, pilot usage, joint use of certain inputs (e.g. laboratories), contract research, or joint innovation projects. As far as cooperation requires face-to-face communication (Nohria and Eccles, 1992), close location of actors may be conducive for the establishment of such relationships.

Investigating the importance of locational proximity for spillovers, Jaffe, Trajtenberg, and Henderson (1993) compared the geographic location of patent citations with the location of the originating patents and detected that these paper trails of knowledge spillovers are, to quite a considerable degree, geographically localized (for a similar approach see Almeida and Kogut, 1997). However, the effect of geographic coincidence between the citation and the cited patent seems to fade away over time. A number of studies focused on the impact of university research in a region on innovation output of private firms. In his pioneering study based on patent data, Jaffe (1989, p. 968) found "only weak evidence that spillovers are facilitated by geographic coincidence of universities and research labs within the state." However, if information on product innovations instead of patents is used in the analysis, the effect of spatial proximity comes out to be considerably stronger (Acs, Audretsch, and Feldman, 1992; Anselin, Varga, and Acs, 1997a, 1997b).[5] With regard to the direction of R&D spillovers, Jaffe (1989) as well as Anselin, Varga, and Acs (1997a, 1997b) conclude from their investigations that university R&D may lead to important spillovers for innovation in private firms located within the same region but that there is no evidence that university R&D benefits from spillovers generated by private innovation activities taking place inside or outside the region.

Despite these results, there remains a severe lack of information about how such local spillovers become effective. Particularly, we do not know much about the importance of different kinds of ties and actors within a regional innovation system for innovation processes and spillovers. If cooperative relationships with actors within the same region tend to be conducive to innovation, is it more the cooperation with suppliers and customers, with public research institutions, or is it horizontal cooperation with firms of the same industry which is important for a locational

[5]   There is considerable evidence that small firms benefit more from university R&D located in the same region than large firms (Link and Rees, 1990; Acs, Audretsch, and Feldman, 1994).

advantage to come into existence? Case study evidence suggests that cooperative relationships with nearby firms of the same industry may be favorable for the spillover of relevant information and that universities may act as an incubator for the emergence of industrial districts (Saxenian, 1994). Vertical relationships within producer–supplier networks may also play an important role (Lundvall, 1992).[6] However, as Audretsch and Stephan (1996) point out, the importance of location may vary for different kinds of cooperative relationships. According to their analysis, spatial proximity seems to be conducive mainly for informal relationships and relatively unimportant for formal relationships.

Empirically, one can find severe differences between regions with regard to main characteristics of their innovation systems and the way these innovation systems work (for an overview see Tödtling, 1995). In this respect it would be plausible to assume that the appropriateness of a regional innovation system depends on a number of factors like population density, its geographical position in the global economy, or the characteristics of the dominant technological field. Notwithstanding, the assertion that a high degree of intra-regional cooperation or local networking stimulates innovation and regional development seems to be widely accepted in the literature.[7] But we still lack convincing empirical evidence that could confirm this hypothesis.

4   The data

4.1   General information

Our analysis is based on data gathered by postal questionnaires in three German regions.[8] Different questionnaires were sent to establishments in manufacturing, business-oriented services, and to publicly funded

---

[6] Another vehicle for the diffusion of innovation-relevant knowledge within a region, which remains neglected in our analysis, is the regional labor market: knowledge spills over when employees change their affiliation or start a new firm on their own.

[7] See, for example, Sabel (1989; 1992) and the literature on "innovative milieux" mentioned above.

[8] The research was designed as a joint project with four teams involved, all founded by the German Science Foundation. The research institutions and the respective project leaders are: Department of Economic Geography at the University of Hanover (Prof. Dr. Ludwig Schätzl), Department of Economic and Social Geography at the University of Cologne (Prof. Dr. Rolf Sternberg), Fraunhofer Institute of Systems Analysis and Innovation Research in Karlsruhe (Dr. Knut Koschatzky, Prof. Dr. Frieder Meyer-Krahmer), and the Faculty of Economics and Business Administration at the Technical University Bergakademie Freiberg, Research Unit Innovation Economics (Prof. Dr. Michael Fritsch). In a next step of this research project, seven non-German regions

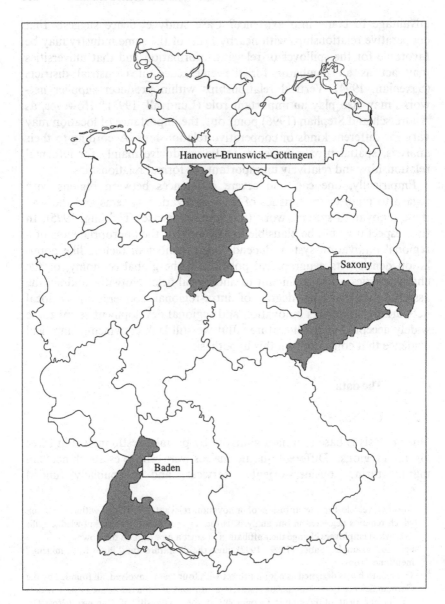

Figure 7.1 Case study areas

research institutions (universities, etc.) in the regions under inspection.[9] These surveys are part of a larger project aiming at identifying the causes for regional differences in innovation performance and growth. The regions under inspection here are (see figure 7.1):[10]

Baden, the south-western part of the State of Baden-Württemberg, a prosperous region characterized by a far above-average performance with regard to innovation. According to conventional wisdom, transfer institutions and cooperative relationships are well developed in this region (Cooke, 1996; Semlinger, 1993). The share of small establishments is considerably above the national average.

The region Hanover–Brunswick–Göttingen in the State of Lower Saxony. The region has a high share of employment in large-scale industries (e.g., automobiles, steel) and the proportion of employment in new innovative industries is comparatively low. Despite various policy attempts to improve innovation performance in this region, the innovation system is said to have considerable deficiencies (Schasse, 1995).

Saxony, one of the new German States until 1990 under a socialist regime. The region has a long tradition in manufacturing, particularly in the mechanical engineering industry. Due to the breakdown of the manufacturing sector after the fall of the Iron Curtain it is dominated by small establishments. About 50 percent of the manufacturing establishments in our sample located in this region have less than 35 employees. Large establishments are rather rare.

In this contribution we restrain ourselves to the data on the manufacturing establishments. The respective questionnaire had been sent out to all manufacturing establishments with ten or more employees.[11] Our data set contains information on certain characteristics of the establishments like number of employees, turnover, product program, the resources devoted to innovation, etc., and on the cooperative relationships

(Barcelona, Gironde, South Holland, Slovenia, South Wales, Stockholm, and Vienna) will be investigated using the same questionnaires.

[9] One should bear in mind that - at least in the regions under inspection here - there are nearly no private universities in Germany.

[10] Our current data set also includes information on the region of Alsace (France) which is neglected here in order not to complicate the analysis by an international comparison.

[11] The response rate for the questionnaires sent to manufacturing establishments amounted to 17.8 percent in Baden, 20.6 percent in Hanover, and 27.7 percent in Saxony. Because the focus of the questions was on innovation one could expect a relatively low representation of non-innovative establishments in the data. A non-response analysis revealed that there is no such bias with respect to the share of innovative establishments, however, the innovative establishments in the sample tend to have a slightly higher share of R&D personnel than the entire population of establishments.

with other firms as well as with public research institutions. Particularly, information on the number of cooperative relationships and the regional distribution of the respective partners was gathered. For the three German regions our data set contains more than 1,800 establishments.[12] Analyzing regional differences of innovation performance based on these data, we find Baden in the leading position while Hanover comes out to be second and Saxony occupies the last place in this ranking (cf. Fritsch, Franke, and Schwirten, 1998).

4.2   Indicators for cooperation

To gather information on cooperation includes a definition of what is cooperation. However, the definition of cooperative relationships is a delicate task. In our questionnaire, we tried to assess the existence of cooperative relationships with different types of partners separately. These types of partners were

customers,
manufacturing suppliers,
"other" firms, and
publicly funded research institutions.

The "other" firms are non-vertically related businesses, particularly including competitors. We assume that most of the relationships to "other" firms are horizontal in nature. In a first question we asked if in the last three years the establishments maintained relationships with customers, manufacturing suppliers, or "other" firms which in character went beyond "normal" business interactions. In the following question four categories of such cooperative relationships were given that consti-tute a closer definition. For cooperative relationships with customers and manufacturing suppliers these categories were "casual contact for infor-mation purposes," "organized exchange of information and experi-ences," "involvement in planning and operation of projects," and "pilot use of an innovation." For the assessment of cooperations with "other" firms, the last two categories were substituted by "joint use of equipment or laboratories" and "joint R&D projects." With regard to cooperation with publicly funded research institutions, the categories for the type of relationship were "use of equipment or laboratories," "research con-tracts," "joint R&D projects," and "collaboration with regard to theses." Respondents were asked to attach weights to these types of cooperative

---

[12] For more detailed information on the sample and some analyses based on this data set see Fritsch, Brœskamp, and Schwirten (1996) and Fritsch, Franke, and Schwirten (1998).

Table 7.1 *Share of establishments with a certain kind of cooperative relationship (percentages)*

Type of relationship	Share of establishments with respective type of relationship (percent)	
	All establishments	Establishments with / without innovation
Customers	61.6	68.6 / 37.6
casual contact for information purposes	52.6	58.2 / 33.8
organized exchange of information and experiences	40.0	44.3 / 25.0
involvement in planning and operation of projects	44.0	49.7 / 24.5
pilot use of an innovation	32.2	37.7 / 13.3
Suppliers	49.5	55.7 / 28.2
casual contact for information purposes	40.8	45.9 / 23.3
organized exchange of information and experiences	31.2	35.4 / 16.8
involvement in planning and operation of projects	36.1	41.5 / 17.5
pilot use of an innovation	21.4	24.9 / 9.3
"Other" firms	32.5	36.2 / 19.8
casual contact for information purposes	25.6	28.5 / 15.7
organized exchange of information and experiences	19.3	21.6 / 11.3
joint use of equipment or laboratories	12.8	15.0 / 5.3
joint R&D projects	14.6	17.7 / 4.3
Publicly funded research institutions	33.8	40.6 / 10.4
use of equipment or laboratories	16.5	29.9 / 5.0
research contracts	14.9	18.7 / 2.2
joint R&D projects	22.2	27.0 / 6.0
thesis collaboration	18.8	23.1 / 4.0

relationships on a three-grade scale ranging from "unimportant" (= no such kind of cooperation) to "very important."

We also gathered information on the number of cooperative relationships (according to the first question) to manufacturing suppliers, customers, "other" firms, and publicly funded research institutes and we

166   Michael Fritsch and Rolf Lukas

also know the number of cooperative relationships with partners in certain regional categories ("same Federal State," "rest of Germany," "abroad").

5   How common is (which kind of) cooperation ?

Generally we find that cooperation is a quite widespread phenomenon. Slightly more than 60 percent of the manufacturing establishments in our sample have cooperative relationships with their customers, nearly 49 percent maintain cooperation with their manufacturing suppliers, 33 percent with publicly funded research institutions, and about 31 percent cooperate with "other" establishments (table 7.1).

Looking at the different kinds of cooperative relationships with suppliers, customers, and "other" firms we find that casual contacts for information purposes make the highest share. For cooperation with vertically related firms the involvement in planning and operation of projects constitutes the second important type followed by an organized exchange of information and experiences. About 30 percent of establishments which maintain cooperative relationships with their customers stated that these customers act as pilot users of products. The share of establishments which have a role as pilot users for their suppliers amounts to nearly 20 percent. In the cooperative relationships with "other" firms we find the second highest share for an organized exchange of information and experiences followed by joint R&D projects (14.0 percent) and joint use of equipment or laboratories (12.3 percent). With regard to the relationships with publicly funded research institutions, joint R&D projects and thesis collaboration play the most prominent roles followed by use of equipment or laboratories and contracted research. Interestingly, but not surprising, the share of establishments maintaining cooperative relationships is always higher among those establishments that stated that they have been innovative during the preceding three years than for those establishments that had not introduced significant product or process innovation during that time. This finding corresponds to the hypotheses concerning the relationship between innovation and cooperation stated above (section 2).

6   Who cooperates?

Differences in the propensity to cooperate between establishments may be caused by a number of factors that are not specific to their location. In order to identify such region specific differences, we conducted multivariate analyses that accounted for characteristics of those establishments that maintain cooperative relationships compared to those establishments that did not. By including dummy variables for location of establishments in the analysis we are able to assess regional effects, i.e., if establishments in a certain region are more or less likely to cooperate than their counterparts in the other regions.

6.1   Hypotheses and indicators

What kind of establishments can be expected to maintain cooperative relationships? A great part of the theoretical literature on the determinants of R&D cooperation concentrates on firm characteristics (e.g., innovativeness), market structure, strategy of firms, and characteristics of the relevant technology (e.g., appropriability of generated knowledge).[13] Empirical analyses of the propensity to cooperate on R&D are few and do not arrive at a clear pattern of variables or factors that are conducive for explaining cooperative relationships (cf. Fusfeld and Haklish, 1985; Kleinknecht and Reijnen, 1992; König, Licht, and Staat, 1994). According to these studies, the main characteristics of firms that cooperate on R&D compared to firms that do not cooperate are larger firm size, relatively high R&D intensity, as well as certain features of the respective technology and of the relevant market that are identified by variables for the industry of the respective firm.[14]

In our data we find that one crucial characteristic of establishments that maintain R&D cooperation is establishment size. Assuming that there exists a given probability for cooperation per unit of value added, we can expect that large establishments are more likely to cooperate than smaller establishments. We use the natural logarithm of the number of employees as an indicator for size. As far as cooperation is related to innovation, we may expect that the likelihood or the need for cooperation rises with the R&D intensity of the respective establishment. Our measure of R&D intensity is the share of R&D employees. R&D intensity may also be interpreted as an indicator for the absorptive capacity of an establishment, i.e., its ability to identify and use relevant external knowledge for internal innovation activities (Cohen and Levinthal, 1989; 1990). The literature suggests that certain characteristics of an establishment's interface with its economic environment may also be

---

[13]   Katz and Ordover (1990), Teece (1986, 1992).

[14]   König, Licht, and Staat (1994) find that the propensity to cooperate rises with firm size (number of employees) but that the impact of R&D intensity of the respective firm is hardly significant. In the work by Kleinknecht and Reijnen (1992), size and R&D intensity only matter for cooperation with research institutions but not for relationships with other private firms.

important for cooperation. A basic issue in this respect is the existence of a "gatekeeper," i.e., a person that systematically monitors external information. We may hypothesize that the existence of such a gatekeeper increases the probability for R&D cooperation (cf. Cohen and Levinthal, 1989, 1990). Our gatekeeper variable has the value 0 if no gatekeeper exists. If there is a gatekeeper in the establishment, the effect may vary according to the extent that he or she is systematically transferring information to the relevant department or person. For establishments with a gatekeeper who is not systematically transmitting information, the gatekeeper variable has the value 1; if such a transfer occurs occasionally, the value is 2; and, if such transfer is routinized, the value of the gatekeeper variable is 3.

Our data set provides a number of variables on the objectives and on certain features of R&D activities. With respect to product innovation, respondents were asked to indicate on a three grade scale how far they aim at generating completely new products in contrast to further development of products that are already part of their product program (product modification). The answers may be regarded as an indication of the aspiration level of product innovation activities. We also asked respondents for an assessment of the importance of different objectives of process innovation activities on a three grade scale. The answers to the response category "reduction of total production time" may be interpreted as an indication of the emphasis lying on rationalization effects in process innovation activities.[15] We include the share of value added to turnover in order to test if cooperation constitutes a substitute or a complement for internal R&D. If cooperation works as a substitute, then the share of value added to turnover should be relatively low for establishments that maintain cooperative relationships; if it is complementary to internal R&D, the share of value added to turnover should be higher for firms that cooperate. Dummy variables for the 13 industry groups to which the establishments belong control for effects of technology and market structure.[16] Regional dummy variables for location in

[15] On a firm or establishment level, cost savings are very frequently due to a reduction of production time which represents a good indicator for many kinds of rationalization effects. The other response categories were "reduction of negative effects on the environment," "increased flexibility of production," "reduction of unit labor costs," "improvement of product quality," "reduction of energy or materials input," and "improvement of working conditions." None of these variables proved to be significant when introduced in addition to "reduction of total production time" in the model.

[16] The control group is the medicine technology and optical instruments industry. The industry groups are based on the German two-digit classification which has 22 industries in manufacturing. We had to aggregate some of these industries in order to secure a sufficient number of cases in each industry group.

Baden and in the Hanover–Brunswick–Göttingen region are included to test for regional differences.

A number of further variables had been tested but did not make a significant contribution. One of these variables was an estimation of the average length of the product life cycle of the main product based on a three grade scale. Our hypothesis was that the probability for establishments to enter a cooperative relationship may rise if product life cycles are relatively short because R&D cooperation can contribute to a reduction of time to market. Also, no statistically significant impact could be found for the age of the establishment, the share of exports, and for the assessment of the importance of certain inputs for innovation activities.[17]

6.2   Results

Tables 7.2 and 7.3 show the results of logit analyses trying to identify the characteristics of establishments that maintain a cooperative relationship with a certain type of actor. The dependent variable has the value of 1 if at least one relationship with the respective type of partner exists and it is 0 if there is no such relationship.[18] The set of variables included as well as the number of cases differ considerably between these tables. The reason is that in the questionnaire not all establishments were asked to answer all of the questions. We suspected that many respondents in establishments which did not innovate would refuse to answer numerous detailed questions concerning innovation activities which were not relevant for them. Accordingly, after some basic information was gathered, those establishments which stated not to have introduced any considerable product or process innovations during the preceding three years were advised to leave out a number of innovation-specific topics and pass on to the questions on cooperative relationships. The issues that have been left out by the non-innovators included the questions on main objectives of product and process innovation activities as well as the gatekeeper question. Therefore, two versions have been estimated. In a first version, (table 7.2) all establishments, innovators, and non-innovators, were included while the gatekeeper indicator as well as the indicators for the

---

[17] E.g., "training of personnel," "analysis of market conditions," "purchase of licenses or certain components," "experience with certain technologies."

[18] Estimations for the different kinds of relationship with a certain type of cooperation partner arrived at about the same results. In these estimations, the pseudo R^2 tended to be highest for relatively intense forms of cooperation (e.g., "joint R&D projects") and lowest for those kinds of cooperative relationships that are characterized by a low level of involvement (e.g., "casual contact for information purposes").

Table 7.2 *The propensity to cooperate with customers, suppliers, other firms and public research institutions – logit models including all establishments*[+]

	Customers	Suppliers	"Other" firms	Research institutions
Number of employees (ln)	0.324**	0.406**	0.190**	0.843**
	(6.24)	(8.08)	(3.87)	(13.56)
R&D-intensity	2.317**	1.751**	1.845**	5.173**
(share of R&D employees)	(3.96)	(3.55)	(3.82)	(8.57)
Share of value added to				
turnover	0.003	−0.100**	0.003	0.007*
(in percent)	(1.06)	(3.17)	(1.01)	(2.18)
Dummy for location in	−0.258	0.070	−0.246	−1.070**
Hanover region	(1.17)	(0.61)	(0.67)	(6.18)
Dummy for location in Baden	−0.265	−0.312*	−0.603**	−0.513**
	(1.90)	(2.27)	(4.00)	(3.18)
Industry dummies				
Food, beverages and tobacco	−0.871**	−0.316	−0.285	−0.540
	(2.80)	(1.04)	(0.88)	(1.58)
Textiles, clothing, leather	−0.248	−0.091	−0.382	−0.495
	(0.82)	(0.31)	(1.22)	(1.55)
Wood (excl. furniture)	−0.548	−0.228	−0.250	−1.000*
	(1.60)	(0.67)	(0.67)	(2.31)
Paper, printing, publishing	−0.492	−0.071	−0.340	−1.025**
	(1.65)	(0.24)	(1.15)	(3.00)
Furniture, jewelry, musical	−0.490	−0.216	−0.382	−0.956*
instruments, toys	(1.49)	(0.67)	(1.08)	(2.54)
Mineral oil, chemicals	0.066	−0.172	0.093	−0.343
	(0.19)	(0.52)	(0.27)	(0.93)
Rubber and plastics	−0.201	0.112	−0.155	−0.637
	(0.64)	(0.37)	(0.48)	(1.83)
Stone, ceramics and glass	−0.133	0.021	−0.028	−0.478
	(0.43)	(0.07)	(0.09)	(1.44)
Primary and fabricated metal	−0.290	−0.193	0.118	−0.726**
products, recycling	(1.13)	(0.78)	(0.46)	(2.62)
Mechanical engineering	0.083	0.094	0.094	0.029
	(0.31)	(0.38)	(0.03)	(0.11)
Vehicles	0.291	−0.051	−0.145	−0.278
	(0.73)	(0.144)	(0.39)	(0.70)
Data processing, electrical	0.409	0.142	0.081	−0.574
and electronic equipment	(1.30)	(0.49)	(0.28)	(1.83)
Model summary				
Chi-square for covariates	109.58	121.95	59.74	359.53
Significance Chi-square	0.00	0.00	0.00	0.00
Pseudo R$^{2\ adj.}$	0.053	0.057	0.03	0.181
Number of cases	1 546	1 540	1 539	1 537

Notes: + Estimated logit coefficients. Asymptotic t-values in parentheses. ** Statistically significant at the 1 percent level. * Statistically significant at the 5 percent level.

Table 7.3 *The propensity to cooperate with customers, suppliers, other firms and public research institutions – logit models including only establishments with innovations*[+]

	Customers	Suppliers	"Other" firms	Research institutions
Number of employees (ln)	0.141*	0.031**	0.162**	0.767**
	(2.01)	(4.79)	(2.62)	(9.99)
R&D-intensity	0.599	1.488*	1.766**	4.858**
(share of R&D employees)	(0.81)	(2.22)	(2.74)	(5.95)
Share of value added to turnover	0.002	−0.009*	0.004	0.004
(in percent)	(0.53)	(2.37)	(1.15)	(0.33)
Gatekeeper	0.287**	0.221**	0.105	0.241**
	(4.38)	(3.52)	(1.61)	(3.30)
Importance of new products as an objective of product	0.206**	0.044	0.171*	0.174*
innovation effort	(2.71)	(0.63)	(2.42)	(2.24)
Importance of cost reduction as an objective of process	0.075	0.212*	−0.131	−0.079
innovation effort	(0.70)	(2.13)	(1.32)	(0.07)
Dummy for location in	−0.187	0.055	−0.199	−1.178**
Hanover region	(0.93)	(0.29)	(1.09)	(5.56)
Dummy for location in Baden	−0.213	−0.284	−0.439*	−0.532**
	(1.05)	(1.53)	(2.31)	(2.56)
Industry dummies				
Food, beverages and tobacco	−0.683	0.095	0.029	−0.041
	(1.66)	(0.24)	(0.74)	(0.09)
Textiles, clothing, leather	−0.091	0.228	0.026	−0.123
	(0.23)	(0.60)	(0.07)	(0.31)
Wood (excl. furniture)	0.035	−0.129	0.229	−0.778
	(0.07)	(0.28)	(0.49)	(1.45)
Paper, printing, publishing	−0.074	0.231	0.639	−0.733
	(0.18)	(0.60)	(0.07)	(1.72)
Furniture, jewelry, musical	−0.216	−0.286	−0.055	−0.898
instruments, toys	(0.50)	(0.69)	(0.13)	(1.94)
Mineral oil, chemicals	−0.119	−0.324	0.361	−0.284*
	(0.28)	(0.83)	(0.93)	(0.66)
Rubber and plastics	−0.038	0.289	0.079	−0.165
	(0.09)	(0.72)	(0.19)	(0.38)
Stone, ceramics and glass	0.286	−0.080	−0.154	−0.173
	(0.66)	(0.21)	(0.39)	(0.41)
Primary and fabricated metal	0.026	−0.106	0.360	−0.642
products, recycling	(0.07)	(0.32)	(1.14)	(1.83)
Mechanical engineering	0.254	0.029	0.225	0.288
	(0.75)	(0.09)	(0.73)	(0.87)
Vehicles	0.380	0.077	0.305	−0.039
	(0.72)	(0.15)	(0.66)	(0.07)
Data processing, electrical and	0.605	−0.081	0.258	−0.361
electronic equipment	(1.48)	(0.23)	(0.74)	(0.94)

172   Michael Fritsch and Rolf Lukas

Table 7.3 (*cont.*)

	Customers	Suppliers	"Other" firms	Research institutions
Model summary				
Chi-square for covariates	67.88	81.00	41.84	240.38
Significance Chi-square	0.00	0.00	0.002	0.00
Pseudo R$^{2 \text{ adj.}}$	0.06	0.063	0.033	0.187
Number of cases	944	940	939	938

Notes: + Estimated logit coefficients. Asymptotic t-values in parentheses. ** Statistically significant at the 1 percent level. * Statistically significant at the 5 percent level.

objectives of innovation activities had to be left out. The second version was restricted to those establishments that had introduced considerable innovation during the preceding years and accounted for these three indicators (table 7.3).[19]

In the estimations for all establishments (innovators and non-innovators; table 7.2), size and R&D intensity are always statistically significant. According to the parameter estimates the importance of the two variables is considerably higher for cooperative relationships with research institutions than for cooperation with other types of actors. The coefficient for the share of value added to turnover shows a statistically significant negative sign in the estimation for cooperative relationships with suppliers. This indicates that cooperation with suppliers in many cases works as a substitute for own innovation activities. However, the positive sign of this variable in the estimation for cooperation with public research institutions suggests that cooperation with this type of partner tends to be complementary to internal R&D.

When restricting the estimations to the innovative establishments and including the gatekeeper variable as well as the indicators for main objectives of innovation activities (table 7.3) the impact of size and R&D intensity comes out to be much weaker. The gatekeeper appears to be important for cooperative relationships with suppliers, customers, and with research institutions but not for cooperation with "other" firms. The more product innovation activity is aiming at developing new products in contrast to a further development of already existing products the higher the propensity for R&D cooperation with customers, research institutions, and "other" firms. High importance of

[19] The difference with regard to the number of cases between these two approaches is caused by the omission of non-innovative establishments in the second version as well as by a relatively high share of missing values for the indicators for main objectives of product and process innovation.

rationalization for process innovation increases the likelihood for the existence of cooperative relationships with suppliers.

Industry dummy variables turn out to be statistically significant mainly in the first version of the estimations (table 7.2) and only with regard to cooperation with customers and research institutions. In these cases, the coefficients show a negative sign indicating that our control group, the medicine technology and optical instruments industry, is characterized by a relatively high propensity for cooperation. While this industry is rather high tech, those industries for which we find statistically significant coefficients in the estimations for cooperation with public research institutions have in common that they tend to be low tech and less science based. The negative sign for the food, beverage, and tobacco industry in the estimation for cooperation with customers implies that here the demand side (mainly the final consumer) is less involved in innovation activities than in the control group.

With regard to the regional dummy variables, we find that establishments in Baden and the Hanover region exhibit a lower propensity to cooperate with public research institutions than establishments in Saxony. Establishments in Baden are also less likely to maintain cooperative relationships with their suppliers and with "other" firms. These results are quite surprising because regional innovation systems in Baden and the Hanover region are well established while the innovation system in Saxony had to undergo radical changes during the transformation from a socialist to a market driven system in the last years. In this process public research institutions in Saxony have been subject to drastic reorganization and many of them experienced a severe turnover of personnel. Likewise, almost all of the manufacturing firms that survived the transition had to undergo fundamental changes with respect to the number of employees, their internal structure, and their market relations (Fritsch and Mallok, 1998). Many of the "old" networks have been destroyed by these developments so that a large part of cooperative relationships within Saxony's innovation system needed to be established anew. In contrast to that, Baden is said to be characterized by a sophisticated transfer infrastructure and a high level of interfirm cooperation (Cooke, 1996; Semlinger, 1993).

There are mainly three possible explanations for the higher propensity of establishments in Saxony to cooperate with public research institutions. The first explanation could be that many persons formerly employed in public research now work in private firms and that many of the "old" ties to research institutions have survived the transformation. Second, research institutions in the socialist innovation system, even if engaged in basic research, were characterized by a pronounced orientation towards the application of their results and this attitude of research personnel may be still widespread in Saxony leading to a relatively high level of cooperation with private firms. A third explanation could be based on differences in the local supply of respective research institutions between the regions.[20] All three explanations could only be plausible if locational proximity is important for cooperative relationships with public research institutions. This issue will be treated in the next section.[21]

7   Regional distribution of cooperation partners

From the responses to our questionnaire we know the number of cooperation partners by type of partner and region. Looking at the share of cooperation partners we find that a relatively high proportion are located in the respective Federal State (figure 7.2). This holds particularly for cooperative relationships with non-vertically related firms and with publicly funded research institutions. In 55.6 percent of all cooperative relationships with public research institutions the cooperation partners are located in the same region.[22] A somewhat similar picture can be found for cooperative relationships with non-vertically related firms. However, here the share of relationships with partners in the region is a little smaller but still amounts to more than 49.0 percent. The lowest

---

[20] In the questionnaire respondents were asked to assess the quality of certain characteristics of their regional environment for innovation activities. With regard to the response category "supply of research" we found that establishments in Saxony judged the supply of research in the region more positive than the establishments in the other two regions. However, this difference is only statistically significant with regard to Hanover, not with regard to Baden.

[21] It appears not very plausible to assume that the higher propensity to cooperate in Saxony is the result of the relatively high level of subsidies in East Germany because policy programs aimed at stimulating R&D cooperation of private firms have been operating in both parts of the country during the time under inspection here to a comparable degree, and respective support has been available already to West German firms before German unification.

[22] The importance of publicly funded research institutions within the same region becomes also quite clear if we look at the share of those manufacturing establishments maintaining only relationships with institutions within the same region. We find that for 67.7 percent of those establishments that maintain at least one relationship with publicly funded research institutions, these partners are entirely located in the same region. Of establishments that have a relationship with a partner outside their region, 72.5 percent also have at least one such relationship with a partner inside the region they are located. Note that for the Hanover–Brunswick–Göttingen region we have no information on the number of cooperative relationships with public research institutions so that figure 7.2 is based on the data for Saxony and Baden only.

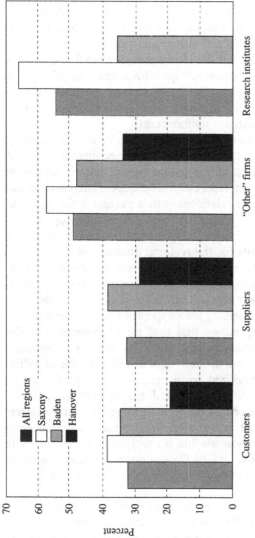

Figure 7.2 Share of cooperative relationships with customers, suppliers, "other" firms, and public research institutions located in the same region

share of cooperative relationships with partners in the same region (about 32 percent) can be found for customers.

To a certain degree, this general pattern holds for all three regions under inspection here. However, there are some striking differences. Remarkably, establishments in Saxony have the highest share of cooperative ties with customers, "other" firms, and public research institutions inside their region, while for the Hanover region we find the lowest share of regional cooperative relationships with respect to all types of (private) partners. This suggests that networks of establishments in Saxony are highly concentrated in their region while in Hanover local networking appears to be relatively unimportant.

In order to shed some more light on these regional differences we performed logit analyses for the propensity of establishments to maintain a cooperative relationship with a certain type of partner within the region and outside the region separately. The dependent variable had the value of 1 if a cooperative relationship to a partner inside (outside) the region existed and it is 0 if there was no such relationship. The set of explanatory variables is identical to those estimations reported in table 7.2. Based on the results for the regional dummy variables we can judge if the establishments in a region are less or more likely to maintain a cooperative relationship with a certain type of partner located inside or outside their region than the rest of the sample (table 7.4). Looking first at the propensity for cooperative relationships with a partner inside the same region, we find that establishments in Baden and in Hanover are significantly less likely to have a cooperative relationship with "other" firms in their region and that the establishments in Baden are characterized by a relatively low propensity to cooperate with research institutions located nearby. Obviously, local networking is more pronounced in the transforming innovation system of Saxony than in Baden and in Hanover. With regard to relationships with partners outside the region we find a relatively low propensity to cooperate with external customers in Hanover while establishments in Baden are more likely to cooperate with research institutions located elsewhere.

This evidence should, however, be interpreted with great care. We still do not know the causes of these differences and what they mean for regional performance with regard to innovation and growth. One reason for this reservation is that the propensity for having a cooperative relationship with a certain type of partner in a certain region depends – among other factors – on the supply of such partners in that region. Another reason is that the effect of having cooperative relationships with actors inside the region should not be overestimated. On the one hand, local

Table 7.4 *Logit analyses for the propensity of a cooperative relationship with different kinds of partners inside or outside the respective region including all establishments – results for regional dummy variables*[+]

	Dummy variable for location in	
Cooperative relationship with ...	Baden	Hanover
Customers		
inside the region	n.s.	n.s.
outside the region	n.s.	_*
Suppliers		
inside the region	n.s.	n.s.
outside the region	n.s.	n.s.
"Other" firms		
inside the region	_*	_*
outside the region	n.s.	n.s.
Public research institutions		
inside the region	_**	not tested
outside the region	+*	not tested

Notes: + ** Statistically significant at the 1 percent level. * Statistically significant at the 5 percent level. n.s. not statistically significant.

networking and the exploitation of agglomeration economies may have a significant effect on economic development of a region. However, the contribution of cooperative relationships depends on the needs of the respective actor as well as on the type and the structure of the relationships in question. Maximizing the number or share of (local) ties is not a strategy to be recommended at all (Grabher and Stark, 1997). On the other hand, local networks also need considerable ties to the "outer world" in order to be able to quickly absorb external knowledge for their innovation activities. There is little doubt that local cooperation matters but being more or less purely local in this respect may work as a disadvantage.

8 Regional systems of innovation

Our results clearly suggest that location matters for cooperation and that geographic distance tends to be unfavorable for the establishment of cooperative relationships. Therefore, we can conclude that innovation systems possess a pronounced regional dimension. Regions are

178   Michael Fritsch and Rolf Lukas

characterized by specific innovation systems that should be analyzed in order to understand the forces that make some areas competitive while others fall behind. Furthermore, our results suggest that having the appropriate supply of public research institutions and of non-vertically related firms located within the same region is more important than vertical ties to manufacturing suppliers or customers. Since the cooperative relationships with the non-vertically related firms are horizontal in nature, our results indicate the importance of localization economies. This corresponds to the empirical finding that innovation activities of a certain kind are concentrated in space (Audretsch and Feldman, 1996; Feldman, 1994). According to our analysis, cooperative relationships to suppliers and customers are far less pronounced with regard to their regional dimension.

Relating the propensity to maintain cooperative relationships to the performance of the respective innovation system in the three regions under inspection here, we can conclude that if local networking is conducive to innovation, this effect may be overcompensated by other factors. Further analysis of our data shows (cf. Fritsch, Franke, and Schwirten, 1998) that establishments in Baden perform much better with regard to innovation than those located in Saxony whereas a simple "cooperation is good for innovation" hypothesis would lead us to expect the reverse. But this only tells us what we already should know, i.e., that simple mono causal explanations do not suffice. Things are much more complex than that and deserve further careful analysis.

References

Acs, Zoltan J., David B. Audretsch, and Maryann P. Feldman (1992), "The Real Effects of Academic Research: Comment," *American Economic Review*, 82: 363–367.
    (1994), R&D "Spillovers and Recipient Firm Size," *Review of Economics and Statistics*, 76: 336–340.
Almeida, Paul and Bruce Kogut (1997), "The Exploration of Technological Diversity and the Geographic Localization of Innovation," *Small Business Economics*, 9: 21–31.
Anselin, Luc, Attila Varga, and Zoltan J. Acs (1997a), "Entrepreneurship, Geographic Spillovers and University Research: A Spatial Econometric Approach," Cambridge: ESRC Working Paper 59, University of Cambridge.
    (1997b), "Local Geographic Spillovers Between University Research and High Technology Innovation," *Journal of Urban Economics*, 42: 422–448.
Audretsch, David B. and Maryann P. Feldman (1996), "R&D Spillovers and the Geography of Innovation and Production," *American Economic Review*, 86: 630–640.

Audretsch, David B. and Paula E. Stephan (1996), "Company–Scientist Locational Links: The Case of Biotechnology," *American Economic Review*, 86: 641–652.

Axelsson, B. (1992), "Corporate Strategy Models and Networks – Diverging Perspectives," in B. Axelsson and G. Easton (eds.), *Industrial Networks: A New View of Reality*, London: Routledge, pp. 184–204.

Aydalot, P. and David Keeble (eds.) (1988), *High Technology Industry and Innovative Environments: The European Experience*, London.

Camagni, R. (ed.) (1991), *Innovation Networks: Spatial Perspectives*, London: Belhaven-Pinter.

Cohen, Wesley and D.A. Levinthal (1989), "Innovation and Learning: The Two Faces of R&D – Implications for the Analysis of R&D Investment," *Economic Journal*, 99: 569–596.

——— (1990), "Absorptive Capacity: A New Perspective on Learning and Innovation," *Administrative Science Quarterly*, 35: 128–152.

Cooke, Phillip (1996), "The New Wave of Regional Innovation Networks: Analysis, characteristics and strategy," *Small Business Economics*, 2: 159–171.

Dertouzos, Michael L., Richard K. Lester, and Robert M. Solow (1989), *Made in America: Regaining the Productive Edge*, Cambridge, Mass.: MIT Press.

Feldman, Maryann P. (1994), *The Geography of Innovation*, Boston: Kluwer.

Fritsch, Michael, Annette Broeskamp, and Christian Schwirten (1996), "Innovationen in der Sächsischen Industrie – Erste Ergebnisse einer Befragung" (Innovation in Saxony's manufacturing – First results), Freiberg: Working Paper 96/13, Faculty of Economics and Business Administration, Technical University Bergakademie Freiberg (in German).

Fritsch, Michael, Grit Franke, and Christian Schwirten (1998), "Innovationen im Verarbeitenden Gewerbe – Ein Ost–West Vergleich" (Innovation in manufacturing – An East–West comparison), in Michael Fritsch, Frieder Meyer-Krahmer and Franz Pleschak (eds.), *Innovationen in Ostdeutschland – Potentiale und Probleme*, Heidelberg: Physica, pp. 119–144 (in German).

Fritsch, Michael and Jörn Mallok (1998), "Surviving the Transition: The Process of Adaptation of Small and Medium-Sized Firms in East Germany," in Horst Brezinski, Egon Franck, and Michael Fritsch (eds.), *The Microeconomics of Transition and Growth*, Cheltenham/Brookfield: Edward Elgar Publishers, pp. 163–184

Fusfeld, H. and C. Haklish (1985), "Cooperative R&D for Competitors," *Harvard Business Review*, 63: 60–76.

Galaskiewicz, J. (1985), "Interorganizational Relations," *Annual Review of Sociology*, 8: 281–304.

Grabher, Gernot and David Stark (1997), "Organizing Diversity: Evolutionary Theory, Network Analysis and Postsocialism," *Regional Studies*, 31: 533–544.

Grotz, Reinhold and Boris Braun (1997), "Territorial or Trans-Territorial Networking: Spatial Aspects of Technology-Oriented Cooperation within the German Mechanical Engineering Industry," *Regional Studies*, 31: 545–557.

Jaffe, A.B. (1989), "Real Effects of Academic Research," *American Economic Review*, 79: 957–970.

Jaffe, A.B., M. Trajtenberg, and R. Henderson (1993), "Geographic Localization of Knowledge Spillovers as Evidenced by Patent Citations," *Quarterly Journal of Economics*, 108: 576–598.

Jewkes, J., D. Sawers, and R. Stillerman (1969), *The Sources of Invention*, 2nd. revised and enlarged edn, London: Macmillan.

Katz, Michael L. and Jamusz A. Ordover (1990), "R&D Cooperation and Competition," *Brookings Papers on Economic Activity – Microeconomics*, 137–203.

Kleinknecht, Alfred and Jeroen O.N. Reijnen (1992), "Why Do Firms Cooperate on R&D? An Empirical Study," *Research Policy*, 21: 347–360.

König, Heinz, Georg Licht, and Matthias Staat (1994), "F&E-Kooperationen und Innovationsaktivität" (*R&D Cooperation and Innovation Activity*), in Bernhard Gahlen, Helmut Hesse, and Hans-Jürgen Ramser (eds.), *Europäische Integrationsprobleme aus wirtschaftswissenschaftlicher Sicht*, Tübingen: Siebeck, pp. 219–242 (in German).

Link, Albert N. and John Rees (1990), "Firm Size, University Based Research, and the Returns to R&D," *Small Business Economics*, 2: 25–31.

Lundvall, Bengt-Ake (1992), "User-Producer Relationships, National Systems of Innovation and Internationalisation," in Bengt-Ake Lundvall (ed.), *National Systems of Innovation: Towards a Theory of Innovation and Interactive Learning*, London: Pinter, pp. 45–67.

(1993), "Explaining Interfirm Cooperation and Innovation – Limits of the Transaction-Cost Approach," in Gernot Grabher (ed.), *The Embedded Firm – On the Socioeconomics of Industrial Networks*, London: Routledge, pp. 52–64.

Maillat, Dennis, Olivier Crevoisier, and Bruno Lecoq (1994), "Innovation Networks and Territorial Dynamics: A Tentative Typology," in Börje Johansson, Charlie Karlsson, and Lars Westin (eds.), *Patterns of a Network Economy*, Berlin: Springer, pp. 33–52.

Nohria, Nitin and Robert Eccles (1992), "Face-to-Face: Making Network Organizations Work," in Nitin Nohria and Robert Eccles (eds.), *Networks and Organizations: Structure, Form, and Action*, Boston: Harvard Business School Press, pp. 288–308.

Powell, Walter W. (1990), "Neither Market Nor Hierarchy: Network Forms of Organization," *Research in Organizational Behavior*, 12: 295–336.

Sabel, Charles F. (1989), "Flexible Specialization and the Reemergence of Regional Economies," in P. Hirst and J. Zeitlin (eds.), *Reversing Industrial Decline*, New York: St. Martin's Press, pp. 17–70.

(1992), "Studied Trust: Building New Forms of Cooperation in a Volatile Economy," in Frank Pyke and Werner Sengenberger (eds.), *Industrial Districts and Local Economic Regeneration*, Geneva: International Institute for Labour Studies, pp. 215–250.

Saxenian, Annalee (1994), *Regional Advantage*, Cambridge, Mass.: Harvard University Press.

Schasse, Ulrich (1995), "Produkt- und Prozeßinnovationen in Niedersachsen" (*Product and Process Innovation in Lower Saxony*), in Ulrich Schasse and Joachim Wagner (eds.), *Erfolgreich produzieren in Niedersachsen*, Hanover: Niedersächsisches Institut für Wirtschaftsforschung (NIW-Vortragsreihe, Bd. 10), pp. 61–82.

Semlinger, Klaus (1993), "Economic Development and Industrial Policy in Baden-Württemberg: Small Firms in a Benevolent Environment," *European Planning Studies*, 1: 435–463.

Spencer W.J. and P. Grindley (1993), "SEMATECH after Five Years: High-Technology Consortia and US Competitiveness," *California Management Review*, 35: 9–32.

Storper, Michael (1992), "The Limits of Globalization: Technology Districts and International Trade," *Economic Geography*, 28: 60–93.

Teece, David J. (1986), "Profiting from Technological Innovation – Implications for Integration, Collaboration, Licensing and Public Policy," *Research Policy*, 15: 285–305.

(1992), "Competition, Cooperation and Innovation – Organizational Arrangements for Regimes of Rapid Technological Progress," *Journal of Economic Behavior and Organization*, 18: 1–15.

Thorelli, H. B. (1986), "Networks: Between Markets and Hierarchies," *Strategic Management Journal*, 7: 37–51.

Tödtling, Franz (1995), "The Innovation Process and Local Environment," in Sergio Conti, Edward J. Malecki, and Päivi Oinas (eds.), *The Industrial Enterprise and Its Environment: Spatial Perspectives*, Aldershot: Avebury, pp. 171–193.

8 Industry clusters: biotechnology/biomedicine and polymers in Ohio and Sweden

Bo Carlsson and Pontus Braunerhjelm

1 Introduction

Since the mid 1970s, economic growth at the macro level has been much slower and the unemployment rate much higher in Europe than in the United States and Japan. But performance has varied considerably among countries, regions, and industries. For example, Sweden has had particularly slow growth, its GDP per capita sliding from among the very top in international comparison in 1975 to below the OECD average in 1996. In the United States, too, there have been marked regional variations ranging from sharp contractions, particularly in manufacturing, in the early 1980s in the mid-west to stellar performance in the same region more recently, and with generally higher growth in the sunbelt and on the west coast throughout the period. Ohio is part of the industrial heartland (often referred to as the "rustbelt" in the 1980s) of the United States and constitutes an example of a heavily industrial region which suffered a disastrous economic decline in the early 1980s but is now recovering by retooling in some areas of previous strength while at the same time generating new activities, particularly in services.

Two sectors which have had consistently high growth during the last two decades, wherever they are present, are those based on biotechnology/biomedical engineering and polymers. Similarly to many other

Financial support from the Swedish Employers' Confederation and the Swedish National Board for Industrial and Technical Development, as well as research assistance by Dilek Karaomerlioglu and Dan Johansson, is gratefully acknowledged. We would also like to thank Dorothy Baunach, Rinaldo Evangelista, Frank Samuel, and the participants in the conference on "The impact of technological change on firm and industry performance," 29–30 August 1997. Tinbergen Institute, Erasmus University Rotterdam, as well as the participants in the Workshop on Innovation and Services at the Centre for Research on Innovation and Competition, the University of Manchester, March 16–18, 1998, for helpful comments on previous drafts.

industries, the activity in these sectors tends to cluster in certain regions. What is it that enables regions to foster innovation, entrepreneurship, and growth in these particular sectors? That is the question motivating this study.

We take the view that economic activity takes place within the context of a *technological system* consisting of networks of agents (firms, organizations, and individuals) who interact with each other under a particular infrastructure made up of academic institutions, research institutes, financial institutions, government agencies, and industry associations (Carlsson and Stankiewicz, 1991, p. 111).[1] Some aspects of the infrastructure may be specific to a country or region, while others are specific to industries or fields of technology. The geographic boundaries of a technological system do not necessarily coincide with national borders, but a technological system in a region within a country may be heavily influenced by certain national characteristics and institutions.[2] The role and composition of the infrastructure clearly vary from one field of technology to another and influence both market and non-market interaction. The market interaction among agents is governed also by the general rules of the economic game, for example with regard to entrepreneurship, the functioning and openness of markets for capital, labor, goods, and services, as well as by other aspects of the business climate. The non-market interaction is influenced particularly by social, cultural, historical, and political factors.

There are several reasons for studying Sweden and the state of Ohio. Given the variations among regions within Europe and the United States, it makes sense to study smaller, more homogeneous regions of similar size experiencing the same problems but also exhibiting differences in infrastructure and economic performance. Sweden and the state of Ohio are of similar size (8.7 and 10.8 million inhabitants, respectively, in 1993), overall level of development (GDP/capita in 1993 of $16,800 in Sweden and $23,300 in Ohio), and industrial structure (18.3 percent versus 21.5 percent of the total labor force in manufacturing in 1993). Both have suffered a severe economic decline in the last two decades and are struggling to restructure and build for the future.

But most important among all the reasons for comparing Ohio and Sweden is the following. Although the existing economic structures are similar, Ohio entered its severe economic crisis about a decade before

---

[1] For further discussion of technological systems, see Carlsson (1995) and Carlsson (1997).

[2] Thus, technological systems and so-called National Systems of Innovation (Freeman 1988; Lundvall 1988 and 1992; and Nelson 1988 and 1993) are complements, not substitutes.

Sweden and has now come a long way toward recovery while Sweden is only now beginning to recover. What lessons are there to be learned from the Ohio experience?

Even though dealing with the economic crisis involves restructuring of existing activities and shifting to new activities, the new activities do not emerge out of thin air. As will be shown below, the path dependence is strong: the infrastructure and areas of competence built in the past determine, in large measure, the activities that are likely to prosper in the future.

Among the new lines of economic activity which have become focal points in both Ohio and Sweden are biomedicine/biotechnology and polymers.[3] Both of these fields are based on new discoveries in science and engineering and are also strongly tied to existing industrial capabilities. However, they do not correspond well to any particular Standard Industrial Classification codes. They represent *technologies and competencies* in a broad sense rather than *industries* and are found in many different types of businesses. They also go beyond the "industry" in that they encompass entities outside the market process, in addition to firms within the "industry" and those in upstream and downstream activities.

It is useful to define the relationships among three key concepts used in the present study. *Industry* is used in the conventional way as referring to groups of firms producing similar products. *Clusters* refer to groups of firms whose activities are closely related (and geographically close) even if they are not in the same industry. Clusters are sometimes narrower, sometimes broader than industries in their makeup; they may consist of subsets of firms in several industries. *Technological systems* constitute the broader framework within which clusters function. As stated earlier, they are made up of networks of actors (not just business firms) interacting with each other both via markets and outside the market. They include the infrastructure.

The focus of the study is on the origins, extent and composition of the technological systems surrounding activities involving biomedicine/biotechnology and polymers in each region. Who are the main actors both in the industrial/commercial arena and in the science, research, and institutional infrastructure? What is the nature of clustering of activity, both geographically and in other dimensions, within each region? To

---

[3] As explained below, biomedicine/biotechnology refers to biopharmaceuticals, medical devices, and health-care software. Thus this system is not a "pure" technological system but consists of a cluster of technologies; the boundaries of the system are defined by the users: health-care providers and consumers.

Polymers are defined as "naturally occurring or synthetic substances consisting of giant molecules formed from smaller molecules of the same substance and often having a definite arrangement of the components of the giant molecules" (Webster's *New World Dictionary*).

what extent are today's growth sectors rooted in traditional industrial know-how? What are the characteristics of the networks holding these systems together, not only in terms of user–producer relationships but also problem-solving and informal networks? What has been the role of public policy in shaping these clusters? What are the policy implications for the future for both private entities and public policy makers?

The paper is organized as follows. In the next section we provide the historical background concerning the macroeconomic performance in Ohio and Sweden, the present industrial structure, and the need to restructure. We then present the methods we have used to identify the biomedical/biotechnology and polymer clusters. This is followed by a brief description of each cluster in both countries, and their recent development. In the concluding section we compare the results across clusters and countries and discuss some of the implications for policy and further research.

2   Historical background

Macroeconomic Performance

As shown in figure 8.1, GDP has grown more slowly in Ohio and Sweden than in the United States as a whole and in the OECD area since 1975. The Ohio economy went into a severe decline in 1979, bottomed out in 1982, and has since rebounded nicely, particularly in the early 1990s. Meanwhile, the Swedish economy stagnated in the mid 1970s and then grew only slowly compared with other OECD countries. Sweden's GDP even declined in absolute terms during 1991–1993, similarly to the development in Ohio for 1980–1982.

Manufacturing output also took a nosedive in Ohio 1979–1982 but has since made a comeback, interrupted by another recession in 1991; the growth has continued even more strongly in the last few years. In Sweden, manufacturing output kept pace with that in the US and OECD until 1989 and then fell sharply, but has grown rapidly since 1993.

Figure 8.2 shows that in spite of Ohio's poor performance in manufacturing in the 1980s, it has done quite well in creating jobs – better than the OECD area over the period as a whole – while Sweden has done extremely poorly in this regard in the last few years.

Entrepreneurial activity is difficult to measure. A partial (and certainly not ideal) indicator is the net increase in the number of firms in any given activity.[4] Over the period 1981–1993, the number of establishments in all

---

[4]   Gross entry and exit of firms would be a better measure, but such data are not available for the present study.

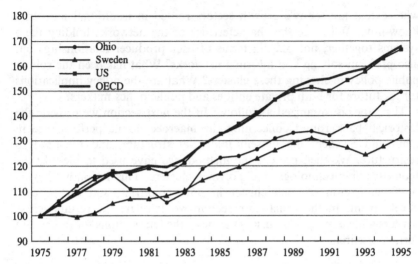

Figure 8.1   GDP in Ohio, Sweden, United States, and OECD, 1975–1995 (Index, 1975 = 100).

Sources: Ohio: H.L. Friedenberg and R.M. Beemiller, 1997. Sweden and the United States: IMF, 1991 and 1996, *International Financial Statistics*; OECD, 1993; OECD, 1996.

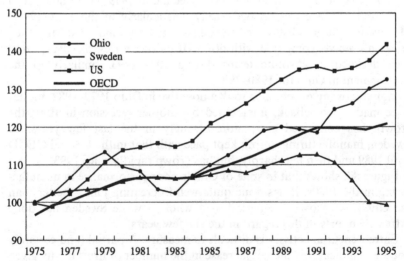

Figure 8.2   Civilian employment in Ohio, Sweden, the United States, and OECD, 1975–1995 (Index, 1975 = 100).

Sources: OECD, Sweden, and the United States: OECD, various issues, *Historical Statistics*; Ohio: Regional Financial Associates.

sectors rose by nearly 45 percent in the United States, while it increased by only 24 and 26 percent in Sweden and Ohio, respectively.

Industry Structure

Thus, all of these macroeconomic measures indicate lagging performance in both Ohio and Sweden relative to the United States in the last two decades. Some of the reasons for this poor performance are structural. In another study (Braunerhjelm and Carlsson, 1998) we have compared the composition of industries in Ohio and Sweden to that in the United States. We found that Ohio is most heavily over-represented in primary metal products; rubber and miscellaneous plastics products; and fabricated metal products. Moreover, during the period 1975–1995, Ohio's share of US activity increased in these industries, even though both primary metals and fabricated metal products declined in employment in Ohio. In other words, these industries declined even faster elsewhere in the US.

The corresponding data for Sweden show that metal mining; communications; health, education, and social services; and paper and allied products are the relatively largest industries in Sweden. Except for health, education, and social services and transportation services, all of the relatively largest industries saw their employment decline in relation to that in the United States between 1975 and 1993, contrary to the development in Ohio. But similarly to Ohio, the labor force in these large industries was reduced (again with the exception of the health, etc., sector; transportation services; and construction). Also, the number of establishments increased in most of these industries, in spite of declining employment.

These developments provide an important explanation for the relatively poor performance of both Ohio and Sweden relative to the United States in terms of employment growth over the last two decades. They either gained shares in declining industries (this is true for Ohio) or lost shares in declining industries with only modest gains in other sectors (as in Sweden).

A similar picture emerges if we look at clusters of industries. Rather than looking at each industry as being independent of all others, we take into account the fact that many industries are actually closely related to others (see Braunerhjelm and Carlsson (1998) for further details). It turns out that the largest clusters in Ohio are industrial machinery and equipment; fabricated metal products; transportation equipment; primary metal products; rubber and miscellaneous plastics products; and stone, clay, and glass products. The clusters identified in Sweden contain a mixture of service and manufacturing industries. The largest is transportation services.[5] The other identified clusters are traditional

[5] This result is somewhat surprising; it is due in large measure to a high location quotient in 1993 which, in turn, reflects the inclusion of government workers in this sector in the

manufacturing industries for which Sweden has long been known: industrial machinery and equipment; fabricated metal products; transportation equipment; primary metal industries; and paper and allied products. This list contains no surprises. Thus, the largest manufacturing clusters are exactly the same in Ohio and Sweden.

As noted earlier, all of these clusters are characterized by slow growth or even decline. This is clearly one of the factors behind the relatively poor macroeconomic performance of both Ohio and Sweden in the last couple of decades; there is a high degree of path dependence. The question that arises is: to what extent is it possible to find ways to turn this around and to build new clusters, either in entirely new and expansive areas – loosening the grip of the past – or perhaps even in clusters drawing upon old strengths put to new uses – turning old knowledge into new assets?

As will be explained in what follows, the biotechnology/biomedical cluster is an example of activity in an emerging field, whereas the polymer-based cluster is rooted in existing industries looking to expand through application of new technology as well as new applications of existing technology.

3   Cluster definition: methodology and data

Neither of the clusters in which we are interested is well represented by any particular industry. Given that they are both based on *generic technologies*[6] with application in a variety of *industries*, the coverage in industrial statistics is fragmented. There is no industry whose output consists entirely of goods produced with the generic technology, and there are many industries some of whose output is produced using the generic technology.[7] Thus, if one wants to study these clusters, the first task is to define the activities and boundaries of each.

The biotechnology/biomedical cluster in Ohio and Sweden

Given all the attention devoted to biotechnology in recent years, it is tempting to start with the assumption that the application of genetic

Swedish data but not in the Ohio data. Further exploration of this finding is certainly warranted.

[6]   These technologies are based on biomedical engineering, biotechnology, and macromolecular science.

[7]   This problem is not unique to these technologies but is more important here than in most other "industries."

Table 8.1 *Biotechnology/biomedical industry in Ohio and the United States, 1983 and 1994*

SIC	Industry	Employment	
		1983	1994
283	Pharmaceutical industry		
	Ohio	3,658	2,975
	US	167,259	200,284
	Ohio's share, %	2.19	1.49
384	Medical instruments and supplies		
	Ohio	4,842	11,961
	US	145,803	271,771
	Ohio's share, %	3.32	4.40
8071	Medical laboratories		
	Ohio	2,298	5,315
	US	65,904	150,921
	Ohio's share, %	3.49	3.52
3821, 3823,	Measuring and controlling devices excl.		
3824, 3826,	environmental controls and		
3827, 3829	instruments to measure electricity		
	Ohio	6,144	10,098
	US	96,162	170,989
	Ohio's share, %	6.39	5.90
	Total of above		
	Ohio	16,942	30,349
	US	475,128	793,965
	Ohio's share, %	3.57	3.82

Source: US Bureau of the Census, *County Business Patterns*, 1983 and 1994.

engineering is the appropriate focus. Indeed, most studies have focused on drugs developed with genetic engineering techniques, i.e., biopharmaceuticals. This amounts to the assumption that the pharmaceutical industry constitutes the core of the cluster. But as will be made clear below, that is not the most appropriate assumption if one wants to study significant activity in Ohio and Sweden.[8]

[8] Using the Ohio input/output table for 1994 (which is based on three-digit SIC level data), we added together those industries whose interaction with the drug industry exceeded 10 percent of that industry's total purchases (inputs) or sales (outputs). The resulting cluster turned out to have an employment level in 1995 of over 650,000, representing 14.6 percent of total employment in Ohio (a slight decline from just over 15 percent in 1985). This is much too broad, since it included all of the employment in a large number of industries which have only a minor connection with the drug industry in Ohio.

Taking the drug industry as defined by the respective region's official statistics (SIC 283), only a subset of the biotech/biomedical activities are captured. Using this definition, the drug industry has declined in Ohio (but not in Sweden). This approach suffers from several weaknesses. Most important is that only a fraction of drugs produced today are based on biotechnology (genetic engineering); in that sense, the pharmaceutical industry is too broad. Alternative definitions may again yield completely different figures. For instance, as suggested by Berry (1996), if the definition is based on the industries whose main output consists of products used in the health care sector, then the number of employees in Ohio is found to have almost doubled over the last decade. Taking the end user (rather than the product) as the departure point implies that medical instruments and laboratories, together with measuring and controlling devices, are also included in the biotech/ biomedicine area.

Clearly a cluster definition which is useful in the present context would have to cut across several industries. Even so, the Census Bureau data include neither upstream and downstream activities nor any kind of non-market interaction among agents within the technological system. Therefore, we decided to pursue a different approach.[9] After reviewing recent literature about biomedical and biotechnology developments in Ohio, we consulted with the Edison BioTechnology Center (EBTC). EBTC is one of seven "centers of excellence" in the Ohio Edison program which constitutes the core of Ohio's technology policy. In spite of its name, EBTC is concerned with a far broader range of activities than biotechnology alone. Its mission is to strengthen the Ohio economy by creating, retaining, growing, and attracting companies in the fields of *biopharmaceuticals, medical devices, and health-care software*.[10] We decided to take as a starting point a directory of biotechnology and biomedical firms in Ohio put together biannually by the EBTC. It is based on a survey of companies with activities in relevant fields. The coverage is consistent with EBTC's mission. One of the problems with the data is that they are

[9] Yet another approach which we are also pursuing (although not in this chapter) is to examine patent citation data. By analyzing the patents obtained by Ohio firms with regard to the patents cited in each application, it is possible to get an idea of the linkages and boundaries of the supporting knowledge network.

[10] *Biotechnology* is defined by EBTC as pharmaceutical products based on biologically derived substances rather than chemically based substances. This definition excludes applications in other industries (e.g., agriculture, food, and beverages). *Medical devices* are health-care products that, unlike drugs, do not achieve their intended purpose through chemical action in the body. *Health-care software* is computer software applied to the manufacture, testing, and use of health-care products.

Table 8.2 *Distribution by industry of biomedical and biotechnology firms in Ohio, 1996*

SIC	Industry	Employment	% of emp.	Number of firms	% of firms
384	Medical instruments and supplies	10,602	20.5	62	14.5
283	Drugs	7,275	14.1	37	8.7
284	Soap, cleaners, and toilet goods	7,226	14.0	8	1.9
873	Research and testing services	4,470	8.6	52	12.2
5912	Drug and proprietary stores	2,499	4.8	1	0.2
382	Measuring and controlling devices	2,468	4.8	22	5.2
26	Paper and allied products	2,190	4.2	6	1.4
8711+ 8742	Engineering services & mgmt consulting services	1,865	3.6	46	10.8
35	Industrial machinery and equipment	1,835	3.5	24	5.6
308	Misc. plastics products, nec	1,608	3.1	10	2.3
289	Misc. chemical products	1,581	3.1	5	1.2
3069	Fabricated rubber prdts, NEC	1,462	2.8	7	1.6
282	Plastics materials and synthetics	645	1.2	4	0.9
	Other industries	6,027	11.6	143	33.5
	Total	51,753	100.0	427	100.0

Sources: Edison Bio Technology Center, 1996, *Directory of Ohio Biomedical & Biotechnology Companies, 1996,* Cleveland: EBTC.
Harris Registry of Manufacturing Companies.

not classified by industry and thus are difficult to use for the kind of study we have in mind. However, by combining data in the EBTC directory with the Harris Directory of firms in manufacturing, as well as other sources, we have managed to classify all but 87 of the 427 firms in the directory. The results are summarized in table 8.2.

The table shows that the single largest three-digit industry represented among the Ohio biomedical/biotechnology firms is medical instruments and supplies. It makes up about 20 percent of the total employment of the companies in the directory. The pharmaceutical industry and companies manufacturing soap, cleaners, and toilet goods represent about 14 percent each. These three industries together represent about half of the total employment in the directory firms. If we rank by the number of firms instead, the largest industries are medical instruments and supplies; research and testing services; and engineering and management consulting services.

In the case of Sweden, the data currently available emanate from private surveys undertaken by Bioprint Publishing and Consulting AB (Grönberg, 1996 and 1997). If the firms in the agriculture and the food industries are removed, there are approximately 230 biomedical/biotech firms in Sweden. The data on firms are limited to the geographic location, their specialization in production, the number of employees (in broad size classes), and the year of establishment. By combining the directory data with information obtained for the same firms from the Sweden Statistics (*Företagsregistret*, The Firm Register) we were also able to get data on sales and more precise employment data. In terms of employment, the top two industries in this cluster in Sweden are pharmaceuticals and medical instruments and supplies.

The Polymer Cluster in Ohio and Sweden

Polymers have applications in many different products and industries. Thus, we encounter the same problem in defining "the polymer cluster" as in "the biomedical/biotech cluster." Again, having considered and tried various approaches, we ended up using the *Ohio Polymer Directory* published by the Edison Polymer Innovation Corporation, another one of the "centers of excellence" within the Ohio Edison program. The directory provides information on the names, addresses, and main products of polymer-related firms in Ohio, classified in six major categories: machinery manufacturers, materials manufacturers, mold manufacturers, processors, service providers, and tool and die manufacturers. These categories do not correspond directly to the Standard Industrial Classification codes. In order to classify the firms by industry and to obtain information on employment and sales, we turned to the Harris Directory and were thus able to classify the 2,800 firms in the directory. The industries represented, ranked in declining order of employment in the directory firms, are listed in table 8.3. If all the four-digit industries in SIC 30 (plastic and rubber products) are added together, they represent 33 percent of the total employment in the polymer sector. Other industries which are represented, although at lower levels of total employment and with much less industry coverage, are motor vehicles and parts (SIC 37) and industrial machinery (SIC 35).

Table 8.3 *Polymer industry in Ohio 1996 (based on directory listings)*

SIC	(Primary)	Number of establishments	% of total	Employ- ment	% of total
3089	Plastic prdts	683	24.12	56,887	20.81
3069	Fabricated rubber prdts, NEC	116	4.10	21,590	7.90
3544	Dies, tools, jigs, fixtures and ind. molds	277	9.78	12,957	4.74
3714	Motor vehicle parts and access	30	1.06	7,186	2.63
3559	Special ind. machinery, NEC	67	2.37	6,487	2.37
3562	Ball and roller bearings	1	0.04	6,300	2.30
2899	Chemical preparations, NEC	33	1.17	5,508	2.01
8731	Commercial physical research	20	0.71	5,374	1.97
3599	Machinery, except electrical, NEC	153	5.40	5,277	1.93
3312	Blast furnaces, coke ovens, steel and rolling mills	3	0.11	5,030	1.84
2891	Adhesives and sealants	37	1.31	4,824	1.76
2869	Industrial organic chemicals, NEC	14	0.49	4,246	1.55
2851	Paints, varnishes, lacquers, enamels	41	1.45	4,229	1.55
2671	Paper coating and laminating for packaging	4	0.14	4,136	1.51
2821	Plastics, mtrls and non-vulcanizable elastomers	57	2.01	3,324	1.22
2621	Paper mills	3	0.11	3,250	1.19
3011	Tires and inner tubes	10	0.35	3,107	1.14
	Other industries	1,283	45.30	113,701	41.59
	Total reported in directory	2,832	100	273,413	100

Sources: Edison Polymer Innovation Corporation (EPIC), 1996 *Ohio Polymer Directory*, Brechsville, OH: EPIC. US Bureau of the Census, *County Business Patterns, 1994*.

Also the Swedish polymer cluster is much larger than the biotech/ biomedical cluster. Altogether it contains 1,400 firms and represents approximately 10 percent of employment in the Swedish manufacturing sector. Most of the firms are small or medium sized and are involved in manufacture of relatively simple plastic components. Both manufacturing and service firms are included in the population of polymer firms which have been derived primarily from industry directories, but also other sources have been implemented Ekonomisk Litteratur AB (1996), Skandinavisk plantindustri 97 (*Scandinavian Plastics Industry 97*), Stockholm: Almquist & Wicksell AB. One indication of the difference as compared to the official Swedish statistics on the chemical industry is that the polymer cluster employment is about 35 percent larger.

Interviews

In addition to the above data on commercial activity we also have obtained data on the non-market aspects of each technological system: academic research, venture capital, bridging institutions between academic research and industry and between new startups and venture capital, networks of contacts involving all types of entities within each system, as well as other aspects of infrastructure. The primary means of collection of these data has been interviews, but we have also consulted various other sources. Thus far we have made 27 interviews in Ohio (13 in biotech/biomedicine, ten in polymers, and four with venture capitalists) and 18 in Sweden (five in biotech/biomedicine, ten in polymers, and three with venture capitalists).

4   Size, composition, and origin of each technological system

The biomedical/biotechnology system in Ohio

The industrial/commercial cluster

The biomedical/biotechnology system in Ohio consists of a large number of actors in research, goods and service production, finance, and technology policy. The number of goods- and service-producing companies is about 425 firms with a total employment exceeding 50,000 and estimated sales of about $15 billion in 1996. The cluster may be divided into three main groups: one based on drug manufacture and related services, one consisting primarily of medical supplies (intermediary products used by health care providers and drug companies, as well as products used directly by patients/consumers), and one focused on medical hardware (apparatus and instruments). The first group represents nearly half of the firms, employment, and estimated sales in the cluster. The other half is divided roughly equally between medical supply and hardware companies. The drug companies tend to be older and larger than other firms in the cluster, while service providers (companies producing software, laboratory services, and manufacturing and engineering services) tend to be the youngest and smallest (see table 8.4).

About half of the sales in the biomedical/biotechnology cluster in Ohio are made up of medical and diagnostic equipment. Three of the largest companies, each with annual sales exceeding $700 million, are Picker International (manufacturer of CAT scanners and other imaging equipment), Invacare (the world's largest manufacturer of wheelchairs), and Steris (manufacturer of sterilization equipment). Picker International was established in 1915 and Invacare in 1971; the manufacturing

Table 8.4 *Comparison of firms in the biomedical/biotech cluster in Sweden and Ohio, 1996*

	Number of firms		No. of employees		Sales, $ million		Establishment year		Employees/firm		Sales/firm, $ million	
	Sweden	Ohio	Sweden	Ohio	Sweden	Ohio	Sweden	Ohio	Sweden	Ohio	Sweden	Ohio
Diagnostics	18	77	314	7,257	38	3,886	1986	1979	17.4	94.2	2.1	50.5
Medical equipment	71	138	8,771	14,476	1,833	4,043	1981	1971	123.5	104.9	25.8	29.3
Medical supplies	111	101	2,812	13,880	403	795	1982	1966	25.3	137.4	3.6	7.9
Software	13	30	195	2,054	15	257	1989	1987	15.0	68.5	1.2	8.6
Pharmaceuticals	17	51	13,676	11,025	3,839	4,138	1973	1960	804.5	216.2	225.8	81.1
Mfg and eng. services		25		3,483		1,879		1981		139.3		75.2
	230	422	25,768	52,175	6,128	14,998	1981	1972	112.0	123.6	26.6	35.5

activities of both these companies are closely related to the industrial machinery cluster which has long dominated the industrial landscape in Ohio. Steris was founded much more recently (1987), with both capital input and other support from Invacare. The manufacturing know-how in these companies is part of the old manufacturing base in Ohio, while the marketing is oriented to a "new" area, namely the medical sector. The older companies (particularly Picker International and Invacare) have continued to grow rapidly as a result of broadening of the product base and market expansion both domestically and overseas. Their linkages to the Ohio economy are becoming weaker as a result of this process and also because inputs such as electronic devices and highly trained and specialized labor are sourced globally, not locally. This does not mean that firms are leaving the area, only that the determinants for originally locating in the area are no longer important.

Most if not all of the companies interviewed indicated that the Ohio location was either favorable or of minor importance. Among the most important factors for new firms is the availability of venture capital in the form of local venture capitalists as well as venture capital firms based in other parts of the United States where the competition for venture capital is keener. Proximity to major markets and attractive living conditions (including low housing costs) were also often mentioned as favorable factors.

The biomedical/biotechnology cluster also includes a number of younger and smaller companies in entirely new areas. Some of these are biotech companies which are much more research intensive than their older counterparts. In fact, many of them have no products at all to sell; all their revenues consist of research funding in the form of research grants as well as seed or venture capital. Several of these companies are university spin-offs or have other important ties to academic research, particularly at Case Western Reserve University (CWRU). Once the companies are established, their local ties become less important as they network with and recruit from universities everywhere. Other companies are software companies, consulting firms, and specialized manufacturing, engineering, and other service companies. An interesting question for further research is the extent to which these companies would exist at all in Ohio if it were not for the prior existence of a strong manufacturing base in closely related areas and of a significant research base in relevant fields.

The Infrastructure

In addition to the cluster of commercially oriented firms, the technological system also encompasses a number of other entities which together form the infrastructure: research units in universities and hospitals, medical clinics, policy organizations and other institutions, as well as venture capitalists and other financial entities. In biomedical engineering research the largest units in northeast Ohio are The Cleveland Clinic Foundation (created by The Cleveland Clinic, one of the largest hospitals in the United States) and Case Western Reserve University (CWRU) whose Department of Biomedical Engineering is one of the leading institutions in its field in the United States (in terms of number of faculty and size of both graduate and undergraduate programs as well as research funding). Other engineering departments as well as the School of Medicine at CWRU, other hospitals in the Cleveland area, and the University of Akron are other important research units. Together these institutions spend about $17 million on biomedical engineering research annually.[11] To this amount should be added the research which is conducted in other parts of Ohio (The Ohio State University in Columbus, The University of Cincinnati, and other universities and hospitals) for which no data are currently available. We estimate that the total amount spent annually on academic biomedical engineering research in Ohio is about $25–30 million. Most of this research is funded by the National Institutes of Health, the National Science Foundation, and other federal sources.

The Edison BioTechnology Center (EBTC) plays an important dual role as a "bridging institution" between academic research (particularly at CWRU) and industry and between new startups and potential financiers. EBTC, founded in 1987, is an independent non-profit organization affiliated with the Ohio Edison Program. It works closely with the leading universities and medical institutions, businesses, foundations, and civic and state organizations in Ohio. EBTC also collaborates with Enterprise Development, Inc. (EDI), a joint venture between the Weatherhead School of Management at CWRU and the Edison Program. EBTC's primary task is to encourage and support the creation of new firms based on biomedical engineering and biotechnology. This is done through technical and business assistance and advice (especially in writing business plans), training courses and seminars, and especially through two business incubators in which newly started companies have free access to office space, laboratory facilities and equipment, office

---

[11] Data obtained from Cindy Brogan, unpublished scientific paper, EBTC. The total expenditures on medical (not just biomedical engineering) research in Ohio are, of course, many times larger. According to the National Institutes of Health, total NIH funding of medical research in Ohio in 1997 amounted to $307 million. More than half of this amount, $156 million, went to northeast Ohio, with CWRU alone receiving about $120.

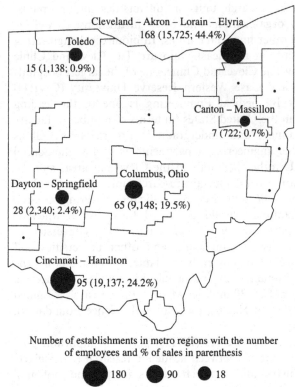

Figure 8.3 Regional distribution of biomedical/biotechnology firms in Ohio, 1996.

services, and advice in exchange for a modest rent over a maximum of five years.[12] An important function of EDI is to arrange conferences a few times each year to bring together people interested in presenting their business plans with venture capitalists.

There are currently 17 venture capital firms in Ohio with a total capital of $9.6 billion, about $2 billion of which is estimated to be committed to biomedicine/biotechnology. All but four of these firms were founded after 1980. In addition to these local companies there are also venture capitalists whose main activities are outside Ohio. There are also "business angels" who are willing to provide "seed" and "startup" capital.

[12] It is important to note that these incubators are specialized in biotechnology/ biomedicine. There are eight other Edison incubators in Ohio, plus a number of incubators not associated with the Edison Program.

In addition to the roughly $30 million spent annually in Ohio on academic research in biomedical engineering there is considerable research and development work (particularly the latter) in private companies in these fields. While no data are available, a conservative estimate would be that at least 5 percent of sales revenue – and probably much more – is spent on R&D. This would mean a minimum of $1 billion per year.

The biomedical/biotechnology firms are heavily concentrated in the major metropolitan areas where the major universities are also located (see figure 8.3). About three-quarters of the firms and employment and almost 90 percent of the sales are associated with firms in Cleveland, Cincinnati, and Columbus, the three largest metropolitan areas. These three regions also have a disproportionate share of the newest firms. The chemically based drug industry is most prominently represented in Cincinnati (strongly associated with Procter & Gamble), while the biotechnology-based sector is tied primarily to Cleveland.

The biomedical/biotechnology system in Sweden

The industrial/commercial cluster

The core of this cluster in Sweden is made up of pharmaceutical companies. These represent nearly two-thirds of total sales in the biomedical/biotechnology cluster, with medical equipment firms making up another 30 percent. There are 230 companies in total with combined sales of about $6 billion in 1996 (about $3.5 billion if the drug companies are excluded) and total employment of approximately 26,000 persons (including 14,000 in pharmaceutical companies). Thus, the drug companies make up a much higher share than in Ohio (see table 8.4).

The pharmaceutical industry has a long history in Sweden and has enjoyed extraordinary sales growth in the 1980s and 1990s while at the same time undergoing rapid consolidation. The number of drug companies was reduced from seven major companies in the late 1970s to only two today (Stankiewicz, 1997, p. 95): Astra and Pharmacia-Upjohn, the latter the result of a 1995 merger of Pharmacia with the US Upjohn company. The rapid sales growth has been generated by extremely successful innovation in the form of new drugs, including the first beta blocker to be approved by the Food and Drug Administration in the United States and Losec, the peptic ulcer drug which is currently (1998) the world's best-selling drug.

The medical equipment industry in Sweden is dominated by Gambro (founded in 1964). Similarly to the Ohio medical equipment companies, Gambro may be seen as closely related to the industrial machinery industry base, with sales oriented to the medical sector rather than other manufacturing industries.

There is also a large number of small medical supply firms in Sweden. This is the only field in the biomedical/biotechnology area in which there are more firms in Sweden than in Ohio. But these are generally quite small firms; they are similar in size to those in the software and diagnostics sectors. These latter companies are much more heavily represented and are also much larger in Ohio than in Sweden.

The Infrastructure
In addition to the industrial and commercial cluster of firms, the technological system consists of other actors, particularly in academic research. In biotechnology, the Cancer Foundation, the Swedish National Board for Industrial and Technical Development (NUTEK), the Technology Research Council (TFR), the Medical Research Council (MFR), and the Science Research Council (NFR) are among the leading research units. In the field of medicine as a whole, the Swedish academic research expenditures in 1995/1996 amounted to around $500 million. Most of these expenditures are concentrated in the Stockholm–Uppsala region, with the Karolinska Institute as the largest unit. In Göteborg the publicly financed research amounts to about $125 million and in Lund to about $100 million. Among the private companies Astra is the most important actor with a total research budget of about $1 billion, half of which is spent in Sweden. We estimate that there are about 100 research units in Sweden in the medical field, including universities, research institutes, and private companies. The expenditures on biomedical research appear to have increased during the 1990s.

It appears that although there are venture capital firms active in this field in Sweden, they are much fewer in number than in Ohio. Thus far, we have been able to identify only a handful of firms, some of them foreign. But this does not mean that there is a shortage of capital. Our interviews indicate that there are also plenty of ideas; what is in short supply is management and marketing competence – the primary input by venture capitalists. We will return to this point below.

Similarly to Ohio, the geographic location of economic activity in this field is strongly tied to universities with high research capability (see figure 8.4). The Stockholm–Uppsala region dominates, with other clusters based in Göteborg and Lund and also in Linköping and Umeå. There is a certain amount of specialization among the regions. The Linköping region is relatively large in biomedical software; Göteborg is specialized in medical instruments and supplies; while Uppsala is biggest in diagnostics. However, the Stockholm region is largest in most areas.

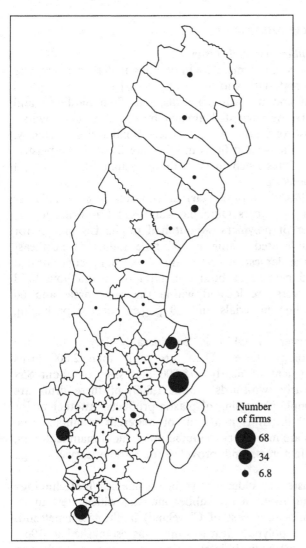

Figure 8.4 Regional distribution of biomedical/biotechnology firms in Sweden, 1996.

The polymer technology system in Ohio

The industrial/commercial cluster

The major applications of polymers are in building materials; fibers, and textiles; packaging materials and coatings; transparent and optical materials; biological and medical materials; and fluid modifiers and suspension stabilizers. As suggested already by this list, the polymer-based industry consists of firms in a great variety of industries. Currently, about half of the polymer-based firms in Ohio are listed in the plastics industry, with many firms listed in the rubber, automotive parts, and building materials industries.

Northeast Ohio has the world's largest concentration of polymer industry. In the last few years Ohio has surpassed California as the leading US producer of polymers. About half of the US market for plastics products is located within a 500 mile radius of northeast Ohio. Several of the largest markets are even more concentrated regionally: about 75 percent of both the automotive and household appliance manufacturers are located within the same area, and 60 percent of the building materials and 50 percent of the packaging materials industries.

The polymer cluster in Ohio is considerably larger than the biomedical/biotechnology cluster. There are more than 2,800 firms with a total employment of nearly 275,000 and sales of about $59 billion in 1996. Nearly two-thirds (about 1,800) of these firms are engaged in fairly simple processing of plastic products. Another major segment (nearly 400 firms) is made up of materials manufacturers. The remaining firms are machinery manufacturers, mold manufacturers, tool and die manufacturers, and providers of various services (e.g., distribution).

The polymer cluster is older than the biomedical/biotechnology cluster, having strong roots in the rubber industry which grew up in Akron (about 40 miles southeast of Cleveland) in the late nineteenth century. (The average polymer firm in Ohio was established in 1962, whereas the average biomedical/biotechnology firm was established in 1976.) At one time, all the major tire companies in the United States were based in Akron. For a variety of reasons (especially, high labor costs and poor management) the tire companies either withdrew from the tire industry, moved their tire manufacturing operations elsewhere, or merged with other companies (some of which are foreign owned). As a result, tires are no longer manufactured in Akron, but the polymer-related know-how which constitutes much of the technology base of the rubber industry still remains. Much of the research capability has its origin in the efforts, funded by the US government during World War II, to make synthetic rubber in response to the curtailment of the supply of natural rubber.

The Infrastructure

The concentration of the United States rubber industry to northeast Ohio is the main reason why two of the top three academic polymer research institutions in the United States are located in Akron and Cleveland: the College of Polymer Science at the University of Akron and the Department of Macromolecular Science at Case Western Reserve University in Cleveland. (The third and perhaps leading institution in the United States is the University of Massachusetts at Amherst.) The polymer-related research budget at the University of Akron is approximately $9 million per year and that at CWRU about $5 million. Together with the University of Cincinnati, the Ohio State University, and other universities, the academic polymer research in Ohio is estimated at about $20 million annually. (There appears to be no similar concentration of academic polymer research anywhere else in the world, the leading rivals being in Germany (Max Planck Institute and the University of Mainz) and Japan (the universities of Tokyo and Kyoto).)

Similarly to the biotechnology case, the Ohio Edison Program has established a "bridging institution," the Edison Polymer Innovation Corporation (EPIC), to support polymer research and technology at Ohio universities in collaboration with local industry. EPIC has a research budget of about $2 million a year to support such efforts; none of the research is done in-house. For a variety of reasons (especially, the substantial in-house capabilities of the major polymer-related companies and limited research needs (and even more limited capabilities) of the bulk of firms which only concern themselves with materials processing), EPIC appears to play a more modest role in generating new firms and activities than does EBTC in the biomedical/biotechnology cluster. One of the major reasons for this difference is found in the nature of research and its commercial application pertaining to the two areas. There have been complaints from industry (particularly from smaller companies) that the research funded by EPIC is too academically oriented, i.e., insufficiently oriented toward commercial exploitation, to warrant the membership fees. This is not surprising, given the limited receiver competence (absorptive capacity) in the small firms. At the same time, the large firms have excellent research capabilities in-house and thus are not dependent on academic research. To the extent they are, they can go anywhere in the world, not just to local sources. But they often prefer to do their own R&D, for reasons of appropriability. This is EPIC's dilemma.[13]

The academic research is important (especially as a producer of Ph.D.s, less so as a producer of research results), even though it is literally dwarfed by the R&D carried out by major corporations. Goodyear alone spends about $300 million a year on R&D, but only a small portion of that is fundamental research. Other major companies with polymer-related R&D are BF Goodrich, Firestone, Gen. Corp., Loral, and BP Chemicals. According to industry sources, a good guess is that somewhere around 2–3 percent of sales of materials manufacturers is spent on R&D. This would mean that corporate polymer-related R&D in Ohio is in the neighborhood of $400–600 million a year, and perhaps as much as twice that amount if machinery, mold, and tool and die manufacturers are also included.

Thus, it appears that the academic research base in polymers is somewhat smaller than that in biomedicine/biotechnology, but the commercial activity supported by that base is much larger. The commercial R&D appears to be of the same order of magnitude in both clusters, but the total sales are twice as large in polymers.

Although there is venture capital available in the polymer field in Ohio, our impression is that it is much more rare than in the biotech/ biomedical field. One venture firm told us that they had withdrawn from further funding in polymers. Our tentative interpretation is that the large firms who dominate both research and industrial activity have sufficient internal funding and that the many small firms have insufficient management and technical competence to be of interest to venture capitalists.

Similarly to the biomedical/biotech cluster, the polymer cluster is concentrated in the major metropolitan areas in Ohio (see figure 8.5). Further study shows that the materials manufacturers are heavily concentrated in the Cleveland–Akron–Lorain metropolitan area (with 45 percent of employment and sales), as one would expect, given the dependence on polymer research (both academic and commercial) which is also heavily concentrated in the same region. But in contrast to the biomedical/biotechnology case, the R&D does not seem to create new firms as much as it generates more activity in existing firms: the materials manufacturers in the Cleveland area are slightly older (average establishment year 1941) than the Ohio average (average establishment year 1949)

---

[13] By contrast, in the biomedical field, the small startup companies are often academic spin-offs with high research capability (and not yet many products to sell), whereas the larger firms spend a lower percentage of sales on research. But by virtue of large total research volume, these firms have sufficient capabilities to tap into research around the world, not just locally.

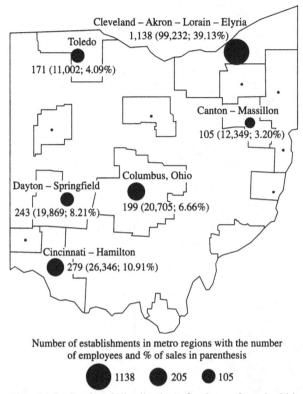

Number of establishments in metro regions with the number
of employees and % of sales in parenthesis

● 1138   ● 205   ● 105

Figure 8.5   Regional distribution of polymer firms in Ohio, 1996.

for the same group of firms – which, in turn, is older than the average for
all Ohio polymer firms (established in 1962). The youngest firms are the
service providers (established in 1967, on average).

The Polymer Technology System in Sweden

The industrial/commercial polymer cluster in Sweden consists of about
1,400 firms with about 75,000 employees and sales of about $18 billion in
1996. Thus, there are about half as many firms and one-third the
employment and sales as in the corresponding cluster in Ohio. It is
estimated that polymer-oriented research in Swedish universities
amounts to about $12 million annually (compared to $20 million in
Ohio), with Stockholm and Göteborg dominating (about $4 million
each), followed by Lund, and the rest allocated roughly equally among
the other universities. The magnitude of industrial R&D is not known,
but since many large chemical companies active in Sweden are foreign-

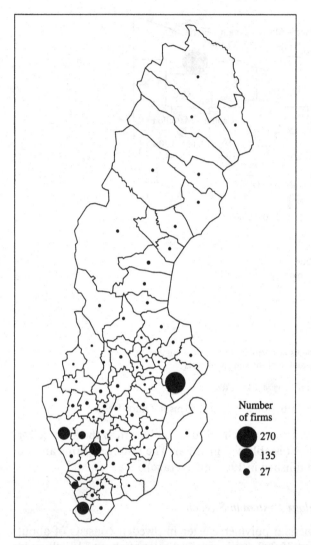

Figure 8.6   Regional distribution of polymer firms in Sweden, 1996.

owned (e.g., BASF Svenska AB, Bayer Sverige AB, Borealis Industrier AB, Norsk Hydro Sverige AB, and Akzo Nobel AB), much of their research is concentrated in the parent companies, thus reducing the R&D intensity in Sweden.

An international expert panel who visited Sweden in 1989 reviewed about 60 research projects carried out by 19 groups (STU, 1989). They estimated that a total of about 60 million SEK (about $9 million) was spent annually on polymer-related research in Sweden at that time, with almost half being funded by the Swedish National Board for Industrial and Technical Development (then STU, currently NUTEK). It was estimated that only 2 million SEK was spent on fundamental work in polymer chemistry and physics. A group of industry representatives with whom the experts met expressed concern about the inadequate amount of polymer science in the training of college graduates. The large international companies in Sweden can get their research needs met both in Sweden and abroad, and the industrial representatives were found to be well aware of, and well connected to, both Swedish universities and research units elsewhere. The problem of access to research was found to be greatest at the large majority of small- and medium-sized firms. The expert panel also recommended that the research be consolidated to fewer but larger units.

Thus, the academic and research infrastructure for polymers in Sweden seems to be somewhat inadequate. Our own interviews also did not find any evidence of presence of venture capital in the polymer field.

As shown in figure 8.6, the geographic distribution of the Swedish polymer-based firms is radically different from that in the biomedical/biotechnology cluster. The distribution is not as highly concentrated and not at all as tightly connected to university cities. A regional cluster which does not appear in the biomedical sector is centered at Värnamo and Gislaved, an area known for private entrepreneurship but not for any university or research links. The earlier location of a major rubber company at Gislaved, and a few other fairly large plastics companies (Borealis, Gnosjöplast, and others), seems to have anchored this cluster. The relatively simple technology and minor reliance on research have led to a greater geographic diffusion of production than in the case of biomedicine/biotechnology.

5   Analysis and comparison of the systems

Age and size structure

A comparison of the age distribution of firms provides additional insight. Table 8.5 gives an overview of the firms in each cluster established in the 1990s compared with all the firms. Nearly 32 percent of the Swedish firms in biomedicine/biotechnology were established during the period 1990–1996, compared with 26 percent in Ohio. The corresponding figures for polymers are 17 percent and 3 percent, respectively. Thus, the relative rate of firm formation appears to be higher in these fields in Sweden than in Ohio – dramatically so in polymers.

Table 8.5 *Comparison of biomedical/biotech and polymer firms in Sweden and Ohio, 1996*

	Number of firms		No. of employees		Sales, $ billion		Employees/firm		Sales/firm, $ million	
	Sweden	Ohio	Sweden	Ohio	Sweden	Ohio	Sweden	Ohio	Sweden	Ohio
Firms established 1990–1996										
Biomedicine/biotech	73	108	982	1,791	0.1	1.7	13.5	16.6	1.8	15.4
Polymers	242	94	6,268	6,166	1.1	1.6	25.9	65.6	4.7	16.5
All firms										
Biomedicine/biotech	230	422	25,768	52,175	6.1	15.0	112.0	123.6	26.6	35.5
Polymers	1,387	2,832	76,271	273,413	18.1	58.7	55.0	96.5	13.1	20.7

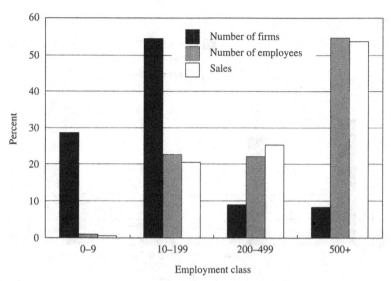

Figure 8.7 The distribution of number of firms, number of employees, and sales in the Ohio biotechnology/biomedical cluster, 1996.

However, the picture is quite different when the growth of the newly established firms is considered. In polymers, the 94 new firms in Ohio created as many jobs as the 242 in Sweden, and their total sales were nearly 50 percent larger. This means that each new polymer firm in Ohio was 2.5 times larger than its Swedish counterpart in terms of employment and 3.5 times as large in terms of sales. In biomedicine/biotechnology the difference is even more dramatic. The 108 new firms in Ohio generated 1,791 jobs, compared with 982 in the 73 Swedish firms. The Ohio firms had a combined sales volume in 1996 of $1,700 million versus only $100 million in Sweden. As a result, the Ohio firms were 23 percent larger in terms of employment and 8.5 times larger in sales per firm!

Figures 8.7 and 8.8 show the size distribution of firms in the biomedical/biotechnology cluster in Ohio and Sweden, respectively. Firms with 0–9 employees represent 29 percent of the total number of firms in Ohio, compared with 50 percent in Sweden. In the next larger size classes (10–199 and 200–499 employees) we find 63 percent of the firms in Ohio versus 45 percent in Sweden. As a result, the total employment and sales are much more evenly distributed among the firms of various sizes in Ohio than in Sweden.

Figures 8.9 and 8.10 present similar data for the polymer clusters. The smallest and largest firms represent 52 percent of the number of firms

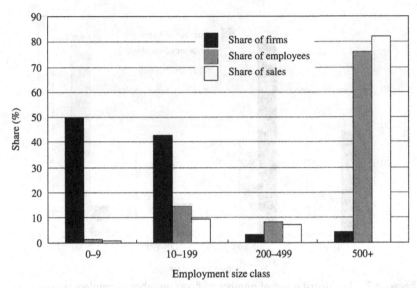

Figure 8.8 The distribution of number of firms, number of employees and sales in the Swedish biotechnology/biomedical cluster, 1996.

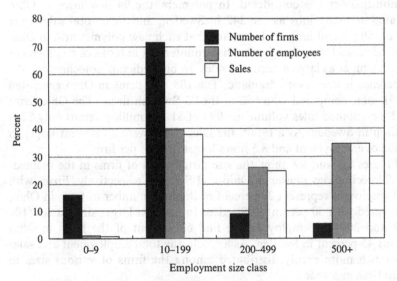

Figure 8.9 The distribution of number of firms, number of employees, and sales in the Ohio polymer cluster, 1996.

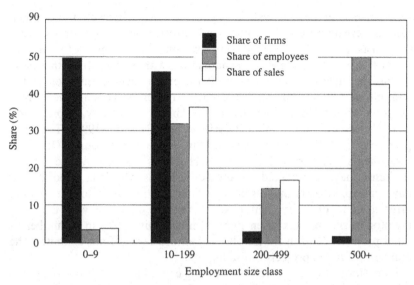

Figure 8.10 The distribution of number of firms, number of employees, and sales in the Swedish polymer cluster, 1996.

and 54 percent of total employment in Sweden, while the corresponding figures for Ohio are 20 percent and 35 percent, respectively.

This confirms the often noted small share of economic activity in medium-size firms in Sweden compared to other countries. In a recent paper, Henrekson and Johansson (1997) hypothesize that the failure of Swedish firms to grow to medium or large size is caused by a number of institutional impediments: the level of taxation and design of the tax system, credit market regulation, the Swedish wage negotiation system, the negative effects of the pension system on private savings, the labor security legislation with particularly detrimental effects on small firms, and the dominance of the public sector in services which could be produced in small firms. For further analysis of these and similar issues, see Andersson *et al.* (1993) and Jakobsson *et al.* (1998).

Our results are consistent with such a view. Certainly the more rapid economic growth in Ohio and in the United States as a whole compared to Sweden and other parts of Europe, as well as the proximity to major domestic markets, have given Ohio firms an advantage over Swedish firms during the last decade. But it also seems quite plausible that certain institutional features have also played a role in explaining the differences in behavior of new firms in the two regions. In particular, the presence in Ohio of bridging institutions which can assist in commercializing academic research results (along with greater incentives and better mechanisms for commercializing academic research results) and which can also create an effective interface between new startups and venture capitalists, provide a part of the explanation. The existence of numerous venture capital firms (at least in comparison with Sweden and other parts of Europe) also seems important. It is not primarily a question of the amount of risk capital made available; rather, it is fundamentally a question of economic competence: the ability to identify, exploit, and expand business opportunities (Carlsson and Eliasson, 1994). The competence to evaluate risky business ventures is a scarce resource. Often the assessments will vary widely. A project that is rejected by one venture capitalist may be accepted by another. That is why it is important to have multiple agents making independent judgments. Also, the venture firms need to diversify their risks. A venture capitalist who is a lead investor in one project often plays a more limited role in a number of other projects. Thus, if the number of venture capital firms is limited, the number of funded projects is also limited.

In addition, without a well-functioning capital market, it is difficult for venture capital firms to sell their holdings in order to redeploy their capital in new ventures. The existence of a well-established IPO (Initial Public Offering) function and over-the-counter market (such as the Nasdaq exchange) in the United States offer much more depth and breadth than their European counterparts, thus providing an advantage for new startups in the United States.

6   Conclusion

The main findings in this study are summarized in tables 8.6 and 8.7. Table 8.6 shows that the biomedical/biotechnology system in Ohio is about twice as large as that in Sweden in terms of employment and number of firms and more than three times as large in terms of sales. The Ohio firms are about nine years older, on average, than the Swedish firms. Their sales per firm are twice as large, even though they have about the same employment. Sweden appears to have a larger research base in the medical field as a whole, while Ohio has more in biomedical research.

In polymers also, Ohio has twice as many firms as Sweden and three times as large sales volume. The Ohio firms are also somewhat older and larger, on average. The research base is considerably larger in Ohio, particularly on the industrial side.

Table 8.7 summarizes the key differences between Ohio and Sweden. The number of new startups and the volume of medical academic research are greater in Sweden, but Ohio leads in all the other categories. This is particularly true when it comes to the growth of new firms, once

Table 8.6 *Overview of the biomedical/biotechnology and polymer clusters in Sweden and Ohio, 1996*

	Sweden	Ohio
Biomedicine/biotechnology		
Number of firms	230	422
Annual sales, $ billion	6	15
Employment, thousands	26	52
Sales/firm, $ million	27	36
Employment per firm	112	124
Average year established	1981	1972
Academic research		
Medicine, $ million/year	437.5	300
of which biomedical engineering research	?	25–30
Industrial R&D, $ million/year	>500	>1,000
Polymers		
Number of firms	1387	2832
Annual sales, $ billion	18	59
Employment, thousands	76	273
Sales/firm, $ million	13	21
Employment per firm	55	97
Average year established	1969	1962
Academic research		
Chemistry, $ million/year	75	
of which polymer research, $ million/year	12–16	20
Industrial R&D, $ million/year	?	375–625

they are established. Better mechanisms and incentives for commercialization of academic research in combination with better bridging institutions, a larger and more differentiated venture capital market with a greater number of firms, more opportunities for interaction between startup firms and venture capitalists, and a generally better climate for entrepreneurial activities are among the factors which have contributed to the generally better performance in Ohio than in Sweden in the last decade. A faster economic growth in the US economy than in Europe and proximity to large domestic markets have undoubtedly also contributed.

The primary issues for public policy which follow from this study are the following. The first issue is how to create better mechanisms for commercial exploitation of research, both academic and industrial. A related issue is how to create larger, deeper, and more differentiated

214   Bo Carlsson and Pontus Braunerhjelm

Table 8.7 *Key differences between Ohio and Sweden*

Feature	Ohio	Sweden
● Cluster size and density	+	
● Number of new startups		+
● Growth rate of new firms	++	
● Industrial R&D	+	
● Volume of academic research		+
● New firms/jobs generated by academic R&D	+	
● Commercialization of academic research; bridging between research and market	+	
● Differentiated risk capital market, access to venture capital, business angels	+	
● Active bridging between new startups and venture capitalists	+	
● Entrepreneurial climate, favorable economic incentives	+	

markets for venture capital. What is needed is not primarily financial capital but rather a larger number of independent firms with sufficient management and marketing competence. Finally, removing the more general obstacles which prevent small firms from growing large must be assigned a high priority.

References

Andersson, T., P. Braunerhjelm, B. Carlsson, G. Eliasson, S: Fölster, L. Jagrén, E. Kazamaki Ottersten, and K.R. Sjöholm (1993). *Den långa vägen – den ekonomiska politikens begränsningar och möjligheter att föra Sverige ur 1990-talets kris* (The Long Road – The Limitations and Possibilities of Economic Policy to Bring Sweden out of the Crisis of the 1990s), Stockholm: IUI.
Berry, Daniel (1996). "Technological Innovation and Diffusion in Cleveland's Biomedical/Biotechnology Industries," mimeo, Case Western Reserve University.
Braunerhjelm, Pontus and Bo Carlsson (1998). "Industry Clusters in Ohio and Sweden," *Small Business Economics*, forthcoming
Carlsson, Bo (ed.) (1995), *Technological Systems and Economic Performance: The Case of Factory Automation*, Dordrecht, Boston, and London: Kluwer Academic Publishers.
Carlsson, Bo. (ed.) (1997), *Technological Systems and Industrial Dynamics*, Dordrecht, Boston and London: Kluwer Academic Publishers.
Carlsson, Bo and Gunnar Eliasson (1994), "The Nature and Importance of Economic Competence," *Industrial and Corporate Change*, 3 (1): 687–711.

Carlsson, Bo and Rikard Stankiewicz (1991), "On the Nature, Function, and Composition of Technological Systems," *Journal of Evolutionary Economics*, 1 (2): 93–118.

Dosi, Giovanni, C. Freeman, R.R. Nelson, G. Silverberg, and L. Soete (eds.) (1988), *Technical Change and Economic Theory*, London: Francis Pinter.

Freeman, Christopher (1988), "Japan: A New National System of Innovation?" in Dosi (eds.), *et al*. (1988), pp. 330–348.

Friedenberg, Howard L. and Beemiller, Richard M. (1997), "Comprehensive Revision of Gross State Product by Industry, 1977–94," *Survey of Current Business*, 77 (June): 15–45.

Grönberg, Ann-Marie (1996), *Nordiska företag i medicinsk teknik* (Nordic Firms in Medical Technology), Huddinge: Bioprint Publishing and Consulting AB.

Grönberg, Ann-Marie (1997), *Nordiska företag i bioteknik* (Nordic Firms in Biotechnology), Huddinge: Bioprint Publishing and Consulting AB.

Henrekson, Magnus and Dan Johansson (1997), "Institutional Effects on the Evolution of the Size Distribution of Firms," Working Paper, October, IUI, Stockholm.

Jakobsson, U., L. Bergman, P. Braunerhjelm, S. Fölster, and M. Henrekson (1998), *Entrepreneurship in the Welfare State. Summary and Conclusions. SNS Economic Policy Group Report 1998*, Stockholm: SNS.

Lundvall, Bengt-Åke (1988), "Innovation as an Interactive Process: From User-Supplier Interaction to the National System of Innovation," in Dosi *et al*. (eds.) (1988), pp. 349–369.

Lundvall, Bengt-Åke (ed.) (1992), *National Systems of Innovation: Towards a Theory of Innovation and Interactive Learning*, London: Pinter Publishers.

Nelson, Richard R. (1988), "National Systems of Innovation: Preface" and "Institutions Supporting Technical Change in the United States," in Dosi *et al*. (eds.) (1988), pp. 309–329.

Nelson, Richard R. (ed.) (1993), *National Systems of Innovation. A Comparative Analysis*, Oxford: Oxford University Press.

OECD (1993), *National Accounts. Main Aggregates, volume 1, 1960–1991*, Paris: OECD.

OECD (1996), *Main Economic Indicators*, January, Paris: OECD.

Stanhiewicz, Rikard (1997), "The Development of Beta Blockers at Astra-Hässle and the Technological System of the Swedish Pharmaceutical Industry" in Carlsson (ed.) (1997), pp. 93–137.

STU (Swedish National Board for Technical Development) (1989), *Report of the International Evaluation Committee on Swedish Polymer Research and Technology, STU-info no. 723-1989*, Stockholm: STU.

9 How and why does knowledge spill over in biotechnology?

David Audretsch and Paula Stephan

The late twentieth century has witnessed a scientific gold rush of astonishing proportions: the headlong and furious haste to commercialize genetic engineering. This enterprise has proceeded so rapidly – with so little outside commentary – that its dimensions and implications are hardly understood at all.

Michael Crichton, Introduction to *Jurassic Park*

1 Introduction

The starting point for most theories of innovation is the firm. In such theories the firm is assumed to be exogenous and its performance in generating technological change is endogenous (Arrow, 1962). For example, in the most prevalent model in the literature of technological change, the *knowledge production function*, formalized by Zvi Griliches (1979), the firm exists exogenously and then engages in the pursuit of new knowledge as an input into the process of generating innovative activity. The most important source of new knowledge is generally considered to be R&D. Certainly a large body of empirical work has found a strong and positive relationship between knowledge inputs, such as R&D, and innovative outputs (Griliches, 1984).

However, the recent wave of studies revealing that small enterprises serve as the engine of innovative activity in certain industries (Audretsch, 1995; Acs and Audretsch, 1988 and 1990) is particularly startling, because the bulk of industrial R&D is undertaken in the largest corporations; small enterprises account for only a minor share of R&D inputs (Scherer, 1991; and Cohen and Klepper, 1992). Thus, the model of the

We would like to thank the participants at the conference on "The impact of technological change on firm and industry performance," 29–30 August, 1997, Tinbergen Institute, Erasmus University, Rotterdam, for their useful comments and suggestions. All errors and omissions remain our responsibility.

knowledge production function seemingly implies that innovative activity favors those organizations with access to knowledge-producing inputs of large organizations. The more recent evidence identifying the role of small firms as a source of innovative activity raises the question: Where do new and small firms get the innovation producing inputs, that is the knowledge?

One suggested answer is that although the model of the knowledge production function may certainly be valid, the implicitly assumed unit of observation which links the knowledge inputs with the innovative outputs – at the level of the establishment or firm – may be less valid. Instead, a new literature suggests that knowledge spills over from the firm or research institute producing it to a different firm commercializing that knowledge (Griliches, 1992). This view is supported by theoretical models which have focused on the role that spillovers of knowledge across firms play in generating increasing returns and ultimately economic growth (Romer, 1994, 1990, and 1986; Krugman, 1991a and 1991b; and Grossman and Helpman, 1991).

An important theoretical development is that geography may provide a relevant unit of observation within which knowledge spillovers occur. The theory of localization suggests that because geographic proximity is needed to transmit knowledge and especially tacit knowledge, knowledge spillovers tend to be localized within a geographic region. The importance of geographic proximity for knowledge spillovers has been supported in a wave of recent empirical studies by Jaffe (1989), Jaffe, Trajtenberg, and Henderson (1993), Acs, Feldman, and Audretsch (1992 and 1994), Audretsch and Feldman (1996), and Audretsch and Stephan (1996).

While this literature has identified the important role that knowledge spillovers play, they provide little insight into the questions of why knowledge spills over and how it spills over. What happens within the black box of the knowledge production is vague and ambiguous at best. The exact links between knowledge sources and the resulting innovative output remain invisible and unknown. This has moved Paul Krugman (1991a, p. 53) to argue that economists should abandon any attempts at measuring knowledge spillovers because "knowledge flows are invisible, they leave no paper trail by which they may be measured and tracked."

While Krugman's (1991a) observation is undeniably true, the creation of a new firm, especially in a high-technology, science-based industry, such as biotechnology, produces an event that leaves traces for studying the knowledge production function. One of the most striking features of firms making Initial Public Offerings (IPOs) in biotechnology is that they

218   David Audretsch and Paula Stephan

are typically able to raise millions of dollars in the absence of having a viable product at the time when they go public. Indeed, new firms are founded and receive financing on the prospects of transforming technological knowledge created at another source into economic knowledge at a new firm through the development and introduction of an innovative product. Thus, the establishment of a new firm in a knowledge-based industry such as biotechnology provides an opportunity for examining properties of the knowledge production function, and especially the links between the creation of knowledge and its commercialization.

The purpose of this chapter is to shed some light on the questions, Why does knowledge spill over? and How does knowledge spill over? We suggest that the answer to these questions lies in the incentives confronting scientists to appropriate the expected value of their knowledge considered in the context of their path-dependent career trajectories. In the metaphor provided by Albert O. Hirschman (1970), if voice proves to be ineffective within incumbent organizations, and loyalty is sufficiently weak, scientists will resort to exit from a corporation or a university to form a new biotechnology company.

2   Appropriability and incentives

A large literature has emerged focusing on what has become known as the appropriability problem. The underlying issue revolves around how firms which invest in the creation of new knowledge can best appropriate the economic returns from that knowledge (Arrow, 1962). Audretsch (1995) proposes shifting the unit of observation away from exogenously assumed firms to individuals – agents with endowments of new economic knowledge. When the lens is shifted away from the firm to the individual as the relevant unit of observation, the appropriability issue remains, but the question becomes: How can economic agents with a given endowment of new knowledge best appropriate the returns from that knowledge? Stephan (1996) and Levin and Stephan (1991) suggest that the answer is: It depends – it depends on the career trajectory of the individual scientist and whether (s)he is coming from an academic or an industrial background.

Stephan and Levin (1992) analyze how different work contexts have different incentive structures. The academic sector encourages and rewards the production of new scientific knowledge. Thus, the goal of the scientist in the university context is to establish *priority*. This is done most efficiently through publication in scientific journals (Stephan, 1996). By contrast, in the industrial sector, scientists are rewarded for the production of new economic knowledge but not necessarily new scientific knowledge *per se*. In fact, scientists working in industry are often discouraged from sharing knowledge externally with the scientific community through publication. As a result of these differential incentive structures, industrial and academic scientists develop distinct career trajectories.

The appropriability question confronting academic scientists can be considered in the context of the human capital model. Life-cycle models of scientists suggest that early in their careers scientists invest heavily in human capital in order to build a reputation (Levin and Stephan, 1991). In the later stages of their career, scientists trade or *cash in* this reputation for economic return. Thus, early in their careers, scientists invest in the creation of knowledge in order to establish a reputation that signals the value of that knowledge to the scientific community. With maturity, scientists seek ways to appropriate the economic value of the new knowledge. But how should a scientist best appropriate the value of her/his human capital? Alternatives abound, such as working full time or part time with an incumbent firm, licensing the knowledge to an incumbent firm, or starting or joining a new firm.

Scientists working in the private sector are arguably more fully compensated for the economic value of their knowledge. This will not be the case for academic scientists unless they *cash out*, in terms of Dasgupta and David (1994), by selling their knowledge to a private firm. This suggests that academic scientists seek affiliation with a commercial venture in a life-cycle context. By contrast, industrial scientists consider leaving the incumbent firm when a disparity arises between the firm and the individual concerning the expected value of their knowledge. In the former situation, age is a good predictor of when the scientist establishes ties with industry. In the latter case, factors other than age are expected to play a more important role in determining when the scientist leaves the incumbent firm.

3   The database

This chapter will use a database drawn from the prospectuses of 60 firms that made an initial public offering (IPO) in biotechnology during the period March 1990 to November 1992 to examine the sources and incentives for commercializing new knowledge. Prospectuses for the offerings were carefully read in order to identify the scientific founders of the new firms. In cases where it proved difficult to identify founders from the prospectuses, telephone calls were made to the firm. In addition, firm histories were checked and confirmed in *BioScan*. Founders having a Ph.D. or an M.D. were coded as scientific founders for the purposes of this research. In addition, several individuals who did not have a doctorate but were engaged in research were included as scientific founders. All told, we were able to identify 101 scientific founders for 52 firms making an initial public offering during this period.

Biographical information was also collected from the prospectuses and was supplemented by entries from standard reference works such as *American Men and Women of Science*. Four types of job experience were identified – academic experience (which includes positions at hospitals, research foundations, and the government), experience with pharmaceutical companies, training experiences (as a student, post-doc, or resident), and "other" experience. This information was used to distinguish among five distinct career trajectories followed prior to the founding of the company:

1   the *academic trajectory* describes scientists who had spent all of their time since completing their training employed in the academic research sector;
2   the *pharmaceutical trajectory* describes those scientists whose careers subsequent to receiving training had been entirely spent working in the drug industry;
3   the *mixed trajectory* describes scientists who had worked in both the pharmaceutical industry and the academic research sector;
4   the *student trajectory* describes individuals who went directly from a training position to founding a biotechnology firm; and
5   the *other trajectory*, which includes scientists who have been employed by non-pharmaceutical firms.

Additional biographical information was ascertained concerning date of birth and educational background. Citation counts to first-authored published scientific articles were measured using the 1991 *Science Citation Index* produced by ISI and are used here as an indicator of scientific reputation.

4   Preliminary results

Summary data, presented in table 9.1, show that 50 percent of the scientific founders' careers followed an academic trajectory, slightly more than 25 percent followed a pharmaceutical trajectory. Half of this latter group had established their careers exclusively with large pharmaceutical companies such as SmithKline and Beckman; half had come from smaller pharmaceutical firms, some of which, like Amgen, were a first generation biotech firm. Table 9.1 also indicates that approximately an eighth of the founders had a mixed career in the sense that prior to founding the firm they had held positions in both a pharmaceutical

Table 9.1 *The age and citation record of founders*

	Birth date				Citations		
	N	M	SD	N_{known}	M	SD	N_{known}
All scientific founders	101	1943.18	10.20	96	92.13	171.05	99
All academic founders	50	1940.55	10.06	49	149.32	226.51	49
Part time	35	1938.79	10.29	34	172.71	259.03	35
Full time	15	1945.06	8.54	15	72.21	78.70	15
All drug founders	28	1945.61	9.20	28	29.71	46.28	28
Small	14	1945.93	9.84	14	30.30	57.40	14
Big	12	1947.00	7.67	12	34.00	34.41	14
Mixed career	13	1943.80	8.76	13	62.69	57.56	13
Student career	6	1957.00	3.54	5	58.17	83.72	6
All full time	57	1945.64	9.61	57	46.59	60.69	57
All part time	40	1939.42	10.03	37	159.30	245.52	37

Notes: N is number of observations, M is mean, SD is standard deviation, and N_{known} is number of observations for which the variable is known.

company as well as a university or non-profit research organization. A handful of founders moved directly from a training position such as a residency or post-doctorate appointment to the startup firm, thereby short-circuiting the traditional trajectories from pharmaceutical firms and/or academe. The career trajectory of the remaining scientists was either indeterminate or followed another type of path.

The employment status of the founders with the biotechnology company was also determined. We find that 59 of the 101 scientific founders were working full time with the new firm at the time of the public offering; 41 were working part time, and almost all (35) of these had followed an academic trajectory. This means that 70 percent of the academic founders maintain full-time employment with their academic institutions, serving as consultants or members of the Scientific Advisory Boards to the startup firms. Only 15 of the academic founders had moved to full-time employment with the firm by the time the IPO was made. By contrast, all 28 scientists whose careers had been exclusively in the pharmaceutical sector held full-time positions with the firm at the time of the IPO; nine of the 13 whose careers followed a mixed trajectory were full time.

The evidence from table 9.1 supports the hypothesis that the incentive structure varies considerably between the pharmaceutical founders and the academic founders. Those founders coming from universities and non-profit research organizations have the option of having their cake and eating it too, by maintaining formal contacts with their previous employer, often in a full-time position. Even those from the academic sector who are full time with the new firm are often able to maintain some connection with the non-profit sector as adjunct or clinical faculty. By contrast, those scientists who have a career path in pharmaceuticals take full-time positions with the company, at least by the time the company goes public.

There are other differences between those scientists coming from an academic trajectory and those scientists coming from a pharmaceutical trajectory. The most notable is the difference in age at the time the public offering was made. On average, those coming from universities were born approximately five years earlier than those coming from the pharmaceutical sector, a difference which is statistically significant at the 95 percent level of confidence. As would be expected, we also find that those following the academic trajectory have significantly more citations than those coming from a pharmaceutical trajectory.

Of perhaps even greater interest are the differences between the part-time academics and the full-time academics. Academic founders who remain full-time with their institution, working but only part-time for the new firm, were, for example, born more than six years earlier than academic founders who leave their institution to go full time with the firm. The part-timers are not only older; they are also more eminent, having significantly more citations than academics who go full time with the firm. This suggests that eminence gives these scientists the luxury of hedging their bets; both the firm and their research institution welcome a chance to claim them as affiliates. And, although we have not yet measured the incidence, such individuals often serve as directors and members of Scientific Advisory Boards of additional startup firms. The full-timers, by contrast, have developed sufficient human capital to be recognized as experts but lack the luster to hold "dual" citizenship. In terms of both citation counts and date of birth they are remarkably similar to their fellow founders who followed a pharmaceutical trajectory.

These preliminary observations suggest that the incentive structure depends upon the career trajectory that the scientist has followed as well as upon whether the scientist has established sufficient eminence to be able to sustain multiple roles. Scientists working in incumbent pharmaceutical firms face the well-known problem of deciding whether to remain with the incumbent firm or start a new firm. Furthermore, the goal of an incumbent firm to capture their economic knowledge seldom permits a scientist to establish a reputation based solely on publication. Instead, their scientific reputations are typically established in terms of the products they helped to develop and are known primarily to "insiders" in the industry. Scientists in academe, however, face a different incentive structure. They live in a world where publications are essential for the establishment of reputation. Early in their careers they invest heavily in human capital in order to build a reputation. In the later stages of their career, scientists may trade or cash in on this reputation for economic returns. A variety of avenues are available to do this, including the establishment of a new firm.

The data suggest that this *cashing out* pattern is determined in part by eminence. As noted, a number of academic founders have established sufficiently strong reputations as to be able to have their cake and eat it too. They maintain their full-time jobs in academe, while seeking part-time opportunities to gain economically from their knowledge and scientific reputation. The economic returns are tied to the shares they own in the startup companies. A subset of academic scientists, however, go full time with the firm. They, too, hold stock in the firm. But, their rewards are more immediate in terms of the salaries paid to executives in the companies.[1] And, while they have established solid reputations, they are considerably less cited than those academic founders who maintain full-time positions in academe. Although this may be a result of age (they are, after all, about five years younger), it is more likely a characteristic that age cannot alter. Science, as numerous researchers have established, is noteworthy for persistent inequality which age merely amplifies (Stephan, 1996).

5   A hazard model estimating biotechnology startups

What drives a scientist to become a carrier of knowledge in the spillover process? The preliminary evidence presented in the previous section suggests that it is the incentive structure confronting the scientist, which is shaped by the scientist's career trajectory. Other work (Audretsch and Stephan, 1996) suggests that the location of the scientist also plays an important role, through a contagion effect. Those scientists who are exposed to colleagues who have already started a biotechnology firm are more likely to receive vital information reducing the costs and raising the expected value of starting a new firm. This suggests that, *ceteris paribus*, scientists would be expected to start a new firm at a younger age when they are located in the main geographic clusters of biotechnology activity than when they are located outside of biotechnology agglomerations.

To address the question, what drives a scientist to start a new

---

[1]   Note that our data do not permit us to compare the *full-timers* and *part-timers* to university-based scientists who *do not* found firms. One would expect that this group is younger, and less eminent than either of the other groups.

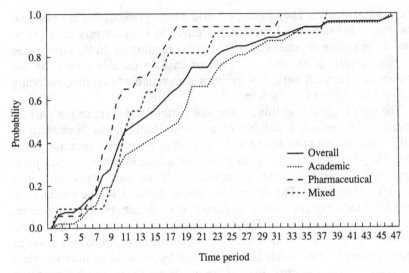

Figure 9.1 Cumulative probability of founding a firm

biotechnology company, we apply a semi-parametric hazard duration model (Cox, 1972 and 1975; and Kiefer, 1988), where the model is defined in terms of $h(t;x)$, where h is the hazard rate for a scientist subsequent to completion of his Ph.D., and x is a vector of covariates, reflecting the influences described above. The hazard model is given by

$$h(t; x) = h_0(t) * \exp(\beta x')$$ (1)

or

$$\ln[h(t; x)/h_0(t)] = \beta x'$$ (2)

where β is a vector of unknown regression coefficients and $h_0(t)$ is an unknown non-negative baseline hazard rate. The second exponential term incorporates the covariates vector x. Estimates of the regression parameters are obtained as follows; let $t_1 \leq t_2 \leq ...t_k$ represent distinct times to the startup of a new biotechnology firm among n observed years. The conditional probability that the ith scientist starts a new biotechnology firm at time t_i^* with a covariate vector x_i, given that a single startup has occurred at t_i, is given as the ratio of the hazards

$$\exp(\beta x_i'). \sum_{j \in R_t} \exp(\beta x_i'),$$ (3)

where $j \in R_i$ corresponds to those scientists that have not started a new

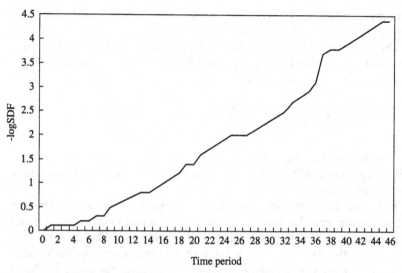

Figure 9.2 Hazard function

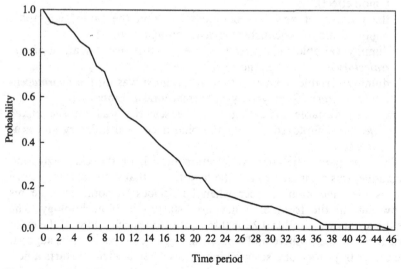

Figure 9.3 Survival function

firm prior to time t_i. The baseline hazard rate is assumed to be the same for all the observations and hence it cancels out.

The partial likelihood function derived from Cox (1972 and 1975) is obtained by multiplying these probabilities together for each of the k incidences of starting a new firm

$$PL(\beta, x_1, x_2, ..., x_n) = \prod_{j \in R}^{k} [\exp(\beta x_i') / \sum \exp(\beta x_i')] \qquad (4)$$

Maximization of the partial likelihood function yields estimators of β with properties similar to those of usual maximum likelihood estimators, such as asymptotic normality.

The estimated regression coefficient indicates the relationship between the covariate and the hazard function. A positive coefficient increases the value of the hazard function and therefore indicates a positive impact on the likelihood of a scientist starting a new biotechnology firm. A negative coefficient indicates that the particular covariate has a negative impact on the likelihood of the scientist starting a new biotechnology firm.

The specific covariates in equation (4) to be estimated in the hazard model include:

1   the cumulative citations of the scientist;
2   the number of other scientists who have started biotechnology firms in the same geographic region where the scientist is located (contagion effect);
3   the number of new biotechnology firms in the same geographic region where the scientist is located (contagion effect);
4   dummy variable indicating that the scientist was on an *academic trajectory* (employed in the academic sector);
5   dummy variable indicating that the scientist was on the *pharmaceutical trajectory* (employed by a pharmaceutical company);
6   dummy variable indicating that the scientist was on the *mixed trajectory* (employed in both the pharmaceutical industry and academic sector).

The semi-parametric hazard duration model, or the Cox-regression technique, was estimated to test the hypotheses that the career trajectory shapes the time in his career when he decides to commercialize his knowledge in the form of a new-firm startup in biotechnology. The results are shown in table 9.2 for three different specifications of the error structure. As the positive and statistically significant coefficients suggest, the career trajectory of a scientist influences when a scientist starts a new biotechnology company. The career trajectory of those scientists who

Table 9.2 *Hazard function estimates of duration to biotechology startup* (standard errors in parentheses)

	Log-logistic	Normal	Gamma
Academic trajectory	1.896	1.934	1.879
	(0.36)	(0.36)	(0.28)
Pharmaceutical trajectory	1.427	1.475	1.341
	(0.39)	(0.37)	(0.32)
Mixed trajectory	1.606	1.730	1.616
	(0.40)	(0.39)	(0.33)
Citations	0.002	0.002	−0.002
	(0.05)	(0.04)	(0.03)
Firm density	−0.017	−0.017	−0.006
	(0.04)	(0.05)	(0.04)
Scientist density	−0.001	0.002	−0.004
	(0.01)	(0.01)	(0.10)
Intercept	0.769	0.844	1.203
	(0.39)	(4.79)	(12.58)
Log-likelihood	−84.760	−290.780	−81.926

have been in university and non-profit research institutes leads them to start new biotechnology companies somewhat later than their counterparts in the pharmaceutical industry. The mixed career trajectory is somewhere in between the academic and pharmaceutical scientists. Thus, the evidence suggests the life-cycle theory that the career trajectory of a scientist shapes the decision to start a new biotechnology.

6   Conclusion

This chapter has attempted to penetrate the black box of the knowledge production function. In addressing the questions how and why knowledge spills over, an assumption implicit to the model of the knowledge production function is challenged – that firms exist *exogenously* and then *endogenously* seek out and apply knowledge inputs to generate innovative output. Although this may be valid some, if not most of the time, the evidence from biotechnology suggests that, at least in some cases, it is the

228   David Audretsch and Paula Stephan

knowledge in the possession of economic agents that is *exogenous*. In an effort to appropriate the returns from that knowledge, the scientist then *endogenously* creates a new firm. Thus, the spillover of knowledge from the source creating it, such as a university, research institute, or industrial corporation, to a new-firm startup facilitates the appropriation of knowledge for the individual scientist(s) but not necessarily for the organization creating that new knowledge in the first place.

This chapter also sheds light on the question which has plagued economists for decades, Where do new industries come from? The answer, at least in the case of biotechnology, appears to have something to do with new knowledge created with perhaps one purpose in mind, but is, in fact, valuable in a very different context. We observe that the participants in the biotechnology industry come from a broad range of diverse backgrounds. Because no biotechnology industry has traditionally existed, no set career paths have been established. Rather, the participants in an emerging industry choose to leave what otherwise would be established career trajectories in more traditional industries. Through the flow of scientists into this new industry, knowledge which was generated with a more traditional context in mind spills over by becoming applied in the process of creating a new industry.

References

Acs, Zoltan J. and David B. Audretsch (1988), "Innovation in Large and Small Firms," *American Economic Review*, 78(4): 678–690.
    (1990), *Innovation and Small Firms*, Cambridge, Mass.: MIT Press.
Acs, Zoltan J., Maryann P. Feldman and David B. Audretsch (1992), "Real Effects of Academic Research," *American Economic Review*, 82(1): 363–367.
    (1994), "R&D Spillovers and Recipient Firm Size," *Review of Economics and Statistics*, 100(2): 336–340.
Arrow, Kenneth J. (1962), "Economic Welfare and the Allocation of Resources for Invention," in R.R. Nelson (ed.), *The Rate and Direction of Inventive Activity*, Princeton: Princeton University Press, pp. 609–626.
Audretsch, David B. (1995), *Innovation and Industry Evolution*, Cambridge, Mass.: MIT Press.
Audretsch, David B. and Maryann P. Feldman (1996), "R&D Spillovers and the Geography of Innovation and Production," *American Economic Review*, 86(3): 630–640.
Audretsch, David B. and Paula E. Stephan (1996), "Company-Scientist Locational Links: The Case of Biotechnology," *American Economic Review*, 86(3): 641–652.
Cohen, Wesley M. and Steven Klepper (1992), "The Anatomy of Industry R&D Intensity Distributions," *American Economic Review*, 82(4): 773–799.

Cox, David R. (1972), "Regression Models and Life Tables," *Journal of the Royal Statistical Society*, 34 (May/August), 187–220.
 (1975), "Partial Likelihood," *Biometrics*, 62(3): 269–275.
Dasgupta, Partha and Paul A. David (1994), "Toward a New Economics of Science," *Research Policy*, 23(5): 487–521.
Griliches, Zvi (1979), "Issues in Assessing the Contribution of R&D to Productivity Growth," *Bell Journal of Economics*, 10(1): 92–116.
 (1992), "The Search for R&D Spillovers," *Scandanavian Journal of Economics*, 94(S): 29–47.
Griliches, Zvi (ed.) (1984), *R&D, Patents, and Productivity*, Chicago: University of Chicago Press.
Grossman, Gene and Elhanan Helpman (1991), *Innovation and Growth in the Global Economy*, Cambridge, Mass.: MIT Press.
Hirschman, Albert O. (1989), *Exit, Voice, and Loyalty*, Cambridge, Mass.: Harvard University Press.
Jaffe, Adam B. (1970), "Real Effects of Academic Research," *American Economic Review*, 79(5): 957–970.
Jaffe, Adam B., Manuel Trajtenberg, and Rebecca Henderson (1993), "Geographic Localization of Knowledge Spillovers as Evidenced by Patent Citations," *Quarterly Journal of Economics*, 63(3): 577–598.
Kiefer, Nicholas M. (1988), "Economic Duration Data and Hazard Functions," *Journal of Economic Literature*, 26(2): 646–679.
Krugman, Paul A. (1991a), *Geography and Trade*, Cambridge, Mass.: MIT Press.
 (1991b), "Increasing Returns and Economic Geography," *Journal of Political Economy*, 99(3) (June): 483–499.
Levin, Sharon G. and Paula E. Stephan (1991), "Research Productivity over the Life Cycle: Evidence for Academic Scientists," *American Economic Review*, 81(4): 114–132.
Prevezer, Martha (1997), "The Dynamics of Industrial Clustering in Biotechnology," *Small Business Economics*, 9(3) (June): 255–271.
Romer, Paul (1986), "Increasing Returns and Long-Run Economic Growth," *Journal of Political Economy*, 94(5) (November): 1002–1037.
 (1990), "Endogenous Technological Change," *Journal of Political Economy*, 94(1): 71–102.
 (1994), "The Origins of Endogenous Growth," *Journal of Economic Perspectives*," 8(1) (Winter): 3–22.
Scherer, F.M. (1991), "Changing Perspectives on the Firm Size Problem," in Z.J. Acs and D.B. Audretsch (eds.), *Innovation and Technological Change: An International Comparison*, Ann Arbor: University of Michigan Press, pp. 24–38.
Stephan, Paula E. (1996), "The Economics of Science," *Journal of Economic Literature*, 34(3): 1199–1262.
Stephan, Paula E. and Sharon G. Levin (1992), *Striking the Mother Lode in Science*, New York: Oxford University Press.

10 Do services differ from manufacturing? The post-entry performance of firms in Dutch services

David Audretsch, Luuk Klomp, and Roy Thurik

1 Introduction

In response to a literature that focused on static relationships in industrial organizations, Mansfield (1962, p. 1023) made a plea some 35 years ago for a greater emphasis on understanding the dynamic process by which industries evolve over time: "Because there have been so few econometric studies of the birth, growth, and death of firms, we lack even crude answers to the following basic questions regarding the dynamic processes governing an industry's structure. What are the quantitative effects of various factors on the rates of entry and exit? What have been the effects on a firm's growth rate? What determines the amount of mobility within an industry's size structure?" Industrial organization scholars responded to Mansfield's plea by undertaking a wave of studies focusing on the various dimensions of industry evolution. The resulting literature on intra-industry dynamics examines the process by which new firms enter an industry, either survive or exit, and grow to even displace incumbent firms in some cases. Paul Geroski (1995) was able to comb through a diverse set of studies spanning a broad spectrum of countries, time periods, and methods of analysis, to uncover a set of Stylized Facts that emerge with remarkable consistency to answer the question: "What Do We Know About Entry?" While the studies upon which Geroski bases his Stylized Facts are disparate in many dimensions, they all have one thing in common – they are all based upon manufacturing. Although never explicitly stated by Geroski, an important qualification to his insightful synthesis of the literature is that whatever it is we know about entry, as well as the dynamic process by which firms and

The authors would like to give special thanks to Statistics Netherlands for providing data. We thank Ad Abrahamse, Martin Carree, Michael Fritsch, and Joachim Wagner for helpful comments. This paper was prepared while Audretsch was visiting the Tinbergen Institute in Rotterdam in 1997.

industries evolve over time, it is about manufacturing. There is virtually nothing known about the entry and post-entry processes in the non-manufacturing sectors. This void in knowledge about industrial organization is particularly striking since manufacturing accounts for less than one-quarter of employment in most of the OECD countries. Most work and economic activity occurs outside of the manufacturing sector. This gap in knowledge about the applicability of findings from manufacturing to services has led Davis, Haltiwanger, and Schuh (1996a and 1996b) to call for the development of longitudinal firm-level data sets for the service industries.

The purpose of this chapter is to fill this gap in knowledge about the role of non-manufacturing in industrial organization, and, in particular, of firms, or what happens to firms subsequent to, entering an industry. The literature on the post-entry performance has a particular focus on the relationships between firm size and age, on the one hand, and survival and growth, on the other. As Geroski (1995) emphasizes, virtually every study undertaken, independent of the country, time period, and methodology employed, has found positive relationships between the likelihood of survival and firm age and size, but negative relationships between firm growth and age and size. In a more recent study, Sutton (1997) reports on similar relationships in his exhaustive survey on Gibrat's Law, i.e., the Law of Proportionate Effect, and the wave of studies on the dynamics of firm size and industry structure that emerged subsequent to Gibrat's pioneering book (Gibrat, 1931).[1] In the second section of this chapter we introduce the longitudinal data base for Dutch firms in the retail and hotel and catering sectors to identify around 13,000 new-firm startups and 47,000 incumbents in the services and track them over subsequent years. Throughout this chapter we will use the term hospitality for the hotel and catering sectors. In the third section, we use this longitudinal data base to identify whether the relevant Stylized Facts from manufacturing pointed out by Geroski also apply to services. In the fourth section we suggest theoretical reasons why the relationships between firm

---

[1] The combination of the Statistical Regularities 1 and 2 in Sutton (1997) is consistent with both the observed positive relationships between the likelihood of survival and firm size and age, and the observed negative relationships between firm growth and age and size, which are the basis for Geroski to constitute his Stylized Result 8 (Geroski, 1995). The Statistical Regularities 1 and 2 in Sutton (1997, p. 46) are:

1 *Size and growth*: (a) the probability of survival increases with firm (or plant) size (b) the proportional rate of growth of a firm (or plant) conditional on survival is decreasing in size.

2 *The life cycle*: For any given size of firm (or plant), the proportional rate of growth is smaller if the firm (or plant) is older, but its probability of survival is greater.

age and size, on the one hand, and survival and growth, on the other, may not be the same in services as they are for manufacturing. We then test to see whether the Stylized Results identified by Geroski based on manufacturing still hold in the services. In the final section we provide a summary and conclusions. The results suggest that while a number of Stylized Facts regarding entry based on manufacturing are confirmed for services, the most fundamental relationships between firm size, age, survival, and growth are strikingly different for services than for manufacturing. This suggests that, in terms of the dynamics of industrial organization, services may, in fact, not simply mirror the manufacturing sector.

2   Measurement

One of the main reasons why so little is known about the dynamics of industrial organization outside of manufacturing is the paucity of comprehensive longitudinal data bases for non-manufacturing firms. All of the pioneering studies examining the dynamics of industrial organization in terms of the entry of new firms, their subsequent survival, and growth or exit, have been based on longitudinal data in manufacturing.

In this chapter we use firm-level data for the services for the period 1985–1988 in the Dutch hospitality and retail sectors. Data were compiled in a yearly survey undertaken by Statistics Netherlands (CBS) in the files, *Statistics of Man-Years and Gross Wages*. Annual observations for each non-manufacturing firm include the number of employees,[2] the year the firm was started,[3] the municipal location, the four-digit industry code (SBI), the legal form, and a firm identifier.[4]

Entrants in any year t are defined as those firms that appeared in the data set in that year for the first time. Conversely, exit in year t is measured as those firms that appear in the data set in year $t-1$ but not in year t. Incumbents are defined as firms that remained in the data set over the entire observation period.

There are three important qualifications about the data base that should be emphasized. First, entry and exit rates overestimate the turnover of firms. This is because only firms with employees are included in the data base. This means that when a firm has an employee in one year but no employee(s) in the subsequent year, the firm is classified as

---

[2] For each firm the number of working days of paid employees is known. For each firm we divided the number by 260. In this way, for each firm, the number of (paid) employees, measured in full-time equivalents (FTE), is obtained.

[3] This is actually the initial year that the firm was registered with Statistics Netherlands.

[4] More details about the data set can be found in chapters 3 and 4 of Klomp (1996).

exiting, when it may still be in operation. This overstatement of exit and entry is greater for small firms than for larger enterprises.

Second, the startup year is measured as the year that a firm appears for the first time in the *Algemeen BedrijfsRegister*, or the General Business Register (ABR).[5] It is certainly possible firms existed before they were registered in the ABR and may be older than are actually recorded.

Finally, the four-digit industry code associated with a firm can change during the observation period. For example, as a result of a (typically slight) change in the share of sales from beverages to meals, the four-digit industry of a firm in the hospitality sector can be changed from cafes to restaurants. In addition, the four-digit industry code for some firms can only be determined correctly after several years of business activities. In such cases the firm is classified as neither exiting nor entering. If the four-digit industry code changes during the observation period the firm is assigned to the industry where it was recorded most recently.

The data base provides longitudinal observations for 66 four-digit retail industries and 13 hospitality industries. For presentation purposes the 66 four-digit industries in retailing are condensed into 18 slightly broader three-digit industries in table 10.1, which lists the number of firms, employment and mean employment size for each industry. The mean firm size in services is remarkably small – the average size of the 44,499 retail firms is 7.5 employees, and of the 18,423 hospitality firms is 4.8 employees.

3   Geroski's Stylized Facts: Are the services different?

The first Stylized Fact Geroski (1995, p. 422) draws attention to in his review of the literature on industry dynamics in manufacturing is "Entry is common. Large numbers of firms enter most markets in most years, but entry rates are far higher than market penetration rates."[6] Table 10.2 confirms that entry is also important for services. The mean entry rate for the 1985–1988 period is 21 percent in retailing and 27 percent in hospitality.[7] These entry rates for Dutch services also exceed the entry

---

[5]   In principle the ABR includes all firms in The Netherlands. The ABR is more fully described in Willeboordse (1986).

[6]   There are, in fact, more Stylized Facts provided by Geroski (1995) than we are able to make comparisons with in this chapter due to the broad range of subjects that he covers. The relevant Stylized Facts which we deal with are Stylized Facts 1, 3, and 4, along with Stylized Result 8.

[7]   The entry rate is based on Dunne, Roberts and Samuelson (1988 and 1989) and is defined as the number of firms entering the industry between 1986–1988 divided by the total number of firms in that industry in 1985.

Table 10.1 *Description of the retail and hospitality industries for the year 1988*

SBI[a]	Industry	No. of firms	Employment (thousands)	Employ-ment per firm
65/66	*Retail trade (total)*	*44,499*	*332.0*	*7.5*
651	Meat, fish, poultry, and dairy products	5,498	17.8	3.2
652	Potatoes, fruit, vegetables, beverages, chocolate, and tobacco	7,720	105.9	13.7
653	Pharmacies	1,106	9.8	8.9
654	Medical and orthopedic goods, perfumery, and toilet articles	1,445	7.3	5.0
655	Clothing	4,995	38.3	7.7
656	Textiles, wool, linen, and dress materials	1,273	9.2	7.3
657	Footwear, leather goods, and travel accessories	1,517	11.2	7.4
658	Floor covering and furnishing fabrics	1,983	9.7	4.9
659	Domestic decoration and electrical household appliances	3,409	19.4	5.7
661	Household utensils and do-it-yourself materials	3,410	19.8	5.8
662	Cars, motor-cycles, and bicycles	2,285	10.4	4.6
663	Gas stations	1,280	5.5	4.3
664	Books, newspapers and magazines	1,213	7.7	6.3
665	Photographic and optical equipment, watches, and jewellery	2,217	9.4	4.3
666	Flowers, plants, and pets	3,103	7.5	2.4
667	Fuel oil, bottled gas, coal, and wood	121	0.4	3.7
668	Games and toys, sports goods, camping articles, and caravans	1,781	7.2	4.0
669	Department stores and mail order houses	143	35.3	246.8
67	*Hospitality (total)*	*18,423*	*88.4*	*4.8*
6711	Restaurants	5,455	27.3	5.0
6712	Cafeterias	3,959	9.9	2.5
6721	Cafes[b]	5,715	12.8	2.3
6741	Hotels	1,595	22.0	13.8
6799	Remaining hospitality industries	1,699	16.3	9.6

Notes:
[a] For the SBI-code the "Standaard BedrijfsIndeling" of the Statistics Netherlands (CBS) of 1974 is used.
[b] The business group of cafes includes both firms which do and do not have a licence to serve wines and spirits.

rates found by Dunne, Roberts, and Samuelson (1988 and 1989) for United States manufacturing.[8] Compared to the findings of Kleijweg and Lever (1994) documenting the role of entry in Dutch manufacturing, entry in services in The Netherlands is at least as important.

In addition, the market penetration of new entrants, measured as the market share of employment of new firms, i.e., new firm employment divided by total industry employment, is considerably less than the entry rates. The market penetration rate is 9.8 percent in retailing, which is less than half as large as the entry rate. Similarly, the market penetration rate is 18.0 percent in the hospitality sector, which is 50 percent less than the entry rate. Thus, the low market penetration rates of new entrants relative to the entry rates in services is similar to Geroski's Stylized Fact for manufacturing.

The third Stylized Fact uncovered by Geroski (1995) is "Entry and exit rates are highly positively correlated, and net entry rates and penetration are modest fractions of gross entry rates and penetration."[9] The exit rates shown in the second column of table 10.2 tend to follow the entry rates in the first column.[10] Those service industries with a low entry rate also tend to experience a low exit rate; those service industries with a high entry rate also tend to experience a high exit rate. This is consistent with the simple correlation coefficient of 0.52 between entry and exit rates across industries. This high degree of correlation found between entry and exit in services is also consistent with that found for manufacturing, not just in The Netherlands (Kleijweg and Lever, 1994), but also in a host of other countries, such as the United States (Dunne, Roberts, and Samuelson, 1988), Portugal (Mata, 1993), Germany (Wagner, 1994), and Canada (Baldwin, 1995).

The net entry rates, or the difference between the gross entry rate and the exit rate, is relatively small in the Dutch services and certainly smaller than the gross entry rates as well as the penetration rates. The mean net

---

[8] See Carree and Thurik (1996) for an extensive review of the empirical literature on the entry and exit of firms.

[9] This Stylized Fact by Geroski is very similar to (the first part of) Sutton's fourth Statistical Regularity (Sutton, 1997, p. 52) which is:

4 *Turbulence*: Across different industries, there is a positive correlation between gross entry rates, and gross exit rates, i.e., the "churning" of the population of firms is greater in some industries than others. However, most of this entry and exit has relatively little effect on the largest firms in the industry.

The last sentence of Statistical Regularity 4 by Sutton is consistent with Geroski's fourth Stylized Fact, which we discuss below.

[10] The exit rate is based on Dunne, Roberts, and Samuelson (1988 and 1989) and is defined as the number of firms exiting the industry between 1986–1988 divided by the total number of firms in that industry in 1985.

Table 10.2 *Measures of entry, exit, their market shares and relative size in services*

	Entry rates	Exit rates	Market share		Relative size	
			Entry	Exit	Entry	Exit
SBI						
Retailing						
Total	*0.211*	*0.243*	*0.098*	*0.179*	*0.399*	*0.679*
651	0.161	0.234	0.193	0.253	1.130	1.109
652	0.189	0.265	0.079	0.119	0.333	0.373
653	0.125	0.115	0.147	0.142	1.214	1.276
654	0.148	0.190	0.097	0.203	0.589	1.083
655	0.235	0.246	0.098	0.122	0.352	0.498
656	0.212	0.348	0.074	0.153	0.247	0.337
657	0.152	0.202	0.139	0.162	0.842	0.764
658	0.158	0.216	0.101	0.148	0.540	0.630
659	0.259	0.265	0.110	0.153	0.358	0.500
661	0.245	0.272	0.116	0.136	0.391	0.422
662	0.267	0.224	0.162	0.145	0.565	0.588
663	0.197	0.205	0.150	0.127	0.705	0.563
664	0.238	0.216	0.128	0.274	0.482	1.366
665	0.173	0.210	0.118	0.135	0.611	0.588
666	0.305	0.230	0.149	0.168	0.439	0.679
667	0.118	0.250	0.049	0.157	0.318	0.562
668	0.328	0.295	0.125	0.201	0.309	0.599
669	0.140	0.280	0.016	0.413	0.089	1.808
Hospitality						
Total	*0.270*	*0.240*	*0.180*	*0.136*	*0.617*	*0.499*
6711	0.214	0.199	0.141	0.113	0.623	0.515
6712	0.330	0.260	0.227	0.161	0.654	0.546
6721	0.337	0.290	0.215	0.173	0.578	0.513
6741	0.115	0.144	0.113	0.097	0.927	0.634
6799	0.247	0.257	0.279	0.180	1.129	0.631

entry rate in retailing is − 3.2 percent, which is considerably smaller than the gross entry rate of 21.1 percent. Similarly, the mean net entry rate in hospitality is 3.0 percent, which is considerably smaller than the gross entry rate of 27.0 percent. The net penetration rates, or the difference between the penetration rate of the entrants and that of the exiting firms, which is shown in the third and fourth columns, is also considerably smaller than the penetration rates of the entrants. Thus, the tendency for gross entry to exceed net entry and for gross penetration by entrants to exceed the net penetration holds for services as well as in manufacturing.

The fourth Stylized Fact regarding industry dynamics for manufacturing uncovered by Geroski is, "The survival rate of most entrants is low, and even successful entrants may take more than a decade to achieve a size comparable to the average incumbent." This Stylized Fact also holds for services, as indicated in table 10.3, which shows the exit rate, market share, and relative size by firm age class. The mean three-year exit rate in retailing declines with age, from 39.6 percent for firms two years old and younger, to 18.9 percent for firms that are at least 11 years old. Similarly, the mean exit rate in hospitality also declines with age, from 37.5 percent for firms two years old and younger, to 15.0 percent for firms that are at least 11 years old.

Table 10.3 also shows that the mean size of firms in an age class relative to the size of all firms in the industry is greater for older firms than for younger firms. The mean size of firms is defined as the number of employees in the industry divided by the number of firms. Retail firms that are at least 11 years old are, on average, 31 percent larger than the industry mean size. By contrast, retail firms that are between 6 and 10 years old are only 54.9 percent as large as the industry mean size. One surprising finding that differs from that in manufacturing is that the youngest firms in retailing are actually slightly larger than the mean firm size for the entire industry. But this may be the result of the large size of new firms in industry 652, potatoes, fruit, vegetables, beverages, chocolate, and tobacco. By contrast, in hospitality, the youngest firms are only 61.6 percent as large as the mean firm size in the industry. Even firms that are between six and ten years old are only 81.9 percent as large as the mean firm size for the entire industry. Firm size only starts to increase significantly for firms that are at least 11 years old, which have a mean size of 77.6 percent greater than that for the entire industry. Thus, not only does the likelihood of survival tend to be low in services, but older firms tend to be larger than their younger counterparts, in a manner that is similar to that found in manufacturing.

Based on three of the Stylized Facts about entry and subsequent post-entry performance that Geroski was able to uncover from a large and diverse body of studies for the manufacturing sector, the evidence presented here suggests that these Stylized Facts tend to hold up quite well for the services. That is, the entry of new firms is common and involves a high number of entrants, but the market penetration of those new entrants is considerably lower than the actual entry rates. In addition, entry rates tend to be highly correlated with exit rates. Finally, the likelihood of new-firm survival is low in services, just as it is in manufacturing.

Table 10.3 *Exit rate, market share, and relative size by age class*

	Exit rate by age class (years)				Market share[a] by age class (years)				Relative size[b] by age class (years)			
	0–2	3–5	6–10	11+	0–2	3–5	6–10	11+	0–2	3–5	6–10	11+
SBI												
Retailing												
Total	*0.396*	*0.316*	*0.265*	*0.189*	*0.081*	*0.093*	*0.171*	*0.655*	*1.088*	*0.804*	*0.549*	*1.313*
651	0.406	0.330	0.261	0.172	0.035	0.124	0.240	0.601	0.477	1.201	0.736	1.209
652	0.404	0.303	0.281	0.225	0.139	0.112	0.134	0.615	1.823	0.954	0.424	1.254
653	0.173	0.094	0.130	0.100	0.069	0.098	0.237	0.596	0.593	0.716	1.047	1.145
654	0.518	0.233	0.204	0.162	0.018	0.032	0.363	0.587	0.486	0.541	1.448	0.899
655	0.411	0.346	0.275	0.169	0.084	0.085	0.134	0.698	0.817	0.597	0.523	1.396
656	0.500	0.487	0.355	0.255	0.029	0.325	0.197	0.449	0.259	2.499	0.560	1.107
657	0.311	0.252	0.243	0.169	0.021	0.078	0.164	0.737	0.372	0.958	0.656	1.203
658	0.383	0.311	0.226	0.178	0.061	0.106	0.156	0.677	1.030	0.974	0.659	1.137
659	0.418	0.435	0.295	0.207	0.050	0.120	0.217	0.613	0.715	1.065	0.672	1.240
661	0.385	0.351	0.301	0.220	0.034	0.079	0.196	0.691	0.508	0.654	0.640	1.364
662	0.343	0.326	0.260	0.173	0.018	0.069	0.237	0.667	0.585	0.665	0.698	1.285
663	0.243	0.211	0.259	0.153	0.048	0.079	0.301	0.571	0.848	0.700	0.787	1.277
664	0.402	0.312	0.266	0.143	0.022	0.057	0.234	0.688	0.281	0.430	0.934	1.273
665	0.318	0.287	0.233	0.173	0.071	0.062	0.213	0.654	0.942	0.797	0.741	1.156
666	0.406	0.247	0.229	0.186	0.030	0.093	0.382	0.495	0.400	0.687	0.873	1.405
667	n.a.[c]	n.a.[c]	0.236	0.254	n.a.[c]	n.a.[c]	0.547	0.397	n.a.[c]	n.a.[c]	1.095	0.854
668	0.525	0.404	0.265	0.220	0.047	0.097	0.273	0.583	0.510	0.591	0.727	1.584
669	0.333	0.235	0.186	0.329	0.106	0.010	0.046	0.838	0.690	0.090	0.169	1.803
Hospitality												
Total	*0.375*	*0.289*	*0.238*	*0.150*	*0.066*	*0.157*	*0.250*	*0.527*	*0.616*	*0.766*	*0.819*	*1.776*
6711	0.321	0.234	0.188	0.127	0.080	0.186	0.280	0.454	0.650	0.862	0.842	1.592
6712	0.358	0.316	0.248	0.178	0.082	0.197	0.338	0.383	0.789	0.851	0.812	1.571
6721	0.426	0.332	0.277	0.183	0.126	0.175	0.323	0.376	0.508	0.751	0.685	1.587
6741	0.278	0.180	0.161	0.115	0.047	0.086	0.203	0.664	0.729	0.806	0.780	1.168
6799	0.436	0.345	0.272	0.154	0.019	0.167	0.171	0.642	0.196	0.937	0.488	1.723

Notes:
[a] The market share of an age class in an industry is defined as the employment in that age class divided by the total employment in the industry.
[b] The relative size in an age class of an industry is defined as the average size in that age class divided by the average size in that industry.
[c] Not available due to the small number of firms in the age class.

4 Why are services different?

Despite the seeming similarities in the dynamics of new-firm entry and their post-entry patterns between services and manufacturing documented in the previous section, there are theoretical reasons to believe that, in fact, the services would not be expected to mirror manufacturing, particularly with respect to the central focus of the literature on the post-entry performance of firms – growth and survival. Beginning with the pioneering studies by Evans (1987a and 1987b) and Hall (1987) along with Dunne, Roberts, and Samuelson (1988 and 1989) a central finding of this literature is that firm growth is negatively related to firm size and age and that firm survival is positively related to size and age. These findings have been confirmed in virtually every other study undertaken, despite differences in country, time period, and methodology used, leading Geroski (1995, p. 434) to infer the existence of a Stylized Result that: "Both firm size and age are correlated with the survival and growth of entrants."

Despite the robustness of this Stylized Result for manufacturing, there are strong theoretical reasons why it may not hold for services. An important reason for this doubt comes from a secondary result about the relationships between growth and survival, on the one hand, and firm size and age, on the other, from the manufacturing industries. While these relationships have been found to hold for manufacturing firms in general, studies find that they actually vary systematically across industries, depending upon particular characteristics specific to each industry. In particular, the likelihood of new-firm survival is found to be systematically lower in industries where scale economies play an important role and systematically higher in industries with no significant economies of scale. Similarly, the growth of new firms is found to be greater in those industries with high scale economies but lower in industries where scale economies are negligible.

Why should the extent of scale economies influence the likelihood of survival and post-entry growth? The answer provided by Jovanovic (1982), which presents the common theoretical framework for this literature, has to do with the conditions under which people start firms. In his theory of noisy learning, Jovanovic (1982) argues that new firms are started by entrepreneurs who have limited knowledge about their ability to manage a firm and therefore about the viability of the new startup.[11] Although entrepreneurs may start a new firm based on an

[11] Recent extensions of the Jovanovic model can be found in Hopenhayn (1992) and Ericson and Pakes (1995).

expected post-entry performance, they only discover or learn about their true ability on the basis of actual firm performance. Those entrepreneurs who discover that their ability exceeds expectations expand the scale of operations, while those who are disappointed are unable to grow.

But what happens to those new firms unable to grow? If scale economies are negligible in the industry, the firm can remain operating at a small scale of output indefinitely without incurring any cost disadvantage. However, if there are extensive economies of scale, a small firm will be confronted by sizeable cost disadvantages. The inability of the new firm to grow will force it to exit from an industry characterized by high scale economies but not in industries with negligible scale economies. At the same time, any cost disadvantage resulting from scale economies will be reduced as the firm size increases. As the empirical evidence in manufacturing suggests, the likelihood of new-firm survival tends to be lower but growth rates of surviving new firms higher in industries where scale economies are substantial (Audretsch, 1995; Baldwin, 1995; Mata, 1994; Audretsch and Mahmood, 1995; and Wagner, 1994). The consequences of not being able to grow and attain the minimum efficient scale (MES) are a cost disadvantage which will ultimately lead to exit.

The different impacts of size and age on growth and survival across different industries is also evidenced from the disparities in the empirical findings on the validity of Gibrat's Law, which assumes that firm growth is independent of size, between samples of smaller firms and larger firms. At first glance, the empirical evidence testing the validity of Gibrat's Law seems ambiguous and confusing. For example, Schmalensee (1989) concludes that Gibrat's Law seems to hold in older studies but not in newer studies. But what differs between the older and more recent studies is the size composition of firms included in the data base. In fact, most studies consisting of larger firms, which tend to be the older studies, have found Gibrat's Law to hold. Growth appears to be independent of size for large firms. But the evidence is strikingly different for studies including small firms. As Geroski (1995) characterizes as a Stylized Result from these studies, firm size tends to be negatively correlated with growth. Actually Mansfield (1962) anticipated the reconciliation between these seemingly inconsistent results when he warned that Gibrat's Law should only hold for firms having attained the MES level of output. Those firms operating at a suboptimal scale of output need to grow in order to survive, resulting in the observation of a negative relationship between growth and firm size but a positive relationship between survival and firm size.

One of the main differences between services and manufacturing, at least in The Netherlands, is the absence of scale economies in services. There has been a long and vibrant tradition of small-scale enterprise in the Dutch services. As table 10.1 suggests, the Dutch are an economy of small shopkeepers when it comes to services, at least up until now. Clearly, this is consistent with the observation from table 10.1 of the mean employment size of fewer than eight employees in retailing and fewer than five employees in hospitality. While these averages include incumbents as well as new firms, the mean size of just *startups* in manufacturing has been found to be slightly greater in OECD countries as diverse as the US (Dunne, Roberts, and Samuelson, 1988), Germany (Wagner, 1994), Canada (Baldwin, 1995), and Portugal (Mata and Portugal, 1994).

The relative absence of scale economies in the Dutch services imply a different selection process for new firms in the services than has been found in manufacturing. New entrants are not compelled to grow in order to survive. Negligible scale economies in services ensure that new firms can remain small without being confronted by any cost disadvantage. In the absence of any pressure to grow in order to reduce costs, no systematic relationships would be expected to be found between growth and survival, on the one hand, and firm size and age, on the other. What is currently referred to as a Stylized Result in the literature may only apply to manufacturing but not services.

We expect that growth rates for services are distributed more or less independently of firm size and age. We do not expect to observe a relationship between the likelihood of survival and firm size either. However, since the learning process described by Jovanovic (1982) should be as valid in services as it is in manufacturing, we would expect the likelihood of survival to increase with age. These four propositions are tested in the next section.

5   Linking growth and survival to firm size and age

While there have been numerous methodologies and frameworks used to link firm growth to size and age, and survival to size and age in the studies of manufacturing, to examine these relationships for services we adapt not only the methodology, but also the exact functional form, used in the pioneering studies by Evans (1987a and 1987b).[12] Firm growth, G,

---

[12] A linear functional form (which Evans, 1987a and 1987b did not estimate), was also estimated but the results are not reported here because inclusion of the quadratic terms substantially increases the fit of the model.

is determined by size, S, and age, A, in a second-order expansion in a (natural) log specified model

$$\ln G_{t'} = [\ln S_{t'} | \ln S_t]/d = \beta_0 + \beta_1 \ln S_t + \beta_2 \ln A_t +$$
$$\beta_3(\ln S_t)^2 + \beta_4(\ln A_t)^2 + \beta_5(\ln S_t) \times (\ln A_t) + u_t \qquad (1)$$

where the annual firm growth rate, G, is measured by the number of employees in 1988 divided by the number of employees in 1985 and divided by 3. Firm size is measured as the number of employees in 1985,[13] and age is the number of years the firm has been in operation in 1985.[14] The time period t', refers to 1985 and t refers to 1988, so that $t' \geq t, d = t' - t$, and u is a normally distributed disturbance term with mean zero and possibly non-constant variance across observations.

Survival is similarly estimated by

$$E[I_{t'} | A_t, S_t] = \Phi[\gamma_0 + \gamma_1 \ln S_t + \gamma_2 \ln A_t + \gamma_3(\ln S_t)^2 +$$
$$\gamma_4(\ln A_t)^2 + \gamma_5(\ln S_t) \times (\ln A_t)] \qquad (2)$$

where $E[I_{t'} | A_t, S_t]$ is the conditional expectation of survival I given the size and age in period t, $I_{t'} = 1$ if a firm survives from 1985 through 1988, $I_t = 0$ if a firm exits between 1985 and 1988, and Φ is the cumulative distribution for a (standard) normal variable. We obtain estimation results for firm survival in the probit equation (2) using the maximum likelihood (ML) method. The estimation of the growth equation (1) cannot be carried out in a straightforward manner. As a result of sample selection and heteroskedasticity, the estimation needs to be corrected to obtain unbiased coefficients in equation (1). We shall first discuss these issues of sample selection and heteroskedasticity.

[13] There is a difference in the measurement of the employment size between incorporated and non-incorporated firms. This discrepancy occurs because non-incorporated firms do not include the owner as being employed, while the managing director of an incorporated firm is. We reconcile this discrepancy by increasing the number of recorded employment in non-incorporated firms by one. Because some incorporated firms with only part-time employees are sufficiently small to have full-time equivalent (FTE) employment of less than one, they are excluded from the data base.

[14] To avoid having undefined observations when taking the log of the age of new firms, the age of each firm is augmented by one year. In addition, the age of the firm tends to be somewhat underestimated as a result of the lag between the startup date and the time the firm is recorded in the data base. An approximation about the age of old firms had to be made since the General Business Register (ABR) started in 1967, so that no firm births were recorded prior to 1967. The estimated age of firms born before 1967 is based on fitting a log-normal distribution of the age data. The approximated mean firm age for these older firms in 1985 is 27 in hospitality and 31 in retailing.

There have been two main sources of sample selection bias in the studies linking firm survival and growth to size and age in manufacturing. First, sample selection has occurred because large firms are overrepresented in the data set.[15] Larger firms in many of the studies have a higher probability of being selected in the data base than smaller firms. This source of sample selection is not likely to impose a bias on the data base used in this study because all firms with paid employees are included in the data base: all small and large firms have an equal chance of being included in the data base, which, in principle, should be 100 percent. The second source of selection bias in most studies occurs because growth can only be observed and measured for surviving firms. Since virtually every study for manufacturing finds that survival is positively related to size and age, the estimated relationships between firm growth and size and firm growth and age will be biased downwards.[16] We estimate the probit equation (2) and add Heckman's λ (Heckman, 1979) to equation (1) to correct for sample selection bias.[17]

There is a complication involved in adding Heckman's λ to equation (1). First, inclusion of the variable λ causes severe multicollinearity in the growth equation. The variable λ is a non-linear function of the independent variables in the survival equation, which are the same as those in the growth equation. The introduction of λ results in imprecise estimates of the coefficients in the growth equation. Therefore, we estimate the probit equation for each of the 18 three-digit retail industries and for each of the five four-digit hospitality industries, as defined in table 10.1. We then use the coefficients of the industries to calculate the variable λ.[18]

If the growth rates of firms vary less for larger and older firms it is reasonable to expect heteroskedasticity in the growth equation (1). We follow White's (1980a) procedure and regress the squared residuals upon

[15] Mata (1994) points out that this form of sample selection bias has occurred in most of the studies in manufacturing linking firm survival and growth to age and size.

[16] Mansfield (1962) implicitly introduced the possibility of sample selection bias by conjecturing that the inverse relationship between firm growth and size is an artefact of the greater likelihood of exit exhibited by slow-growth firms. Evans (1987a and 1987b) and Hall (1987), as well as subsequent studies, found that the observed negative relationship between growth and firm size is robust with respect to sample censoring.

[17] If the coefficient for the variable λ differs significantly from zero, the standard errors for all coefficients in equation (1) are understated. We followed the procedure suggested by Heckman (1979) and corrected by Greene (1981) to obtain consistent estimates of the standard errors.

[18] The use of the coefficients of the three- and four-digit industries to calculate the variable λ reduces the value of the R^2 between the variable λ and the (five) other independent variables from 0.999 to 0.833 in the retail sector and from 1.000 to 0.919 in hospitality.

the regressors used in equation (1),[19] and afterwards the squared estimated residuals are used to obtain weighted least squares (WLS) results.[20]

The estimated results of equations (1) and (2) are presented in table 10.4 based on 45,158 firms in retailing and 17,610 firms in hospitality. Estimation of quadratic relationships make it difficult to unequivocally interpret whether an explanatory variable has a positive or negative impact. Only by calculating the turning point and then the number of firms included in each part of the curve can such an inference be made. The results of such calculations are given in table 10.5, which shows the share of firms included in the increasing and decreasing parts of the functions.[21]

In the growth equations for retailing, the negative coefficient of firm size combined with the positive coefficient of size-squared suggests that growth rates tend to decline as firm size increases up to a certain size and then increases with subsequent increases in firm size. As table 10.5 shows, 91.6 percent of the firms are operating on the negative part of this curve; only the largest 8.4 percent of the firms have a sufficient size to be operating on the positive part of the curve.[22] This means that for almost all firms in retailing, firm growth declines with size.

Similarly, the negative coefficient of age combined with the positive coefficient of age-squared suggests that age has a negative impact on growth for smaller firms but a positive impact for larger firms. As table 10.5 shows, 82.7 percent of the firms are operating on the negative part of this curve and only the largest 17.3 percent are on the positive part. This means that all but the largest of the retail firms experience a negative relationship between firm growth and age.

Thus, the results from estimation equation (1) for all retail firms imply that the relationships between firm growth and size, and growth and age are similar to those that have emerged in manufacturing. The finding of generally negative relationships between growth, on the one hand, and

[19] We do not include third-order expansion terms in the regression due to strong multicollinearity.

[20] The degree of heteroskedasticity is modest and the OLS and WLS estimates are close, although the OLS estimates generally do not pass the White (1980a) test. The slight differences between the OLS and WLS estimates indicate that no further non-linearity than the second-order expansions in equation (1) is needed. See White (1980b).

[21] The impact of size and age on firm growth and survival is calculated by computing the partial derivatives of (logarithmic) growth and survival with respect to (logarithmic) size and (logarithmic) age.

[22] These calculations are based on the estimated regression for firm growth in table 10.4 using weighted least squares (WLS) and corrected for sample selection bias.

size and age, on the other, are independent of whether the estimated growth equation is corrected for sample selection bias.

The probit estimation of survival for all retailing firms results in a positive coefficient between firm size and the likelihood of survival but a negative coefficient between firm size squared and the likelihood of survival. This suggests that the likelihood of survival increases with firm size up to a point and then decreases with subsequent increases in firm size. As table 10.5 shows, 97.8 percent of the retail firms operate in the upward sloping part of this curve; only 2.2 percent of the retail firms are actually in the downward sloping part of this curve. The vast majority of retail firms are subject to a positive relationship between firm size and the likelihood of survival.

Similarly, the positive coefficient of age combined with the negative coefficient of age squared implies that the likelihood of survival increases as firms mature until a critical age and then decreases as the firm ages. Table 10.5 shows that 91.0 percent of the retail firms are on the upward slope of this curve, while only 9.0 percent are on the downward slope.

Tables 10.4 and 10.5 also show virtually identical results for the hospitality firms. In particular, 94.5 percent of the firms are found to experience negative relationships between firm size and growth and 80.3 percent between firm age and growth. Similarly, 97.9 percent of the firms are found to experience a positive relationship between the likelihood of survival and firm size, while all the firms experience a positive relationship between the likelihood of survival and firm age. Thus, the generally positive impact of size and age on the likelihood of firm survival in both hospitality as well as retailing seems to mirror the Stylized Result found in manufacturing.

The previous section predicts that, based on the findings from manufacturing industries, the impacts of age and size on growth and survival should be lower or even non-existent for firms that have attained the MES level of output.[23] This suggests that the results from table 10.4 may be sensitive to inclusion of the smallest firms in the sample.[24] The

---

[23] An important characteristic of hospitality and retailing in The Netherlands is the absence of significant scale economies.

[24] One reason for this is due to statistical problems associated with regression to the mean. As Mata (1994) points out, firms with no or just several employees cannot experience a measured decrease in employment growth. If such a tiny firm experiences negative growth, it will, by definition, disappear. Therefore, the lower bound of measured growth rates for firms with no employees is 0 percent and cannot, by definition, be negative. Only firms with more than a handful of employees can experience negative growth and still be in existence.

Table 10.4 *Empirical results for firm growth and firm survival (equations (1) and (2) are estimated for all firms)*

	Retail industries			Hospitality industries		
	Firm growth: WLS[a]	Firm survival: ML[b]	Firm growth: WLS and CSS[c]	Firm growth: WLS[a]	Firm survival: ML[b]	Firm growth: WLS and CSS[c]
Variable						
ln S	−0.1072	0.5840	−0.0881	−0.1399	0.6703	−0.1566
	(0.0048)[d]	(0.0323)	(0.0066)	(0.0086)	(0.0521)	(0.0156)
ln A	−0.1010	0.3230	−0.0907	−0.1099	0.2652	−0.1182
	(0.0068)	(0.0421)	(0.0074)	(0.0104)	(0.0662)	(0.0121)
(ln S)^2	0.0163	−0.1294	0.0124	0.0179	−0.1368	0.0206
	(0.0008)	(0.0048)	(0.0012)	(0.0020)	(0.0098)	(0.0030)
(ln A)^2	0.0129	−0.0595	0.0112	0.0146	−0.0219	0.0154
	(0.0014)	(0.0093)	(0.0015)	(0.0025)	(0.0172)	(0.0025)
(ln S) x (ln A)	0.0093	0.0944	0.0102	0.0211	0.0789	0.0214
	(0.0016)	(0.0116)	(0.0017)	(0.0034)	(0.0227)	(0.0034)
Constant	0.2529	−0.3395	0.1996	0.2595	−0.3119	0.3018
	(0.0088)	(0.0501)	(0.0153)	(0.0124)	(0.0693)	(0.0341)
Heckman λ	—	—	0.0546	—	—	−0.0430
			(0.0127)			(0.0323)
R^2	0.0640	0.0758[e]	0.0645	0.058	0.0830[e]	0.0600
N	34,519	45,158	34,519	13,484	17,610	13,484

Notes:
[a] WLS stands for weighted least squares.
[b] ML stands for maximum likelihood.
[c] WLS and CSS stands for weighted least squares estimates which are corrected for sample selection bias.
[d] Standard errors are given between parentheses.
[e] R^2 is defined as the proportion of the variance of firm survival rates that is explained by the probit equation.

prevalence of small-scale operations in the Dutch services suggests a virtual absence of scale economies in all but the tiniest enterprises. Thus, we re-estimate the growth and survival equations leaving out firms with fewer than five employees. The results, which are reported in table 10.6, are strikingly different when the smallest firms are omitted. While the sign of the coefficients in the growth equations are the same as in table 10.4, their impacts are considerably weaker. For the hospitality industries there is no significant relationship between growth and the size and age of firms when the smallest firms are omitted from the sample. None of

Table 10.5 *The effects of firm size and age on growth and survival (statistics based on the estimation results of table 10.4)*

		Retail industries	Hospitality industries
	Partial derivative		
g_s	mean	−0.031	−0.061
	standard deviation	0.022	0.036
	fraction positive	0.084	0.055
	fraction negative	0.916	0.945
g_a	mean	−0.019	−0.024
	standard deviation	0.019	0.029
	fraction positive	0.173	0.197
	fraction negative	0.827	0.803
S_s	mean	0.159	0.169
	standard deviation	0.086	0.091
	fraction positive	0.978	0.979
	fraction negative	0.022	0.021
S_a	mean	0.038	0.069
	standard deviation	0.033	0.021
	fraction positive	0.910	1.000
	fraction negative	0.090	0.000
	Elasticity		
$Es_t S_t$	mean	0.969	0.939
	standard deviation	0.022	0.036
$Es_t A_t$	mean	−0.019	−0.024
	standard deviation	0.019	0.029
ESs_t	mean	0.227	0.244
	standard deviation	0.165	0.164
ESA_t	mean	0.053	0.096
	standard deviation	0.066	0.044

Note:

g_s is the partial derivative of (logarithmic) growth with respect to (logarithmic) size in the preceding year.

g_a is the partial derivative of (logarithmic) growth with respect to (logarithmic) age in the preceding year.

S_s is the partial derivative of survival with respect to (logarithmic) size in the preceding year.

S_a is the partial derivative of survival with respect to (logarithmic) age in the preceding year.

$Es_t S_t$ is the elasticity of size in a certain year with respect to size in the preceding year.

$Es_t A_t$ is the elasticity of size in a certain year with respect to age in the preceding year.

ESs_t is the elasticity of survival with respect to size in the preceding year.

ESA_t is the elasticity of survival with respect to age in the preceding year.

248   David Audretsch, Luuk Klomp, and Roy Thurik

the coefficients of size and age in the growth equations of table 10.6 in hospitality are statistically insignificant. For retailing, the coefficients of size and age in table 10.6 are statistically significant (at the 5 percent level), but are sufficiently small as to render the impact of size and age on growth meaningless. Using the F-test proposed by Leamer (1978) leads to the conclusion that growth rates are independent of size and age, even in the retail industries.[25] In addition, in the growth equation the R^2 for retailing falls from 0.0645 in table 10.4 to 0.0109 in table 10.6, and in hospitality from 0.0600 in table 10.4 to 0.0035 in table 10.6.

To ensure that these results do not reflect the aggregation of firms from different industries, the growth equations were estimated for each of the 16 retail three-digit industries and five hospitality industries. Using a 1 percent level of significance, the hypothesis that there are no size and age effects is accepted in 15 of the 16 retail industries, and in four of the five hospitality industries.

The results from the probit survival estimates in table 10.6 also show that firm survival is not related to size in either retailing or hospitality. The coefficients of size and size-squared are not statistically significant in either of these service industries. However, as the statistically significant coefficients of age suggests, the likelihood of survival is still shaped by firm age, even when the smallest firms are deleted from the sample. On average, a 1 percent change in age leads to a 0.064 percent change in the probability of survival in retailing, and a 0.075 percent change in the likelihood of survival in hospitality.[26]

To summarize the results of growth and survival, the four propositions stated at the end of the previous section have been largely confirmed. In particular, the results when the smallest service firms are omitted in table 10.6 are strikingly different from the Stylized Result reported by Geroski (1995) based on manufacturing. Firm growth is not systematically related to either size or age. Rather, Gibrat's Law holds for all but the smallest of firms in the services, suggesting that firm growth is independent of size. While Evans (1987a, p. 579) concluded that in manufacturing "firm growth decreases at a diminishing rate with firm size," the evidence from services suggests that Gibrat's Law actually holds in the

[25] The calculated F-values for the hypotheses that there are no age and size effects on growth are 6.89 and 5.98, respectively. The critical F-value is 9.13 for the retail industries.
[26] The average elasticities of firm survival with respect to age in table 10.6 approximate those from table 10.4, which are reported in table 10.5. The higher age of the firms included in the samples used in table 10.6 compared to that in table 10.4 offsets the higher coefficients for the age and size variables in table 10.6 compared to those in table 10.4.

Table 10.6 *Empirical results for firm growth and firm survival (equations (1) and (2) are estimated for firms with at least 5 (full time) employees)*

	Retail industries			Hospitality industries		
	Firm growth: WLS[a]	Firm survival: ML[b]	Firm growth: WLS and CSS[c]	Firm growth: WLS[a]	Firm survival: ML[b]	Firm growth: WLS and CSS[c]
Variable						
ln S	−0.0274	0.1256	−0.0279	−0.0261	0.0505	−0.0210
	(0.0125)[d]	(0.0931)	(0.0139)	(0.0388)	(0.2042)	(0.0465)
ln A	−0.0739	0.8910	−0.0577	−0.0396	0.6800	−0.0028
	(0.0190)	(0.1348)	(0.0221)	(0.0389)	(0.2445)	(0.0496)
$(\ln S)^2$	0.0024	−0.0024	0.0026	−0.0005	−0.0285	−0.0010
	(0.0013)	(0.0101)	(0.0014)	(0.0060)	(0.0284)	(0.0072)
$(\ln A)^2$	0.0069	−0.0903	0.0053	0.0028	−0.1097	−0.0008
	(0.0033)	(0.0252)	(0.0037)	(0.0071)	(0.0508)	(0.0087)
$(\ln S) \times (\ln A)$	0.0074	−0.0734	0.0067	0.0121	0.0670	0.0117
	(0.0031)	(0.0241)	(0.0035)	(0.0096)	(0.0596)	(0.0115)
Constant	0.1430	−0.3839	0.1006	0.0612	0.0099	−0.0483
	(0.0334)	(0.2296)	(0.0410)	(0.0748)	(0.4166)	(0.1027)
Heckman λ	—	—	0.0655	—	—	0.1914
			(0.0296)			(0.0878)
R^2	0.0116	0.0207[e]	0.0109	0.0012	0.0516[e]	0.0035
N	9,166	10,564	9,166	2,980	3,341	2,980

Notes:
[a] WLS stands for weighted least squares.
[b] ML stands for maximum likelihood.
[c] WLS and CSS stands for weighted least squares estimates which are corrected for sample selection bias.
[d] Standard errors are given between parentheses.
[e] R^2 is defined as the proportion of the variance of firm survival rates that is explained by the probit equation.

services for all but the tiniest firms. Similarly, the likelihood of survival is independent of size for all but the smallest service firms. Unlike in manufacturing, beyond just a handful of employees, additional increases in firm size will neither influence growth nor secure a higher likelihood of survival. Of all four relationships involved in Geroski's Stylized Result based on manufacturing, only the link between age and survival is found to hold for services.

6   Conclusion

Are the services different from manufacturing? The answer is somewhat ambiguous. On the one hand, the relationships between firm survival, growth, age, and size, which have emerged so consistently in manufacturing as to constitute a Stylized Result (Geroski, 1995) or Statistical Regularities (Sutton, 1997), do not exist in the services for all but the smallest firms. The post-entry dynamics appear to be strikingly different in services than in manufacturing.

On the other hand, further reflection suggests that firms in services are subject to the same selection process as their manufacturing counterparts. As Jovanovic (1982) indicated, entrants need to learn about the viability of their new enterprise. The positive impact of age on the likelihood of survival in both services as well as in manufacturing argues that in the initial post-entry period new startups have a high propensity to exit, presumably because they learn that their new venture is not feasible.

In addition, firms with only a handful of employees are found to be confronted with a lower likelihood of survival in the services, just as in manufacturing. And, those tiny service firms that do manage to survive have systematically higher growth rates than do their larger counterparts. Just as has been found in manufacturing, these tiny service firms need to grow in order to survive. This pressure, however, is lower than in manufacturing. Apparently, this necessity to grow disappears once the service firms have reached the size of five employees.

What is different in services than manufacturing is the apparent absence of scale economies, so that the role of size in the selection process of new entrants diminishes quickly and disappears once the minimal size of about five employees has been attained. By contrast, the mean startup size in manufacturing is considerably larger than five employees. The differences between services and manufacturing found in this chapter were in some way anticipated by Mansfield (1962), even before any of the empirical studies on post-entry performance of firms were undertaken. Mansfield emphasized that the assumption of Gibrat's Law, that growth is independent of size, should hold only for firms that have attained the MES level of output and exhausted scale economies. Sub-optimal scale firms need to grow in order to attain the MES level of output and reduce average cost to a minimum. By contrast, large firms experiencing even negative growth will not be penalized by a cost disadvantage. Many of the ambiguities in the literature on Gibrat's Law are attributable to neglecting Mansfield's distinction about the role of scale economies in shaping the firm size–growth relationship some three decades ago.

The suggestion that the dynamics of industrial organization in services mirrors that in manufacturing appears naïve and is not supported by the evidence. Therefore, what emerges as a Stylized Fact in manufacturing may not hold in services. The evidence from this chapter suggests that services, at least in the European context, differ from manufacturing in that scale economies are negligible, resulting in a different post-entry performance in the services than in manufacturing. Of course, Europe remains a continent where family-owned lodging houses have not yet been replaced by large hotel chains and where local independent restaurants and retail stores have not yet been overtaken by national and international mega-store chains. Whether our findings would hold in the very different context of North America can only be confirmed by undertaking the necessary research.

References

Audretsch, D.B. (1995), *Innovation and Industry Evolution*, Cambridge, Mass.: MIT Press.

Audretsch, D.B. and T. Mahmood (1995), "New-Firm Survival: New Results Using a Hazard Function," *Review of Economics and Statistics*, 77: 97–103.

Baldwin, J.R. (1995), *The Dynamics of Industrial Competition: A North American Perspective*, Cambridge, Mass.: Cambridge University Press.

Carree, M.A. and A.R. Thurik (1996), "Entry and Exit in Retailing: Incentives, Barriers, Displacement and Replacement," *Review of Industrial Organization*, 11: 155–172.

Davis, S.J., J. Haltiwanger, and S. Schuh (1996a), *Job Creation and Destruction*, Cambridge, Mass.: MIT Press.

(1996b), "Small Business and Job Creation: Dissecting the Myth and Reassessing the Facts," *Small Business Economics*, 8: 297–316.

Dunne, T., M.J. Roberts, and L. Samuelson (1988), "Patterns of Firm Entry and Exit in US Manufacturing Industries," *Rand Journal of Economics*, 19: 495–515.

(1989), "The Growth and Failure of US Manufacturing Plants," *Quarterly Journal of Economics*, 104: 671–698.

Ericson, R. and A. Pakes (1995), "Markov-Perfect Industry Dynamics: a Framework for Empirical Work," *Review of Economic Studies*, 62: 53–82.

Evans, D.S. (1987a), "The Relationship between Firm Growth, Size, and Age: Estimates for 100 Manufacturing Industries," *Journal of Industrial Economics*, 35: 567–581.

(1987b), "Tests of Alternative Theories of Firm Growth," *Journal of Political Economy*, 95: 657–674.

Geroski, P.A. (1995), "What Do We Know About Entry?" *International Journal of Industrial Organization*, 13: 421–440.

Gibrat, R. (1931), *Les Inégalités Économiques*, Paris: Librairie du Receuil Sirey.

252   David Audretsch, Luuk Klomp, and Roy Thurik

Greene, W.H. (1981), "Sample Selection Bias as a Specification Error: Comment," *Econometrica*, 49: 795–798.

Hall, B.H. (1987), "The Relationship between Firm Size and Firm Growth in the US Manufacturing Sector," *Journal of Industrial Economics*, 35: 583–606.

Heckman, J.J. (1979), "Sample Selection Bias as a Specification Error," *Econometrica*, 47: 153–161.

Hopenhayn, H.A. (1992), "Entry, Exit and Firm Dynamics in Long Run Equilibrium," *Econometrica*, 60: 1127–1150.

Jovanovic, B. (1982), "Selection and the Evolution of Industry," *Econometrica*, 50: 649–670.

Kleijweg, A.J.M. and M.H.C. Lever (1994), "Entry and Exit in Dutch Manufacturing Industries," EIM Research Report 9409/E, EIM Small Business Research and Consultancy, Zoetermeer.

Klomp, L. (1996), "Empirical Studies in the Hospitality Sector," Ph.D. thesis, Ridderkerk: Ridderprint.

Leamer, E.E. (1978), *Specification Searches: Ad Hoc Inference with Nonexperimental Data*, New York: John Wiley & Sons.

Mansfield, E. (1962), "Entry, Gibrat's Law, Innovation, and the Growth of Firms," *American Economic Review*, 52: 1023–1051.

Mata, J. (1993), "Firm Entry and Firm Growth," *Review of Industrial Organization*, 8: 567–578.

(1994), Firm Growth During Infancy," *Small Business Economics*, 6: 27–39.

Mata, J. and P. Portugal (1994), "Life Duration of New Firms," *Journal of Industrial Economics*, 42: 227–246.

Schmalensee, R. (1989), "Inter-Industry Studies of Structure and Performance," in R. Schmalensee and R.D. Willig (eds.), *Handbook of Industrial Organization*, volume II, Amsterdam: North-Holland, pp. 951–1009.

Sutton, J. (1997), "Gibrat's Legacy," *Journal of Economic Literature*, 35: 40–59.

Wagner, J. (1994), "The Post-Entry Performance of New Small Firms in German Manufacturing Industries," *Journal of Industrial Economics*, 42: 141–154.

White, H. (1980a), "A Heteroscedasticity-Consistent Covariance Matrix Estimator and a Direct Test for Heteroscedasticity," *Econometrica*, 48: 817–838.

(1980b), "Using Least Squares to Approximate Unknown Regression Functions," *International Economic Review*, 21: 149–170.

Willeboordse, A.J. (1986), "Towards a 'Demography' of Firms," *Netherlands Official Statistics*, 1(2): 5–11.

11 Who exits from German manufacturing industries and why? Evidence from the Hannover Firm Panel study

Joachim Wagner

1   Introduction

When a firm dies, unfortunately, there is no coroner called to testify the reasons why. Therefore, we have no evidence from official statistics on reasons for exits – we often even lack reliable information on the number of firms that left an industry during a period, and the basic characteristics of these firms (age, size, ownership status, etc.). Given that exits constitute one crucial element of the dynamics of an industry, in times of high and persisting unemployment this lack of knowledge is an important shortcoming.

Usually, only the net change in the number of firms in an industry between two points in time are reported in official statistics, and the number of gross entries and exits is not known. Gross numbers can be computed from longitudinal data sets built from (official) cross-section surveys linked over time, and this type of data has been used in a number of recent studies on the interindustry and interregional variation of entry and exits, and on the post-entry performance (i.e., growth, decline, or failure) of new firms.[1]

Despite the important insights that are uncovered in empirical investigations of this type, they tend to suffer from an inherent shortcoming of

---

This paper uses data from the project *Das Hannoveraner Firmenpanel*, funded by the Volkswagen-Stiftung.

[1] Carree and Thurik (1996, table III) list 44 studies published between 1962 and 1994 based on data from various countries. Important recent contributions using data from the US and Canada include Audretsch (1995), Baldwin (1995), and Davis, Haltiwanger, and Schuh (1996). For Germany, see the surveys of studies based on data from official statistics of firms in manufacturing industries by Gerlach and Wagner (1997), and of work done with data computed from the statistics of employees covered by social insurance in Fritsch (1997); Harhoff, Stahl, and Woywode (1995) use firm data from a credit rating agency to investigate exits.

these data sets, namely the scarcity of information available about the firms that exit (or survive). For example, in the longitudinal data set built from cross-section surveys from official statistics covering all establishments in manufacturing industries in the German state of Lower Saxony that I used in various studies of the kind mentioned above, the only information available is the number of employees and the amount of total sales of a firm for each year (between 1978 and 1994), plus the industry affiliation (at the four-digit level of the German classification system *SYPRO*), the county (*Kreis*) affiliation, and whether the local production unit is part of a multi-establishment enterprise or not. While the data cover the population of enterprises and, therefore, are (by and large) suitable to identify exits, and to compute exit rates for industries or regions, this type of data is not rich enough in information to investigate the reasons why some firms exit and others not. Furthermore, given the great amount of heterogeneity between firms in an industry, linking information from other sources based on the industry affiliation is no solution.

This chapter contributes to the literature on exits by exploring a rich longitudinal data set that was collected by annual personal interviews in some 1,000 establishments from German manufacturing between 1994 and 1996. The rest of the chapter is organized as follows: *section 2* introduces the data set and discusses some measurement issues. *Section 3* presents basic descriptive information on the number of exits and some of their characteristics compared to surviving firms, and reports results from empirical models that investigate the survival status of the firms. *Section 4* concludes with a discussion of the findings.

2   Data issues

The data used in this inquiry were collected in interviews conducted between 1994 and 1996 as the first three waves of a panel study investigating various aspects of firm behavior and firm performance. The research project in question, *Das Hannoveraner Firmenpanel*, will contain at least one additional wave to be performed late in 1997. The population covered encompasses all manufacturing establishments with at least five employees (including the owner and members of his family) that were active in 1994 in the state of Lower Saxony. Note that, therefore, micro firms with up to four employees are not covered by the survey. The sample of establishments is stratified according to firm size and industry, with oversampling of larger firms. Accordingly, in the descriptive evidence presented below the data are weighted to correct for this stratified sampling procedure.

The data were collected in personal interviews by Infratest Sozial-forschung, a leading German survey and opinion research institute. Interviews were held with the owner or top manager of the firm, often assisted by personnel management in the larger firms. Full information on the sampling frame, interviews, and data editing procedure are provided in Infratest Sozialforschung (1995).

1,025 firms or 51 percent of all those approached agreed to take part in the first wave conducted late in 1994. Note that despite the relatively high attrition rate the deviation between the actual and planned stratification in the net sample is relatively small. Twenty four of these firms closed down before the second wave and a further 151 indicated that they would not participate in the second wave, though 76 of these stated that they might be willing to take part in subsequent waves. The second wave sample thus comprises 849 firms, yielding a response rate of 85 percent of the survivors. The third wave comprised 694 of the firms from wave 2, plus 25 of the group of 76 firms not participating in wave 2. By the time of the third wave, another 24 firms had closed down. Seven hundred and nineteen firms participated in the third wave, and a further 182 firms indicated that they were not willing to do so. These 901 (719 plus 182) firms form the group of survivor firms, because we know from their participation/non-participation reaction that they were alive at the time the field work for the third wave was conducted late in 1996. The 24 firms that closed down between wave 1 and wave 2 plus the 24 firms that closed down between wave 2 and 3 form the group of 48 exits. Note that "closed down" means that the professional interviewers sent out to contact the firms were not able to locate the establishment at the old address, or to find out where it had moved to (if it moved). Establishments that changed the owner, or merged with other firms, are not considered as exits as long as they still produce at the old location. All in all, the subsample considered in the empirical investigation performed in this chapter is made of 949 establishments – 901 survivors and 48 exits. The balance between these 949 firms and the 1,025 firms that participated in wave 1 is made of the 75 firms which were approached in wave 2 and which stated explicitly that they did not want to be approached in the future (in this case, according to the German data protection law, it is illegal to try to get in contact with a firm in the future), plus one firm that moved between wave 1 and 2 without leaving a new address (*unbekannt verzogen*). Stated differently, we have 76 cases with missing values on the exit/survivor status variable in 1996.

Note that the data do not allow to distinguish between exits that are voluntary liquidations (without losses to creditors) and bankruptcies as forced liquidations.

Note further that the sample was drawn in 1994. New firms that were established after this point were not added to the panel, with the exception of those businesses created by or spun off from sample firms (at wave 2) if these businesses were also in the production sector and located in Lower Saxony. In practice, just two such newly founded firms have to be added to the total of 719 firms reported earlier for wave 3, and given that important information for these two units is lacking due to the structure of the questionnaire they were not included in the sample considered here.

The survey *Erfolgreich Produzieren in Niedersachsen* asks approximately 90 numbered questions. In fact, the questions vary by wave because the first and third waves focus on "the labor market, employment and remuneration" whereas the second and fourth waves concentrate on "international cooperation, market and innovation dynamics, and environmental measures." English translations of the 1994 and 1995 survey questionnaires are contained in Brand *et al.* (1996).

Further aspects of the survey will be noted below, but we should finally note here that according to the strict data protection laws of the Federal Republic, and agreements entered into with the firm participants, any dissemination of the micro data is prohibited. A public use file preserving the anonymity of the establishments will, however, be published after completion of the project.

3   Who exits and why?

The overall share of exits between 1994 and 1996 in all firms covered by the *Hannover Firm Panel* study is 7.16 percent, giving an annual rate of exits of about 3.6 percent.[2] This order of magnitude is in accordance with evidence from panel data covering all manufacturing establishments in Lower Saxony (including micro firms with less than five persons that are excluded from the sample used here): 1,090 (or 16.95 percent) of the 6,429 firms that produced in 1990 were no longer active in 1994, meaning an average annual exit rate of 4.2 percent. To see who exits and why, we will begin by comparing certain characteristics of exits and survivors, one at a time, based on results reported in table 11.1.

David Audretsch (1995, p. 149) mentions as one of the stylized facts that have emerged from the recent wave of studies (mostly based on US

---

[2]   Note that all descriptive information reported in table 11.1, and discussed in this section, is based on *weighted* data to correct for the stratification of the sample of the *Hannover Firm Panel* study.

data) examining exit that the likelihood of a firm exiting apparently
declines

Table 11.1 *Characteristics of exits versus survivors*

	Exits	Survivors
Overall shares of exits and survivors 1994–1996 (%)	7.16	92.84
Shares of exits and survivors by age class (%)		
Age class 1 (founded before 1960)	7.92	92.08
Age class 2 (founded between 1960 and 1989)	3.45	96.55
Age class 3 (founded between 1990 and 1994)	19.56	80.44
Shares of exits and survivors from an age class in all exits and survivors (%)		
Age class 1 (founded before 1960)	59.74	53.97
Age class 2 (founded between 1960 and 1989)	17.86	38.86
Age class 3 (founded between 1990 and 1994)	22.40	7.16
Average number of employees in exits and survivors in 1994	22.75	52.40
Shares of exits and survivors by size class (%)		
Size class 1 (less than 20 employees in 1994)	7.72	92.28
Size class 2 (20 to 49 employees in 1994)	7.50	92.50
Size class 3 (50 to 249 employees in 1994)	4.62	95.38
Size class 4 (250 and more employees in 1994)	1.63	98.37
Shares of exits and survivors from a size class in all exits and survivors (%)		
Size class 1 (less than 20 employees in 1994)	75.41	69.54
Size class 2 (20 to 49 employees in 1994)	16.97	16.15
Size class 3 (50 to 249 employees in 1994)	6.91	11.10
Size class 4 (250 and more employees in 1994)	0.71	3.31
Shares of exits and survivors by establishment status (%)		
Branch plant (1994)	16.60	83.40
No branch plant (1994)	6.43	93.57
Shares of exits and survivors by liability statute (%)		
Limited liability (1994)	7.58	92.42
No limited liability (1994)	6.40	93.60

Shares of exits and survivors by product innovator

status (%)

	Exits	Survivors
Firms with (at least) one new product in 1993	9.99	90.01
Firms without a new product in 1993	5.83	94.17

Table 11.1 (*cont.*)

	Exits	Survivors
Shares of exits and survivors by state of technology (%)		
Firms with state-of-the-art machinery in 1993	3.99	96.01
Firms without state-of-the-art machinery in 1993	8.47	91.53
Average share of jobs which need a polytech or university degree in exits and survivors in 1994	3.47	2.72
Average value of labor productivity proxied by sales per employee in exits and survivors in 1993 (in DM)	138,428	197,982
Average value of labor productivity proxied by value added per employee in exits and survivors in 1993 (in DM)	77,577	103,667
Shares of exits and survivors by profit situation (%)		
Profits in 1993 considered as		
very good	0.47	99.53
good	5.11	94.89
not so good	5.08	94.92
bad	16.38	83.62
very bad	15.70	84.30
Shares of exits and survivors by broad industry groups (%)		
Firms from basic products and producer goods industries	3.57	96.43
Firms from investment goods industries	14.35	85.65
Firms from consumer goods industries	1.73	98.27
Firms from food and beverages industries	8.43	91.66
Shares of exits and survivors from a broad industry group in all exits and survivors (%)		
Firms from basic products and producer goods industries	8.61	17.92
Firms from investment goods industries	66.52	30.63
Firms from consumer goods industries	8.10	35.51
Firms from food and beverages industries	16.77	14.21

Source: Own calculations based on data from the *Hannover Firm Panel*; weighted data.

with both age and size, suggesting that the bulk of firms exiting from the industry tends to be new and small enterprises. Similarly, Harhoff, Stahl, and Woywode (1995, table 3) report a negative relationship between both size and age of firms and exit rates in their study using German data. As regards *size* (measured by the number of employees, including owners and members of his family, in the firm at the time of interview late in 1994) we find the same pattern in our data: the average number of employees in surviving firms is about 2.3 times larger than in exits, with the share of exits declining over size classes, and three quarters of all exits coming from the smallest size class covering firms with less than 20 employees. Looking at *age*, however, gives a different picture: although the share of exits is largest among the youngest age class (covering firms founded between 1990 and 1994), it is higher among the "old" firms (founded before 1960) than among the "middle-aged" firms (founded between 1960 and 1990). Furthermore, 60 percent of all exits come from the oldest firms.

A breakdown of exits and survivors by establishment status (branch plant versus single establishment or parent company with subsidiaries) shows that the risk of failure is considerably higher for establishments that are subsidiaries of a company. This might be due to the role of "secondary production sites" often played by branch plants.

Comparing firms with different liability statutes (limited liability versus other) shows no big difference as regards the proportion of exits in both groups. Harhoff, Stahl, and Woywode (1995) argue that under limited liability, projects with more growth potential but also higher risk of failure tend to be chosen, and they find that limited liability firms are characterized by an above-average rate of insolvency, while they do not play a major role in voluntary business closings. As said in the discussion of the data, we are not able to distinguish between these two types of exit with the data from the *Hannover Firm Panel*, and this might explain the rather similar exit rates for firms with and without limited liabilty in our sample.

Turning to the role of innovation in shaping the risk of failure, we find that being a product innovator is no way to insure against exit. Contrary to this, the share of exits among firms that introduced (at least) one new product in 1993 is nearly double the share among the non-innovator firms. Evidently, introducing a new product is a chance to pick a piece of the cake – however, it might be the wrong thing in the wrong place at the wrong time as well.

Looking at technology and productivity, we find that the proportion of exits is about twice as high in firms that report that their machinery is not of a state-of-the-art type than in firms with an up-to-date capital stock. Labor productivity (proxied either by sales per employee, or by value-added per employee) is distinctively lower in exits than in surviving firms. This evidence fits well into the picture that emerges from a look at panel data covering all manufacturing establishments in Lower Saxony between 1990 and 1994, where about two-thirds of all exits belonged to the bottom 50 percent of the labor productivity distribution in 1990. At odds with these findings is the fact that the average share of jobs which need a polytech or university degree is higher in exits than in surviving firms, because these employees tend to go hand in hand both with a modern capital stock, and a high value of labor productivity (see Addison and Wagner, 1997).

Finally, as a catch-all indicator for the "goodness" of a firm we look at its profit situation in 1993 according to the subjective assessment by the owner/top manager. While exits are more frequent among firms with bad or very bad profits, not all of these firms do exit, and some firms with good profits in 1993 exit in the years to come, too. To put it another way, there is a link between the profit situation and the propensity to exit, but it is not too strong. Bad profits can be tolerated for a while, especially if there is hope for change in the near future, or if closing down is even more costly due to fixed costs; ultimately, however, this often leads to exit. Good profits today, on the other hand, are by no means a guarantee for good profits in the future – bad luck, mistakes, or any kind of negative shock can turn things against a firm.

At the bottom of table 11.1 a breakdown of exits and survivors by broad industry groups shows that the percentage of exits differs widely between industries, and that two-thirds of all exits come from investment goods industries.

Obviously, firm characteristics listed in table 11.1 are related – consider size and age, productivity and profitability, etc. Comparing certain characteristics of exits and survivors one at a time, therefore, can be misleading when investigating the reasons why some firms exited and others did not. To take account of this, we will next look at the results from a multivariate analysis. Table 11.2 reports results of failure estimates based on empirical models of the probability of exit as a function of various firm characteristics.

Modeling the probability of exit as a function of firm age alone (model 1) does not point to any statistically significant differences among the age groups considered (the reference group here is made of the "old" firms founded before 1960). This holds true if firm size is controlled for additionally (model 2), and in models that are augmented by several other firm characteristics, too (see models 3 and 4). From these results we conclude that, *ceteris paribus*, there is no nexus between firm age and the probability to exit.

Table 11.2 *Results of failure estimates*
Endogenous variable: Exit (Dummy; 1 = yes)/Method: PROBIT

Exogenous variables	Model	1	2	3	4
Age class 2 (founded between		0.023	−0.021	−0.013	0.020
1960 and 1989)	t	0.15	−0.014	−0.08	0.11
Age class 3 (founded between		0.502	0.421	0.259	0.212
1990 and 1994)	t	1.70	1.43	0.62	0.51
Number of employees in 1994			−0.002	−0.003	−0.003
	t		−2.06*	−2.09*	−2.15*
Squared number of employees			1.04e-7	8.34e-7	8.69e-7
in 1994	t		1.94	2.00*	2.04*
Branch plant (1994)				0.497	0.550
[Dummy; 1 = yes]	t			1.99*	2.19*
Limited liability (1994)				0.040	0.058
[Dummy; 1 = yes]	t			0.20	0.28
Firm introduced (at least)					
one new product in 1993				0.055	0.026
[Dummy; 1 = yes]	t			0.34	0.16
Firm had state-of-the-art					
machinery in 1993				−0.002	0.007
[Dummy; 1 = yes]	t			−0.02	0.05
Share of jobs which need a					
polytech or university				−0.002	−0.006
degree (1994)	t			−0.18	−0.47
Value of labor productivity					
proxied by sales per				−1.26e-6	−1.32e-6
employee (1993)	t			−2.08*	−2.35*
Profit situation in 1993					
[Index; 1 = very good, …,				0.175	0.183
5 = very bad]	t			2.36*	2.49*
Firm from basic products and					
producer goods industries					−0.167
[Dummy; 1 = yes]	t				−0.78
Firm from consumer goods					
industries					−0.277
[Dummy; 1 = yes]	t				−1.47
Firm from food and beverages					
industries					0.195
[Dummy; 1 = yes]	t				0.74
Constant		−1.671	−1.482	−1.779	−1.688
	t	−19.55**	−13.33**	−5.22**	−4.50**
Number of observations		949	949	786	786

Source: Own calculations based on data from the *Hannover Firm Panel*.
Note: * (**) = significant at 0.05 (0.01) level.

Looking at firm size (measured by the number of employees in 1994) it turns out that the probability of failure declines with firm size, *ceteris paribus*. Note that this decline is non-linear – the estimated coefficient of the squared number of employees is negative. From model 4 the minimum of the quadratic function describing the c.p. influence of size on failure is calculated as 1,632 employees. In the sample used to estimate models 3 and 4 only three firms had more than 1,632 employees in 1994 (with a maximum number of 2,800), and, therefore, we find a negative impact of firm size on exit in the models estimated.

From models 3 and 4 it can be seen that three conclusions from the "one-characteristic-at-a-time" descriptive analysis conducted above hold *ceteris paribus*, too: branch plants have a higher probability of failure than other types of firms; the exit probability declines with higher values of labor productivity; and the worse the profit situation, the higher is the probability of failure.

On the other hand, according to the results reported in table 11.2, neither the liability statute of a firm, nor its product-innovator status, nor the state-of-the-art character of its machinery, nor the share of jobs that demand a degree are related to the probability of exit, *ceteris paribus*, and the same holds for the broad industry groups considered here. It should be added that these findings are corroborated by the results from a large number of variants of these models with various subsets of the variables included in the full model 4.

The bottom line, then, is that the risk of failure is higher for smaller firms, branch plants, firms with low labor productivity, and with bad profit accounts, while firm age and innovativeness does not matter, *ceteris paribus*.

4   Creative destruction, revolving doors, or what?

To put the results reported above into perspective, in this section we will relate this evidence to two metaphors of industry evolution that according to David Audretsch (1995, pp. 149ff.) may shape the types of firms exiting – the metaphor of displacement of tired old incumbent enterprises by new firms with the entrepreneurial spirit, or Schumpetarian creative destruction, and the metaphor of the revolving door, where the bulk of exiting firms tends to be comprised of new entrants that do not manage to survive past the very short run.

Looking at table 11.1 reporting the descriptive results, we find evidence for both metaphors – some 60 percent of all exits are from the group of old firms (in line with the creative destruction metaphor), but the risk of exit is much higher for the very young firms compared to older firms (in line with the revolving door metaphor). However, as is documented in table 11.2 this relationship between firm age and risk of exit vanishes when other characteristics of the firms are taken into account simultaneously. Furthermore, we find no influence of product innovations, modern machinery, or the share of highly skilled employees on the propensity to exit – all of these variables, however, are related to the creative destruction metaphor.

Audretsch (1995, pp. 149ff.) argues that the process of firm selection will not be constant across industries. While in industries characterized by substantial scale economies the revolving door model should fit better because most of the new entrants will not grow large enough to displace incumbents, the creative destruction model should be more appropriate in industries where small firms tend to have the innovative advantage and where entrants with their new products can shift away demand from incumbents. While the evidence from US data presented by Audretsch is in line with this reasoning, we cannot test whether this is the case in Germany, too, because the industry classification used in the *Hannover Firm Panel* study is much too broad to allow a distinction between industries belonging to one type or the other, and important information for such a classification, the small firm innovation rate by industry, is unavailable.

This said, neither of the two metaphors – creative destruction or revolving doors – tends to describe the pattern of firms that exited from German manufacturing. We have evidence that a third one fits better, the "survival of the fittest," meaning that firms – whether old or young – that (for whatever reasons) do not manage to grow or stay big enough to realize high labor productivity and to make good profits have a higher risk of failure than their fitter counterparts. This suggests an answer to the "Who exits ..." part of the title question of this chapter, but it does not answer the "... and why" part satisfactorily, because we do not know from the data and their analysis why some firms grow, have high productivity, and good profits. Given that we have no information about the owners or managers of the firms, and about the conditions characterizing the – often small and local – markets the firms are active in, we cannot expect to learn much about the role of knowledge, strategies, and luck in making a survivor from the data at hand. Evidently, further research in this area is needed.

References

Addison, John T. and Joachim Wagner (1997), "The Changing Skill Structure of Employment in German Manufacturing: A Peek Inside the Industry Black

Box," Paper presented at the conference "Globalization, Technological Change, and the Welfare State," American Institute for Contemporary German Studies AICGS, Washington, DC, June 9–10.

Audretsch, David B. (1995), *Innovation and Industry Evolution*, Cambridge, Mass. and London, England: MIT Press.

Baldwin, John R. (1995), *The Dynamics of Industrial Competition*, Cambridge: Cambridge University Press.

Brand, Ruth, Vivian Carstensen, Knut Gerlach, and Thomas Klodt (1996), "The Hannover Panel," Das Hannoveraner Firmenpanel Diskussionspapier Nr. 2, Universität Hannover: Forschungsstelle Firmenpanel, May.

Carree, Martin and Roy Thurik (1996), "Entry and Exit in Retailing: Incentives, Barriers, Displacement and Replacement," *Review of Industrial Organization*, 11: 155–172.

Davis, Steven J., John C. Haltiwanger, and Scott Schuh (1996), *Job Creation and Destruction*, Cambridge, Mass. and London, England: MIT Press.

Fritsch, Michael (1997), "Analyse des Gründungsgeschehens auf der Grundlage der Beschäftigtenstatistik: Ansatz und Überblick," in Jürgen Kühl, Manfred Lahner and Joachim Wagner (eds.), *Die Nachfrageseite des Arbeitsmarktes – Ergebnisse aus Analysen mit deutschen Firmenpaneldaten*, Nürnberg: IAB, S. 103–133.

Gerlach, Knut and Joachim Wagner (1997), "Analysen zur Nachfrageseite des Arbeitsmarktes mit Betriebspaneldaten aus Erhebungen der amtlichen Statistik – Ein Überblick über Ansätze und Ergebnisse für niedersächsische Industriebetriebe," in Jürgen Kühl, Manfred Lahner, und Joachim Wagner (eds.), *Die Nachfrageseite des Arbeitsmarktes – Ergebnisse aus Analysen mit deutschen Firmenpaneldaten*. Nürnberg: IAB, S. 11–82.

Harhoff, Dietmar, Konrad Stahl, and Michael Woywode (1995), "Growth and Exit of West German Firms – An Empirical Investigation on the Impact of Liability Statutes," ZEW Discussion Paper No. 95–15, Mannheim: Zentrum für Europäische Wirtschaftsforschung, May.

Infratest Sozialforschung (1995), *Das Hannoveraner Firmenpanel – Methodenbericht*, Munich: Infratest Sozialforschung.

12 Technology intensity, demand conditions, and the longevity of firms

José Mata and Pedro Portugal

1   Introduction

One of the most robust findings emerging from the recent literature that studies the entry of new competitors and their subsequent performance is that many of the firms that appear in the economy never reach maturity. This has been recognized as one of the key features of the process of post-entry performance of firms, and lead Paul Geroski, in his influential survey on entry, to write: "The survival rate of most entrants is low and even successful entrants take more than a decade to achieve a size comparable to the average incumbent" (1995, p. 434). The description above fits the Portuguese case like a glove. In fact, almost one half of the total number of firms created in Portuguese manufacturing in 1983 failed within the four years following their birth. Failure rates among these new firms are considerably higher than among their older counterparts. About 20 percent of the newly created firms failed during the first year and, even though the hazard rates decrease in subsequent years, it is still about 10 percent at the fourth year. In contrast, during the same period, the hazard rates confronting the whole set of firms that were born before 1983, remain roughly stable at the 6 percent level (Mata, 1994).

The first studies to analyze the determinants of firm survival focused on exit between two particular moments in time (e.g., Evans, 1987a and 1987b; Dunne, Roberts, and Samuelson, 1989). More recently, however, industrial economists have followed the example of their colleagues in the field of labor economics, and started using econometric duration models to study the determinants of the lifespan of firms. Duration models are particularly efficient for the task of analyzing the survival of firms, because they use information on all the lifespan of firms, rather than on one single point in time. (Kiefer (1988) provides a good survey on econometric duration models.) Examples of application of such models to the duration of firms include a paper by Audretsch and

Mahmood (1994), with a data base covering startups in the United States, who found the probability of survival to be negatively related to startup size. In addition, they employed industry-level variables as explanatory variables, and found that American plants last longer in fast-growing industries, and in those where innovation and R&D are less important. This research was developed by Mahmood (1992), who found that the hazard rates vary between low- and high-tech industries. In one of the earliest non-American studies of the kind, Mata and Portugal (1994) estimated different models of the determinants of duration of new firms in Portuguese manufacturing. They concluded that, in addition to firm startup size, the number of plants operated by the newly created firm, and the industry growth and entry rates were important to the duration of new firms.

In this chapter, we extend that analysis by investigating the stability of these relationships under different environments. In particular, we study the effect of demand and technological conditions on new firms' longevity. We classify industries according to three aspects (technological intensity, employment growth rate, and scope for product differentiation) and apply the same econometric duration model to the samples defined according to the criteria above. With this exercise, we expect to gain some new insights into whether the demand and technological conditions prevalent in the industry where entry takes place, significantly alter the determinants of new firms' longevity. After reviewing the expected effects of the different environments on the new firms' duration (section 2), we present the statistical model employed (section 3) and discuss our empirical results (section 4). Section 5 concludes the chapter.

2   Firm duration in different environments

Previous work on entry, exit, and growth of firms provided us with a stylized picture of the life cycle of firms. For a number of reasons, such as liquidity constraints and imperfect knowledge, firms are, in general, small when they start. Before actual operation in the market is experienced, firms are unaware of the adequacy of their products to the tastes of buyers as well as their own ability to meet the normal levels of cost in the industry. Their initial presence in the market can be regarded as a trial period during which new information regarding these abilities is conveyed to the firms. Some firms find that they are not efficient enough to cope with market competition and are forced to exit. Others discover that they are efficient and grow. Such a story can be found, for example, in Jovanovic (1982).

Jovanovic's model is built upon the assumption that firms are all of the same size at the time of birth. However, firms do startup with various sizes and these diverse initial sizes exert an important influence on their survival.[1] There are two broad types of reasons for new firms to be created in different sizes. The first includes firm-specific considerations, such as differences in the managerial abilities of new firms' founders (Lucas, 1978), their beliefs about these abilities (Frank, 1988) and their financial constraints (Evans and Jovanovic, 1989). The second consists of those motives that affect all firms operating in the industry in which entry takes place. Here technology, ease of exit and the dynamics of industry evolution exert a major influence.[2]

The destiny of firms after entry is also likely to vary dramatically according to the different environments in which entry occurs. In particular, the demand and technological conditions in the industry where entry takes place affect the abilities required for new firms to compete and are likely to determine their survival patterns. The first characteristic of demand that is alleged to be important in determining the new firms' prospects of survival is the scope for product differentiation in the industry. New firms may find it easier to survive in industries with higher potential for product differentiation (even if they operate with a scale disadvantage *vis à vis* their established competitors), provided they are able to find market niches to serve (Bradburd and Ross, 1989). However, finding the right niche and the right product specification is not an easy task, and the likelihood that a new competitor appears in the market with a product designed for the same niche and better suited to the buyers' needs is much greater in such markets than in markets with homogeneous products.

It has also been suggested by Gort and Klepper (1982) that the lifespan of firms in a particular industry depends on the stage of the industry life cycle that the particular firm encounters when it starts its activities. In the earlier stages of the industry life cycle, when products and technology are not yet well established, firms enter essentially by introducing new products or processes, which may or may not be accepted in the market. In fact, most of the new firms created in these environments quickly find themselves unable to match their competitors and thus leave the market. As the industry evolves and an industry-specific technology becomes

[1] In our sample, although more than three-quarters of the total number of new firms with more than four employees employed fewer than 20 people, entrants employing more than 49 people are still 7 percent of the total number of new firms, and the corresponding figure for entrants with more than 99 people is 3 percent.

[2] See Mata (1996) for a study on the impact of entrepreneurs' human capital attributes on the size of new firms and Mata and Machado (1996) for an analysis of the effect of industry environments.

more developed, innovations introduced from outside the industry become rarer, and possession of large R&D facilities becomes crucial to the ability to innovate and, therefore, to survive (Audretsch and Acs, 1991). This evolution has two important consequences with respect to entrants. On the one hand, given the increased importance of economies of scale, fewer firms consider entry, but those that enter do so on a larger scale. On the other hand, as products and technology become more established, the capital goods required to operate in the industry become more industry specific, and the entry investment becomes more sunk as a result. Both reasons suggest that the duration of firms should increase as industries go into this stage of their life cycle. Finally, when industries move to a more mature state and products and technology become standardized, cost minimization prevails as the central concern for firms in the industry, and exploitation of economies of scale and the ability to operate efficiently become the key competitive advantage. In these latter stages, markets are enlarged and the entry impediments are reduced. Capital goods for the industry are also more standardized; as second-hand and rental markets for them develop, they become less sunk. More entry occurs and, concomitantly, entrants last less time in the market than before. Empirical studies have found that the lives of entrants are shorter in highly innovative environments (Audretsch, 1995) and in environments characterized by high rates of entry (Mata and Portugal, 1994).

The stages of the industry life cycle are often deemed to be related to the rate of industry output growth, the earlier periods being the fast-growing ones. Because of this, White (1982, p. 45) expressed that "the newer the industry, the more unsettled are the conditions in the industry, the greater the uncertainties, and the more likely that small business will do well. Alternatively, a high growth rate could be seen simply as an indication of an area in which there are expanding possibilities and one in which smaller firms, capable of moving quickly, could flourish." This first view suggests that, in periods of rapid growth, firm turnover should be greater and that firm duration should be shorter. Evidence for Portugal has, however, failed to confirm the alternative suggestion that new and small firms should have a greater presence in the fastest-growing industries. Small firm presence has been found to vary negatively with industry growth (Mata, 1993), and the only group of entrants that has been found to respond to industry growth rates is the group of large-scale entrants (Mata, 1991). Moreover, industry growth has an additional effect upon firm longevity. In the fastest-growing industries, new-firm entry does not necessarily occur at the expense of established firms' market shares as it does in contracting or stable industries. This reduces the incentives for incumbents to react aggressively and fosters the prospects of new-firm survival. Empirical studies have confirmed that this is the most important effect of industry growth on firm duration, both for Portugal (Mata and Portugal, 1994) and the US (Audretsch and Mahmood, 1994).

3   The statistical framework

The duration model specifies the firm's duration as a random outcome of a survival process. More precisely, the hazard rate, $h(t)$, is the probability of exiting the activity state in the time interval $[t, t+\Delta t]$ conditional on having survived until t

$$h(t) = \frac{P(t \leq T \leq t + \Delta t | T \geq t)}{\Delta t} \tag{1}$$

where T is the firm duration. Assuming that T has the distribution function $F(t)$ and density function $f(t)$, as $\Delta t \rightarrow 0$

$$h(t) = \frac{f(t)}{1 - F(t)} \tag{2}$$

where the survival function, $S(t)=1-F(t)$, is the probability of surviving to t, or not having failed by t. The hazard rate may be written as a conditional function of observed variables which we denote by vector X. Using a proportional hazards model, the effect of a unit change in a covariate is to produce a constant proportional change in the hazard rate

$$h(t|X) = h_0(t)\phi(X) \tag{3}$$

Equation (3) thus specifies the hazard function as a product of two components. The former component is known as the baseline hazard, and the role of the vector X is to shift its location. Letting $\phi(X) = exp(X\beta)$ and taking logarithms, we have

$$\ln h(t|X) = \ln h_0(t) + X\beta \tag{4}$$

It is conventional to assume a particular parametric form for the baseline hazard, and then maximize the likelihood function constructed from the implied distribution of spell lengths. Since our interest is in the coefficient vector β, and given the risk of assuming an incorrect function for the baseline hazard, we shall adopt the Cox (1972) semi-parametric estimation technique. In other words, $h_0(t)$ is not given a specific functional form.

Information on β is available in the ranking of firms by spell length. If firms with certain characteristics X_j have longer spells than other firms with a lower value of X_j the hazard rate will be negatively correlated with X_j, and a negative value will be assigned to β_j. Expressed another way, a negative coefficient will translate into an increase in firms' duration.

The likelihood function for the semi-parametric proportional hazards model may be written as (Kalbfleish and Prentice, 1980)

$$L = \prod_{i=1}^{k} \frac{\exp(s_i\beta)}{\left[\sum_{l \in R(t_{(i)})} \exp(X_l\beta)\right]^{\delta_i}}$$

where $t_{(i)}$ is observed failure time ($i = 1,...,k$; $t_{(1)} < t_{(1)} < ... t_{(k)}$); $R(t_{(i)}$ identifies the risk set (that is, the number of firms in activity) at $t_{(i)}$. $s(i) = \Sigma X_{ij}$; and, finally, δ_i is the number firms failing by $t_{(i)}$. The likelihood function given in equation (5) accommodates right-censored duration data resulting from ongoing spells.

The estimation equation can be described as follows

$$\ln(h(t)) = \ln h_0(t) + \beta_1 \text{ Startup Size} + \beta_2 \text{ Ownership} + \beta_3 \text{ Growth} +$$
$$\beta_4 \text{ Entry} + \beta_5 \text{ Industry Size} + \beta_6 \text{ MediumTechnology} +$$
$$\beta_7 \text{ HighTechnology} \tag{6}$$

where the independent variables are defined as follows

Startup Size – Logarithm of the number of people employed in the firm in 1983.

Ownership – Number of establishments operated by the firm in 1983.

Growth – Employment growth rate in the industry (1982–1983).

Entry – Logarithm of the number of entrants in the industry in 1983.

Industry Size – Logarithm of the number of firms in the industry in 1983.

Medium Technology – Dummy variable. 1 if the industry is classified as being of medium technology, 0 otherwise.

High Technology – Dummy variable. 1 if the industry is classified as being of high-technology, 0 otherwise.

4   Empirical results

For the research reported in this study, we used unpublished data from an annual survey (*Quadros de Pessoal*) conducted by the Ministry of Employment. This is a comprehensive survey, to which all the firms employing paid labor are required to report. As we worked with the raw files, we were able to use firms' identifiers to locate and follow entrants over time.

After deleting 246 firms due to minor data problems, we could recognize the 3,169 manufacturing firms that were registered for the first time in the Ministry of Employment files in 1983. Comparing these firms' identifiers with the files for the subsequent years, we learned that from these newly born firms, only 2,161 were still active in the next year, and that in 1987 the number had been further reduced to 1,649. This means that more than 20 percent of the firms created in 1983 died during the first year and that almost one half failed before they reached the age of four.

Before going to the discussion of regression results, it is useful to take a look at some descriptive material, namely the empirical survival rates produced by the Kaplan–Meier estimator. These estimates were produced for the full sample and for six subsamples, defined according to the growth, consumption, and technology criteria. Industries were defined as high-tech, med-tech, and low-tech industries, following an OECD classification given in Hughes (1992). The three categories were retained to define two dummy variables to be included in the regression, but for purposes of splitting the sample according to the technology, the medium- and high-tech industries were kept together. Industries were classified as expanding if the 1982–1983 employment growth was positive and as consumer oriented if, according to a table made available by the official statistical agency (*INE*), no less than 40 percent of their output was directed to final consumption.

The results in table 12.1 concur with our previous statement that roughly one fifth of the new born firms failed during the first year of their lives and that only about one half survived after four years of economic activity. A few other patterns are also worth mentioning. First, entrants in expanding industries seem to have better chances of survival than do those in contracting ones. Second, the consumption distinction does not appear to imply discernible differences among the survival functions. Third, entry in medium- and high-technology sectors slightly enhances the prospects of survival.

Table 12.1 also exhibits an estimate of the Weibull shape parameter, which was obtained from the Kaplan–Meier survival rate estimates (Lawless, 1982). Those values were computed from a simple linear regression of $\log[-\log(\hat{S}(t))]$ on $\log(t)$. This parameter provides information on the shape of the baseline hazard function. A Weibull shape parameter greater than one implies positive duration dependence, that is, hazard rates that increase with time. Conversely, when the Weibull parameter is less than one, negative duration dependence is implied. In our case, there is a clear indication of negative duration dependence, i.e., that hazard rates decrease with time, the null hypothesis of constant hazard (an exponential duration distribution) being soundly rejected.

Table 12.1 *Empirical survival rates for different sample configurations*

Survival rates	Full sample	Growth		Industries characterized by Consumption		Technology	
		Positive	Negative	High	Low	Med/High	Low
After 1 year	0.776	0.801	0.760	0.777	0.802	0.801	0.773
After 2 years	0.682	0.719	0.658	0.688	0.706	0.702	0.679
After 3 years	0.590	0.637	0.559	0.615	0.605	0.624	0.585
After 4 years	0.520	0.568	0.489	0.547	0.531	0.561	0.515
Weibull parameter	0.594	0.587	0.602	0.544	0.660	0.594	0.595
	(0.001)	(0.002)	(0.001)	(0.001)	(0.002)	(0.003)	(0.001)
N	3.169	1.249	1.920	1.303	1.026	362	2.807

Note: Standard errors in parentheses.

Finally, we note that the hazard rates seem to decrease at a faster rate for firms producing consumption goods than for firms producing producer-oriented goods.

In table 12.2 industries are ranked by their survival rates after four years. Additional information regarding the classification of industries according to the criteria defined above is also provided. Again, we would like to emphasize three aspects. First, there is a wide range of survival experiences across industries – whereas three out of four entrants disappear from economic activity after four years in the fish preserving industry, the chances of surviving are six out of seven in the glass products industry. Second, a disproportionate number of industries characterized by negative growth show up at the lower tail of the survival function. Symmetrically, a relatively large number of expanding industries are present in the top ten surviving industries. Third, it is interesting to note that medium/high-tech industries do not exhibit particularly low or high survival rates. Rather, they seem to be positioned at the medium range, which may reflect the compounded effect of stronger capital requirements which are invested in a "risky business."

The regression results are presented in table 12.3. For comparative purposes, the results obtained when the model is estimated using the full sample and the complete set of explanatory variables previously defined are reported in the first column.[3] In this column, the results for the first five variables are basically the same as in our previous study (Mata and Portugal, 1994). They suggest that firm failure decreases with firm startup size, with the number of plants operated by the firm and with industry growth, and increases with the extent of new-firm creation in the industry. Although the t-values of the dummy variables associated with the technological regime never allow rejection of the null hypothesis of zero coefficients, the estimated coefficients always carry the expected sign. Moreover, given that the absolute values of the coefficients associated with these variables increase from *medium technology* to *high technology*, a further indication is given that the hazard rate decreases as the industries' technological content increases.

In the remaining columns, the results of estimating the model on the different subsamples are presented. The most noticeable result across these columns is that the effect of firm startup size remains remarkably constant at the 0.2 level. The only exception seems to be the subsample of

---

[3] A dummy variable, defined as 1 if 40 percent or more of the total output in the industry is directed to final consumption and 0 otherwise was also included in preliminary runs. However, this variable never reached statistical significance and its inclusion did not change the other coefficient estimates. Moreover, since this variable is defined only for 2,329 firms, we decided to drop it from the reported results.

Table 12.2 *The industries with the lowest and the highest survival rates*

CAE	Industry*	N	Survival rates after				Growth	Consumption	Technology
			1 Year	2 Years	3 Years	4 Years			
31.142	Fish preserving	12	0.500	0.417	0.333	0.250	positive	high	low
31.172	Pastry	72	0.653	0.542	0.417	0.347	negative	n.a.	low
32.201	Made-to-measure clothing	58	0.741	0.638	0.431	0.379	negative	n.a.	low
32.122	Household textile products	22	0.682	0.591	0.500	0.409	positive	n.a.	low
36.102	Pottery	17	0.647	0.529	0.471	0.412	negative	n.a.	low
36.911	Clay products for construction	19	0.579	0.526	0.526	0.421	negative	low	low
36.993	Cement products	82	0.756	0.634	0.476	0.427	negative	low	low
39.099	Manufacturing n.e.c.	18	0.833	0.611	0.556	0.444	negative	n.a.	low
38.199	Fabricated metal products n.e.c.	43	0.721	0.607	0.512	0.465	negative	low	low
38.320	Radio and TV communication equipment	19	0.790	0.632	0.579	0.474	negative	low	high
38.249	Mach. for the industry n.e.c.	13	0.769	0.692	0.692	0.615	negative	n.a.	medium
32.310	Tanning and dressing of leather	11	0.636	0.636	0.636	0.636	positive	high	low
37.109	Iron and steel industry	14	0.857	0.786	0.643	0.643	positive	low	low
32.409	Footwear n.e.c.	26	0.923	0.846	0.654	0.654	negative	high	low
36.995	Cut store and stone products	64	0.875	0.813	0.688	0.656	positive	low	low
32.130	Knitting industry	67	0.910	0.851	0.746	0.657	positive	high	low
31.111	Slaughtering	22	0.909	0.909	0.818	0.682	positive	n.a.	low
32.112	Spinning, weaving and finishing of wood	13	1.000	0.923	0.769	0.769	negative	low	low
32.113	Spin. weav. and finish. of cotton. art. and synth. fibres	21	0.905	0.905	0.857	0.810	positive	low	low
36.202	Glass products	14	1.000	0.929	0.929	0.857	negative	high	low

Note: * Industries with less than ten entrants were excluded from this table.

Table 12.3 Determinants of firm survival for different sample definitions (proportional hazards model)

Survival rates	Full sample	Industries characterized by					
		Growth		Consumption		Technology	
		Positive	Negative	High	Low	Med/High	Low
Startup size	−0.209	−0.201	−0.200	−0.203	−0.216	−0.345	−0.190
	(7.375)	(4.997)	(5.462)	(5.038)	(4.391)	(3.933)	(6.858)
Ownership	−0.431	−0.821	−0.220	−0.110	−1.157	−0.890	−0.369
	(1.466)	(1.372)	(0.660)	(0.309)	(1.241)	(0.402)	(1.214)
Growth	−0.625			−0.268	−0.844	−1.105	−0.560
	(2.085)			(0.431)	(1.445)	(1.632)	(1.631)
Entry	0.157	0.258	0.028	0.365	0.129	0.088	0.154
	(2.076)	(2.341)	(0.258)	(2.217)	(0.787)	(0.674)	(1.928)
Industry size	−0.192	−0.323	−0.052	−0.448	−0.132	−0.173	−0.188
	(2.361)	(2.808)	(0.434)	(0.148)	(0.787)	(0.796)	(2.190)
Medium technology	−0.111	−0.157	−0.089	−0.148	−0.089		
	(1.054)	(1.054)	(1.054)	(1.054)	(1.054)		
High technology	−0.140	−0.287	−0.093	−0.452	−0.093		
	(0.967)	(0.910)	(0.541)	(1.176)	(0.541)		
Chi square	87.07	40.90	34.97	33.79	36.90	22.94	66.51
N	3.169	1.249	1.920	1.303	1.026	362	2.807

Note: Absolute values of asymptotic t statistics in parentheses.

industries with medium/high technology, in which the estimated coefficient experiences a notable increase. This result suggests that for the firms' survival prospects, the higher the industries' technological content, the greater is the importance of starting on a comparatively larger scale. This is not an unexpected result, given the argument made in section 2. In a certain way, it complements the point already made that the hazard rates decrease with the increase in the technological content. Moreover, this finding seems to be quite robust to the different sample definitions. Although the coefficients associated with the technology variables are never statistically significant, the estimated coefficients are always negative and the *high technology* coefficient is always greater (in absolute value) than the *medium technology* one.

The result that presents the clearest differences according to the diverse sample partitions is the estimated effect of the entry rate. The extent of entry in the industry seems to be a particularly important determinant of new-firm failure in expanding industries, in consumer-oriented industries, and in those industries with lower technological content. Note that it is the entry rate effect that is particularly important, as evinced by the fact that the statistical significance of the entry variable parallels the significance of the industry size variable. These results seem to confirm our previous conjectures. In the consumer-oriented industries, new entrants typically enter by offering products that are, in one way or another, different from those sold by their competitors. If successful, they may easily displace their competitors, thereby presenting a more powerful threat to firms already in the market. The results for the sample partition according to the growth rate give some support to the suggestion made by Gort and Klepper (1982), that a very high entry rate in a fast-growing industry would be an indication of a young industry, where entry is normally associated with the introduction of innovations, involving a high risk of failure. Finally, we argued in section 2 that in all the high-tech industries, the capital requirements are higher and that sunk costs are more important than in industries that have already achieved the standardization stage, and we hypothesized that firm duration should, therefore, be longer. We were not able to find statistically different patterns of duration between these groups of firms, but the results obtained for entry, as well as those for startup size, are consistent with this conjecture. If capital goods are more specific, thus involving greater sunk costs, the influence of the entry flows on the exit decisions will be less important (see Dixit and Shapiro, 1986). Moreover, as larger firms normally employ the capital factor more intensively, this implies that, in these environments, larger firms have a disproportionately higher share of costs that are sunk, which may also explain why the effect of firm startup size on the hazard rate is so important.

Our results for the full sample suggest that growth is an important determinant of the hazard rates, and growth was the only one of the three criteria that we employed that proved to generate statistically different survival distributions. When the sample is split according to the other two criteria, however, the effect of growth is less evident, and the estimated coefficients are not (or are only marginally) statistically significant. However, their absolute values reveal that, if any effect exists, the effect seems to be greater in the producer-oriented and high-tech industries.

5 Conclusion

In this chapter, we seek the answers to the following two questions. Does the life expectancy of new firms vary with the demand and technological conditions prevailing in the industries in which the firms operate? Do the determinants of firms' survival change from one type of industry to another?

Our answer to the first question is yes, although in a somewhat limited way. Our results show that the growth criterion generates statistically different duration experiences, while the consumption criterion indicates dissimilar duration dependence patterns. Finally, industries with higher technology seem to exhibit lower mortality rates and to benefit more from larger startup size. Although this empirical evidence clearly deserves further investigation, it nevertheless seems to be indisputable that the demand and technological conditions affect the duration of firms. With respect to the second question, we discovered that the extent to which entry in the industry affects the lifespan of entrants is quite different, depending on the type of industry under scrutiny. In particular, the effect of the entry rate as a determinant of the life expectancy of entrants was found to be important only in the faster-growing, consumer-oriented, and low-tech industries.

We investigated the influence of industry structure characteristics relative to demand and technology on the duration of new firms. We did not investigate how the firms' decisions regarding product differentiation or technology affect their hazard rates. Yet, it seems plausible to hypothesize that the ability to engage in product differentiation activities or to carry out R&D within the firm may alter the firms' survival prospects. To incorporate such aspects of firm behavior in our model, one would need a much more detailed data base than the one we have available. However, this is an obvious extension of our work that deserves to be taken into account in further research.

References

Audretsch, D. (1995), "Innovation, Growth and Survival," *International Journal of Industrial Organization*, 13 (4): 441–458.

Audretsch, D. and T. Mahmood (1994), "The Rate of Hazard Confronting New Firms and Plants in U.S. Manufacturing," *Review of Industrial Organization*, 9 (1): 41–56.

Audretsch, D. and Z. Acs (1991), "Innovation as a Means of Entry: an Overview," in P. Geroski, and J. Schwalbach (eds.), *Entry and Market Contestability: An International Comparison*, Oxford: Basil Blackwell.

Bradburd, R. and D. Ross (1989), "Can Small Firms Find and Defend Strategic Niches? A Test of Porter Hypothesis," *Review of Economics and Statistics*, 71 (2 May): 258–262.

Cox, D. (1972), "Regression Models and Life Tables," *Journal of the Royal Statistical Society, Series B*, 34(2): 187–202.

Dixit, A. and C. Shapiro (1986), "Entry Dynamics with Mixed Strategies," in L. Thomas III (ed.), *The Economics of Strategic Planning*, Lexington, Mass.: Lexington Books.

Dunne, T. M. Roberts, and L. Samuelson (1989), "The Growth and Failure of US Manufacturing Plants," *Quarterly Journal of Economics*, 104(4): 671–688.

Evans, D. (1987a), "Tests of Alternative Theories of Firm Growth," *Journal of Political Economy*, 95(4): 657–674.

(1987b), "The Relationship Between Firm Growth, Size, and Age – Estimates for 100 Manufacturing Industries," *Journal of Industrial Economics*, 35(4): 567–581.

Evans, D. and B. Jovanovic (1989), "An Estimated Model of Entrepreneurial Choice Under Liquidity Constraints," *Journal of Political Economy*, 97(4): 808–827.

Frank, M. (1988), "An Intertemporal Model of Industrial Exit," *Quarterly Journal of Economics*, 103(2): 333–344.

Geroski, P. (1995), "What Do We Know About Entry?" *International Journal of Industrial Organization*, 13 (4): 421–440.

Gort, M. and S. Klepper (1982), "Time Paths in the Diffusion of Product Innovations," *Economic Journal*, 92(367): 630–653.

Hughes, K. (1992), "Technology and International Competitiveness," *International Review of Applied Economics*, 6(2): 166–183.

Jovanovic, B. (1982), "Selection and Evolution of Industry," *Econometrica*, 50(3): 649–670.

Kalbfleish, J. and R. Prentice (1980), *The Statistical Analysis of Failure Data*, New York: John Wiley.

Kiefer, N. (1988), "Econometric Duration Data and Hazard Functions," *Journal of Economic Literature*, 26(2): 646–679.

Lawless, J. (1982), *Statistical Models and Methods for Lifetime Data*, New York: John Wiley.

Lucas, R. (1978), "On the Size Distribution of Business Firms," *Bell Journal of Economics*, 9(3): 508–523.

Mahmood, T. (1992), "Does the Hazard Rate for New Plants Vary Between Low- and High-Tech Industries," *Small Business Economics*, 4 (3): 201–209.

Mata, J. (1991), "Sunk Costs and Entry By Small and Large Plants," in P. Geroski and J. Schwalbach (eds.) *Entry and Market Contestability: An International Comparison*, Oxford: Basil Blackwell.

(1993), "Small Firms in the Portuguese Manufacturing Industries," in Z. Acs and D. Audretsch (eds.), *Small Firms and Entrepreneurship: An East–West Perspective*, Cambridge: Cambridge University Press.

(1994), "Firm Growth During Infancy," *Small Business Economics*, 8 (1): 27–39.

(1996), "Markets, Entrepreneurs and the Size of New Firms," *Economics Letters*, 52(1): 89–94.

Mata, J. and J. Machado (1996), "Firm Start-Up Size: A Conditional Quantile Approach," *European Economic Review*, 40(6): 1305–1323.

Mata, J. and P. Portugal (1994), "Life Duration of New Firms," *Journal of Industrial Economics*, 42 (3): 227–246.

White, L. (1982), "The Determinants of the Relative Importance of Small Business," *Review of Economics and Statistics*, 64(1): 42–49.

13 Does startup size influence the likelihood of survival?

David Audretsch, Enrico Santarelli, and
Marco Vivarelli

1 Introduction

The literature identifying the economic role of new and small firms is schizophrenic. On the one hand is a large and compelling literature suggesting that the emergence of networks of small firms has generated an alternative industry structure to that based on large corporations. In particular, seminal studies by Pyke and Sengenberger (1990) and Brusco (1990) argue that small and new firms enjoy a high degree of stability when supported by networks. A rich literature has provided a compelling body of case studies, spanning the textile industries of northern Italy to the metal working firms of Baden-Wuerttenberg (Piore and Sabel, 1984), documenting the long-term viability and stability of small and new firms embedded in such industrial districts.

As John Sutton's (1997) recent survey article on *Gibrat's Law* in the *Journal of Economic Literature* makes clear, the assumption underlying Gibrat's Law that firm growth is independent of size is certainly consistent with the view that small firms are not disadvantaged *vis-à-vis* their larger counterparts.

On the other hand is more literature suggesting exactly the opposite – that small and new firms are burdened with a greater likelihood of failure, reflecting their inherent size disadvantage and propensity to pursue new ideas. According to this view (Audretsch, 1995), entrepreneurs start new firms and workers agree to be employed in them because they believe in the economic value of a new idea that is not being pursued by an incumbent enterprise. This evolutionary view suggests that new firms represent *agents of change*. Entrepreneurs start new firms in an

We would like to thank the helpful suggestions and comments of the participants at the Conference on Innovation, Industry Evolution, and Employment, sponsored by the Tinbergen Institute and School of Policy Studies at Georgia State University, August 1997, and the careful research assistance of Valentine Aiello.

effort to appropriate the value of an idea that they were unable to appropriate with an incumbent enterprise. They then discover whether the idea is viable as a result of actual post-entry market performance. Those new entrants that discover that they are based on a viable idea grow and ultimately survive; those new firms learning that their idea is not viable tend to stagnate and ultimately exit from the market. A rich body of literature has emerged testing the validity of this view of new firms as *agents of change*. The resulting empirical evidence is so compelling that it led Paul Geroski (1995, p. 434) to declare the emergence of a new *Stylized Result*: "Both firm size and age are correlated with the survival of entrants."

The purpose of this chapter is to reconcile these two views about the economic role of small firms. We do this by comparing the relationship between firm size and the likelihood of survival in two countries – Italy and the United States. A positive relationship between firm size and the likelihood of survival supports the evolutionary view of small firms. By contrast, if firm size is found to exert no effect on the likelihood of survival, as implied by Gibrat's Law, then the network view of small firms is more likely to be correct.

2   The post-entry performance of firms: two views

Pyke and Sengenberger (1990) argue that through the support of an industrial district, small firms are able to compensate for what would otherwise be an inherent size disadvantage. According to Pyke and Sengenberger (1990), an industrial district is a geographically defined productive system, involving a large number of enterprises engaging in production at a wide range of stages, and typically involved in the production of a homogeneous product. A particularly significant feature of Italian industrial districts is that almost all of the firms are small or even micro-enterprises. Examples of such industrial districts include: Prato, Biella, Carpi and Castelgoffredo which specialise in textile (collants in Castelgoffredo); Vigevano, Montebellune and Montegranaro where shoes are manufactured (ski boots in Montebellune); Pesaro and Nogara which manufacture wooden furniture; Sassuolo where ceramic tiles are produced.

Brusco (1990) emphasizes the cooperation among network firms within an industrial district. Such cooperation presumably reduces any size-inherent disadvantages and improves the viability of small firms operating within the network. According to Pyke and Sengenberger (1990, p. 2), "A characteristic of the industrial district is that it should be conceived as a social and economic whole. That is to say, there are close inter-relationships between the different social, political and economic spheres, and the functioning of one, say the economic, is shaped by the functioning and organization of the others. The success of the districts, then, lies not just in the realm of the 'economic'. Broader social and institutional aspects are just as important." Grabher (1993) similarly argues that the social structure underlying industrial networks contributes to the viability of small firms that would otherwise be vulnerable if they were operating in an isolated context.

The implication concerning the economic role of small firms in industrial districts is that it provides an alternative industrial organization – flexible specialization (Piore and Sabel, 1982 and Van Dijk, 1995) – to the large vertically integrated corporation. Through the support of the network embedded in the industrial district the small firm is able to offset any size-inherent cost disadvantages. Thus, the likelihood of survival should not be related to firm size.

This view is consistent with the stochastic theories about the post-entry performance of new firms. The *stochastic theories*, dating back to Gibrat's Law, contend that variations in performance are attributable solely to chance. In his exhaustive survey in the *Journal of Economic Literature*, John Sutton (1997, p. 40) recently observed that publication of *Inegalites Economiques* by Robert Gibrat (1931) triggered, "One of the most important strands in the literature on market structure." Sutton points out that what is commonly referred to as *Gibrat's Law* is something of a misnomer. Rather than constituting a bona fide *Law*, what Gibrat proposed is actually an assumption that the probability of the "next opportunity is taken up by any particular active firm is proportional to the current size of the firm" (Sutton, 1997, p. 43). From this simple proposition follows the equally simple prediction of *proportional effect*, that growth rates should be independent of size, which Mansfield (1962, pp. 1030–1031) characterized as, "the probability of a given proportionate change in size during a specified period is the same for all firms in a given industry regardless of their size at the beginning of the period."

The theoretical model of *noisy selection*, introduced by Boyan Jovanovic (1982) provided a bridge between the stochastic models and the evolutionary models of post-entry performance. Jovanovic presents a model in which the new entrants, which he terms entrepreneurs, face costs that are not only random but also differ across firms. The likelihood of survival is therefore random across all new entrants. In this sense, his model adheres to the stochastic approach. However, a central feature of his model is that a new firm does not know what its cost function is – that is, its relative efficiency – but rather discovers it through the process of learning from its actual post-entry performance. In particular, Jovanovic assumes that entrepreneurs are uncertain about their ability to manage a new-firm startup and are therefore uncertain about their prospects of success (Jovanovic, 1994). Although entrepreneurs may launch a new firm based on a vague sense of expected post-entry performance, they only discover their true ability in terms of managerial competence and of having based their firm on an idea viable in the market once their business is established. Those entrepreneurs who discover that their firm is, in fact, efficient will survive and grow. Those who discover that their firm is inefficient will tend to exit from the industry. The firm will typically have a small startup size, since actual experience in the industry is necessary for the entrepreneur to discover whether the new firm is able to gain a significant share in the market or not. But the salient feature of Jovanovic's theory is that, a priori, a new firm has no expectation about its post-entry performance, suggesting that the likelihood of survival is simply stochastically distributed across firms. However, a second implication of Jovanovic's theory is that new-firm survival should be positively related both to firm size and firm age. In an *ex post* sense, larger and older firms have learned on the basis of market experience that they are viable and are less likely to exit from the market. Thus, Jovanovic introduced a very different view of small firms than is characterized in the models of the Italian industrial districts.

Audretsch has extended this *ex post* perspective in the Jovanovic model to introduce an evolutionary view of the post-entry performance of new firms. According to this evolutionary view, the likelihood of new-firm survival will not be identical across industries but rather shaped by characteristics specific to the industry. In particular, the degree of scale economies will influence the likelihood of new-firm survival. In industries where the minimum efficient scale (MES) level of output is high, those firms unable to grow and approach the MES level of output will be confronted with a cost disadvantage and forced to exit from the industry, resulting in a low likelihood of survival. By contrast, in industries characterized by a low MES, neither the need for growth, nor the consequences of its absence are as severe, so that relatively lower growth rates but higher survival rates would be expected. Empirical evidence for the United States (Audretsch, 1991; Audretsch and Mahmood, 1995), United Kingdom (Dunne and Hughes, 1994), Portugal (Mata and Portugal, 1994), and Germany (Wagner, 1994) supports the theory that the likelihood of survival tends to be lower in industries characterized by a greater degree of scale economies.

Similarly, Dixit (1989) and Hopenhayn (1992) both argue that the post-entry performance of firms will be influenced by the amount of sunk costs in the industry. A greater degree of sunk costs should reduce the likelihood of exit and lead to lower observed growth rates of surviving firms. Empirical evidence linking the extent of sunk costs to a lower likelihood of exit and lower observed growth rates of surviving firms has been provided by Audretsch (1991 and 1995) and Baldwin (1995).

The innovative environment of the industry has also been hypothesized to influence the post-entry performance of firms. Geroski (1995) has observed that entry serves as an important vehicle for innovative activity. However, the importance of entry as a vehicle should vary from industry to industry, not only because the relative importance of innovative activity varies systematically across industries, but also because the opportunity for new firms to generate that innovative activity varies from industry to industry. In such industries, those firms that successfully innovate will have a greater likelihood of survival, but those unable to successfully innovate will be confronted with a lower likelihood of survival. Since the likelihood of any given firm successfully innovating is relatively low, the likelihood of survival confronting a new entrant is also low. Empirical evidence for the United States (Audretsch, 1991 and 1995; Amirkhalkhaly and Mukhopadhyay, 1993) suggests that the likelihood of new-firm survival tends to decrease as the degree of innovative activity in an industry increases.

Several theories in the evolutionary tradition have also argued that characteristics specific to the firm also influence their post-entry performance (Audretsch, 1995). For example, a greater startup size of the firm increases the likelihood of survival, since the cost disadvantage confronting a firm operating at a sub-optimal scale level of output will be reduced. At the same time, the greater the size of the firm, the less it will need to grow in order to exhaust potential scale economies, and ultimately survive. That is, if the startup size of the firm is large enough relative to the MES of the industry, the firm need not grow at all and will still be viable in the long run. Both a positive relationship between firm size and the likelihood of survival, and a negative relationship between firm size and post-entry growth rates have been found in the United States (Hall, 1987; Dunne, Roberts, and Samuelson, 1988 and 1989; Audretsch, 1991 and 1995; and Audretsch and Mahmood, 1995), United Kingdom (Dunne and Hughes, 1994), Portugal (Mata and Portugal, 1994; Mata, Portugal, and Guimaraes, 1995), Germany (Wagner, 1994), and Canada (Baldwin, 1995).

In addition, other studies (Doms, Dunne, and Roberts, 1995) show that firm-specific factors such as capital intensity and the use of specific advanced manufacturing technologies influence the post-entry performance of new firms. Taken together, the wave of recent empirical studies therefore provides systematic evidence that post-entry performance is not stochastic across firms and industries, but is specific to factors particular to the firm and industry.

3 New-firm survival

3.1 Measurement

The greatest obstacle to the direct measurement and analysis of the post-entry performance of firms has been the lack of panel data sets tracking the evolution of firms subsequent to their birth. In this chapter we use for Italy a data set from the National Institute for Social Security (INPS). All private Italian firms are compelled to transfer to INPS national security payments for their employees (Santarelli, 1998). When a new firm is registered as "active" in the INPS files an entry can be identified, while a firm cancellation denotes a failure (this happens when a firm ultimately stops paying national security fees). Sometimes – for administrative reasons – cancellation is preceded by a period during which the firm results are suspended. In this chapter, suspended firms of this kind have been classified as having exited from the market at the month of their transition from the status of "active" to that of being a "suspended" firm. Of course, firms which suspended operations only temporarily (for one or a few months) during the subsequent periods and were "active" in January 1993 have been classified as having survived. The INPS identifies new manufacturing firms (with at least one paid employee) founded in January 1987. The subsequent performance of each firm is then tracked at monthly intervals until January 1993. Information on firms that have no paid employees is not available from the INPS file. However, these firms usually identify as being self-employed and only occasionally become true entrants with positive post-entry growth rates.

The original INPS file has been subjected to an editing procedure aimed at correctly identifying the entry and failure time periods as well as detecting inconsistencies in individual records resulting from administrative causes, problems related to file truncation in January 1993, and cancellations due to firm transfers and takeovers. This editing procedure effectively reduces the total number of firms included in the data base from 1,889 to 1,570. Table 13.1 shows the survival and hazard rates for the 1,570 new manufacturing firms identified in the INPS data base as being founded in January 1987. The survival rate is defined as the share

Table 13.1 *Survival and hazard rates of new firms in Italian manufacturing,*
1987–1993

Month	Survival		Hazard	
	Surviving firms	Survival rate[a]	Exiting firms	Hazard rate[b]
1/87	1,570			
1/88	1,435	91.1%	141	9.4%
1/89	1,286	81.6%	149	11.0%
1/90	1,183	75.1%	103	8.3%
1/91	1,077	68.3%	106	9.4%
1/92	988	62.7%	89	8.6%
1/93	932	59.1%	56	5.8%

Notes:

[a] Share of new firms started up in January 1987 still in existence as of January of
each subsequent year.

[b] Ratio of firms escaping from operation in each year following startup to the
average number of firms surviving during that year (mean of the absolute values
at the beginning and the end of the relevant year).

of new firms started in January 1987 that were still in existence as of
January of each subsequent year. Thus, one year subsequent to startup,
91.1 percent of the new firms still existed. By contrast, the survival rate
after six years is considerably smaller, 59.1 percent.

The hazard rate shown in table 13.1 is defined as the risk of failure at
each point in time, on the condition that the firm had survived until the
previous time period. Thus, the one-year hazard rate is 9.4 percent, and
then rises to 11.0 percent for the two-year hazard rate, before falling to
5.8 percent for the six-year hazard rate.

Table 13.2 shows the number of new entrants in each manufacturing
sector, the mean startup size (measured in terms of employment) and
the mean survival rate between 1987 and 1993. There is no clear
evidence that the likelihood of survival tends to be higher in those
sectors in which the startup size is larger. There are some sectors, such
as mining and transformation of metals, and rubber and plastics, where
a very small startup size is associated with high survival rates. The
substantial variations in survival rates across manufacturing industries
are consistent with the findings of Audretsch (1991 and 1995) that
characteristics specific to each particular industry shape the post-entry
performance of firms in that industry. For example, in the traditional
consumer goods sectors the mean survival rates tend to be below the
mean survival rate for manufacturing, 59.1 percent. For example, in the

Table 13.2 *New firm entry (absolute value), average startup size, and survival rate compared across manufacturing industries, 1987–1993*

Industry	New firm entry, 1987	Average startup size*	Survival rate, 1993
Mining and trans. of metals	16	7.9 (13.08)	81.3%
Metal working	29	28.4 (74.86)	65.5%
Mining and trans. of other minerals	20	6.3 (7.05)	60.0%
Stone, clay, glass	73	13.73 (22.41)	57.5%
Chemicals	49	65.88 (196.20)	55.1%
Fabricated metal products	118	9.11 (13.43)	55.9%
Mechanical engineering	101	20.24 (48.46)	70.3%
Office machinery and computers	7	7.43 (14.05)	37.5%
Electrical and electronic engineering	129	12.43 (38.92)	64.3%
Other means of transportation	20	19.5 (38.86)	55.0%
Instruments	214	12.17 (30.18)	61.2%
Food	82	11.07 (25.16)	47.6%
Sugar, beverages, and tobacco	27	14.6 (31.23)	66.7%
Textiles	102	15.6 (29.55)	52.9%
Leather products	54	9.74 (15.84)	61.1%
Footwear and clothing	231	14.61 (34.62)	48.5%
Wood and furniture	115	11.51 (24.58)	60.9%
Paper and printing	109	10.23 (24.57)	55.0%
Rubber and plastics	85	7.23 (9.60)	77.6%

Note: * Standard deviation in brackets.

footwear and clothing sector, only 48.5 percent of the new firms started in January 1987 were still in existence as of January 1993. Similarly, the six-year survival rate of startups in the food industry is 47.6 percent. Not only are these sectors of traditional strength in Italy, but they are also characterized by relatively low barriers to entry, low market concentration, and require a negligible degree of sunk costs. The rate of entry is remarkably high in these sectors. However, most firms exit the industry before attaining the MES level of output. This seems to be consistent with the process of discovery and learning described by Audretsch (1995).

At the same time, mechanical engineering and electrical and electronic engineering provide a contrast. These sectors are also traditional strengths of Italian manufacturing and have been generally identified as holding the international competitive advantage. However, these industries are typically characterized by high barriers to entry and a high degree of sunk costs. Market concentration is still low in these industries. The six-year survival rates are 70.3 percent in mechanical engineering and 64.3 percent in electrical and electronic engineering, suggesting that in these industries the process of market selection is stronger and more effective at the pre-entry stage. Only those entrepreneurs facing a relatively high likelihood of survival actually enter the industry. Such startups are relatively large.

3.2   Startup size and the likelihood of survival

In order to test the hypothesis that the likelihood of survival is shaped by what the literature has identified as being the most important observable characteristic specific to the firm – its size – it is essential to control for industry-specific factors. While Audretsch (1991 and 1995), Audretsch and Mahmood (1995), Wagner (1994), and Mata, Portugal, and Guimaraes (1995) all control for industry-specific characteristics by directly including measures reflecting various factors specific to the industry, here we follow the examples of Dunne, Roberts, and Samuelson (1988 and 1989), Doms, Dunne, and Roberts (1995), and Hall (1987), by separately estimating a model for new-firm survival for each manufacturing sector.

The first specification used is a logit model, where the dependent variable takes on the value of one if it was still in existence at the end of the estimation period, and zero if it was not. The results are shown in table 13.3. Not only is the coefficient negative in a number of the sectors, it is too small in any of the sectors to be statistically significant. Thus, on the basis of logit estimation there does not appear to be any relationship between firm size and the likelihood of survival.

Table 13.3 *Logit model estimates: survival on startup size for new firms in selected manufacturing industries, 1987–1993*

Industry	Constant	Startup size	N
Stone, clay, glass	0.440	−0.010	73
	(1.57)	(−0.97)	
Chemicals	0.302	−0.002	49
	(0.32)	(−0.91)	
Fabricated metal products	0.177	0.007	118
	(0.79)	(0.46)	
Mechanical engineering	0.566	0.022	101
	(2.13)	(1.51)	
Electrical and electronic engineering	0.567	0.002	129
	(2.93)	(0.37)	
Instruments	0.37	0.005	214
	(2.60)	(0.94)	
Food	−0.072	−0.002	82
	(−0.30)	(−0.26)	
Textiles	−0.065	0.012	102
	(−0.28)	(1.38)	
Leather products	0.038	0.051	54
	(0.10)	(0.04)	
Footwear and clothing	−0.157	0.007	231
	(−1.03)	(1.16)	
Wood and furniture	0.455	−0.001	115
	(2.16)	(−0.15)	
Paper and printing	0.140	0.006	109
	(0.66)	(0.71)	
Rubber and plastics	1.430	−0.024	85
	(4.00)	(−0.98)	

Note: t statistics in brackets.

The second specification we use for the size–survival relationship is to measure the dependent variable in terms of number of months survived using the framework of Tobit estimation. As described in the previous section, the INPS data base tracks the post-entry performance of firms started in January 1987 until January 1993. As a consequence, when testing for the likelihood of survival of new firms, we may only consider the interval, termed follow-up time, which consists of the period between $t = 1$ (where 1 corresponds to January 1987) and $t = T$ (with T corresponding to January 1993), during which N firms survived in each industry. If a firm exited the industry at any time between t and T, the failure time is correctly reported. Otherwise, the duration period exceeds

Table 13.4 *Tobit model estimates: duration (in months) on start-up size for new firms in selected manufacturing industries, 1987–1993*

Industry	Constant	Start-up size	N
Stone, clay, glass	81.28	−0.155	73
	(9.97)	(−0.63)	
Chemicals	78.00	−0.03	49
	(9.13)	(−0.90)	
Fabricated metal products	73.70	0.210	118
	(10.67)	(0.57)	
Mechanical engineering	59.00	0.064	101
	(26.46)	(1.50)	
Electrical and electronic engineering	89.48	0.043	129
	(11.41)	(0.26)	
Instruments	56.63	0.655	214
	(34.50)	(1.09)	
Food	66.07	−0.134	82
	(9.60)	(−0.26)	
Textiles	67.27	0.330	102
	(11.29)	(1.56)	
Leather products	66.88	1.580	54
	(5.41)	(1.38)	
Footwear and clothing	25.73	0.127	231
	(5.31)	(0.62)	
Wood and furniture	82.46	6.071	115
	(10.73)	(0.32)	
Paper and printing	72.91	0.11	109
	(11.85)	(0.50)	
Rubber and plastics	12.71	−0.890	85
	(6.80)	(−0.96)	

Note: t statistics in brackets.

T. To analyze this truncated distribution, we follow Greene (1993, pp. 691–697) in defining a new random variable, y, transformed from the original one, y^*, by $y = T$ if $y^* \geq T$, and $y = y^*$ if $0 \prec y^* \prec T$.

The regression model based on the above discussion is a common censored regression model, or Tobit model, for which the general formulation is represented by the index function $y_i = \beta' x_i + \varepsilon_i$, where $y_i = T_i$ if $y_i^* \geq T$, and $y_i = y_i^*$ if $0 \prec y_i^* \prec T$.

The results from the estimation of the Tobit model, where the dependent variable is the number of months that each new-firm startup survives, are presented in table 13.4. As the results indicate, there is virtually no evidence to link firm size to the likelihood of survival.

Although there is a positive coefficient in nine of the 13 sectors, the *t*-statistic is sufficiently low so that the coefficient cannot be interpreted as being statistically different from zero.

3.3   An Italian–US comparison

How does the post-entry performance of Italian manufacturing firms compare with their counterparts in other countries? Table 13.5 provides a comparison between the Italian and US survival and hazard rates over three distinct periods. The US data are from the USELM file of the US Small Business Data Base (SBDB). The SBDB data were derived from the Dun and Bradstreet (DUNS) market identifier file (DMI). The USELM file provides biennial observations between 1976 and 1986. Table 13.5 shows the survival and hazard rates of 11,661 US manufacturing firms (Audretsch, 1995) that were founded in 1976 and then tracked throughout the subsequent six years.

Table 13.5 *A comparison of Italian and US survival and hazard rates*

Period	Survival rate (%)		Hazard rate (%)	
	Italy	US	Italy	US
2 years	81.6	72.4	11.0	25.2
4 years	68.3	63.1	9.4	20.5
6 years	59.1	45.4	5.8	35.4

There are several striking comparisons between the post-entry performance of Italian and US startups. The survival rate of American startups is always substantially lower than that of new startups in Italy, regardless of the time period. After six years subsequent to startup, nearly 60 percent of the Italian firms survived. By contrast, only 45 percent of their American counterparts survived. Similarly, the hazard rates are strikingly different between the two countries. The hazard rate confronting new-firm startups is considerably greater in the United States than in Italy, independent of the time duration considered.

The mean startup size and six-year survival rates are compared between American and Italian firms in table 13.6. Again, striking contrasts emerge. The mean startup size is greater in Italy than in the US in every sector except primary metals and rubber and plastics, although, as already noticed in section 3.1, it should be borne in mind that in the case of Italy only firms with at least one paid employee are taken into

292   David Audretsch, Enrico Santarelli and Marco Vivarelli

Table 13.6 *Mean startup size and survival rates across manufacturing sectors for Italy and the US**

	Mean startup size		Six-year survival rate (%)	
	Italy	US	Italy	US
Primary metals	7.90	9.88	81.3	48.8
Stone, clay, and glass	13.73	7.42	57.5	45.1
Chemicals	65.88	6.36	55.1	51.6
Fabricated metal products	9.11	7.85	55.9	51.2
Mechanical engineering	20.24	5.79	70.3	54.0
Electrical engineering	12.43	6.99	64.3	40.8
Transportation	19.5	7.68	55.0	34.3
Instruments	12.17	6.76	61.2	47.1
Food	11.07	8.92	47.6	42.8
Textiles	15.60	12.54	52.9	36.0
Leather	9.74	7.22	61.1	41.0
Footwear	14.61	13.40	48.5	38.4
Furniture	11.51	7.44	60.9	44.0
Printing	10.23	4.76	55.0	45.3
Rubber and plastics	7.23	7.43	77.6	48.1

account. Besides, the survival rate of Italian startups exceeds that of their American counterparts in every manufacturing sector.

The impact of startup size on the likelihood of survival is compared between Italy and the US in table 13.7. The US results are taken from Audretsch (1995). This comparison clearly shows that while startup size has a clear impact on the likelihood of survival in the US, there is no similar impact in Italy. A positive relationship between size and the likelihood of survival is found in every US manufacturing sector except one. By contrast, no such relationship exists in any Italian manufacturing sector, within which even very small firms are not clearly disadvantaged with respect to their larger counterparts in terms of their likelihood of survival.

4   Conclusion

The post-entry performance of firms in Italy apparently does not replicate that found in most other countries. Based on evidence from countries such as Germany, Portugal, the United Kingdom, and the United States, Geroski (1995) was able to conclude that the consistently observed positive relationship between firm size and the likelihood of survival

Table 13.7 *Comparison of impact of start-up size on survival between Italy and the US*

	Coefficient from logit estimation	
Sector	Italy	US
Stone, clay, and glass	−0.010	0.059*
Chemicals	−0.002	0.078*
Fabricated metal products	0.007	0.024*
Mechanical engineering	0.022	0.177
Electrical engineering	0.002	0.047*
Instruments	0.005	0.095*
Food	−0.002	0.010*
Textiles	0.012	0.019*
Leather	0.051	0.092*
Apparel	0.007	0.032*
Furniture	−0.001	0.023*
Printing	0.006	0.037*
Rubber	−0.024	0.090*

Note: * Statistically significant at the 95% level of confidence.

constituted a *Stylized Result*. However, the results of the present study suggest that this Stylized Result is not sufficiently robust to automatically apply to every country and every situation. Rather, the empirical evidence we have found suggests a markedly different post-entry performance in Italy where size has no impact on the likelihood of survival.

The differences in post-entry performance identified between the United States and elsewhere and Italy may reflect a different institutional context. The prevalence of industrial districts and interfirm linkages embodied in the rich networks may provide new firms with a different role and support structure. The evidence clearly suggests that new-firm startups tend to be considerably larger in almost every manufacturing sector in Italy than in the United States. It may be that the economic and social roles of new firms are heterogeneous not just with respect to industries, as Audretsch (1995) showed, but also with respect to different countries.

References

Amirkhalkhaly, Saleh and Arun K. Mukhopadhyay (1993), "The Influence of Size and R&D on the Growth of Firms in the U.S.," *Eastern Economic Journal*, 223–233.

Audretsch, David B (1991), "New Firm Survival and the Technological Regime," *Review of Economics and Statistics*, 73(4): 520–526.

(1995), *Innovation and Industry Evolution*, Cambridge, Mass.: MIT Press.

Audretsch, David B. and Talat Mahmood (1995), "New Firm Survival: New Results Using a Hazard Function," *Review of Economics and Statistics*, 77(1): 97–103.

Audretsch, David B. and Marco Vivarelli (1995), "New Firm Formation in Italy," *Economics Letters*, 48(2): 77–81.

Baldwin, John R. (1995), *The Dynamics of Industrial Competition: A North American Perspective*, Cambridge: Cambridge University Press.

Baldwin, John R. and Garnett Picot (1995), "Employment Generation by Small Producers in the Canadian Manufacturing Sector," *Small Business Economics*, 7(4): 301–315.

Baldwin, John R. and Mohammed Rafiquzzaman (1995), "Selection versus Evolutionary Adaptation, Learning and Post-Entry Performance," *International Journal of Industrial Organization*, 13(4): 501–522.

Brusco, Sebastiano (1990), "The Idea of the Industrial District: Its Genesis," in Frank Pyke, Giacomo Becattini, and Werner Sengenberger (eds.), *Industrial Districts and Inter-Firm Co-operation in Italy*, Geneva: International Institute for Labour Studies, pp. 10–19.

Brusco, Sebastiano, Enrico Giovannetti, and Werter Malagoli (1979), "La relazione tra dimensioni e saggio di sviluppo nelle imprese industriali: una ricerca empirica," Universita di Modena, Facolta di Economia e Commercio, *Studi e Ricerche dell'Istituto Econnomico*, No. 5.

Cabral, Luis (1995), "Sunk Costs, Firm Size and Firm Growth," *Journal of Industrial Economics*, 43(2): 161–172.

Caves, Richard E., Bradley T. Gale, and Michael E. Porter (1977), "Interfirm Profitability Differences: Comment," *Quarterly Journal of Economics*, 91(4): 667–675.

Chesher, Andrew (1979), "Testing the Law of Proportionate Effect," *Journal of Industrial Economics*, 27(4): 403–411.

Dixit, Avinash (1989), "Entry and Exit Decisions under Uncertainty," *Journal of Political Economy*, 97(2): 620–638.

Doms, Mark, Timothy Dunne, and Mark J. Roberts (1995), "The Role of Technology Use in the Survival and Growth of Manufacturing Plants," *International Journal of Industrial Organization*, 13(4): 523–542.

Dunne, Paul and Alan Hughes (1994), "Age, Size, Growth and Survival: UK Companies in the 1980s," *Journal of Industrial Economics*, 42(2): 115–140.

Dunne, Timothy, Mark J. Roberts, and Larry Samuelson (1988), "Patterns of Firm Entry and Exit in U.S. Manufacturing Industries," *Rand Journal of Economics*, 19(4): 495–515.

(1989), "The Growth and Failure of U.S. Manufacturing Plants," *Quarterly Journal of Economics*, 104(4): 671–698.

Geroski, Paul A. (1995), "What Do We Know About Entry?" *International Journal of Industrial Organization*, 13(4): 421–440.

Geroski, Paul A. and Steve Machin (1993), "The Dynamics of Corporate Growth," unpublished manuscript, London Business School.

Geroski, Paul A. and Joachim Schwalbach (eds.) (1991), *Entry and Market Contestability: An International Comparison*, Oxford: Basil Blackwell.

Gibrat, Robert (1931), *Les Inegalites Economiques*, Paris: Librairie du Recueil Sirey.

Giunta, Anna and Domenico Scalera (1995), "Sopravvivenza e mortalita delle piccole imprese meridionali: un'applicazione dei modelli di durata," paper presented at the XIX Annual Conference of L'Industria, Ravello (Italy), 29–30 September.

Grabher, Gernot (ed.) (1993), *The Embedded Firm: On the Socioeconomics of Industrial Networks*, London: Routledge.

Greene, William H. (1993), *Econometric Analysis*, Englewood Cliffs, NJ: Prentice Hall.

Hall, Bronwyn (1987), "The Relationship between Firm Size and Firm Growth in the US Manufacturing Sector," *Journal of Industrial Economics*, 36(2): 583–606.

Hart, Peter E. and Nicholas Oulton (1996), "Growth and Size of Firms," *Economic Journal*, 106(3): 1242–1252.

Hart, Peter E. and S.J. Prais (1956), "The Analysis of Business Concentration: A Statistical Approach," *Journal of the Royal Statistical Society*, 119, series A: 150–191.

Hopenhayn, Hugo (1992), "Entry, Exit and Firm Dynamics in Long Run Equilibrium," *Econometrica*, 60(5): 1127–1150.

Hymer, Stephen and Peter Pashigian (1962), "Firm Size and the Rate of Growth," *Journal of Political Economy*, 70(4): 556–569.

Ijiry, Yuji and Herbert A. Simon (1964), "Business Firm Growth and Size," *American Economic Review*, 54(1): 77–89.

Jovanovic, Boyan (1982), "Selection and Evolution of Industry," *Econometrica*, 50(3), 649–670.

(1994), "Firm Formation with Heterogeneous Management and Labor Skills," *Small Business Economics*, 6(3): 185–191.

Kumar, Manmohan S. (1984), *Growth, Acquisition and Investment*, Cambridge: Cambridge University Press.

Lucas, Robert E., Jr. (1967), "Adjustment Costs and the Theory of Supply," *Journal of Political Economy*, 75(4): 321–334.

(1978), "On the Size Distribution of Business Firms," *Bell Journal of Economics*, 9(2): 508–523.

Mandelbrot, Benoit (1963), "New Methods in Statistical Economics," *Journal of Political Economy*, 71(3): 421–440.

Mansfield, Edwin (1962), "Entry, Gibrat's Law, Innovation, and the Growth of Firms," *American Economic Review*, 52(5): 1023–1051.

Marris, Robin (1979), *Theory and the Future of the Corporate Economy and Society*, Amsterdam: North-Holland.

Mata, Jose and Pedro Portugal (1994), "Life Duration of New Firms," *Journal of Industrial Economics*, 42(3): 227–246.

Mata, Jose, Pedro Portugal, and Paulo Guimaraes (1995), "The Survival of New

296   David Audretsch, Enrico Santarelli and Marco Vivarelli

Plants: Startup Conditions and Post-entry Evolution," *International Journal of Industrial Organization*, 13(4): 459–482.

McCloughan, Patrick (1995), "Simulation of Concentration Development from Modified Gibrat Growth-Entry-Exit processes," *Journal of Industrial Economics*, 43(4): 405–433.

Mueller, Dennis C. (ed.) (1990), *The Dynamics of Company Profits: An International Comparison*, Cambridge: Cambridge University Press.

Pakes, Ariel and Richard Ericson (1994), "Empirical Implications of Alternative Models of Firm Dynamics," unpublished manuscript, University of Wisconsin-Madison.

Penrose, Edith T. (1959), *The Theory of the Growth of the Firm*, Oxford: Basil Blackwell.

Piore, Michael J. and Charles F. Sabel (1984), *The Second Industrial Divide*, New York: Basic Books.

Pyke, Frank, Giacomo Becattini, and Werner Sengenberger (eds.) (1990), *Industrial Districts and Inter-Firm Co-operation in Italy*, Geneva: International Institute for Labour Studies.

Pyke, Frank and Werner Sengenberger (1990), "Introduction," in Frank Pyke, Giacomo Becattini, and Werner Sengenberger (eds.), *Industrial Districts and Inter-Firm Co-operation in Italy*, Geneva: International Institute for Labour Studies, pp. 1–9.

Santarelli, Enrico (1998), "Start-up Size and Post-entry Performance: The Case of Tourism Services in Italy," *Applied Economics*, 30(2): 157–163.

Simon, Herbert A. and Charles P. Bonini (1958), "The Size Distribution of Business Firms," *American Economic Review*, 58(4): 607–617.

Singh, Ajit and Geoffrey Wittington (1975), "The Size and Growth of Firms," *Review of Economic Studies*, 42(1): 15–26.

Solinas, Giovanni (1995), "Le imprese nuove nate e la legge di Gibrat," *Economia e Lavoro*, 26(1): 117–139.

Sutton, John (1995), "The Size Distribution of Business, Part I: A Benchmark Case," London School of Economics, The Economics of Industry Group, Discussion Paper Series, No. EI/9.

(1997), "Gibrat's Legacy," *Journal of Economic Literature*, 35, 40–59.

Van Dijk (1995), "Exports, Firm Size, and Firm Dynamics," *Small Business Economics*, 7(1): 15–28.

Van Kijk and Pieter Meine, "Flexible Specialisation, The New Competition and Industrial Districts," Small Business Economics, 7 (1 February), 15–28.

Wagner, Joachim (1992), "Firm Size, Firm Growth, and Persistence of Chance: Testing Gibrat's Law with Establishment Data from Lower Saxony," *Small Business Economics*, 4(2): 125–131.

(1994), "The Post-Entry Performance of New Small Firms in German Manufacturing Industries," *Journal of Industrial Economics*, 42(2): 141–154.

You, Jong-Il (1995), "Small Firms in Economic Theory," *Cambridge Journal of Economics*, 19(3): 441–462.

14 Barriers to growth of firms in developing countries: evidence from Burundi

Micheline Goedhuys and Leo Sleuwaegen

1 Introduction

After independence, most African countries expected economic development to come from a solid industrial base generated by large-scale investments undertaken by the state and foreign investors and supported by heavy protection from foreign competition. However, when the large state- and foreign-owned enterprises generated disappointing results, the focus of attention shifted toward smaller enterprises. During the last decade, most African governments undertook further policy reforms in order to liberalize their economy and "restore market forces." Within this new approach, competition among firms through an open market mechanism was considered a better instrument for allocating resources to more efficient organizations within a thriving private sector.

However, so far the results remain disappointing in most countries. Besides what is left of former large-scale investments, a large number of micro-enterprises and small firms struggle for survival and face important barriers preventing them from growing into a larger size. In many developing countries, product markets and markets for inputs are still ill developed and characterized by a low number of market participants and high transaction costs. Market failures weaken the process of competition among firms as an effective selection mechanism.

Accounting for the conditions of the institutional environment contributes to a better understanding of the process by which resources are allocated, and firms able to grow, in developing countries. In a related

We would like to thank the participants of the conference "The impact of technological change on industry and firm performance," 29–30 August 1997. Tinbergen Institute, Erasmus University Rotterdam for comments on a related study and in particular we are grateful to David Audretsch, Martin Carree, and Steven Klepper. Financial support from the Belgian Fund for Scientific Research (FWO-G.0196.96 N) is gratefully acknowledged.

study on the growth of manufacturing firms in Côte d'Ivoire (Sleuwaegen and Goedhuys, 1998), firm growth is found to result from a complex process in which institutional and structural factors interact. Similar conditions seem to apply to Burundi, the country under study in this chapter.

In the early years after its independence, the Burundian state had taken up and consolidated an overly dominating role in the ownership and management of productive assets, especially as its influence was even more strengthened by a tight regulation of the economy. Following a period of severe crisis and macro-economic imbalances, the government embarked in 1986 on its first comprehensive adjustment programme. By the end of 1993, Burundi was considered one of Sub-Saharan Africa's most liberal trade regimes (World Bank, IDA, 1992). Still, the manufacturing sector in Burundi remains relatively small. In most sectors a very small number of formal firms occupy a dominant position in the local market. The informal sector is very strongly represented, especially in the rural areas. Burundi's past and current structural problems as well as the characteristics of its manufacturing sector are typical of the much larger region of Sub-Saharan Africa and make it a good representative country for studying the dynamics of firm growth in this region of the world.

The second section of this chapter presents an analytical framework which integrates institutional factors into the more traditional literature on firm growth. After presenting the data in section 3, the empirical model is proposed in section 4 and tested against data on a heterogeneous group of manufacturing firms in Burundi. In section 5, an analysis of labor productivity differences among firms, as well as an analysis of the perceptions of growth barriers by the owners and managers of the sample firms, provide corroborating evidence on the determinants of firm growth. Section 6 concludes.

2   Growth of firms in developing countries

Research on the size distribution of firms and the underlying firm dynamics commonly starts from Gibrat's law of proportionate effect (LPE) which implies that firms grow each year following a random drawing from a distribution of growth rates. This stochastic growth model, as well as the whole generation of growth models based on weaker assumptions of the LPE, generate skewed distributions (lognormal, Pareto, Yule) which fit the observed size distributions of firms in Western economies strikingly well (Ijiri and Simon, 1964).

In spite of the apparent power of Gibrat's law, an increasing number of empirical studies find evidence which goes against it. Most studies find a significant negative relationship between firm growth and firm size (Mansfield, 1962; Evans, 1987a; Kumar, 1985; and Dunne and Hughes, 1994). In industries characterized by the existence of economies of scale, small efficient firms grow faster than their larger counterparts as they overcome their initial scale disadvantage and invest relatively more than larger firms. Audretsch (1995) finds evidence suggesting that a larger gap between the minimum efficient scale and firm size is related to higher growth rates of surviving firms. Moreover, a negative relationship is often observed between the variability in growth rates and firm size (Mansfield, 1962; Kumar, 1985; Dunne and Hughes, 1994; Dunne, Roberts, and Samuelson, 1989). Similarly, Gibrat's law is violated by a negative relationship between firm growth and firm age (Evans, 1987a; and Dunne and Hughes, 1994) and between the variability in growth and firm age.

Using an alternative theoretical approach, Lucas (1978) argued that the equilibrium size distribution of firms is determined by the underlying distribution of managerial abilities within the population. Deepening this line of reasoning, Jovanovic (1982) claimed that, once firms are established in the industry, they learn about their efficiency. The process of competition forces the least efficient firms to exit. The more efficient firms expand their activities when their managers observe that their guesses about their managerial efficiency turn out to have understated their true efficiency. As a firm ages, the manager's guess about his efficiency becomes more accurate and the probability decreases that the output will differ widely from one year to another. Older firms, therefore, grow more slowly than young firms and their growth rates are relatively stable. Pakes and Ericson (1990) extended the passive learning model of Jovanovic. In their view, managers not only uncover their efficiency through learning, they are also able to increase their efficiency over time through human capital formation.

Focusing more on the particular characteristics of markets in developing countries and pointing to the failure of existing theories to explain the frequently observed dual market structure in developing countries, institutional economists have increasingly drawn attention to the role of institutional influences on firm growth. The underdevelopment of both input and product markets, the too low number of market participants and the resulting high transaction costs tend to shift growth opportunities among firms. The argument is mainly developed around the effect of the relative underdevelopment of markets for credit and equity on the size of firms (Nugent and Nabli, 1989, 1992; see also Nugent (1996) for an empirical testing with respect to Korea).

Along the same line of reasoning, organizational ecology models view firm growth primarily as determined by a process of diffuse competition, in which firms essentially compete for scarce resources. Firms competing for an identical set of resources are residing in the same "niche." The growth of one firm or selected group of firms, therefore, impedes or severely depresses the growth rates of other firms in the niche which are deprived of inputs. Moreover, a firm's access to resources is facilitated to the extent that the firm is "legitimated" in the industry, i.e., socially accepted and benefiting from an institutional standing in the eyes of other contracting parties such as clients, suppliers, financial institutions, law enforcing agents, and other key actors (Hannan, Ranger-Moore, and Banaszak-Holl, 1990; Hannan and Carroll, 1992; Winter, 1990).

In a related study, Sleuwaegen and Goedhuys (1998) presented an approach which integrates the implications of organizational ecology models into the market selection processes suggested by the models of learning. Using data on a heterogenous group of manufacturing firms in Côte d'Ivoire, they find that firm growth is explained by size and age effects as a result of efficiency seeking through scale enlargements and learning, but it is strongly moderated by processes of diffuse competition and by formal legitimation in the industry.

This chapter develops a similar model using a unique data set of manufacturing firms in Burundi. The chapter seeks to provide further evidence on firm growth in developing countries and to explain the particular barriers which exist for some groups of firms.

3   Data

The empirical analysis is based on a data set covering the growth of a representative sample of 120 manufacturing firms located in Burundi. The data are obtained from a survey conducted within the framework of the World Bank project RPED ("Regional Program on Enterprise Development in Africa") in April–May 1993. The firms are selected from one of the four main industrial sectors: agro-industries, textiles, wood working, and metal working as shown in table 14.1.

Both formal and informal sector firms are included. In line with other studies (McPherson and Liedholm, 1996; Mead and Morrisson, 1996), firms are defined as "formal" if they are registered, fulfil all tax obligations and respect labor and other regulations. Following this definition, the formal firms were selected from the population of firms which contribute to the INSS (Institut National de Sécurité Social) or are registered with the ISTEEBU (Burundi Institute of Statistics and Economic Studies), the Ministry of Commerce and Industry, or the

Table 14.1 *Firms included in the sample*

	Number of firms	Average size	Standard deviation
All firms	120	75.7	215.9
By start-up year			
1947–73	18	146.8	227.2
1974–83	24	129.5	346.6
1984–88	34	20.0	22.7
1989–93	44	60.2	193.7
By sector			
Agro-industries	40	132.6	267.8
Textiles	31	85.0	285.1
Wood working	25	18.5	19.5
Metal working	24	28.3	39.0
By formal status			
Formal	79	112.2	259.2
Informal	41	5.4	5.7

Burundi Chamber of Commerce, Industry, Agriculture and Handicraft.[1] Of the group of informal firms, on the other hand, no traces can be found in the national statistics.[2] The informal firms included in the sample were selected randomly.

As most industrial activity is located in the capital of Bujumbura, the majority of the sample firms are also located there. The more important firms located in other regions of the country, including Gitega, Mur-amvya, Ngozi, and Rumonge, are also included in the survey. A limited number of smaller and informal sector firms was surveyed on each field trip outside Bujumbura.

Despite the government's commitment to privatize state-owned enter-prises, the process has been very slowly implemented. The dominance of state ownership is still an important feature of the manufacturing sector

[1] These firms respect fiscal obligations including company taxes, transaction taxes on goods and services, property taxes on land and vehicles collected by the local government, tax on increases in capital, and taxes levied on dividends. On the other hand, they have full access to all business support services organized by state agencies and can benefit from tax exemptions provided by the investment code.

[2] Informal firms are at most registered in their urban district. They pay municipal taxes but no income taxes and they do not adhere to official labor regulations which prior to the adjustment programmes used to be considered extremely restrictive, both to the hiring and firing of workers. None of the informal firms have access to business support services and training programs.

302 Micheline Goedhuys and Leo Sleuwaegen

which explains why a number of firms in the sample is partially or entirely state owned.

Foreign investment and ownership had declined in the early 1980s. Some of the structural adjustment measures are designed to promote foreign investment particularly in export-oriented ventures. In 1993 foreign investors came mainly from Europe and the Indian subcontinent.

4   Empirical model

Similar to earlier work on firm growth (Evans, 1987a; McPherson, 1996), the proposed model follows a general growth function g in size and age:

$$G = \frac{S_{t'}}{S_t} = g(S_t, A_{t'}) \tag{1}$$

where $S_{t'}$ and S_t are the size of a firm in period t' and in period t respectively and $A_{t'}$ is the age of the firm in period t'. Following the arguments proposed by organizational ecology models, this functional relationship is assumed to be moderated through a set of environmental and firm-specific variables X which are hypothesized to interact with the basic function in the following way:

$$G = g(S_t, A_{t'})e^{bX} \tag{2}$$

Approximating the growth function g through a second-order logarithmic expansion of a generalized function relating growth to size and age, the estimating equation corresponds to the following form:

$$\frac{\log(S_{t'}) - \log(S_t)}{d} = a_0 + a_1 \log(S_t) + a_2[\log(S_t)]^2 + a_3 \log(A_{t'}) +$$

$$a_4[\log(A_{t'})]^2 + a_5 \log(S_t)^* \log(A_{t'}) + \sum_{i=1}^{n} b_i X_i \tag{3}$$

where d stands for the number of years over which growth is measured and a and b are coefficient vectors. The dependent variable in equation 3 corresponds to an average annual growth rate.

The relationship between firm growth and size and between firm growth and age can subsequently be analyzed by calculating the respective partial derivatives (Evans, 1987a and 1987b; Variyam and Kraybill, 1992). The partial derivatives $g_s = (d\ln G/d\ln S)$ and $g_a = (d\ln G/d\ln A)$ allow us to test for alternative theories of firm growth. Gibrat's law implies that the partial derivative g_s equals zero. Alternatively a negative relationship between firm size and growth implies that $g_s < 0$. Models of learning suggest that $g_a < 0$. The elasticity of end-of-period size with respect to beginning-of-period size is $E_S=1+dg_s$, while the elasticity of end-of-period size with respect to age is $E_A=dg_a$.

Variables

The dependent variable is the average annual growth rate of employment calculated over the period 1986–1993, covering the years the structural adjustment programme came into effect. The analysis is also performed analyzing growth over the entire period of existence of the firm, from birth to 1993.[3]

Following the proposed estimating equation, the set of explanatory variables includes firm size (SIZE), and firm age (AGE) as basic determinants of firm growth. Size is measured at the beginning of the period under consideration, startup and 1986 respectively, while age is measured in 1993.

The environmental moderators of the growth relationship include the sector to which the firm belongs and the region where it is located. Three binary variables account for possibly different growth performance in textiles, wood-working and metal-working industries (WOOD, TEX-TILES, METAL), the reference sector being agro-industries.

From interviews it is clear that owners and managers view access to local resources as an important determinant for the choice of the geographical location.[4] This is especially true for firms located in the more remote areas of Rumonge, Muramvya, Ngozi, and Gitega. However, Burundi's mountainous terrain, and its landlocked position additionally constrain these firms' access to local product markets. Clearly, the largest market is found in the capital city,[5] Bujumbura, where firms are also more likely to engage in networking and

---

[3] As some respondents could not remember the number of employees in 1986 or at start-up, especially for older firms, historical employment data were not consistently available for all firms and the number of observations is reduced in the growth equation. In order to use the maximum information available from the data set the size of the sample may therefore differ across estimating models. Running the model on different subsamples did not produce any different results.

[4] Sixty-seven percent of the firms located outside Bujumbura mention availability of industrial land and access to raw materials as the main location determinant.

[5] Being close to clients and competitors is a relatively more important location determinant for firms in Bujumbura (57 percent of the firms) than for firms located in the more remote areas (11 percent of the firm). In Bujumbura, there is also better provision of infrastructure and a larger supply of skilled labor. The availability of industrial sites and infrastructure and access to raw materials and skilled labor were mentioned as the main location determinant by one-third of the firms located there.

subcontracting. A binary variable (OUTBUJA) is included to capture the geographical niche effect of being located outside Bujumbura.

Sourcing from abroad is taken into account by the variables EURO-PEAN and ASIAN which equal one if the majority of the equity capital is of European or Asian origin, respectively. In a similar way, a binary variable SOE denotes state-owned enterprises which have a soft budget constraint and have access to bank loans under state guarantee. Their status, moreover, facilitates the relationship with other market partici-pants.

In order to take further account of the firm's legitimation in the industry, a binary variable FORMAL is included. The variable takes the value one for formally registered firms which are able to advertise themselves in the industry, and zero for the informal firms, which refrain from officially registering primarily for tax purposes and to alleviate regulatory burdens.

Results

A two-stage estimation procedure, instrumenting the variable FORMAL, is adopted to account for the possible bias originating from endogeneity of the latter variable. It should also be noted that only surviving firms are included in the data set. However, a recent study by McPherson (1996) on the growth of firms in five southern African countries analyzes the possible selection bias resulting from the exclusion of exiting firms on the growth relationship and finds this bias to be insignificant.

Table 14.2 shows the estimated coefficients and t-ratios for the growth regressions over the two different periods from 1986 until 1993 and from startup until 1993. The average annual growth rate equals 0.10 and 0.11 over the period 1986–1993 and start–1993 respectively.

The relationship between age and growth is negative as suggested by the models of learning. This result holds for the different periods over which growth is measured. Evaluated at the sample means, the partial derivative of growth to log age equals -0.18 for the period 1986–1993 and -0.17 for the entire period from startup until 1993. The elasticity of size with respect to age equals -0.93 and -1.39 for the respective periods.

The relationship between size and growth is negative, implying that smaller firms grow faster than larger ones. This is consistent with studies conducted in other countries. The partial derivatives of the growth rate to log size evaluated at the sample mean are negative. The derivative equals -0.13 for the period 1986–1993 and -0.12 for startup until 1993. The elasticity of end-of-period size with respect to beginning-of-period

Table 14.2 *Regression results for employment growth over the period start-up–1993 and 1986–1993*

	1986–1993	Start–1993
AGE	−0.610 ***	−0.504 *
	(−2.577)	(−1.919)
AGE^2	0.081	0.076
	(1.380)	(1.405)
SIZE	−0.233 ***	−0.155
	(−3.001)	(−1.164)
SIZE^2	0.000	−0.006
	(0.023)	(−0.327)
AGE*SIZE	0.057	0.033
	(1.490)	(0.815)
FORMAL	0.444 ***	0.310 ***
	(4.441)	(5.241)
EUROPEAN	−0.022	−0.071
	(−0.249)	(−1.299)
ASIAN	−0.055	−0.062
	(−0.946)	(−1.145)
SOE	0.242	0.235 *
	(1.481)	(1.651)
OUTBUJA	−0.103 *	−0.126 **
	(−1.653)	(−2.339)
WOOD	0.193 **	0.103
	(2.100)	(1.213)
TEXTILES	0.062	0.034
	(0.696)	(0.370)
METAL	0.075	0.052
	(0.852)	(0.742
Constant	0.802 ***	0.752 **
	(3.193)	(2.208)
R-Adj.	0.3133	0.1812
F (13,60)	3.562	
F (13,65)		2.328

Notes: To correct for heteroskedasticity, standard errors are estimated using White's consistent estimator (White, 1980).
Asymptotic t-ratios are in parentheses; Significance levels: *** 99%; ** 95%; * 90%.

size is 0.35 and 0.04 for both models. These results go against Gibrat's law of random growth behavior.

The hypothesis that growth is moderated through different environmental and institutional conditions is also supported by the data. The coefficient of the variable FORMAL is positive and significant at the 99 percent level. The formal character of a firm increases its estimated annual growth rate over the period 1986–1993 by 0.44. For the period start–1993 the formal status increases the expected annual growth rate by 0.31. The results suggest that, besides competition, the process of formal legitimation is important. Formal firms tend to grow faster as scarce resources are allocated to established firms which have legitimated themselves in markets characterized by high transaction costs.

The geographical location also appears to have an impact on the development of firms. Being located outside Bujumbura has a negative impact on growth indicating that the better supplied Bujumbura region is more conducive to firm development than the less accessible and more remote regions. External scale economies and urbanization economies relax competition for resources and explain differences in growth performance between firms located in different regions. Being located in Bujumbura increases, on average, the expected growth rate by 0.10 (1986–1993) and 0.13 (start–1993).

State-owned firms tend to expand employment faster. The effect is significant for growth over the period from startup until 1993. In Burundi, state-owned firms have traditionally occupied a very strong position in manufacturing and a large share of the productive assets were channelled toward these firms. Under the structural adjustment program it is the purpose to reverse this trend and to strengthen the private sector. The effect of state ownership on firm growth during the period of adjustment is still positive but not significant.

The presumed effects of foreign ownership, offering firms the opportunity of sourcing abroad, are not significant. The coefficients of the sectoral variables are all positive indicating that firms in agro-industries, which is the reference sector, tend to grow more slowly.

The empirical results support the view that firm growth is essentially a process of learning over time with younger firms being able to reap strong returns in the initial years of operation as they observe that they can increase efficiency through scale enlargement. The growth process is, however, moderated by institutional factors which tend to shift the growth opportunities toward firms with better access to resources. Legitimation in the industry through obtaining a formal status tends to facilitate access to resources thereby relaxing the barriers to growth. In a similar way, being located outside the industrial core region depresses the expected growth rate. State ownership tends to increase the firm's expansion opportunities, especially during the period before the structural adjustment program, when the institutional environment was discriminating in favor of these firms.

Following the reasoning of the models of learning, the more efficient firms survive and grow into a larger size, suggesting that older and larger firms exhibit a higher level of efficiency. Inefficient firms are forced to exit, unless, as suggested by organizational ecology models, they have an advantage over other firms in securing a share of the scarce resources for themselves which enables them to survive. In order to shed additional light on the determinants of growth, the next section presents a productivity analysis to unravel the characteristics of the more productive firms in relation to size, age, and formal status. The section also investigates in more detail the kind of and severity of growth barriers as they are perceived by the owners and managers of the firms.

5   Productivity and growth barriers

Labor productivity differences

Labor productivity in the growth process of firms is determined by several factors. Technologies exhibiting scale economies may explain why larger firms display substantially higher levels of labor productivity, while, through ageing, firms are able to grow into a scale at which these economies are fully exploited. Implementation of new and improved technologies may shift labor productivity to a higher level. Productivity also depends on the actual organization of the firm which likewise improves through learning over time. Using similar technologies, productivity differences among firms may be due to differences in plant layout, division of labor, delegation of responsibilities, business culture, and incentive systems. As a result, foreign-owned firms may benefit from important transfers of organizational capabilities which may stimulate higher productivity levels. It is often argued that, if competition is not pushing firms to a maximum use of resources, they may become X-inefficient. Within this framework, state-owned firms which are less constrained by profit requirements are often alleged to be less productive.

To test these implications empirically, labor productivity is measured by the logarithm of value-added per employee (LPROD). The explanatory variables include firm size, measured by the logarithm of sales (LSALES). Firms are classified into three age categories. The binary variable AGE1 equals one for firms aged between ten and 20 years while AGE2 equals 1 for firms of over 20 years of age, the reference group

Table 14.3 *Regression results for labour productivity differences*

dependent variable: log (value-added/employee)

LPROD= 3.61   +0.58 LSALES +1.35 INDSHARE −0.01 WHITECOL −0.02 TECACT
         (20.64) (6.00)   (1.98)   (−0.01)   (−0.05)

         +0.04 WOOD +0.50 TEXTILES −0.98 METAL +0.30 AGE1 +0.94 AGE2
         (0.19)   (2.48)   (−4.17)   (1.34)   (2.55)

         −0.70 FORMAL −0.14 EUROPEAN +1.83 ASIAN −1.58 SOE
         (−3.82)   (−0.26)   (2.27)   (−1.96)

adj. R^2=0.48; F(13,73)=5.183

Notes: Results are corrected for heteroskedasticity; Asymptotic t-ratios are in parentheses.

being younger firms of less than ten years of age. A number of variables are included to measure technological effects. INDSHARE, the share of indirect costs in total costs, is included as a proxy for capital intensity of production. The number of managers and administrative and commercial personnel as a percentage of total employment (WHITECOL) is a proxy for the human capital employed by the firm. TECACT is a binary variable equal to one if the firm spends funds on R&D or has obtained licenses. The binary variables EUROPEAN, ASIAN, SOE equal one if the majority of the equity capital is European, Asian, or state owned respectively. Sectoral effects are captured by three binary variables WOOD, TEXTILES, and METAL, leaving agro-industries as the reference sector. The effect of being formally registered is captured by the variable FORMAL. Estimation results are presented in table 14.3.

As expected, scale effects are important in explaining labor productivity differences. Higher levels of capital intensity also substantially increase firms' labor productivity. The coefficient of INDSHARE is positive and significant at the 95 percent level. The coefficient of TECACT is not significantly different from zero. The greater use of white-collar workers in the firm does not appear to have a net effect on labor productivity. The results might be influenced by a high correlation between both variables and with the variable INDSHARE. Firms in the textiles sector tend to exhibit higher levels of labor productivity while firms in the metal-working sector show lower levels than firms in agro-industries.

The most striking result is to observe that formal firms, while growing faster, seem to use labor input in a significantly less productive way. In a similar way, state-owned enterprises show higher levels of employment growth, but tend to have significantly lower levels of labor productivity.

This may point to the great importance of institutional factors interacting in the distribution of scarce resources.

Controlling for firm size, older firms are more productive than younger ones, and the effect increases with the age category as indicated by the coefficient of AGE1 and the even larger coefficient of AGE2. This result is supportive of models of learning, which suggest that firms operating in an industry are not only able to uncover their level of efficiency over time, but may also be able to improve it over time through learning and developing a more performing organization.

In general these results provide corroborating evidence that higher levels of efficiency are obtained through becoming larger scale and through active and passive learning over time. However, institutional factors inhibit firms from having equal access to resources and thereby depress their effective growth rates, which results in misallocation of resources and reduced overall productivity. In what follows, the different kinds of growth obstacles are further analyzed in relation to the different types of firms.

Obstacles to firm growth: the owner and manager's perception

In the RPED survey, the manager or owner of the firm was asked to quantify a list of 15 factors according to the degree to which they actually constitute an obstacle to the growth of their firm. The analysis of the manager's perception complements the previous findings and contributes to a better understanding of how certain growth obstacles are related to different types of firms.[6] The list of 15 growth hampering factors was regrouped into four different types of obstacles.[7] The first and most important obstacle is *access to credit*. The second group of obstacles relates to *market conditions*, with insufficient demand, and competition from local competitors and imports as constituent factors. *Regulation* on social capital, activities and location, labor regulations, price and foreign exchange controls, taxes, and problems in obtaining licenses form a third type of obstacle. Finally, a lack of infrastructure and business support

---

[6]   The answers to the questions were the respondents' subjective and personal views. The questions were intended to show the sources of obstacles to growth at the moment the interview took place in 1993 and these are not necessarily identical to past growth hindrances. Nevertheless, it may be assumed that the main constraints to growth are not too variable over time.

[7]   The respondents quantified the severeness of 15 growth hampering factors on a numeric scale ranging from 1 to 5, where 1 = no obstacle and 5 = severe obstacle. A lack of credit was perceived as the most constraining factor with an average score of 3.3, followed by insufficient demand (3.0) and taxes (2.8).

services and high prices of public utilities as growth obstacles are regrouped in the variable *"infrastructure."*

Each variable corresponds to the average of the constituent factors and ranges continuously on a scale from one to five. In order to uncover systematic effects, a two-way censored Tobit model relates the height of the growth obstacle to the type of firm. Three binary variables classify firms in different size classes: MICRO (1–4), SMALL (5–25), and MEDIUM (26–100). The reference group taken up in the constant term are large firms with over 100 employees. The age of the firm in 1993, in logarithmic value, is represented by the variable LFIRMAGE. Sectoral, locational and ownership and formal status variables are defined as before.

The estimation results are shown in table 14.4.

A lack of credit seems most constraining to the smallest firms and decreases systematically with the size of the firms, as indicated by the magnitude of the coefficient of the size classes. Older firms also seem to complain significantly less about credit as a growth obstacle. This is not surprising as, within the learning view, older firms should have proven over time to be among the more efficient ones. Moreover, their age also grants them an advantage of creditworthiness over younger equally efficient firms if financial markets are characterized by high transaction costs.

Market conditions, and in particular insufficient demand, are experienced as obstacles to the growth of micro-enterprises. While the low purchasing power of the population is generally considered as one of the major problems for development, micro-enterprises, which often serve the lowest segment of the market, are thereby severely hampered from growing into a larger size. Older firms complain significantly less about being constrained by market conditions, probably because they have established a position in the local market. The severity of the market constraint is also sector related; firms in the textiles sector and in metal working complain significantly more about insufficient demand and tough competition. Firms in the informal sector complain less about market conditions, which point to the smaller niches which they define as their relevant market.

Regulation seems to be less constraining for micro-enterprises and small firms, whose scale of operation and type of activity are less subject to regulation. It is more constraining for formal firms than for informal ones as, by definition, informal firms circumvent most of the regulatory obligations. Regulation is less an obstacle to growth for older firms and firms owned by Asians, while the opposite holds for European owned firms and firms in metal working.

Table 14.4 *Perceived obstacles to growth*

Dep. Var:	Access to credit	Market conditions	Regulation	Infrastructure
D-MICRO	9.647 **	1.146 *	−0.443 **	0.461
	(5.444)	(3.076)	(5.172)	(0.963)
D-SMALL	5.376	−0.250	−0.307 **	−0.322
	(2.697)	(0.209)	(4.036)	(0.686)
D-MEDIUM	3.127	0.246	0.025	−0.136
	(1.014)	(0.219)	(0.030)	(0.129)
LFIRMAGE	−2.119 *	−0.541 ***	−0.136 **	−0.185
	(3.263)	(8.001)	(5.712)	(1.749)
FORMAL	0.576	1.125 **	0.254 *	0.009
	(0.049)	(5.700)	(2.870)	(0.001)
EUROPEAN	0.340	0.136	0.321 *	−0.126
	(0.011)	(0.055)	(3.829)	(0.089)
ASIAN	0.657	−0.695	−0.364 *	−0.217
	(0.023)	(0.932)	(2.851)	(0.162)
SOE	−4.298	−0.087	−0.115	0.064
	(1.333)	(0.021)	(0.469)	(0.023)
OUTBUJA	−0.067	−0.089	−0.125	0.130
	(0.001)	(0.043)	(0.949)	(0.183)
WOOD	3.191	0.046	−0.193	0.014
	(1.389)	(0.010)	(1.801)	(0.002)
TEXTILES	−1.298	1.036 **	−0.100	−0.446
	(0.264)	(5.728)	(0.612)	(2.056)
METAL	3.245	1.190 **	0.091	−0.005
	(1.414)	(6.272)	(0.419)	(0.001)
constant	1.911	1.579 **	1.659 ***	2.598 ***
	(0.213)	(4.590)	(61.776)	(24.410)
σ	6.931	1.417	0.415	1.063
	(21.5)	(104.2)	(113.2)	(145.8)
N	102	102	99	101
Log likelihood	−114.2	−147.0	−58.6	−140.2

Notes: X^2-ratios are in parentheses; Significance levels: *** 99%; ** 95%; * 90%.

No significant differences across types of firms are observed with respect to the perception of infrastructure and business supporting services as barriers to firm growth.

In sum, the results with respect to the perceived obstacles to growth provide interesting corroborating evidence for the theoretical framework and empirical growth model presented in this chapter. The constraining factors with respect to credit, the different regulatory environment, and the varying competitive regimes for the different groups of firms are at the heart of the underlying firm growth processes observed in developing countries.

6   Conclusion

Consistent with results obtained for developed countries, firm growth in Burundi is subject to a learning process over time. However, the growth process is hampered by several institutional and environmental conditions which are particular to developing countries, including primarily the absence of well-functioning resource and product markets. Among the constraining factors, access to credit for young and smaller firms shows up as a major constraining factor. Formally registered firms, which grow significantly faster than informal firms, report that they are more severely hampered by credit constraints, overregulation, and market conditions. Informal firms, on the other hand, seem to focus on a mere survival objective in an unregulated segment of the economy where small-scale investment and technological upgrading do not pay off.

The present framework offers some interesting perspectives for the development of a more effective and efficient policy with respect to the development of the private sector in developing countries. Firstly, the ongoing implementation of structural adjustment measures requires due attention to the state of development of the credit market and an in-depth analysis of the existing market failures in both product and input markets. Secondly, the absorptive capacity of small- and medium-sized enterprises should be improved to enhance transfer and implementation of technology from larger companies and firms abroad. The focus of policy should therefore become more oriented toward the growth of firms after startup. Lowering the barriers that impede informal firms from participating in the formal economy and engaging in scale enlargement with associated scale economies and learning effects, appears likewise to be crucial for the development of a more solid industrial base.

References

Audretsch, D.B. (1995), *Innovation and Industry Evolution*, Cambridge, Mass.: MIT Press.
Dunne, P. and A. Hughes (1994), "Age, Size, Growth and Survival: UK Companies in the 1980s," *The Journal of Industrial Economics*, 42: 115–140.
Dunne, T., M.J. Roberts, and L. Samuelson (1989), "The Growth and Failure of US Manufacturing Plants," *Quarterly Journal of Economics*, 104: 671–698.
Evans, D.E. (1987a), "The Relationship between Firm Growth, Size and Age: Estimates for 100 Manufacturing Industries," *The Journal of Industrial Economics*, 35: 567–582.

(1987b), "Tests of Alternative Theories of Firm Growth," *Journal of Political Economy*, 95: 657–674.

Gibrat, R. (1931), *Les inégalités économiques*, Paris: Sirey.

Hannan, M.T. and G.R. Carroll (1992), *Dynamics of Organizational Populations: Density, Legitimation and Competition*, New York: Oxford University Press.

Hannan, M.T., J. Ranger-Moore, and J. Banaszak-Holl (1990), "Competition and the Evolution of Organizational Size Distributions," in J. Singh (ed.), *Organisational Evolution: New Directions*, Sage, Newbury Park, CA.: 246–268.

Ijiri, Y. and H. A. Simon (1964), "Business Firm Growth and Size," *The American Economic Review*, 54: 77–89.

Jovanovic, B. (1982), "Selection and the volution of Industry," *Econometrica*, 50: 649–670.

Klepper, S. and E. Graddy (1990), "The Evolution of New Industries and the Determinants of Market Structure," *Rand Journal of Economics*, 21: 27–44.

Kumar, M.S. (1985), "Growth, Acquisition Activity and Firm Size: Evidence from the United Kingdom," *The Journal of Industrial Economics*, 33: 327–338.

Lucas, R.E. (1978), "On the Size Distribution of Business Firms," *The Bell Journal of Economics*, 9: 508–523.

Mansfield, E. (1962), "Entry, Gibrat's Law, Innovation and the Growth of Firms, *The American Economic Review*, 52: 1023–1051.

McPherson, MA. (1996), "Growth of Micro and Small Enterprises in Southern Africa," *Journal of Development Economics*, 48: 253–277.

McPherson, M.A. and C. Liedholm (1996), "Determinants of Small and Micro Enterprise Registration: Results from Surveys in Niger and Swaziland," *World Development*, 24: 481–487.

Mead, D.C. and C. Morrisson (1996), "The Informal Sector Elephant," *World Development*, 24: 1611–1619.

Nugent, J.B. (1996), "What Explains the Trend Reversal in the Size Distribution of Korean Manufacturing Establishments?" *Journal of Development Economics*, 48: 225–251.

Nugent, J.B. and M.K. Nabli (1989), "An Institutional Analysis of the Size Distribution of Manufacturing Establishments: An International Cross-Section Study," CES International Economics Research Paper No. 62, 29 p.

(1992), "Development of Financial Markets and the Size Distribution of Manufacturing Establishments: International Comparisons," *World Development*, 20: 1489–1499.

Pakes, A. and R. Ericson (1990), "Empirical Implications of Alternative Models of Firm Dynamics," Columbia University Working Paper.

Sleuwaegen, L. and M. Goedhuys (1998), "Organisational Ecology and Growth of Firms in Developing Countries, Evidence from Côte d'Ivoire," Working Paper, University of Leuven.

Variyam, J.N. and D.S. Kraybill (1992), "Empirical Evidence on Determinants of Firm Growth, *Economics Letters*, 38: 31–36.

314   Micheline Goedhuys and Leo Sleuwaegen

White, H. (1980), "A Heteroskedasticity-Consistent Covariance Matrix Estimator and a Direct Test for Heteroskedasticity," *Econometrica*, 48: 817–832.

Winter, S.G. (1990), "Survival, Selection and Inheritance in Evolutionary Theories of Organization," in J. Singh (ed.), *Organisational Evolution: New Directions*, Newbury Park, CA.: Sage, pp. 269–297.

World Bank (1991), *Burundi, Private Sector Development in the Industrial Sector*, Report No. 9422–BU, Washington, DC, 123p.

World Bank (IDA) (1992), *Report and Recommendation of the President of the IDA to the Executive Directors on a Proposed IDA Credit of SDR 22 Million to the Republic of Burundi in Support of a Third Structural Adjustment Program*, 31 pp.+ann.

Author index

Subject index

Amgen, 220
Astra, 199, 200
Azko Nobel, 206

BASF Svenska AB, 206
Bayer Sverige AB, 206
BF Goodrich, 204
biotechnology in Sweden and US, 182–3,
    189–92, 194, 199, 200–2, 212–13
Borealis Industrier AB, 206, 207
BP Chemicals, 204

Cancer Foundation, 200
capital/labor ratio, 71, 73, 76n, 77, 80–1
communications revolution, 3–4
competition, 2, 3, 57, 86, 88n, 106
    impact on productivity, 8, 111–13, 300
competitive selection, 8, 111–13, 300
concentration, 114, 120, 121, 124
    effect on innovation, 112
cooperation between establishments, 164–7,
    170–3
corporate governance, 132–4
creative destruction process, 86–7, 89,
    262–3

decentralization, 87
diversification, 72, 75, 76

Edison BioTechnology Center, 190, 191, 197
Edison Polymer Innovation Corporation,
    192, 193, 203
efficiency, 299, 307, 309
Enterprise Development Inc., 197–8
entrepreneurial activity, 88, 93, 94–9
    results in wage differentials, 93
    in small firms, 87, 88, 93, 106
entry and exits of firms, 233–8, 250, 253,
    256–63, 266, 273, 276–7
export intensity, 77–8, 80, 81

exporters in Taiwan, 16–18
exports and wage inequality, 13, 14–15,
    18–19, 21, 49
    dominance of large firms in, 13, 18

Firestone, 204
firm age, 71–2, 75, 76, 266, 273, 280, 283
    as agent of change, 180–1
    in biotechnology, 207–9, 212
    effect on wages, 23–5
    and survival, 231–2, 237–40, 253,
        259–60, 262, 266, 299, 300, 303, 304,
        307–10
firm size, 70, 73, 76, 262
    in biotechnology firms, 207–12
    link with growth, 89–106, 120, 231–2,
        237–40, 253, 259–60, 262, 268, 280,
        281–3, 299–300, 302–4, 306–7, 312
    and innovation, 60, 112, 167, 216–17
    and market structure, 114–15
    policy of promoting small business, 87,
        105
    shift to small firms, 87–8, 99
    at startup, 266, 273–4, 277, 284, 286,
        288–93
firm survival
    effects of economies of scale, 239–41,
        246–9, 250–1, 263
    likelihood of, 281–8, 291–3
    rates of, 265, 270–2, 274, 275, 282–4,
        287, 292
foreign capital, effect on wages, 23–5
foreign ownership of firms, 72, 75, 76,
    307

Gambro, 199
Gen Corp, 204
General Motors, 99
geographical location, importance of, 3, 5,
    87, 157, 159–61, 173–7, 281–3, 303–7

319

venture capital, 197–8, 200–7, 212, 213
Volvo, 3n

wage differentials, 1, 3, 23–5, 57, 82,
  93
  between production and non-production

workers, 14–15, 59–60, 63–7, 70,
  73–4, 75–83
wages, 1, 3, 23–5
  effect of firm size on, 13, 14, 26, 45, 49,
  51, 52
welfare, 87, 88, 106